D1440810

CHURCH PROPERTY

Visit our web site at
www.albahouse.org
(for orders www.stpauls.us)

or call 1-800-343-2522 (ALBA)
and request current catalog

CHURCH PROPERTY

A Commentary on Canon Law Governing Temporal Goods in the United States and Canada

Reverend Monsignor John A. Renken

M.A. (Civil Law), S.T.D., J.C.D.
Professor of Canon Law

Saint Paul University
Ottawa, Ontario
Canada

ST PAULS

Library of Congress Cataloging-in-Publication Data

Renken, John Anthony.
    Church property : a commentary on canon law governing temporal goods in the
United States and Canada / John A. Renken.
        p. cm.
    Includes bibliographical references and index.
    ISBN 978-0-8189-1297-9
    1. Church property (Canon law). 2. Church property—Law and legislation—United
States. 3. Church property—Law and legislation—Canada.   I. Title.
    KBU3320.R46   2009
    262.9'45—dc22
                                            2009009529

Produced and designed in the United States of America by the
Fathers and Brothers of the Society of St. Paul,
2187 Victory Boulevard, Staten Island, New York 10314-6603
as part of their communications apostolate.

ISBN 10: 0-8189-1297-9
ISBN 13: 978-0-8189-1297-9

Printing Information:

Current Printing - first digit   1   2   3   4   5   6   7   8   9   10

Year of Current Printing - first year shown

2009   2010   2011   2012   2013   2014   2015   2016   2017   2018

TABLE OF CONTENTS

INTRODUCTION

The ultimate purpose of the Church is the salvation of souls (see canon 1752). The Church is organized in this world as a society (canon 204 §2) where it performs spiritual and temporal works. The Church has a right to temporal goods needed to perform these works, which canon law identifies principally as: divine worship, the decent support of ministers, works of the apostolate and of charity, especially towards the needy.

From the earliest days, the Church has used material goods to assist in performing its mission.[1] The same is certainly true today. Over the Christian centuries, much canonical legislation has developed concerning the ownership and care of ecclesiastical property in order that it may be protected and used for the proper purposes of the Church. In the Latin Church today, *Book V* of the 1983 *Code of Canon Law*, entitled *The Temporal Goods of the Church*, is devoted to the acquisition, retention, administration, and alienation of temporal goods. Specific application of norms in *Book V* is made to institutes of consecrated life and societies of apostolic life.[2] Several other norms related to temporal goods are also found interspersed throughout other parts of the code.[3] Many canons require the adap-

---

[1] For a brief but concise overview of the Church's use of temporal goods, and particularly legislation about this use, see: JOSEPH POKUSA, "Introduction to a Church Finance Handbook: Background for the Law on Temporal Goods," in *Church Finance Handbook*, Kevin E. McKenna, Lawrence A. DiNardo, and Joseph W. Pokusa (eds.), Washington, CLSA, 1999, pp. vii-xvii; ALBERTO PERLASCA, *Il concetto di bene ecclesiastico*, Tesi Gregoriana, 24, Roma, Pontificia Università Gregoriana, 1997, pp. 7-81.

[2] See Appendix I. Note especially canons 635, 718, and 741 §1.

[3] See Appendix II.

tation of universal norms to particular circumstances through particular law,[4] proper law, and statutes. Administrators of ecclesiastical
goods and all in Church leadership, together with their collaborators,
must be aware of canonical legislation on the temporalities used by
the Church in this world to lead all people to heaven.

Book V, consisting of only 57 canons, is the shortest of the seven
books of the *Code of Canon Law*. The small number of canons governing the Church's temporal goods reflects subsidiarity, a principle
guiding the revision of the entire code. The common norms exist for
the world-wide Catholic Church and particular applications of them
will be necessary in individual settings.

The purpose of this commentary is to assist those charged with
the care of ecclesiastical goods in readily understanding canonical
norms concerning them and in applying them accurately. Such understanding and application will assure the faithful that ecclesiastical
goods are properly acquired, retained, administered, and alienated. It
will protect the goods owned by the Church and will maintain them
safely for future generations by properly employing ecclesiastical
legislation and, in many cases, by applying norms recognized in civil
law with which the Church freely complies. It will assure that the
intentions of donors of gifts legitimately accepted by the Church are
respected and observed. It will manifest appropriate transparency
and collaboration in financial affairs.

This commentary contains the most recent legislation of the
Latin Church, with particular application to the Church in the United
States of America and in Canada. To understand better the current
legislation, a contrast is often made to the prior legislation of the
1917 *Code of Canon Law* which was operative until November 27,
1983, when the revised code became effective. Reference is also
made frequently to the deliberations of those charged with drafting
the 1983 code; this helps one to understand the priorities found in
the current law and can assist in its interpretation and application.
For each canon, brief reference, without extensive commentary, is

---

[4]   See JOHN A. RENKEN, "Particular Law on Temporal Goods," in *Studies in Church Law*, 4 (2008), pp. 447-454.

made to corresponding canons of the 1990 *Code of Canons of the Eastern Churches.* A current extensive bibliography cites works in several languages, including other commentaries, to guide those interested to further research.

This commentary uses the English translation of the 1983 *Code of Canon Law* published by the Canon Law Society of America in 1999.[5] One must understand, of course, that the Latin text alone remains the official law.

---

[5]   *Code of Canon Law: Latin-English Edition*, prepared under the auspices of the CLSA, CLSA, 1999.

LIST OF ABBREVIATIONS

AAS	*Acta Apostolicae Sedis*
CCCB	Canadian Conference of Catholic Bishops
CCEO	*Codex canonum Ecclesiarum orientalium*
CFH	MCKENNA, KEVIN, LAWRENCE A. DINARDO, AND JOSEPH W. POKUSA (eds.), *Church Finance Handbook*
CIC	*Codex iuris canonici, auctoritate Ioannis Pauli PP. II promulgatus*
CIC/1917	*Codex iuris canonici, Pii X Pontificis Maximi iussu digestus*
CLD	*Canon Law Digest*
CLSA	Canon Law Society of America
CLSA AO1	COGAN, PATRICK (ed.), *CLSA Advisory Opinions, 1984-1993*
CLSA AO2	ESPELAGE, ARTHUR (ed.), *CLSA Advisory Opinions, 1994-2000*
CLSA AO3	ESPELAGE, ARTHUR (ed.), *CLSA Advisory Opinions, 2001-2005*
CLSANZ	Canon Law Society of Australia and New Zealand
DPMB	CONGREGATION FOR BISHOPS, *Directory for the Pastoral Ministry of Bishops*
Exegetical Comm	MARZOA, ÁNGEL, et al. (eds.), *Exegetical Commentary on the Code of Canon Law*
FLANNERY 1	FLANNERY, AUSTIN (ed.), *Vatican Council II*, vol. 1
FLANNERY 2	FLANNERY, AUSTIN (ed.), *Vatican Council II*, vol. 2
NCCB	National Conference of Catholic Bishops (until July 1, 2001)
PCLT	Pontifical Council for Legislative Texts
USCCB	United States Conference of Catholic Bishops (since July 1, 2001)

CHURCH PROPERTY

CHAPTER ONE

HISTORY OF THE DEVELOPMENT OF BOOK V

1917 CODE OF CANON LAW. The first Code of Canon Law for the Latin Church was promulgated in 1917 by Pope Benedict XV. It was comprised of five "books." The canons on temporal goods were found in *Book III: About Things,*[1] which contained norms governing six dimensions of Church life: the sacraments, sacred times and places, divine worship, teaching authority, benefices and other non-collegiate ecclesiastical institutions, and temporal goods. The final section of the book, *Part VI: On the Temporal Goods of the Church,*[2] contained 57 canons grouped as follows:

CANONS	SUBJECT MATTER
1495-1498	[Preliminary Canons]
1499-1517	Title XXVII: The Acquisition of Goods
1518-1528	Title XXVIII: The Administration of Goods
1529-1543	Title XXIX: Contracts
1544-1551	Title XXX: Pious Foundations

---

[1] The 1917 code distinguished "persons" (*personae*) from "things" (*res*). The former exist for themselves; the latter are means to ends other than themselves. The 1917 code treated "persons" in Book II, *De personis,* and "things" in Book III, *De rebus.* Temporal goods were listed among "things," i.e., as instruments or means to ends other than themselves. See A. VERMEERSCH and J. CREUSEN, *Epitome iuris canonici,* vol. 2, 7ᵗʰ ed., Rome, 1954, n. 1.

[2] The material which had comprised *Book III* of the 1917 code is distributed in the 1983 code into three distinct books: *The Teaching Function of the Church* (canons 747-833), *The Sanctifying Function of the Church* (canons 834-1253), and *The Temporal Goods of the Church* (canons 1254-1310).

Several other canons concerning Church temporalities comprised *Part V: On Benefices and Other Non-Collegiate Ecclesiastical Institutes,*[3] which was composed of 85 canons grouped as follows:

CANONS	SUBJECT MATTER
1409-1488	Title XXV: Ecclesiastical Benefices
1489-1494	Title XXVI: Other Non-Collegiate Ecclesiastical Institutes

Several other canons concerning Church temporalities are dispersed throughout the remainder of the 1917 code, as is also the case with the 1983 code.

TEACHING OF VATICAN COUNCIL II. Vatican Council II had mentioned temporal goods, including those of the Church, in several documents, particularly:[4]

- Dogmatic Constitution on the Church, *Lumen gentium*, nn. 12, 23
- Pastoral Constitution on the Church in the Modern World, *Gaudium et spes*, nn. 42, 69, 71, 76
- Decree on the Apostolate of the Laity, *Apostolicam actuositatem*, n. 10
- Decree on the Pastoral Office of Bishops in the Church, *Christus Dominus*, nn. 6, 28
- Declaration on Religious Liberty, *Dignitatis humanae*, nn. 4, 13
- Declaration on Catholic Education, *Gravissimum educationis*, n. 8
- Decree on the Mass Media, *Inter mirifica*, n. 3
- Decree on the Up-to-date Renewal of Religious Life, *Perfectae caritatis*, n. 13
- Decree on the Ministry and Life of Priests, *Presbyterorum ordinis,* nn. 17, 20, 21

---

[3] Vatican II called for the gradual elimination of benefices, so the revised code contains legislation on benefices only in canon 1272. The treatment of other non-collegiate ecclesiastical institutes is reflected in canons 1303-1307.

Much of the conciliar doctrine is found in the 1983 code. Indeed, those drafting the proposed new legislation on temporal goods intended to incorporate conciliar teaching into the law. Following the conclusion of the council, Pope Paul VI issued his *motu proprio* entitled *Ecclesiae sanctae*[5] by which he implemented several conciliar decrees; it contains a number of references to the temporal goods of the Church.

REVISION OF THE CODE OF CANON LAW.[6] On January 25, 1959, when Pope John XXIII announced his intention to convoke the Second Vatican Council, he also called for a revision of the 1917 Code of Canon Law. He established the Pontifical Commission for the Revision of the Code of Canon Law on March 28, 1963. When the group met in November of that year, it decided to suspend its activity until the conclusion of the council. The Pontifical Commission began its many meetings on November 20, 1965, only a few days before the council concluded on December 8, 1965.

In January, 1966, one month after the conclusion of Vatican Council II, the Pontifical Commission established ten *coetus* (bodies, groups) to prepare draft legislation of what would become the 1983 Code of Canon Law. One of these ten *coetus* was assigned to revise the law on temporal goods.[7] A deliberate decision was made in 1967 to place the Church's legislation on temporal goods into a separate section of the revised law.[8]

---

4   See VELASIO DE PAOLIS, *De bonis Ecclesiae temporalibus: Adnotationes in Codicem: Liber V*, Rome, Editrice Pontificia Università Gregoriana, 1986, pp. 18-22 (=DE PAOLIS, *De bonis Ecclesiae temporalibus*).

5   PAUL VI, *motu proprio Ecclesiae sanctae, Normae ad quaedam exequenda SS. Concilii Vaticani II decreta statuuntur* (August 6, 1966), in *AAS*, 58 (1966), pp. 757-787; English translation in *CLD*, vol. 8, pp. 264-298.

6   For a brief critical analysis of the history of the revision of the code, see JEAN-CLAUD PÉRISSET, *Les biens temporals de l'Église*, Paris, Éditions Tardy, 1966, pp. 17-27, 275-282.

7   *Communicationes,* 1 (1969), p. 44.

8   The central *coetus* of consultors of the Pontifical Commission for the Revision of the Code of Canon Law had met April 3-7, 1967 and voted on the question, "Whether it is favorable that legislation on temporal goods (or, patrimonial law) of the Church be placed in a separate part?" The ten consultors were unanimously in favor. *Communicationes,* 1 (1969), pp. 107-108.
On May 28, 1968, the plenary Pontifical Commission met and voted in favor of placing

1977 *Schema*. The *coetus* met nine times[9] before, on November 15, 1977, the *Schema* entitled *Liber V: De iure patrimoniali Ecclesiae*[10] was sent to various consultative organs. The *Schema* consisted of 57 proposed canons:

Canons	Subject Matter
1-12	Title I: Preliminary Canons
13-17	Title II: The Subject of Ownership
18-34	Title III: The Administration of Goods
35-44	Title IV: Acquisition, Alienation and Especially Contracts
45-57	Title V: Pious Wills in General and Pious Foundations

The preface[11] of the *schema* mentions that these proposed canons are a revision of *Part V* and *Part VI* of *Book III* of the 1917 code. It explains that the *Schema* includes only one canon on benefices, and that episcopal conferences should develop particular law on benefices in those few regions where they exist. This reflects *Presbyterorum ordinis*, n. 20 which calls for the gradual elimination (or, at least, the reform) of benefices.

---

legislation on temporal goods (or, patrimonial law) into a separate part of the revised code. The results were 33 *placet* and 7 *placet iuxta modum. Communicationes*, 1 (1969), pp. 111-113.

9   The *coetus De bonis Ecclesiae temporalibus* met on January 24-27, 1967 (*Communicationes*, 36 [2004], pp. 236-249); June 5-10, 1967 (*Communicationes*, 36 [2004], pp. 250-267); November 20-24, 1967 (*Communicationes*, 36 [2004], pp. 277-305); February 19-24, 1968 (*Communicationes*, 36 [2004], pp. 306-333); May 13-17, 1968 (*Communicationes*, 37 [2005], pp. 116-138). The *coetus De iure patrimoniali Ecclesiae* met on January 20-25, 1969 (*Communicationes*, 37 [2005], pp. 186-202); May 26-31, 1969 (*Communicationes,* 37 [2005], pp. 203-222); December 15-19, 1969 (*Communicationes*, 37 [2005], pp. 223-255); April 20-22, 1970 (*Communicationes*, 37 [2005], pp. 256-283). See *Communicationes*, 26 (2004), pp. 218-220. The summary of its work through these nine sessions is reported in *Communicationes*, 5 (1973), pp. 94-103.

10   Pontifical Commission for the Revision of the Code of Canon Law, *Schema canonum libri V: De iure patrimoniali Ecclesiae*, Vatican City State, Typis polyglottis Vaticanis, 1977, p. 3 (=1977 *Schema*). This text is contained also in *Communicationes*, 37 (2005), pp. 284-303.

11   1977 *Schema*, Preface, p. 3.

The preface also identifies several conciliar references to temporal goods whose teaching is incorporated in the proposed law: *"Presbyterorum ordinis*, nn. 17, 20, 21; *Apostolicam actuositatem*, n. 10; *Christus Dominus*, n. 28; etc." It reports the intention of the *coetus* to reflect the principle of subsidiarity which had been identified as one of ten principles to guide the revision of the code[12] and which has particular significance in the matter of temporal goods since the circumstances of diverse regions have a special influence on the governance of goods.

In 1979[13] the *coetus De bonis Ecclesiae temporalibus* reviewed the comments forwarded by the consultative organs and made several modifications to the proposed new law. The *coetus* also decided to change the title of the book from *De iure patrimoniali Ecclesiae* to *De bonis Ecclesiae temporalibus*, which seemed to be recommended by the tradition of the Church. Besides, the term "patrimony" seemed to imply a great quantity of goods.[14]

---

[12] In April 1967, a central committee of the Pontifical Commission for the Revision of the Code of Canon Law developed ten principles to direct the task of revising the code. These principles were approved (with a few modifications) by the 1967 SYNOD OF BISHOPS. Principle 5 on subsidiarity extolled the importance of particular law, especially concerning temporal goods: "The importance of these particular laws is to be more accurately described in the new Code of Canon Law especially in temporal administration, since the governance of temporal goods must be ordered for the most part according to the laws of each nation." *Communicationes*, 1 (1969), p. 81. The Synod of Bishops met September 30-October 4, 1967. They voted in favor of principle 5: 128 *placet*, 58 *placet iuxta modum*, 1 *non placet. Communicationes*, 1 (1969), pp. 99-100.

[13] The coetus met on June 17-23, 1979 (*Communicationes*, 12 [1980], pp. 388-414) and November 12-16, 1979 (*Communicationes*, 12 [1980], pp. 414-435). See *Communicationes*, 36 (2004), p. 220.

[14] *Communicationes*, 12 (1980), p. 394. VICTOR G. D'SOUZA comments that the title *De iure patrimoniali Ecclesiae* was abandoned for several reasons: "(a) the word 'patrimony' has different meanings in the code; (b) it signifies a much wider heritage than what is handed on by way of property and investments; (c) its wider connotation goes beyond the reference to temporal goods in its singular meaning, and (d) the term is not accepted unanimously in civil and canon law." In "General Principles Governing the Administration of Temporal Goods in the Church," in *In the Service of Truth and Justice: Festschrift in Honor of Prof. Augustine Mendonça, Prof. Emeritus*, Victor G. D'Souza (ed.), Bangalore, Saint Peter's Pontifical Institute, 2008, pp. 468-469. See also JEAN-PIERRE SCHOUPPE, *Droit canonique des biens*, Montréal, Wilson and Lafleur, 2008, p. 10, fn. 10; DE PAOLIS, *De bonis Ecclesiae temporalibus*, p. 9. The term *patrimony* is found in several canons, with diverse connotations: canons 251, 578, 1283, 3°, 1285, 1291.

1980 *SCHEMA*. On June 29, 1980, the Pontifical Commission for the Revision of the Code of Canon Law issued the *Schema Codicis Iuris Canonici*[15] and invited comments on the new *Schema* from the commission members. This *Schema* incorporated all the proposed canons developed by the several *coetus* into one text containing 1728 proposed canons. *Book V* of the *Schema*, entitled *De bonis Ecclesiae temporalibus*, contained 58 proposed canons on temporal goods:

CANONS	SUBJECT MATTER
1205-1209	[Preliminary Canons]
1210-1223	Title I: The Acquisition of Goods
1224-1240	Title II: The Administration of Goods
1241-1249	Title III: Contracts and Especially Alienation
1250-1262	Title IV: Pious Wills in General and Pious Foundations

The names given to Titles II and III of the proposed canons show that the *coetus* clearly wished to distinguish the administration of goods from the alienation of goods.

The 30 comments on the proposed canons made by the commission members were organized by the secretariat of the commission into the report or *Relatio*,[16] dated July 16, 1981. The *Relatio* also included replies from the secretariat and consultors to the comments of the commission members.

---

[15] PONTIFICAL COMMISSION FOR THE REVISION OF THE CODE OF CANON LAW, *Schema Codicis Iuris Canonici, iuxta animadversiones S.R.E. Cardinalium, episcoporum conferentiarum, dicasteriorum curiae romanae, universitatem facultatumque ecclesiarum necnon superiorum institutorum vitae consecratae recognitum*, Vatican City State, Typis polyglottis Vaticanis, 1980. (=1980 *Schema*).

[16] PONTIFICAL COMMISSION FOR THE REVISION OF THE CODE OF CANON LAW, *Relatio complectens synthesim animadversionum ab Em.mis atque Exc.mis Patribus commissonis ad novissimum schema Codicis Iuris Canonici exhibitarum, cum responsibus a secretaria et consultoribus datis*, Vatican City State, Typis polyglottis Vaticanis, 1981 (=*Relatio*). The comments on *Book V* are found on pages 280-290. The text of the *Relatio* dealing with temporal goods is contained also in *Communicationes*, 16 (1984), pp. 27-37, without reference to the names of the commission members offering remarks.

1981 PLENARY COMMISSION MEETING. The 1980 *Schema* and the 1981 *Relatio* formed the basis of the discussions of the final session of the commission, which occurred in Rome on October 20-28, 1981.[17] The secretariat of the commission had proposed six questions for discussion, and another forty questions were put forth by members of the Pontifical Commission, each having been proposed by at least ten commission members. Question 11 focused on what became canon 1263 on the diocesan tax.[18]

On October 28, 1981, the commission members concluded their plenary gathering with a unanimous vote to present the final version of their work to Pope John Paul II for promulgation as soon as possible.[19]

1982 SCHEMA. The secretariat produced a revised text, dated March 25, 1982, entitled *Codex Iuris Canonici: Schema Novissimum*[20] which was presented to Pope John Paul II. This final proposed text contained 57 canons on temporal goods in *Book V*:

CANONS	SUBJECT MATTER
1254-1258	[Preliminary Canons]
1259-1272	Title I: The Acquisition of Goods
1273-1289	Title II: The Administration of Goods
1290-1298	Title III: Contracts and Especially Alienation
1299-1310	Title IV: Pious Wills in General and Pious Foundations

---

17 The discussions of the 1981 plenary gathering are reported in: PONTIFICAL COUNCIL FOR THE INTERPRETATION OF LEGISLATIVE TEXTS, *Congregatio Plenaria diebus 20-29 octobris 1981 habita*, Vatican City State, Typis polyglottis Vaticanis, 1991 (=*Congregatio Plenaria*).

18 *Congregatio Plenaria*, pp. 486-493. See this commentary on canon 1263.

19 *Congregatio Plenaria*, p. 592.

20 PONTIFICAL COMMISSION FOR THE REVISION OF THE CODE OF CANON LAW, *Codex Iuris Canonici, Schema Novissimum post consultationem S.R.E. Cardinalium, episcoporum conferentiarum, dicasteriorum curiae romanae, universitatum facultatumque ecclesiarum necnon superiorum institutorum vitae consecratae recognitum, iuxta placita Patrum Commissionis deinde emendatum atque Summo Pontifici praesentatum*, Vatican City, 1982 (=1982 *Schema*).

For ten months the Roman Pontiff personally studied the final proposal with the assistance of a small group of canonical experts. He promulgated the new *Codex Iuris Canonici* on January 25, 1983; it became effective on November 27, 1983, the First Sunday of Advent. *Book V* consists of 57 canons grouped as follows:

CANONS	SUBJECT MATTER
1254-1258	[Preliminary Canons]
1259-1272	Title I: The Acquisition of Goods
1273-1289	Title II: The Administration of Goods
1290-1298	Title III: Contracts and Especially Alienation
1299-1310	Title IV: Pious Wills in General and Pious Foundations

CODE OF CANONS OF THE EASTERN CHURCHES. On October 18, 1990, Pope John Paul II promulgated the *Code of Canons of the Eastern Churches*, which became effective on October 1, 1991. Its canons dealing with temporal goods reflect those promulgated by Pope Pius XII on February 9, 1952 by his *motu proprio* entitled *Postquam apostolicis litteris*;[21] these canons became effective on November 21, 1952. The 48 canons on temporal goods in the Eastern code reflect the discipline of the Latin code, but contain several significant differences. The canons are found in *Title XXIII: The Temporal Goods of the Church*:

---

[21] POPE PIUS XII, apostolic letter *motu proprio Postquam apostolicis litteris* (February 9, 1952), in *AAS*, 44 (1952), pp. 65-150.

CANONS	SUBJECT MATTER
1007-1009	[Preliminary Canons]
1010-1022	Title I: The Acquisition of Temporal Goods
1023-1033	Title II: The Administration of Ecclesiastical Goods
1034-1042	Title III: Contracts and Epecially Alienation
1043-1054	Title IV: Pious Wills in General and Pious Foundations

This commentary briefly considers these canons in relation to those of the 1983 code. The reader is advised to refer to each canon for a more thorough understanding of the existing universal legislation for the Eastern Churches.

CHAPTER TWO

PRELIMINARY CANONS
(Canons 1254-1258)

Book V begins with five preliminary canons which lay a foundation for the remaining canons in it. Canon 1254 affirms the innate power of the Church to acquire, retain, administer, and alienate temporal goods independently of any civil power in order to pursue its three principal purposes: to order divine worship, to provide decent support for the clergy and other ministers, and to perform the works of the sacred apostolate and of charity, especially towards the needy. Canon 1255 explains that temporal goods can be owned by the universal Church, the Apostolic See, and other ecclesiastical juridic persons, and canon 1256 attests that temporal goods are owned by the juridic person which has acquired them legitimately. Canon 1257 says that the norms of *Book V* govern only the temporal goods of the universal Church, the Apostolic See, and *public* juridic persons, all of which are called *ecclesiastical goods.* (The temporal goods of *private* juridic persons are governed by their own statutes, unless express provision is otherwise made in the code.) Finally, canon 1258 explains that the term *Church* is used in *Book V* to refer to those who own these ecclesiastical goods, unless it is otherwise apparent from the context or the nature of the matter.

These canons reflect the discipline of the 1917 *Code of Canon Law* in its canons 1495, 1496, 1497 §1, 1498, and 1499 §2. Canon 1257 §2 has no predecessor in the first code.

Corresponding canons in the 1990 *Code of Canons of the Eastern Churches* are canons 1007, 1008 §2, and 1009. No corresponding canon in the Eastern code exists for canons 1257 §2 and 1258.

INNATE RIGHT OF THE CHURCH CONCERNING TEMPORAL GOODS; PROPER PURPOSES OF THE CHURCH

Can. 1254 – §1. To pursue its proper purposes, the Catholic Church by innate right is able to acquire, retain, administer, and alienate temporal goods independently from civil power.

§2. The proper purposes are principally: to order divine worship, to care for the decent support of the clergy and other ministers, and to exercise works of the sacred apostolate and of charity, especially toward the needy.

Canon 1254 affirms before everyone, nations and individuals, the innate right of the Catholic Church, independently from civil power, to acquire, retain, administer, and alienate temporal goods for its own proper purposes, which are identified principally as three: to order divine worship, to care for the decent support of the clergy and other ministers, and to perform works of the sacred apostolate and of charity, especially to the needy.

FOUNDATIONAL PRINCIPLE: THE CHURCH HAS AN INNATE RIGHT TO TEMPORAL GOODS. Canon 1254 §1 asserts a foundational principle which permeates the entire legislation of the code on temporal goods: "the Church has the innate right to own temporal goods." The canon says that this right of the Church[1] is (1) innate, (2) independent of civil power, and (3) for its proper purposes. The Church is "born" with the right to ownership. It exercises this right without interference from others, including civil authorities.[2] This right is complete (i.e., to acquire, retain, administer, and alienate

---

[1]   CIC/1917, canon 1495 §1 had said the innate right to own temporal goods is enjoyed by both the Catholic Church and the Apostolic See." Reference to the Apostolic See was omitted in this canon since it is mentioned in canon 1255.

[2]   CIC/1917, canon 2345 had imposed an automatic excommunication, reserved to the Apostolic See, on those who usurped or detained goods or rights belonging to the Roman Church; if clergy committed the delict, they were to be deprived of dignities, benefices, offices, and pensions, and declared incapable of the same. A lesser penalty is contained in the 1983 code: "Those who impede... the legitimate use of sacred goods or other ecclesiastical goods... can be punished by a just penalty" (canon 1375). This penal law is facultative (see canon 1315 §3) and indeterminate (see canon 1315 §2).

temporal goods). The right exists in order that the Church can attain its proper purposes.

Put another way, by its very nature the Church needs temporal goods to perform its mission in the world. It therefore enjoys full and complete ownership (*dominium*) of its goods. No human power can eliminate this right of ownership, and this right exists even if others, including secular authorities, refuse to recognize it.

ORIGIN OF THE CHURCH'S RIGHT CONCERNING TEMPORAL GOODS. This canon asserts that the ability of the Church to have temporal goods is "by innate right," founded in the very nature of the Church. This right does not exist as a grant from any secular authority.[3] It has its origin from God and is based in divine positive law.[4] This right is asserted against civil governments which, over the centuries and sometimes still, have denied it to the Catholic Church (and other Christian denominations and non-Christian religions).[5] The Church was founded by Christ who gives both its mission (which ultimately is the "salvation of souls": see canon 1752) and the means to achieve it. It is not instituted by secular power and secular authorities are unable to take away its divine rights.

Just as the code claims that the Church has an "innate right" to own temporal goods, the code also claims that the Church also has the "innate right" to require necessary support from the Christian faithful in order to achieve its proper purposes (canon 1260).

EXERCISE OF THE CHURCH'S RIGHT CONCERNING TEMPORAL GOODS. The Church exercises its innate right to temporal goods

---

[3] See JOHN A. GOODWINE, *The Right of the Church to Acquire Temporal Goods*, Washington, The Catholic University of America, 1941; SCHOUPPE, pp. 22-24.

[4] That the Church has its origin from God is also reflected in canon 113 §1 which states: "the Catholic Church and the Apostolic See have the character of a moral person by divine ordinance itself." The "Apostolic See" here is a reference to the See of Peter, not the dicasteries of the Roman curia which do not claim divine origin. Though the code does not so state, the "college of bishops" is also a moral person. The code uses the term "moral person" to illustrate divine origin; aggregates established by competent Church authorities are called "juridic persons." See ROBERT T. KENNEDY, "Juridic Persons" in *New Commentary on the Code of Canon Law*, commissioned by the CLSA, John P. Beal, James A. Coriden, and Thomas J. Green (eds.), New York, Paulist, 2000, pp. 154-156 (=KENNEDY, "Juridic Persons"). (See the discussion on moral, juridic, and physical persons in the commentary on canon 1255.)

[5] See *Communicationes*, 36 (2004), p. 241.

"independently from civil power." This phrase existed in canon 1495 §1 of the 1917 code, but was omitted initially by the *coetus De bonis Ecclesiae temporalibus* because it was considered polemical.[6] Several recommendations on the 1977 *Schema* had voiced objections to that omission. Others favored the continued omission of the phrase because modern ecclesiology understands that the Church is subject to secular powers in caring for its goods. In the end, the *coetus* reinserted the phrase in order to avoid future doctrinal misinterpretation.[7]

Robert T. Kennedy comments that canon 1254 §1 is a statement revealing the Church's stand on Church-State relations:

> If canon 1254 means what it seems to say, it makes a remarkable claim. Independence from civil power is claimed not just for the *origin* of the Catholic Church's right to own property, but for the *exercise* of those rights as well. A claim of independent origin, alone, would not be particularly noteworthy; such a claim could rightly be made by any association of human beings or, indeed, by any individual human being, in whom the right to acquire and use temporal goods is derived not from concession by civil authority but from the dignity of the human person. Canon 1254, however, claims more: it claims, for the Catholic Church, independence from civil authority even in the *exercise* of its property rights. It is a startling claim of separation of Church and State made by the Roman Catholic Church.... The desired independence of the Church is said to flow from the practical application of the "principle of religious freedom."[8]

---

[6] *Communicationes*, 5 (1973), p. 94. CIC/1917, canon 1495 §1 had said the Catholic Church and Apostolic See possess temporal goods "freely" (*libere*). The omission of the word "freely" in the revised code has no significance, since the Church's freedom to own temporal goods is conveyed with the phrase "independently from civil power." DE PAOLIS, "De bonis Ecclesiae temporalibus," p. 27.

[7] *Communicationes*, 12 (1980), p. 396.

[8] ROBERT T. KENNEDY, "The Declaration of Religious Liberty Thirty Years Later: Challenges to the Church-State Relationship in the United States," in *The Jurist*, 55 (1995), pp. 480-482.

Kennedy observes that one of the sources indicated for canon 1254 §1 is *Dignitatis humanae*, the Second Vatican Council's *Declaration on Religious Liberty*, which states:

> Among those things which pertain to the good of the Church and indeed to the good of society here on earth, things which must everywhere and at all times be safeguarded and defended from all harm, the most outstanding is that the Church enjoy that freedom of action which her responsibility for the salvation of men requires. This is a sacred liberty with which the only-begotten Son of God endowed the Church which he purchased with his blood. Indeed it belongs so intimately to the Church that to attack it is to oppose the will of God. The freedom of the Church is a fundamental principle governing relations between the Church and public authorities and the whole civil order....
>
> As the spiritual authority appointed by Christ the Lord with the duty, imposed by divine command, of going into the whole world and preaching the Gospel to every creature, the Church claims freedom for herself in human society and before every public authority. The Church also claims freedom for herself as a society of men with the right to live in civil society in accordance with the demands of the Christian faith.
>
> When the principle of religious freedom is not just proclaimed in words or incorporated in law but is implemented sincerely in practice, only then does the Church enjoy in law and in fact those stable conditions which give her the independence necessary for fulfilling her divine mission. At the same time the Christian faithful, in common with the rest of men, have the civil right of freedom from interference in leading their lives according to their conscience. A harmony exists therefore between the freedom of the Church and that religious freedom which must be recognized as the right of all men and all

communities and must be sanctioned by constitutional law (n. 13).[9]

Nonetheless, the code recognizes that the Church, living in the midst of the world, co-exists with the secular sphere; it therefore urges compliance with civil laws which contradict neither divine law nor canon law (see canon 22).[10] While the Church asserts its rights in the matter of temporal goods independently from civil authority, several canons in *Book V* make reference, explicitly or implicitly, to the observance of civil laws:

1. canon 1259 – the Church has the same right to acquire temporal goods by every just means of civil law (and natural law and canon law) which are permitted to others

2. canon 1268 – prescription, as identified in civil law, is acknowledged as a means to acquire temporal goods and of freeing oneself from obligations (see canons 197-199, 1269-1270)

3. canon 1274 §5 – the institute for clergy support, the institute for social security of clergy, and the common fund are to be established in such a way that they have civil legal recognition

4. canon 1284 §2, 2° – administrators are to take care that the ownership of ecclesiastical goods is protected by civilly valid methods

5. canon 1284 §2, 3° – administrators are to observe the prescripts of civil law (and of canon law and those imposed by a founder, donor, or legitimate authority) and are especially to be on guard so that no damage comes to the Church from the non-observance of civil laws

---

9 FLANNERY I, pp. 809-810.

10 Those drafting the proposed new law acknowledged that "the Church is subjected to the civil juridic order as regards the administrative organization of goods, although both societies are free and independent": *Communicationes*, 12 (1980), p. 396. See WILLIAM W. BASSETT, "Relating Canon Law and Civil Law," in *The Jurist*, 44 (1984), pp. 3-18; ROBERT C. BECKER and JAMES A. SERRITELLA, "Problems of Ecclesiastical and Religious Organizations," in *The Jurist*, 44 (1984), pp. 48-66; PETER E. CAMPBELL, "The New Code of Canon Law and Religious: Some Civil Law Considerations," in *The Jurist*, 44 (1984), pp. 81-109.

6. canon 1286 1° – administrators are to observe civil labor laws and social policies in employment

7. canon 1288 – administrators need the written permission of their ordinary to initiate or contest civil litigation in the name of a public juridic person

8. canon 1290 – the general and particular provisions of civil law on contracts are to be observed with the same effects in canon law, unless the civil laws are contrary to divine law or canon law, and without prejudice to canon 1547

9. canon 1296 – the competent ecclesiastical authority is to decide what type of action is to be taken, if any, when the alienation of ecclesiastical goods is valid in civil law but invalid in canon law (see canon 1281 §3: a juridic person has the right to make recourse against an administrator who damages it by invalid acts; see also canon 639)

10. canon 1299 §2 – the formalities of civil law are to be observed in dispositions *mortis causa*, if possible[11]

When civil laws are observed properly by the Church, ecclesiastical goods obtain civil recognition and protection. These ecclesiastical goods are thereby subject both to canon law and civil law.

ASPECTS OF THE CHURCH'S RIGHT CONCERNING TEMPORAL GOODS. The canon identifies four aspects of the Church's right concerning temporal goods: to acquire, to retain, to administer, and to alienate them.[12] The 1917 code has listed only the first three, and had considered alienation as a kind of extraordinary administration (see CIC/1917, canon 1495 §1). Those revising the code, however,

---

[11] Consider also canon 681 §2 (a written agreement is to be made between a diocesan bishop and the competent superior of a religious institute when the bishop entrusts works to religious; this contract would have civil and canonical ramifications: see canon 1290) and canon 668 §1 (requiring individual religious to make a civilly valid will before final profession).

[12] When listing these four aspects of ownership, canon 634 §1 uses the word *possidere* (to possess) rather than *retinere* (to retain). These is no significance to this difference. Though the 1977 *Schema* had used both *retinere* (canon 1) and *possidere* (canon 2), when the *coetus* revised the draft it deliberately selected to use *retinere* consistently. See *Communicationes*, 12 (1980), p. 396.

judged alienation to be an act distinct from administration of tempo-ral goods: "alienation is not an act of administration."[13] Therefore, a fourth aspect the Church's right is identified in the law.

Put quite simply, to acquire temporal goods means "to obtain them" which the Church may do in the same ways which are lawful (by natural law and positive law) for others (canon 1259). To retain temporal goods means "to keep them as possessors." To administer temporal goods means "to protect them, to help them bear fruit (e.g., revenue), and to use them for their proper ends."[14] To alienate temporal goods means "to convey ownership of them to another."

Elsewhere, the code specifically states that these four aspects of the Church's right apply to religious institutes (canon 634 §1), and to societies of apostolic life (canon 741 §1).[15] By inference, the aspects are also applied to secular institutes (see canon 718).

THE PURPOSES OF THE CHURCH'S RIGHT CONCERNING TEM-PORAL GOODS. The Church exercises its innate right independently from civil power. This is in order that the Church in this world may perform its "proper purposes,"[16] which canon 1254 §2 identifies as principally three:

---

[13] *Communicationes,* 12 (1980), p. 396.

[14] The PONTIFICAL COUNCIL FOR LEGISLATIVE TEXTS observes that the Legislator uses the term *administration* in two ways in the code: (1) in *Book I* of the code, to designate *acts of governance* as a function proper to ecclesiastical authority performing acts of jurisdiction (diverse from acts of legislation and acts of judgment); and (2) in *Book V* of the code, to designate the *administration of economic affairs,* as performing a function "to preserve a patrimonial good, to help it bear fruit, and to better it." In *Nota* La funzione dell'autorità sui beni ecclesiastici (February 12, 2004), in *Communicationes,* 36 (2004), p. 26 (=PCLT, *Nota,* La funzione dell'autorità).

[15] Canon 741 §2 adds that, according to the norm of proper law, the members of societies of apostolic life are also capable of acquiring, possessing, administering and dispos-ing of temporal goods as individuals, but whatever comes to them on behalf of the society belongs to the society. The members' personal goods are not "ecclesiastical goods" (see canon 1257 §1).

[16] VELASIO DE PAOLIS explains that, strictly speaking, these are the proper ends *of the Church.* They are likewise proper ends of public juridic persons, whose ends are the same as the ends of the Church in whose innate right they participate. In *I beni temporali della Chiesa,* Bologna, Ed. Dehoniane, 1995, p. 19 (=DE PAOLIS, *I beni temporali*)

YUJI SUGAWARA comments that these three proper purposes reflect the mission of the Church. In "Le norme sui beni temporali negli istituti religiosi (can. 635)," in *Iustitia*

1. to order divine worship;

2. to care for the decent support (*sustentatio*) of the clergy and other ministers; and

3. to exercise works of the sacred apostolate[17] and of charity, especially toward the needy.[18]

These are also stated, but differently arranged, in canon 222 §1 which identifies the responsibility of all the Christian faithful to assist the needs of the Church so that it has "what is necessary for divine worship, for the works of the apostolate and of charity, and

---

in caritate: Miscellanea di studi in onore di Velasio De Paolis, Rome, Urbaniana University Press, 2005, p. 417 (=SUGAWARA, "Le norme sui beni temporali").

[17] Canon 298 § identifies some works of the apostolate: "initiatives of evangelization, works of piety or charity, and those which animate the temporal order with a Christian spirit." This list of apostolic works is merely illustrative, not taxative. The *DPMB* identifies an *apostolic criterion* guiding the administration of diocesan goods: "This [apostolic criterion] requires that goods be used as instruments in the service of evangelization and catechesis. The same principle governs the use of the media and information technology, as well as the organization of sacred art exhibitions, guided tours of churches and places of religious interest, and similar activities" (n. 189 d).

[18] The 1977 *Schema* had not made explicit reference to the needy (see canon 2). During the consultation process on that *Schema*, several suggestions were made to mention the needy. *Communicationes*, 12 (1980), p. 396. As a result, reference to the needy was inserted into the 1980 *Schema*.

The code mentions the poor (*pauperes*) or one of its cognates in canons:
    222 §2: the Christian faithful are to assist the poor from their own resources;
    529 §1: the pastor is to seek out the poor with particular diligence;
    600: the evangelical council of poverty entails a life which is poor in fact and in spirit;
    1181: the poor are not to be deprived of funerals;
    1274 §3: a diocesan common fund may be established which, among several things, may help richer dioceses to assist poorer ones.

The code mentions the needy (*egentes*) or one of its cognates in canons:
    600: the evangelical counsel of poverty imitates Christ who became poor for us [cf. 2 Corinthians 8:9];
    640: religious institutes should assist the needy from their own resources;
    945 §2: it is recommended that priests offer Mass especially for the needy even without a Mass offering;
    1254 §2: the works of the apostolate toward the needy is one of the proper purposes of the Catholic Church.

Both terms are found in canon 848: the minister of the sacraments is to take care that the needy (*egentes*) are not deprived of the sacraments because of their poverty (*paupertas*). See GARRETT J. ROCHE, "The Poor and Temporal Goods in Book V of the Code," in *The Jurist*, 55 (1995) 299-348.

for the decent support of ministers."[19] Even though ecclesiastical goods exist for these proper purposes, the ownership of each good rests with the juridic person which possesses them.[20]

The text of canon 1254 §2 is taken from *Presbyterorum ordinis*, n.17 of Vatican Council II which says that the Church has temporal goods for "the organization of divine worship, the provision of decent support for the clergy, and the exercise of works of the apostolate and of charity, especially for the benefit of those in need."[21]

The adverb "principally"[22] may lead to the conclusion that the list of these three purposes is not taxative, that is, that other activi-

---

[19]   These diverse arrangements show that the activities are not listed in any priority. Note also canon 114 §1 which says that juridic persons are "ordered for a purpose which is in keeping with the mission of the Church and which transcends the purpose of the individuals." Canon 114 §2 elaborates: "The purposes mentioned in §1 are understood as those which pertain to works of piety, of the apostolate, and of charity, whether spiritual or temporal." Canon 114 §2 does not make reference to all three of purposes identified in canon 1254 §2.

[20]   PCLT, *Nota, La funzione dell'autorità*, p. 24.

[21]   SECOND VATICAN COUNCIL, Decree on the Ministry and Life of Priests *Presbyterorum ordinis* (December 7, 1975), in *AAS*, 58 (1966), pp. 991-1024; English translation in FLANNERY I, 863-902. The canon adds the words "and other ministers" to the second purpose identified in the conciliar decree.
       Canon 1254 §2 developed from CIC/1917, canon 1496 which affirmed the right of the Church, independently from civil power, to require from the faithful "what is necessary for divine worship, for the honest sustenance of clerics and other ministers, and for the remaining ends proper to it." No specific mention was made to "works of the sacred apostolate and charity, especially toward the needy."

[22]   The *coetus* saw no need to list multiple specific ends of the Church (e.g., assistance to missionaries, the promotion of culture, etc.). The group said that "all the other ends that could be added are nothing but the development of the ends already contained under the more general formulation of 'works of the sacred apostolate and of char-ity'." *Communicationes*, 12 (1980) 396-397.
       VELASIO DE PAOLIS observes that the word principally (*praecipue*) was added to the text of *Presbyterorum ordinis*, n. 17 as a clarification to show that this listing of the purposes of the Church is not taxative but illustrative. In "De bonis Ecclesiae temporalibus," p. 29. See also DE PAOLIS, *I beni temporali*, p. 52; CRISTIAN BEGUS, *Diritto patrimoniale canonico*, Vatican City, Lateran University Press, 2007, pp. 35-36 (=BEGUS, *Diritto patrimoniale canonico*).
       ADAM J. MAIDA and NICHOLAS CAFARDI, however, comment about canon 1254 §2: "The statement of the church's ends, given its location in Book V, obviously refers to those ends for which property is used. It is an illustrative, and not an exhaustive, list of the Church's purposes. It is, however, an exhaustive list of the purposes for which property can be held. Property held for reasons other than these is not properly held by the Church." In *Church Property, Church Finances, and Church-Related Corporations*, Saint Louis, The Catholic Health Association of the United States, 1984, p. 10 (=MAIDA-CAFARDI, *Church Property*).

ties may exist which justify the Church's ownership of goods. Yet, given the breadth of activities which may be considered "works of the sacred apostolate," one may reasonably conclude that this list is indeed taxative and that any activity not somehow a manifestation of one of these three purposes is not in keeping with the Church's mission.[23]

The 2004 *Directory for the Pastoral Ministry of Bishops* comments about these purposes:

> In the administration of goods, always presupposing that justice is observed, the Bishop concerns himself first of all with providing for divine worship, charity, the apostolate and the support of clergy: these ends are given precedence over all others.[24]

Although this excerpt does not make specific mention of the needy, the directory explains elsewhere that an "ascetic" criterion guiding the diocesan bishop's administration would result in generosity to the poor:

> In keeping with the spirit of the Gospel, this [ascetic criterion] demands that the disciples of Christ "make use of the world, as though they were not using it" (cf. 1 Cor 7:31). Therefore, they should be moderate and detached, trusting in divine providence and generous towards the needy, always preserving the bond of love.[25]

MARIANO LÓPEZ ALARCÓN comments: "The scope and the content of each of the objectives have to be given a broad interpretation, so that each one might be totally fulfilled." In "Book V: The Temporal Goods of the Church," in *Code of Canon Law Annotated*, 2nd rev. ed., Ernest Caparros and Hélène Aubé (eds.), Montréal, Wilson and Lafleur, 2004, p. 965 (=LÓPEZ ALARCÓN, "Book V").

[23] Several other canons make reference to works within the Church which reflect the three "proper purposes" identified in canon 1254 §2: e.g., to foster a more perfect life (canon 298 §1), to promote Christian doctrine (canons 298 §1; 301 §1), to undertake initiatives of evangelization (canon 298 §1), to animate the temporal order with a Christian spirit (canons 298 §1; 327), to promote the Christian vocation in the world (canon 215), etc.

[24] *DPMB*, n. 188. No explicit reference is made to the decent support of other ministers.

[25] *DPMB*, n. 189 c).

Inasmuch as these purposes are the basis for ownership of temporal goods by the Church, it follows that using these goods for other purposes is not just.[26] Arguably, goods which are accumulated solely for the sake of wealth and security but not for one of the principal purposes identified in canon 1254 §2, have no right to be called ecclesiastical goods.[27]

Administrators of temporal goods, which exist for the proper purposes of the Church, are to fulfill their function with the diligence due a good householder (canon 1284 §1) and according to the norm of law (canon 1282). Administrators have a fiduciary relationship toward these goods, which are not their personal property. Ordinaries are to exercise vigilance over the administration of ecclesiastical goods belonging to juridic persons subject to them (canon 1276 §1). The role of vigilance is also a responsibility of the Roman Pontiff, who is also an "ordinary" (canon 134 §1; see canons 331-333) and who, in addition, is "the supreme administrator and steward of all ecclesiastical goods" (canon 1273). Yet, even the Pope cannot dispose of them as if they were his personal property.[28]

---

[26] VELASIO DE PAOLIS comments that temporal goods "are to be used for church purposes, in the spirit of the Church's mission, not in the spirit and logic of profit and accumulation." In "Temporal Goods of the Church in the New Code with Particular Reference to Institutes of Consecrated Life," in *The Jurist*, 43 (1983), p. 352 (=DE PAOLIS, "Temporal Goods... Consecrated Life"). See also W.B. SMITH, "Unnecessary Security," in *Homiletic and Pastoral Review*, 10 (2002), pp. 67-68.

[27] JORDAN HITE adds, "a juridic person would not be true to its purpose if it engaged in purely secular activity." In *A Primer on Public and Private Juridic Persons: Applications to the Healthcare Ministry*, Saint Louis, The Catholic Health Association, 2000, p. 6 = (HITE, *Public and Private Juridic Persons*).

[28] STANISLAUS WOYWOOD writes: "The title or ownership of ecclesiastical goods is vested in the individual legal ecclesiastical person, but it is an ownership of a peculiar type which in effect approaches trusteeship. The legal person who holds the title to church property and goods, is not free to use and dispose of the goods at will, as the owner of private property can do. Canon law regulates the use and administration of ecclesiastical goods. That the Roman Pontiff is by his very office the supreme administrator and dispensor of all ecclesiastical goods, is evident from the very constitution of the Catholic Church. Great as his powers are as supreme administrator, they are limited by the very nature of ecclesiastical goods, which are held in trust by ecclesiastical persons for the purposes of charity and religion." In *A Practical Commentary on the Code of Canon Law*, rev. by Callistus Smith, New York, Wagner, 1948, vol. 2, p. 202.

CLASSIFICATIONS OF TEMPORAL GOODS.[29] The 1917 code and canonical tradition distinguished a number of categories to classify temporal goods, many of which are also found in the 1983 code:

- corporeal goods[30] – goods which are palpable or that can be perceived by the senses (e.g., a church, hospital, automobile)

  incorporeal goods – goods which are not palpable and cannot be perceived by the senses but only by the mind (e.g., legal rights, patents, stocks)

- immovable goods[31] – corporeal goods which cannot be transferred from place to place naturally (e.g., land, buildings) or legally (e.g., doors, plumbing, windows)

  movable goods – corporeal goods which can be transferred from place to place (e.g., merchandise, livestock, automobiles); these are further distinguished as:

  - fungible movable goods – movable goods which may be replaced in kind and which are consumed when used (e.g., grain, vegetables, fruit)

    non-fungible movable goods – movable goods which are not consumed by their first use (e.g., automobiles, furniture, computers)

- sacred goods[32] designated for divine worship by dedication or blessing (see canons 1171,1205)

---

[29] CIC/1917, canon 1497. See T. LINCOLN BOUSCAREN, ADAM C. ELLIS, AND FRANCIS N. KORTH, *Canon Law: A Text and Commentary*, 4th rev. ed., Milwaukee, Bruce, 1963, pp. 802-802; DE PAOLIS, *De bonis Ecclesiae temporalibus*, p. 11; G. VROMANT, *De bonis Ecclesiae temporalibus*, 3rd rev. ed., Brussels, Éditions De Schuet, 1953, pp. 41-42; JEAN MARIE SIGNIÉ, *Paroisses et administration des biens: Un chemin vers l'autosuffisiance des Églises d'Afrique*, Paris, L'Harmattan, 2007, pp. 82-85; SCHOUPPE, pp. 43-66.

[30] The 1983 code does not refer to *corporeal* and *incorporeal* goods, a category based in Roman Law: "Res corporales sunt, quae tangi possunt; incorporales, quae tangi non possunt" (GAIUS, *Institutiones*, II, 12). This terminology had appeared in CIC/1917, canon 1497 §1. See DE PAOLIS, *I beni temporali*, p. 11, fn. 15.

[31] Immovable and movable goods are mentioned in canon 1270; 1283, 2°; and 1302 §1. Movable goods are mentioned in canons 1285 and 1305. Both immovable and movable goods are mentioned in canon 1376.

[32] See *Communicationes*, 12 (1980), p. 339. Not all ecclesiastical goods are sacred goods, and not all sacred goods are ecclesiastical goods (since sacred goods can be owned privately: canon 1269). Canon 1171 adds that sacred things "are to be treated

profane goods – goods which are not sacred
- precious goods[33] – goods distinguished by age, art, material, or veneration (see canon 1189)
  non-precious goods – goods which are not precious

In addition, the 1983 Code identifies another category of ecclesiastical goods:
- stable patrimony[34] – immovable and movable goods which, by legitimate designation of competent authority through an act of extraordinary administration, form the secure basis of a juridic person so that it can perform its works (see canons 1285, 1291)
  non-stable patrimony – immovable and movable goods which are not legitimately designated as stable patrimony

CORRESPONDING CANON OF THE EASTERN CODE: CANON 1007. The Eastern norm contains the basic discipline of Latin canon 1254, which it combines into one paragraph, but omits the phrase "independently from civil power." The Eastern canon begins with a phrase explaining the relation of temporal goods to the spiritual mission of the Church: "In taking care of the spiritual well-being of people, the Church needs and uses temporal goods insofar as its proper mission demands it." The canon identifies the three principal purposes of temporal goods in a different sequence than canon 1254 §1: "divine worship, works of the apostolate [and] charity, and suit-

reverently and are not to be employed for profane or inappropriate use even if they are owned by private persons." Further, canon 1376 says, "A person who profanes a movable or immovable sacred object is to be punished with a just penalty." This penal law is preceptive (see canon 1344) and indeterminate (see canon 1315 §2).
See PONTIFICAL COUNCIL FOR LEGISLATIVE TEXTS, "La funzione dell'autorità ecclesiastica sui beni ecclesiastici" (February 12, 2004), in *Communicationes,* 36 (2004), p. 25.

[33] Precious goods are mentioned in canons 638 §3; 1189; 1220 §2; 1270; 1283, 2°; and 1292 §2.

[34] See the commentary on canon 1285. The designation of goods belonging to stable patrimony, required by canon 1291, is very significant. The distinction between stable patrimony and non-stable patrimony is the basis for determinations in matters of alienation (canons 1291-1294), contractual transactions which may threaten a public juridic person (canon 1295), diocesan taxation (canon 1263), and charitable donations (canon 1285).

able (*congrua*, rather than "decent," *honesta*) support for ministers." Also, the Eastern law does not make specific mention of charity being directed especially toward "the needy."

SUBJECTS CAPABLE OF TEMPORAL GOODS

Can. 1255 – The universal Church and the Apostolic See, the particular Churches, as well as any other juridic person, public or private, are subjects capable of acquiring, retaining, administering, and alienating temporal goods according to the norm of law.

Following the assertion of canon 1254 §1 concerning the innate right of the Catholic Church concerning temporal goods, canon 1255 identifies those subjects able to acquire, retain, administer, and alienate them (which must be done according to the norm of law):

1. the universal Church[35] (see canon 204)
2. the Apostolic See (see canon 361)
3. the particular Churches[36] (see canon 368)
4. all other juridic persons (public or private) (see canon 116).

Each of these entities has the juridic right to and capacity for temporal goods, even though some outside the Church may not recognize this right and capacity.

---

[35] Canon 113 §1 says that the Catholic Church and the Apostolic See are moral persons established by divine ordinance. The particular Churches, however, are juridic persons *a iure* (canon 373). Canon 1255 legislates that all these persons are capable of temporal goods. In fact, however, the Catholic Church *as such* owns nothing, and nor does the Apostolic See inasmuch as the term, as used in canon 113 §1 refers to the Roman Pontiff (the supreme administrator and steward of all ecclesiastical goods: see canon 1273), not the Roman curia. The identification of the Apostolic See with the Roman Pontiff himself was mentioned in the third meeting of the *coetus De bonis Ecclesiae temporalibus* on January 21, 1967: see *Communicationes*, 36 (2004), p. 244. See also DE PAOLIS, *De bonis Ecclesiae temporalibus*, p. 44.

[36] By the term "particular Churches" are meant dioceses, territorial prelatures, territorial abbacies, apostolic vicariates, apostolic prefectures, stably erected apostolic administrations (canon 368), and military ordinariates (see POPE JOHN PAUL II, apostolic constitution *Spirituali militium curae* [April 21, 1986], in *AAS*, 78 [1986], pp. 481-486; English translation in *CLD*, Vol. 12, pp. 312-317).

Although all the entities listed in this canon may have temporal goods, the term "ecclesiastical goods" (as used technically in *Book V*) is applied only to the universal Church, the Apostolic See, and *public* juridic persons. While canon 1255 acknowledges the capacity of *private* juridic persons for temporal goods, the term "ecclesiastical goods" is not applied to their temporal goods (canon 1257 §1) since private juridic persons do not act "in the name of the Church"[37] and "in view of the public good." Nor is the term applied to the temporal goods of *private* associations of the Christian faithful.[38] Of course, the term is also not applied to goods owned by physical persons who are members of the Church.

Physical persons cannot own the temporal goods of the Church; they can only be the superior, legal representative, or administrator of the juridic persons which own them (see canon 118). Physical persons may not acquire,[39] retain, administer, or alienate ecclesiastical goods in their own name. Ecclesiastical goods are owned by a public juridic person (not its superior, legal representative, or administrator). Those caring for ecclesiastical goods must give an accounting of their stewardship to others[40] and, in many instances, need special intervention (consultation or consent) from others in order to perform certain aspects of their stewardship validly.[41]

The Roman Pontiff is the supreme administrator and steward of all ecclesiastical goods (canon 1273). Under his supremacy, other

---

[37]   This rationale of the *coetus De bonis Ecclesiae temporalibus* is reported in the *Preface* to the 1977 *Schema*, p. 4.

[38]   The temporal goods of *public* associations of the Christian faithful are "ecclesiastical goods" because these associations are *public* juridic persons. Public associations pursue their purposes in the name of the Church (*nomine Ecclesiae*) (canon 313 §1).

[39]   Canon 1269 says that "sacred goods" (see canon 1171) which belong to public juridic persons (and, therefore, are "ecclesiastical goods") can be acquired only by another public juridic person by prescription; if they belong to a private person, another private person can acquire them by this means. Private persons cannot, however, acquire by prescription sacred goods which are ecclesiastical goods owned by a public juridic person.

[40]   See, for example, canons 636 §2; 1284; 1287; and 1307.

[41]   See, for example, canons 1263; 1264; 1265; 1267 §2; 1277; 1279 §1; 1280; 1281; 1283; 1284; 1288; 1291; 1292; 1295; 1296; 1297; 1298; 1302; 1304 §1; 1305; 1308; 1309; and 1310.

ordinaries in the Church exercise vigilance over the ecclesiastical goods of juridic persons subject to them (see canons 1276 §1; 1301 §2; 1302 §2). Yet, neither the Roman Pontiff nor the other ordinaries own the ecclesiastical goods.

The codified law that gives juridic persons the right to have temporal goods is the same law which requires that these goods be acquired, retained, administered, and alienated "according to the norm of law."[42] The law governing these aspects of ownership of goods may be universal law,[43] particular law,[44] proper law,[45] or statutes.

PERSONS: MORAL, JURIDIC, PHYSICAL.[46] In order to understand the legislation of the Church on temporal goods, one needs to understand clearly the concept of the *juridic persons* created by the Church.

A person is a subject of rights and obligations (see canons 96, 113 §2). Canon 113 §1[47] says that the Catholic Church and the

---

[42] Ecclesiastical law can also place limits on the temporal goods by public juridic persons, as is acknowledged in canon 634 §1 which explains that the constitutions of religious institutes can exclude or restrict their capacity for ownership.

[43] Universal laws are for the entire Catholic Church and bind everywhere those for whom they are issued. They are promulgated in the official commentary, *Acta Apostolicae Sedis,* or in some other fashion, and take effect three months after promulgation (unless otherwise specified by the nature of the matter or the law itself). The canons on temporal goods in *Book V* (and elsewhere in the code) are universal laws, many of which require the establishment of particular laws.

[44] Particular laws are for a particular territory and are not personal (unless otherwise evident). They are promulgated in a manner determined by the legislator and bind one month after promulgation (unless otherwise specified by the law). (See canons 8, 12, and 13.)

[45] Proper laws govern institutes of consecrated life and societies of apostolic life.

[46] The 1917 code identified only two kinds of persons: moral (CIC/1917, canon 99) and physical (CIC/1917, canon 87). The 1983 identifies four kinds of persons: moral (canon 113 §1), public juridic (canon 113 §2 and 116 §1), private juridic (canon 113 §2 and 116 §1), and physical (canon 96).

The Eastern code identifies only two kinds of persons: physical (CCEO, canons 909-919) and juridic (CCEO, canons 920-930). Juridic persons are not further distinguished as public or private in Eastern law.

[47] Canon 113 §1 had not existed in the 1977 *Schema* or the 1980 *Schema,* but was inserted after the 1982 final proposed draft of legislation was presented to Pope John Paul II. In explaining the rationale for the omission, the *coetus* had explained that reference to the Catholic Church as a moral person had no need to be mentioned in

Apostolic See are *moral persons* by divine ordinance.[48] Canon 361 explains that in the code the term "Apostolic See" (or, the "Holy See") refers to the Roman Pontiff, the Secretariat of State, the Council for the Public Affairs of the Church, and the other institutes

---

the law since its origin is divine and not juridic; and, reference to the Apostolic See as a moral person was omitted because the *coetus* discovered no consensus among commentators on the CIC/1917 about the proper subject of its personality nor its collegial or non-collegial nature. Therefore, the *coetus* decided it would be better to make no reference to it in the law. The *coetus* envisioned that the norms of the code would legislate only for juridic persons, not moral ones. See *Communicationes*, 9 (1977), p. 240.

[48] The Eastern code does not use the term "moral persons" (see CCEO, canon 920). ROBERT T. KENNEDY describes a moral person: "A moral person is a group or succession of natural persons who are united by a common purpose and, hence, who have a particular relationship to each other and who, because of that relationship, may be conceived of as a single person.... By divine institution the Catholic Church is a group, and the papacy a succession, of natural persons united by a common purpose and conceived of as a single entity." He observes that the college of bishops should also be treated as a moral person of divine origin. He adds that "moral persons" also exist outside the Church. The 1917 code used the term "moral person" to refer also to "juridic persons" (as that term is used in the 1983 code). KENNEDY comments: "The 1983 Code more clearly distinguishes artificial persons (juridic persons constituted by ecclesiastical authority) from groups of persons or accumulations of assets not brought into existence by ecclesiastical authority (moral persons), and among the latter distinguishes moral persons of divine institution (the Catholic Church and Apostolic See) from moral persons of human origin, such as various *de facto* associations or funds." In "Juridic Persons," pp. 154-156.
WILLIE ONCLIN distinguishes moral and juridic persons: *"Persona moralis exsistit in ordine sociologico et constituitur ab ipsis hominibus sine interventu auctoritatis Societatis constituae. Persona iuridica existat in ordine iuridico positivo et oritur vi legis aut actus administrativi competentis in Societate auctoritatis, qua, communius saltem, realitas socialis exstans iuridice confirmatur."* In "De personalitate morali vel canonica," in *Acta conventus internationalis canonistarum, Romae diebus 20-25 mai 1968 celebrati*, Rome, Typis polyglottis Vaticanis, 1968, p. 131.
For an extensive consideration of juridical persons, and a careful analysis of the historical development of the canons on moral and juridic persons in the 1983 code, see: JOSEPH FOX, "Introductory Thoughts about Public Ecclesiastical Juridic Persons and Their Civilly Incorporated Apostolates," in *Public Ecclesiastical Juridic Persons and their Civilly Incorporated Apostolates (e.g., Universities, Healthcare Institutions, Social Service Agencies) in the Catholic Church in the U.S.A.: Canonical-Civil Aspects: Acts of the Colloquium*, Rome, Pontifical University of Saint Thomas Aquinas in Rome, 1998, pp. 231-258 (=Fox, "Introductory Thoughts"); ALBERT GAUTHIER, "Juridical Persons in the *Code of Canon Law*," in *Studia canonica*, 25 (1991) 77-92; JORDAN HITE, *A Primer on Public and Private Juridic Persons*, Saint Louis, The Catholic Health Association, 2000, esp. pp. 5-9; ALBERTO PERLASCA, *Il concetto di bene ecclesiastico*, pp. 231-293; HUGO A. VON USTINOV, "El régimen canónico de los bienes de propriedad de las personas juridicas privadas," in *Anuario Argentino de Derecho Canónico*, 13 (2006), pp. 187-213.

of the Roman Curia.[49] In the context of canon 113 §1, clearly the "Apostolic See" means the Roman Pontiff only, since the institutes of the Roman Curia do not claim divine origin.[50] In the context of canon 1255, however, the "Apostolic See" means all the institutes identified in canon 361. Also, the "universal Church" here refers to the "Latin Church" (since this code contains legislation only for it, not for the several Eastern Catholic Churches). The particular Churches are juridic persons *a iure* (canon 373).

Canon 113 §2 says that in the Catholic Church (a moral person) there are two other kinds of persons: *physical persons*[51] and *juridic persons* (that is, subjects in canon law of obligations and rights which correspond to their nature). A physical person comes to exist in the Church by baptism whereby one acquires the "rights and duties which are proper to Christians in keeping with their condition" (canon 96; see canons 204, 11). A juridic person comes to exist in the Church by action of competent ecclesiastical authority (see canon 114 §1).

Any study of the temporal goods of the Church requires a clear understanding of *juridic persons*:

1. As regards their establishment, juridic persons are of two kinds (canon 114 §1):
   a. those established by law (*a iure*), or
   b. those established by special grant of competent church authority (*ab homine*) given through a decree. Competent church authority is not to confer juridic personality except on aggregates which pursue a truly useful purpose and possess the means foreseen to be sufficient to achieve their designated purpose (canon 114 §3).[52] An aggregate is able to acquire

---

[49] These are further defined by POPE JOHN PAUL II, apostolic constitution, *Pastor bonus* (June 28, 1988), in *AAS*, 80 (1988), pp. 841-921.

[50] VROMANT, p. 18.

[51] *Physical persons* are also known as *natural persons*.

[52] That juridic persons, when erected, must possess sufficient means to achieve their designated purposes indicates that juridic persons must have "stable patrimony." See the discussion of stable patrimony in the commentary on canon 1285; see also DE PAOLIS, "Temporal Goods... Consecrated Life," p. 356.

juridic personality only if competent authority has approved its statutes (canon 117).[53]

2. As regards their composition, juridic persons are of two kinds (canons 114 §1, 115 §1):

    a. aggregates of persons (*universitates personarum*), of which there are two kinds:

        1) collegial: if the members (at least three in number) determine the juridic person's action through participation in rendering decisions, whether by equal right or not, according to the norm of law[54]

        2) non-collegial: otherwise (canon 115 §2)

    b. aggregates of things (*universitates rerum*), also known as "autonomous foundations" (see canon 1303 §1, 1°), which consist of goods or things, whether spiritual or material; these are directed by either one or more physical persons or a college, according to the norm of law and the statutes of the foundation (canon 115 §3)

3. As regards their purposes, all juridic persons are ordered for a purpose which is in keeping with the mission of the Church and which transcends the purpose of the individuals (canon 114 §1). These purposes are:

    a. works of piety

    b. works of the apostolate

    c. works of charity (spiritual or temporal). (canon 114 §2)[55]

4. As regards their functioning in the name of the Church, juridic persons are of two kinds (canon 116):[56]

    a. public juridic persons: constituted so that, within the purposes set out for them, they fulfill *in the name of the Church,*

---

[53]   A juridic person is governed by universal law and its own statutes (see canon 117, which governs juridic persons erected *a iure* and *ab homine*).

[54]   See canon 119 on the collegial acts of elections and of other affairs.

[55]   Compare with canons 222 §1 (on needs of the Church for which all the Christian faithful are bound to offer assistance) and 1295 §1 (on the principal purposes for which the Church has temporal goods).

[56]   The Eastern code does not distinguish *public* and *private* juridic persons (see CCEO, canons 920-930). All juridic persons in the Eastern law "are constituted for a purpose that is in keeping with the mission of the Church" (canon 921 §1).

according to the norm of law, the proper function entrusted to them *in view of the public good*; they come into existence either by the law itself or by special decree of competent authority[57]

b. private juridic persons: all others; they can come into existence only by a special decree of competent authority; they do not act *in the name of the Church*, but instead act in their own name

5. Every juridic person has a representative who acts in its name (canon 118). This legal representative is one whose competence is determined

   a. for public juridic persons: by universal law, particular law, or the statutes;

   b. for private juridic persons: by the statutes (canon 118).

6. As regards their duration, every juridic person is perpetual by its nature (canon 120). Nevertheless, juridic persons can be extinguished.

   a. A public juridic person is extinguished:

      1) by legitimate suppression by a competent authority, or

      2) if it has ceased to exist for 100 years.

   b. A private juridic person is extinguished:

      1) by legitimate suppression by a competent authority, or

      2) if it has ceased to exist for 100 years, or

---

[57] Canon 1257 assigns the term *ecclesiastical goods* only to the temporal goods of *public* juridic persons. This reflects canon 116 which says that public juridic persons carry on their functions "in the name of the Church," meaning in the name of public Church authority, and "in view of the public good" (see canon 313, which states that public associations of the Christian faithful, which are juridic persons *a iure*, pursue their purposes "in the name of the Church"). The same is not said about private juridic persons, who act in their own name. See *Communicationes*, 21 (1989), pp. 144.

JOSEPH FOX reflects: "The mission entrusted to a public juridic person and its activities are public functions of the Church, performed in its name, and not private acts of the juridical person. There are consequently two principal limitations placed on the acts of the public juridic person. One is that it must act within the scope entrusted to it, within its mission; acting beyond these boundaries would be illicit. The other is that it must act *according to the norm of law* (can. 116 §1); its autonomy is exercised within the limits established by Church law. It cannot act in an entirely independent manner." In "Introductory Thoughts," pp. 250-251. See also VELASIO DE PAOLIS, "Dimensione ecclesiale dei beni temporali destinati a fini ecclesiali," in *Periodica*, 84 (1995), pp. 92-95, 102-103.

3) according to the norm of its statutes, or

4) if, in the judgment of competent authority, it has ceased to exist according to its statutes.

If even one of the members of a collegial juridic person survives, and the aggregate of persons has not ceased to exist according to its statutes, that member has the exercise of all the rights of the aggregate.

7. Special norms govern the extinction of a public[58] juridic person (canon 123).

 a. The allocation of its goods, patrimonial rights, and obligations is governed by law and its statutes.

 b. If the statutes are silent, the goods, patrimonial rights, and obligations transfer to the juridic person immediately superior, always without prejudice to the intentions of founders and donors, and acquired rights.

 c. However, the allocation of the temporal goods of a suppressed institute of consecrated life (i.e., religious institutes and secular institutes), like the suppression itself, is reserved to the Apostolic See (canon 584).

8. Special norms govern the joining of public juridic persons (canon 121).[59]

---

[58] The allocation of the goods of a private juridic person is governed by its statutes (canon 123). The same principle applies in the case of the extinction of a private association of the Christian faithful which is not a juridic person: i.e., its statutes must determine the allocation of its goods "without prejudice to acquired rights and the intentions of founders" (canon 326 §2).

[59] In the 1917 code, the canons dealing with the joining, division, and extinction of moral [juridic] persons were treated among the canons on temporal goods in canons 1500-1501. During the early days of discussing the revision of the canons on temporal goods, it was noted that these canons should be transferred to the general section of the code which would deal with persons: *Communicationes,* 26 (2004), p. 246.
The code does not contain canons specifically addressing the joining or division of private juridic persons; their statutes would govern these actions. Canons 120 and 123, however, address the extinction of private juridic persons. Should private juridic persons be joined or divided, of course, the action of the competent ecclesiastical authority will be necessary to erect the newly emerged juridic persons (i.e., the one which results from the joining of the two or more, and the two or more which result from the division of the one). See HITE, *Public and Private Juridic Persons,* p. 8.

    a. If public juridic persons are so joined that from them one new public juridic person results, the new public juridic person obtains the goods, patrimonial rights and obligations of the prior ones.

    b. With regard to the allocation of goods and the fulfillment of obligations, to be respected are the intentions of the founders and donors, and acquired rights.[60]

9. Special norms govern the dividing of a public juridic person (canon 122). If a public juridic person is divided such that either part of it is joined to another juridic person or is erected as a distinct juridic person, the competent authority (personally or through an executor), observing the intentions of founders and donors, the acquired rights, and the approved statutes, must take care:

    a. that common, divisible, patrimonial goods and rights (as well as debts and other obligations) are divided among the juridic persons, with due proportion in equity and justice, after all the circumstances and needs of each have been considered; and

    b. that the use and usufruct of common goods which cannot be divided accrue to each juridic person, and that the obligations proper to them are imposed upon each, in due proportion determined in equity and justice.

10. Juridic persons, public and private, must have their own statutes (*statuta*) which must be approved by competent ecclesiastical authority before an aggregate of persons or an aggregate of things obtains juridic personality (see canon 117). Statutes are

---

[60] A recently reported decree of the Congregation for Institutes of Consecrated Life and Societies of Apostolic Life addresses the union of seven religious institutes into one. Regarding the ecclesiastical goods involved, the decree states: "Furthermore, all goods, both movable and immovable, of the above mentioned seven religious institutes shall be duly ascribed to the new Religious Institute. Special funds or pious bequests, if there be any, must be used for the purpose intended by the donor or testator; likewise, the rights of others, if there be any, must be preserved intact insofar as the case demands." Reported in CLSA, *Roman Replies and Advisory Opinions*, Joseph J. Koury and Shiobhan Verbeek (eds.), Washington, CLSA, 2007, p. 17.

ordinances which define the aggregate's purpose, constitution, government, and methods of operation (canon 94 §1).

 a. If the statutes belong to an aggregate of persons (*universitas personarum*), they bind the legitimate members of the juridic person.

 b. If the statutes belong to an aggregate of things (*universitas rerum*), they bind those who direct the juridic person (canon 94 §2).

Statutes are ordinances which are established by those who have legislative power (see canon 135 §2) in the Church and which are governed by the canons on laws (canon 94 §3).

JURIDIC PERSONS ESTABLISHED BY THE LAW. The code (*a iure*) confers public juridic personality upon a number of entities: seminaries (canon 238 §1),[61] public associations of the Christian faithful (canon 313),[62] particular churches (canon 373),[63] ecclesiastical provinces (canon 432 §2),[64] conferences of bishops (canon 449 §2),[65] parishes (canon 515 §3),[66] religious institutes (canon 634 §1),[67] religious provinces (canon 634 §1),[68] religious houses (canon 634 §1),[69] secular institutes (by inference – see canon 718),[70] societ-

---

[61] See canon 237 on the erection of a seminary.

[62] See canon 312 on the erection of a public association of the Christian faithful, and canon 320 on its suppression. Private associations of the Christian faithful can be granted juridic personality by decree of competent ecclesiastical authority (canon 322 §1). For legislation concerning private associations of the Christian faithful without juridic personality, see canon 310.

[63] Canon 373 also concerns the erection of particular churches.

[64] See canon 431 §3 on the establishment, suppression, and alteration of ecclesiastical provinces.
    Canon 433 §2 says that an ecclesiastical region (established by the Holy See at the request of the conference of bishops but not required by law) can be erected as a juridic person.

[65] See canon 449 §1 on the erection, suppression, and alteration of conferences of bishops.

[66] See canon 515 §2 on the erection, suppression, and alteration of parishes.

[67] See canons 579-585 on the erection, aggregation, division, merger, union, and suppression of institutes of consecrated life.

[68] See canon 581 on the erection and modification of parts ("by whatever name they are called") of institutes of consecrated life.

[69] See canons 608-616 on the erection and suppression of religious houses.

[70] Canon 718 says that the administration of the goods of a secular institute is governed

ies of apostolic life (canon 741 §1),[71] parts of societies of apostolic life (unless the constitutions determine otherwise – canon 741 §1), houses of societies of apostolic life (unless the constitutions determine otherwise – canon 741 §1).[72] All these are public juridic persons who possess temporal goods which are governed by the norms of *Book V.*

JURIDIC PERSONS ESTABLISHED BY DECREE OF COMPETENT ECCLESIASTICAL AUTHORITY. All other juridic persons, public and private, are created by special grant of competent ecclesiastical authority (*ab homine*) through a decree (canon 114 §1). The code identifies two ecclesiastical entities which can achieve juridic personality by such a special grant: an ecclesiastical region (canon 433 §2) and a conference of major superiors (canon 709). Presumably, these two would be *public* juridic persons.

Only the temporal goods of public juridic persons are governed by the norms of *Book V* (and by particular law and their own statutes). The temporal goods of private juridic persons are governed by their own statutes only, unless other provision is made (canon 1257 §1). All juridic persons, both public and private, obtain their capacity to own temporal goods by grant from the Church, inasmuch as juridic persons are created by the Church, whether *a iure* or *ab homine.*[73]

ASSOCIATIONS OF THE CHRISTIAN FAITHFUL. The code acknowledges associations of the Christian faithful in the Church comprised of clergy and/or lay persons which have as their purpose

---

by *Book V: The Temporal Goods of the Church.* Since the ecclesiastical goods considered in *Book V* belong to juridic persons (see canon 1257 §1), it follows that secular institutes are juridic persons *a iure.*

[71] See canon 732 on the establishment of societies of apostolic life.

[72] See canon 733 §1 on the erection of a house of a society of apostolic life.

[73] DE PAOLIS, "De bonis Ecclesiae temporalibus," p. 28. JOSEPH FOX comments about public juridic persons established *ab homine*: "While it is usually the founder(s) requesting that a juridical person be established who propose(s) its purpose, Church law considers the public juridical person as *receiving* its task or purpose from the Church. This *purpose* is effectively synonymous with the *tasks* of the public juridical person and is its *mission*. In this perspective, the public juridical person exists to act, to perform specified tasks, to fulfill a mission entrusted to it by the Church. The *identity* of the public juridical person is intimately connected with its Church entrusted activity." In "Introductory Thoughts," p. 247.

to "strive in a common endeavor to foster a more perfect life, to
promote public worship or Christian doctrine, or to exercise other
works of the apostolate such as initiatives of evangelization, works of
piety or charity, and those which animate the temporal world with a
Christian spirit" (canon 298 §1; see canon 301). Associations of the
faithful may be public (canons 301 §3; 312-321) or private (canons
299; 321-326).[74] All associations are to have their own statutes defining their purpose, seat, government, membership requirements, and
manner of operation (canon 304 §1). All associations, whether public
or private, are subject to the vigilance of competent ecclesiastical
authority (canons 305, 323).

Public associations of the Christian faithful are erected by
competent ecclesiastical authority (canons 301 §1, 312 §1) and are
public juridic persons *a iure* (canon 313). Canon 319 addresses the
goods possessed by public associations:[75]

> **Can. 319 – §1. Unless other provision has been made,
> a legitimately erected public association administers the
> goods which it possesses according to the norm of the
> statutes under the higher direction of the ecclesiastical**

---

[74] There also exist in the Church *de facto* groups which, inasmuch as their statutes are
not reviewed by competent authority, are not even considered private associations of
the faithful (see canon 299 §3). These *de facto* groups of the faithful were the subject
of an April 20, 1987 response of the PONTIFICAL COMMISSION FOR THE AUTHENTIC
INTERPRETATION OF THE CODE OF CANON LAW. The doubt was: "Whether a group
of the Christian faithful (*coetus Christifidelium*), lacking juridic personality and
even the recognition mentioned in canon 299 §3, has active legitimation to propose
hierarchical recourse against a decree of its own diocesan bishop?" and the response
was "*Negative*, as a group; *affirmative*, as individual members of the Christian faithful, acting either jointly or individually, provided that they have a true grievance.
In judging its gravity, however, the judge must have suitable discretion." In *AAS*, 80
(1988), p. 1818.
   This reflects the discipline of canon 310 on private associations which are not juridic
persons: "A private association which has not been established as a juridic person
cannot, as such, be a subject of obligations and rights. Nevertheless, the members of
the Christian faithful associated together in it can jointly contract obligations and
can acquire and possess rights and goods as co-owners and co-possessors; they are
able to exercise these rights and obligations through an agent or proxy."
[75] See OLIVIER ÉCHAPPÉ, "Les 'biens' des associations d'Église," in *L'année canonique*,
47 (2005), pp. 51-62; ALBERTO PIERLASCA, *Il Concetto di bene ecclesiastico*, pp.
295-364.

authority mentioned in can. 312 §1 to which it must render an account of administration each year.

2. It must also render to the same authority a faithful account of the expenditure of offerings and alms which it has collected.

Upon its extinction, the allocation of goods of a public association of the Christian faithful is governed according to the norm of canon 123.

Private associations are not erected by competent ecclesiastical authority (canons 299 §1). They are recognized by the Church only if competent authority reviews their statutes (canon 299 §3). They are not necessarily juridic persons (see canon 310), but they may become juridic persons through a formal decree issued by the competent authority (see canon 322 §1) which, before granting juridic personality, must approve its statutes (canon 322 §2; see canon 117). A *private* juridic person cannot be granted *public* juridic personality.[76] Canon 319 addresses the goods possessed by private associations:

Canon 325 – §1. A private association of the Christian faithful freely administers those goods it possesses according to the prescripts of the statutes, without prejudice to the right of competent ecclesiastical authority to exercise vigilance so that the goods are used for the purposes of the association.

§2. A private association is subject to the authority of the local ordinary according to the norm of can. 1301 in what pertains to the administration and distribution of goods which have been donated or left to it for pious purposes.

Regarding the allocation of the goods of a private association when it ceases to exist, canon 326 §2 states: "The allocation of the goods

---

[76] See ROCH PAGÉ, "Associations of the Christian Faithful," in *New Commentary on the Code of Canon Law*, commissioned by the CLSA, John P. Beal, James A. Coriden, and Thomas J. Green (eds.), New York, Paulist, 2000, p. 416.

of an association which has ceased to exist must be determined
according to the norm of its statues, without prejudice to acquired
rights and the intention of the donors."

In light of these canons, one concludes that the goods of a
public association of the Christian faithful are governed by the
prescriptions of *Book V* and its own statutes; its goods are ecclesiastical goods (see canon 1257). The goods of a private association,
however, are governed only by its proper statutes; its goods are not
ecclesiastical goods.

NORMS FOR MODIFYING PARISHES. Parishes are public juridic
persons *a iure* (canon 515 §3). On March 3, 2006, the Congregation
for Clergy contacted the Most Reverend William Skylstad,[77] president of the USCCB, in order to clarify the disposition of its goods
when a parish is closed. The congregation explains that in the United
States a parish is often said to be suppressed when, in fact, it has
been merged or amalgamated with one or more other parishes. The
norm of canon 123 does not apply in this situation, since the parish is
not juridically suppressed. The goods of the merged parish are to be
passed on to the successor parish(es) whose territory is modified to
encompass that of the merged parish.[78] The communication states:

---

[77] In his July 10, 2006, memorandum to the bishops of the USCCB which covered the
communication from the Congregation for the Clergy, Bishop Skylstad explained: "At
my request, the Committee on Canonical Affairs has reviewed the letter. The Committee notes that the letter fundamentally reconfirms the canonical principles that
would bear on this subject. Care must be taken, moreover, in implementing decisions
about the merger or suppression of parishes. This is especially so in describing the
rights that pertain to a parish as a juridic person under the Church's law. In our civil
legal culture, ambiguous descriptions of the assembly of the faithful as having rights
under Church law could result in the civil courts abandoning their long tradition of
deferring to the decisions of bishops in these matters. Thus, in acting on matters of
merger, dissolution, or suppression of parishes the Committee urges that due attention
be given to precision of expression about the rights and responsibilities enjoyed by
a parish as a public juridic person versus those rights and responsibilities that might
pertain to the assembly of the faithful or individual members of it."

[78] See CIC/1917, canon 1187 which said that when a church is unable to be used for
divine worship, it can be reduced to profane but not sordid use by the local ordinary
and, if the church is parochial, its duties and income are to be transferred to another
church by the local ordinary.

Congregation for the Clergy
Prot. N. 20060481
March 3, 2006
The Most Reverend William Skylstad
President of the United States Conference of Catholic Bishops
3211 Fourth Street, N.E.
Washington, D.C. 20017-1194
U.S.A.
Your Excellency,

This Congregation deems it opportune to write to you regarding the closure of parishes in the dioceses of the United States, since in recent times certain dioceses have wrongly applied canon 123 CIC and stating that a parish has been "suppressed" when in reality it has been merged or amalgamated.

A parish is more than a public juridical person. Canon 369 defines the diocese as a "portion of the people of God which is entrusted to the bishop to be nurtured by him." Similarly, "a parish is a certain community of Christ's faithful, stably established within a particular Church, whose pastoral care, under the authority of the diocesan bishop, is entrusted to a parish priest as its proper pastor." [canon 515 §1]

In light of this, then, only with great difficulty, can one say that a parish becomes extinct. A parish is extinguished by the law itself only if no Catholic community any longer exists in its territory, or if no pastoral activity has taken place for a hundred years (can. 120 §1). When a parish is "suppressed" by competent authority in reality the still existing community of Christ's faithful is actually "merged" into the neighboring community of Christ's faithful and constitutes a larger community, and the territory of the extinguished parish is added to the other, forming a larger territorial unit. While the parish church and the physical parish plant may be closed and the name of a particular parish extinguished, the spiritual needs of the portion of the Faithful which once constituted that parish must continue to be provided for in accord with their rights in law.

In the case where the portion of the Christian Faithful is reallocated among preexisting or newly created parishes, the corresponding patrimony and obligations of the closed parishes must follow the Faithful in an equitable and proportionate fashion in accord with the corresponding responsibilities and pastoral duties assumed by the parishes ad quem. The wishes of any existing founders and benefactors must be respected, as must any acquired rights as expressed in canon 121 or 122.

Often when a bishop calls his action a "suppression" it is in reality a merger of two communities of Christ's faithful. Thus canon 121 applies: "When aggregates of persons or of things which are public juridic persons, are so joined that from them one aggregate is constituted which also possesses juridic personality, this new juridic person obtains the patrimonial goods and rights proper to the previous aggregates...." The "suppression" of a parish is in most cases then a "unio extinctiva." If a parish is divided between more than one existing parish, then can. 122 would apply.

Thus the goods and liabilities should go with the amalgamated person, and not to the diocese. This would also seem to be more consonant with the requirement that the wishes of the founders, benefactors and those who have acquired rights be safeguarded. In most cases, "suppressions" are in reality a "unio extinctiva" or "amalgamation" or "merger" and as such the goods and obligations do not pass to the higher juridic person, but should pertain to the public juridic person which remains or emerges from the extinctive union. The goods and liabilities should go to the surviving public juridic person, that is, the enlarged parish community.

In conclusion, this Congregation notes that the erroneous use of can. 123 in the dioceses of the United States is not uncommon and therefore asks Your Excellency to bring this matter to the attention of the individual members of the Episcopal Conference.

I take this opportunity to renew my sentiments of esteem and with every best wish, I remain,

Yours sincerely in Christ,

/s/ Dario Card. Castrillon-H.

/s/ Csaba Ternyak

Secr.

In light of this communication from the Congregation for the Clergy, special care must be provided to assure that the ecclesiastical goods of a "merged" parish are passed on to the neighboring parish(es) which are also modified by reason of the merger. In fact, only rarely is a territorial parish "suppressed."[79] Rather, its territory is joined to one or more neighboring parishes to whom its assets and liabilities are passed.

CIVIL LEGAL STRUCTURES OF JURIDIC PERSONS. The norms of the Church on juridic persons make it quite simple to prove the existence, nature, and specific purposes of juridic persons. One need only refer to the decrees of the competent ecclesiastical authority establishing them and to the statutes governing them. These decrees and statutes, however, have relevance for the Church, not necessarily for the secular society. Therefore, it is important that the competent ecclesiastical authority consider assuring that juridic persons also have recognition in civil law (see canon 1284 §2, 2°). The civil legal structures chosen for this acknowledgment should reflect as closely as possible the norms of canon law.

Canon law often calls for adherence to civil laws, provided that the civil laws do not contradict divine law or canon law (see canon 22). Several canons on temporal goods in particular mention compliance with civil law (see canons 1268; 1274 §5; 1284 §2, 2°; 1284 §2, 3°; 1286, 1°; 1290; 1296; 1299 §2). Few, if any, civil laws reciprocate by recognizing canonical provisions. Although secular courts in some jurisdictions will turn to the norms of Church law in rendering their decisions, such civil action is not assured in all jurisdictions. More often and assuredly, however, the secular courts will reply upon secular legislation when rendering their decisions on ecclesiastical goods. Therefore, it is important for administrators of

---

[79] Parishes are generally *territorial*, but they may be *personal* – i.e., "determined by reason of the rite, language, or nationality of the Christian faithful of some territory, or even for some other factor" (canon 518).

It would be very rare for a *territorial* parish, as a public juridic person, to become extinguished through a century of inactivity (see canon 120 §2). If such in fact did occur, however, its goods, patrimonial rights and obligations would pass on to the diocese, i.e., the immediate superior juridic person (see canon 123).

It would not be so uncommon, perhaps, for a *personal* parish, also a public juridic person, to cease its activity for a century or to be extinguished by the diocesan bishop, in which case canon 123 would apply, and its assets and liabilities would pass to the diocese.

ecclesiastical goods to see that those goods are protected in a civilly recognized manner.[80]

DEBATE: MAIDA AND MCGRATH.[81] A significant debate occurred in the late 1960's and 1970's in the United States concerning the Catholic ownership of public juridic persons which are incorporated civilly. Monsignor John J. McGrath, associate professor of comparative law at The Catholic University of America, published a work[82] on the canon law and civil law status of institutions operated under Catholic auspices and incorporated civilly. He contended that civilly incorporated institutions are juridically distinct from the Church; they are not juridic persons with canonical rights and obligations. Therefore, they are not subject to the norms of Church law on temporal goods, although they are "Church-related." They are subject solely to the applicable civil law. He wrote:

> The property, real and personal, of Catholic hospitals and educational institutions which have been incorporated as American law corporations is the property of the corporate entity and not the property of the sponsoring body or individuals who conduct the institution.... There is no question of dealing with ecclesiastical property when speaking of the property of Catholic hospitals and higher educational institutions in the United States. The canon law is clear that property is ecclesiastical only when it

---

[80] See JERALD A. DOYLE, *Civil Incorporation of Ecclesiastical Institutions: A Canonical Perspective*, Ottawa, Saint Paul University, 1989; JOHN A. RENKEN, "The Collaboration of Canon Law and Civil Law in Church Property Issues," in *Studies in Church Law*, 4 (2008), pp. 43-80.

[81] The McGrath-Maida debate is explained and analyzed at length in ROBERT T. KENNEDY, "McGrath, Maida, Michiels: Introduction to a Study of the Canonical and Civil-Law Status of Church-related Institutions in the United States," in *The Jurist*, 50 (1990) 351-401 (=KENNEDY, "McGrath, Maida, Michiels"). See also DANIEL C. CONLIN, "The McGrath Thesis and Its Impact on a Canonical Understanding of the Ownership of Ecclesiastical Goods," in *CLSA Proceedings*, 64 (2002), pp. 73-96 (=CONLIN, "McGrath Thesis").

[82] JOHN J. MCGRATH, *Catholic Institutions in the United States: Canonical and Civil Law Status*, Washington, The Catholic University of America Press, 1968. Employing the terminology of the 1917 code, McGrath and Maida speak of "moral persons" which, in the 1983 code, are referred to as "juridic persons."

belongs to some ecclesiastical moral person. Since the institutions under consideration have not themselves been established as moral persons and, since no other moral person in fact holds title to the property of the institution, their assets are not ecclesiastical property.[83]

Should such an institution ever be dissolved, McGrath indicated that its assets are to be distributed on behalf of the public to another non-profit corporation engaged in similar activities, not to the religious institution under whose auspices it had originally operated before civil incorporation.

A strong reaction against the McGrath thesis came from Father Adam J. Maida, then director of finance of the Diocese of Pittsburgh and later Cardinal-Archbishop of Detroit. He published a work[84] on behalf of the Pennsylvania Catholic Conference which was later distributed to every bishop in the United States, in which he countered the McGrath position. He contended that civilly incorporated Catholic institutions are canonically "part and parcel of the moral persons known as the Diocese or Religious Order which brought them into existence in the beginning."[85] Proposing a hypothetical situation wherein a religious order civilly incorporates a hospital which it operates in order to insulate its assets civilly, Maida concluded:

> As demonstrated in the hypothetical, prior to incorpora-
> tion, there is absolutely no controversy concerning the
> canonical reality that the hospital is part of the apostolate
> and a portion of the assets which belong to the Religious
> Order. The fact of incorporation afterwards, canonically,

---

[83] Ibid., p. 24.

[84] ADAM J. MAIDA, *Ownership, Control and Sponsorship of Catholic Institutions: A Practical Guide,* Harrisburg, Pennsylvania Catholic Conference, 1975 (=MAIDA, *Ownership, Control and Sponsorship*). Before composing this work, Maida had challenged the McGrath thesis in two other writings: "Canonical and Legal Fallacies of the McGrath Thesis on Reorganization of Church Entities," in *The Catholic Lawyer,* 19 (1973), pp. 275-286, and "Canon Law/Civil Law Status of Catholic Hospitals," in *Hospital Progress* (August, 1973), pp. 54-61, 80.

[85] MAIDA, *Ownership, Control and Sponsorship*, p. 37.

does nothing; it is permitted or even encouraged so that
the ecclesiastical dimensions may be preserved and protected in an often hostile society.[86]

The so-called "Maida thesis" acknowledged that civilly incorporated
apostolates of public juridic persons operate in two realms, civil and
canonical. Maida wrote:

> Where a moral person or some part of a moral person
> is given an existence and identity in civil law, so that it
> becomes subject to two legal systems in its existence
> and operation, fiduciaries, trustees and administrators
> are under serious obligation to do all things possible, in
> canon and civil law, to protect the interests and purposes
> of the moral person.[87]

On October 7, 1974, the Sacred Congregation for Catholic
Education and the Sacred Congregation for Religious and Secular Institutes issued a letter asking that the Conference of Major Superiors
of Men and Women in the United States collaborate with the NCCB
to conduct an in-depth study of the influence of the "McGrath thesis"
on institutions of Catholic education. The letter directed that Catholic schools be identified as well as those which no longer consider
themselves Catholic (and the reasons for this change and the steps
taken to effect it). It asked that no further changes in the administrative structure or corporate status be made in any such institutions.
The letter stated directly: "We know that in the course of the study,
the influence of the so-called 'McGrath thesis' will emerge as one
of the principal bases for the action of some institutions in regard
to alienation, etc. We wish to make it clear that this thesis has never
been considered valid by our Congregations and has never been accepted."[88] To the contrary, in a private letter to Archbishop Joseph

---

[86]   Ibid.

[87]   Ibid., pp. 21-22.

[88]   Prot. Nos. 427/70/23 (Sacred Congregation for Catholic Education) and 300/74 (Sacred Congregation for Religious and Secular Institutes): *CLD*, vol. 8, p. 369-371.

Bernardin, president of the NCCB, dated April 15, 1975, Arturo Cardinal Tabera, prefect of the Sacred Congregation for Religious and Secular Institutes, commented that "the suggestions made in Father Maida's book will be helpful, as a substitute, until interim guidelines have been formulated"[89] to address this important issue.

The McGrath thesis failed to recognize that many Catholic institutions may have been operating as apostolic works of public juridic persons (e.g., dioceses, institutes of consecrated life) or had been erected as public juridic persons themselves (e.g., The Catholic University of America, established as a moral person in 1889, and Niagara University, established as a moral person in 1956)[90] for many years well before they were civilly incorporated.[91] Civil incorporation was not envisioned as a canonical act of alienation of an asset of a public juridic person. At the same time, the Maida thesis does not apply when the act of civil incorporation includes a transfer of title and property from the public juridic person to the separately incorporated entity not subject to ecclesiastical authority. Such a transfer would, indeed, be a canonical act of alienation, although perhaps not done in accord with canonical requirements and therefore, canonically, invalid.[92]

This brief discussion illustrates the importance of preserving the ownership of the ecclesiastical goods of public juridic persons in ways which are civilly valid. The civil structure exists to protect the ecclesiastical goods in the civil forum; civil incorporation of ecclesiastical goods must not constitute a canonical act of alienation.[93] Administrators of ecclesiastical goods will wisely incorporate them

---

[89] Cited in KENNEDY, "McGrath, Maida, Michiels," p. 368, fn. 47.

[90] See DANIEL C. CONLIN, *Canonical and Civil Legal Issues Surrounding the Alienation of Catholic Health Care Facilities in the United States*, Rome, Pontifical University of Saint Thomas Aquinas *in Urbe*, 2000, p. 97 (=CONLIN, *Canonical and Civil*).

[91] KENNEDY, "McGrath, Maida, Michiels," p. 355, fn. 14; p. 369.

[92] See the discussion at KENNEDY, "McGrath, Maida, Michiels," pp. 371-375.

[93] See the extensive treatment of civil incorporation of Catholic hospitals in CONLIN, "Canonical and Civil," esp. pp. 187-219.

civilly.[94] The secular articles of incorporation and by-laws should reflect the discipline of canon law,[95] something of which civil attorneys assisting administrators of ecclesiastical goods must be aware.[96] Often these civil documents will also contain a list of so-called "reserved powers." "The reserved powers are such that the secular corporation binds itself in its by-laws, or possibly even in its charter, not to act until the required canonical authorizations have been obtained for those specific instances which have been reserved."[97]

Francis G. Morrisey[98] suggests that the following actions be identified in the civil realm as powers to be reserved to the canonical administrators of juridic persons which have been civilly incorporated:

1. To change the philosophy and mission of the work;
2. To have the corporate documents (charters and by-laws) approved, amended, or abrogated;

---

[94] DANIEL C. CONLIN summarizes succinctly: "...alienation of ecclesiastical goods that belong to a public juridic person must follow proper canonical procedure as well as proper civil procedure. The danger in ignoring canon law is that civil law will seem more important than canon law. The danger in ignoring civil law is that ecclesiastical goods may be needlessly endangered." In "McGrath Thesis," p. 95.

[95] Several significant canonical issues which must be guarded in any civil legal structure include: that the public juridic person retains ownership of its ecclesiastical goods; that the canonical procedures will be followed in performing acts of ordinary administration, acts of extraordinary administration (including those acts which can worsen the patrimonial condition of the public juridic person), and acts of alienation. See DANIEL J. WARD, "Temporal Goods," in CLSA, *Procedural Manual for Institutes of Consecrated Life and Societies of Apostolic Life*, Washington, CLSA, 2001, p. 199 (=WARD, "Temporal Goods").

[96] See MADELINE WELCH, "Establishment of a Lay Board and Alienation of Property" in *CLSA AO2*, p. 426.

[97] FRANCIS G. MORRISEY, "Basic Concepts and Principles," in *CFH*, p.14. This list is operative when the civil corporation is established as a membership corporation, i.e., one with members who act on behalf of the corporation and who belong to the ecclesiastical body (e.g., diocese, religious institute, etc.) exercising the apostolate (e.g., hospital, university, etc.) These members alone exercise the "reserved powers." Subordinate to the members is a board of directors or trustees, who do not have the ability to exercise the "reserved powers" but who must refer issues involving the "reserved powers" to the members. When such a civil structure is in place, alienation of ecclesiastical goods is not considered to have occurred.

[98] MORRISEY, "Basic Concepts and Principles," p. 14. See also WARD, "Temporal Goods," pp. 199-200; THE CATHOLIC HEALTH ASSOCIATION OF THE UNITED STATES, *Search for Identity: Canonical Sponsorship of Catholic Healthcare*, Saint Louis, The Catholic Health Association of the United States, 1993, p. 81; MAIDA-CAFARDI, pp. 167-169.

3. To establish subsidiary corporations;

4. To amalgamate the corporation with other corporations, or to suppress it;

5. To encumber the real estate and the funds of the juridic person with indebtedness.

In addition, the corporate documents may also include some or all of the following reserved powers:

6. To designate the chief executive officer and some or all of the members of the board;

7. To appoint the auditor;

8. To approve operating or capital budgets, or both.

The "reserved powers" will assure the continued ownership of the juridic person by the Church.

Today, with the mergers of various apostolic works, the creation of institutional systems, and the involvement in joint ventures (sometimes with non-Catholic or secular groups) by religious institutes and dioceses, the notion of a public juridic person with certain powers reserved in civil law to competent ecclesiastical authority has taken on a new urgency. Canonical norms assuring that the public juridic persons function in the name of the Church and that ethical standards consistent with Church teaching permeate the new structures must be reflected in the civil documents involved.[99] Civil legal structures

---

[99] See SHARON HOLLAND, "Canonical Reflections on Civilly Incorporated Apostolates," in *Public Ecclesiastical Juridic Persons and their Civilly Incorporated Apostolates (e.g., Universities, Healthcare Institutions, Social Service Agencies) in the Catholic Church in the U.S.A.: Canonical-Civil Aspects: Acts of the Colloquium*, Rome, Pontifical University of Saint Thomas Aquinas in Rome, 1998, pp. 325-341; JOHN P. BEAL, "From the Heart of the Church to the Heart of the World: Ownership, Control, and Catholic Identity of Institutional Apostolates in the United States," in *Sponsorship in the United States Context: Theory and Praxis*, Rosemary Smith, Warren Brown, and Nancy Reynolds (eds.), Alexandria, CLSA, 2006, pp. 31-48; WILLIAM J. KING, "Sponsorship by Juridic Persons," in Ibid., pp. 49-72; MELANIE DIPIETRO, "A Juridical Meaning of Sponsorship in the Formal Relationship Between a Public Juridic Person and a Health Care Corporation in the United States," in Ibid., pp. 101-122; MELANIE DIPIETRO, "Incorporated Apostolates," in *CFH*, pp. 279-303; ROBERT GEISINGER, "Some Ongoing Considerations in Canon Law for Treasurers General of Religious Institutes," in *Periodica*, 96 (2006), pp. 236-240.

must be used to protect the ecclesiastical goods owned by public juridic persons in the Church.[100] The statutes of the ecclesiastical juridic person and the documents of the civil legal structure should reflect each other as closely as possible.[101] If the entity complies with both canon law and civil law, both the Church and the secular society will recognize the entity in the respective fora. This will avoid conflicts which may result in serious damage to, or loss of, the temporal goods of the Church.

CIVIL LEGAL STRUCTURES OF PARISHES. The Sacred Congregation for the Council issued a private letter to the ordinaries of the United States on July 19, 1911 in response to a request from some American bishops on the proper method of civilly incorporating parishes. It explained that the "parish corporation" is the preferred method to hold title to, and to administer, Church property:

1.   Among the methods which now are in use in the United States for holding and administering church property, the one known as *Parish Corporation* is preferable to the others, but with the conditions and safeguards which are now in use in the State of New York. The Bishops therefore should immediately take steps to introduce this method for the handling of property in their dioceses, if the civil law allows it. If the civil law does not allow

---

[100] ADAM MAIDA and NICHOLAS CAFARDI conclude that "[w]here the activity [of an entity] is purely intra-Church, and the risk of legal liability is therefore remote, there is no reason why the corporate structure could not vest a reasonably tight control in the [public juridic person] itself.... The principle to follow is the following: the greater legal risk an activity carries, the greater the need to give that activity its own [civil] legal identity. In such cases, the activity should be its own legal person, its own corporation." In *Church Property*, pp. 133-134. Thus, it is not *imperative* that *every* apostolic endeavor of a public juridic person be separately civilly incorporated. Civil incorporation is recommended, however, (1) if the apostolic work performs activities entailing significant risk, lest the public juridic person could be held liable for those activities, and (2) to the measure that the sponsor of the apostolic work has diminished control.

[101] JORDAN HITE reflects: "The fundamental principle to apply in ordering the relationship between the canonical structure and the [civil] legal structure is to provide compatibility and the absence of conflict. These conflicts are most likely to occur at levels of governance and procedures. In each case, the articles of incorporation and bylaws or the partnership agreement should be compared to the canonical organization's statutes and bylaws in order to avoid conflict." In *Public and Private Juridic Persons*, p. 13.

it, they should exert their influence with the civil authorities that it may be made legal as soon as possible.

2. Only in those places where the civil law does not recognize *Parish Corporations*, and until such recognition is allowed, the method commonly called *Corporation sole* is allowed, but with the understanding that in the administration of ecclesiastical property the Bishop is to act with the advice, and in more important matters with the consent, of those who have an interest in the premises and of the diocesan consultors, this being a conscientious obligation for the Bishop in person.

3. The method called *in fee simple* is to be entirely abandoned.[102]

The law of New York, to which the letter refers, provided that an incorporated parish have a five-member board of trustees: three members serve ex officio (the bishop, the vicar general, and the rector of the church) and the other two are lay members of the church chosen by the rest for a one-year term. The law states: "No act or proceeding of the trustees of any such incorporated church shall be valid without the sanction of the Archbishop or Bishop of the diocese to which such church belongs, or in case of their absence or inability to act, without the sanction of the Vicar General or of the administrator of such diocese."[103]

This private letter suggests that parishes in the United States be

---

[102] *CLD*, vol. 2, pp. 443-445. See *Ecclesiastical Review*, 45 (1911), pp. 585- 596. The method of *fee simple* gives ownership of ecclesiastical property to individual persons (e.g., bishops or priests). The corporation sole as a means to hold church property resulted in response to the negative influence of trusteeism. The history of property tenure in the United States, including the background to this private letter from the Sacred Congregation for the Council, is related succinctly by WILLIAM J. KING, "The Corporation Sole and Subsidiarity," in *CLSA Proceedings*, 65 (2003), pp. 107-134. He identifies a number of methods whereby church property is incorporated in the United States today: corporation sole, the charitable trust, the not-for-profit corporation, the corporation aggregate, and aggregates of charitable trusts (p. 123). See also ROBERT L. KEALY, "Methods of Diocesan Incorporation," in *CLSA Proceedings*, 48 (1986), pp. 163-177; MARK E. CHOPKO, "An Overview of the Parish and the Civil Law," in *The Jurist*, 67 (2007), pp. 198-202; MARY JUDITH O'BRIEN, "Instructions for Parochial Temporal Administration," in *Catholic Lawyer*, 41 (2001), pp. 131-136.
[103] *CLD*, vol. 2, pp. 444-445, fn. 1.

incorporated civilly with a board of trustees, and recommends they not be established as corporations sole. Indeed, it urges bishops to exercise their influence to achieve the parish corporation structure in places where such does not yet exist. Obviously, the mind of the congregation in 1911 was that the parish corporation method with five trustees best reflects ecclesiastical legislation, and that the corporation sole method does not. In this regard, Robert T. Kennedy comments:

> In fact, liability considerations in contemporary American society, and the enhanced emphasis on subsidiarity in the 1983 code, argue strongly for the continued inappropriateness of the corporation-sole method of holding civil title to Church-related property. Where such a method remains in use, diocesan bishops and their finance officers and councils should make every effort to see that the Church laws governing the acquisition, retention, administration, and alienation of temporal goods are faithfully fulfilled.[104]

---

[104] ROBERT T. KENNEDY, "Book V: The Temporal Goods of the Church" in *New Commentary on the Code of Canon Law*, commissioned by the CLSA, John P. Beal, James A. Coriden, and Thomas J. Green (eds.), New York, Paulist, 2000, p. 1457 (=KENNEDY, "Temporal Goods"). See also BRIAN LUCAS, "Diocesan Assets and Risk Management," in *CLSANZ Newsletter*, 1 (2008), pp. 57-65;
The dangers inherent in the corporation sole structure of diocesan property are succinctly highlighted in STEPHEN M. BAINBRIDGE and AARON H. COLE, "The Bishop's Alter Ego: Enterprise Liability and the Catholic Priest Sex Abuse Scandal," *Journal of Catholic Legal Studies,* 46 (2007), pp. 70-80. These American civil attorneys comment that "it is impossible to square the use of the corporation sole with canon law" and "incorporation as a corporation sole exposes the assets of parishes and other juridic persons, which in canon law are the property of such persons, to the claims of creditors of the diocese" (pp. 77, 78).
ADAM MAIDA and NICHOLAS CAFARDI, however, favor the corporation sole method of holding diocesan property in civil law: "Today, after the initial legislative reluctance, the device of corporation sole has been enacted in 19 American jurisdictions. The statutes creating this type of corporation sole typically state that the officeholder must have been duly elected or chosen and must act in accordance with the rules and regulations of the particular organization or denomination of which the office is a part. For bishops of individual dioceses, who act as corporation sole on behalf of their dioceses, this means that they be chosen in accordance with canon law. The legal name of such corporations sole is the name of the office, e.g., the Roman Catholic Bishop of

Nonetheless, Mark E. Chopko, formerly General Council of the USCCB, claims that "[c]learly the most common form by which Catholic dioceses are organized in the United States is the corporation sole."[105]

In a recent communication to the bishops of Ontario, the apostolic nunciature in Canada said the corporation sole is incompatible with canon law:

> Acknowledging that the diocese has an obligation in justice to a victim of abuse, it is nevertheless equally true that the diocese has an obligation in justice to the rest of the faithful of the diocese; these two cannot be mutually exclusive.... Since the *corporation sole* is in fact incompatible with the canonical autonomy of the parish, it appears necessary that all dioceses having their bishop holding the civil status of a *corporation sole* look seriously at changing it.... This means re-establishing the primacy of Canon Law in the financial structure of the dioceses....[106]

Canon 1279 says that the administration of ecclesiastical goods belongs to one who immediately governs the person to whom the goods belong, unless another legitimate provision is made. Since the pastor governs the parish, albeit under the authority of the diocesan bishop (canon 519), he is the administrator of the goods of the parish; he is also its legal representative (see canon 532). This exposes the incompatibility of the corporation sole model of civil designation of a parish (i.e., a civil corporation with the bishop as its sole member of the property of all parishes) with canon law: it

---

Chicago, a corporation sole. The device of a corporation sole, where it does exist, is the preferable civil law instrument for the diocese to use in holding title to property. It places in civil law control of diocesan property the canonical steward, the diocesan bishop, by the vehicle of incorporating his office. It accomplishes a very acceptable civil law parallel to canonical reality." In *Church Property,* pp. 128-129.

[105] CHOPKO, p. 200. He also observes: "In the last five years, some dioceses have begun to organize parishes under the statutory corporation sole provisions of the state. In those new structures, the office of the pastor becomes the corporation sole." (p. 199, fn. 24)

[106] Letter of the Apostolic Nunciature, Prot. N. 6088/05, December 14, 2005.

makes the diocesan bishop, rather than the pastor, to be the legal representative of the parish.[107]

Whatever the civil legal structure assuring the ownership of ecclesiastical goods, care must be taken that the civil structure reflects canonical ownership. Dioceses today often search for appropriate models to achieve this purpose and are considering restructuring, perhaps largely in response to concerns stemming from liability issues and the related threat of bankruptcy. Mark E. Chopko comments on the contemporary restructuring of dioceses and parishes:

> Each diocese will have to evaluate the risk versus the possible benefits that would accompany any particular reorganization. Among other things, dioceses should be deciding whether an adequate civil format is available and achievable. Will the diocese be able to capitalize the various entities that it creates? How much self-sufficiency will be allowed the new structures? Can the new constellation of structures be properly administered by the personnel in place and who will be providing for their training and seeing to it that they act in accord with the laws of the Church? … [H]ow much control will prove to be too much, in effect defeating the purpose of setting up new structures, and how much will be too little, opening the door to the possibility that some of our institutions may seek to separate themselves from the denomination?[108]

CORRESPONDING CANON OF THE EASTERN CODE: CANON 1009 §1. The Eastern code contains legislation only on physical persons (CCEO, canons 909-919) and juridic persons (CCEO, canons 920-930). It does not mention any "moral persons" and does not distinguish juridic persons as "private" or "public." Its canon corresponding to Latin canon 1255 simply states: "Any juridic person is a subject capable of acquiring, retaining, administering, and alienating temporal goods according to the norm of canon law."

---

[107] See O'BRIEN, p. 133.
[108] CHOPKO, pp. 218-219.

OWNERSHIP BELONGS TO THE JURIDIC PERSON WHICH ACQUIRED TEMPORAL GOODS

Can. 1256 – Under the supreme authority of the Roman Pontiff, ownership of goods belongs to that juridic person which has acquired them legitimately.

Canon 1256 explains that the ownership of goods (*dominium bonorum*) belongs to the juridic person (public or private) who has acquired them legitimately.[109] The juridic person exercises its ownership under the supreme authority of the Roman Pontiff who, however, does not have ownership of the goods of the juridic person. His administration is a dimension of his universal power of jurisdiction, which is distinct from administration of the more limited economic fashion.[110] The code adds that the Roman Pontiff is the supreme administrator (*administrator*) and steward (*dispensor*) of all ecclesiastical goods (canon 1273). In practice, the Roman Pontiff exercises his supreme authority over ecclesiastical goods through the dicasteries of the Roman Curia.[111]

---

[109] Consequently, if a public juridic person should suffer bankruptcy, it is not the responsibility of a superior juridic person (e.g., a diocese) to resolve outstanding indebtedness. PCLT, *Nota,* La funzione dell'autorità, pp. 25.

For a discussion of the ownership of temporal goods by juridic persons, and the function of the Roman Pontiff and the diocesan bishop to protect that right of ownership, see PCLT, *Nota,* La funzione dell'autorità, pp. 26-27, 30-31.

[110] When one consultor of the *coetus De bonis Ecclesiae temporalibus* had suggested that this canon omit reference to the Roman Pontiff since it attributes ownership of goods to juridic persons, another replied that the reference to the Roman Pontiff should remain "since it denotes the nature of the authority of the Supreme Pontiff over ecclesiastical goods – namely, that this power is not the same as ownership." At the same time, the *coetus* rejected the recommendation that the canon should state explicitly that other ecclesiastical authorities are unable to claim ownership of goods belonging to those subject to their authority; the *coetus* said that the canon as drafted suffices to explain this. *Communicationes,* 12 (1980), p. 398.

CIC/1917, canon 1499 §2 had said that moral persons have *dominium* over their goods "under the supreme authority of the Apostolic See." The revised law is more precise in its reference to the supreme authority of the Roman Pontiff, but the discipline is essentially unchanged. See DE PAOLIS, *I beni temporali,* p. 79.

[111] Further, canon 1276 §1 explains that the ordinary exercises *vigilance* over the administration of public juridic persons subject to him. The code does *not* refer to the ordinary as the *administrator* or steward of the goods of such public juridic persons.

The canon uses the term *dominium*, a concept from ancient Roman law which was used to express the idea that one has a virtually absolute right over a thing (*ius in re*). The owner is clearly identified and the owner's rights are clear. John J. Myers comments about the rights enjoyed by one with *dominium* over a thing:

> Three rights are usually included in the concept of *dominium*: the right to make physical use of a thing and possess it (*utendi*); the right to income gained from it in money, land, or services (*fruendi*); and the right to manage it – well or badly – including conveying it to someone else (*abutendi*). The social policy was to keep these three rights as closely associated as possible – although some exceptions were made – particularly regarding the right to income.[112]

This understanding of *dominium* is not held by common law which may allow various dimensions of ownership to be separated (for example, one person may hold a piece of real estate and another person may have a right to income from it). Canon law holds that *dominium* of ecclesiastical goods rests with the juridic person to whom the goods pertain. "*Dominium* always denotes ownership for a purpose – the holding and use of property or funds to enable the religious, charitable, and spiritual mission of the Church to be conducted in the world."[113] One with *dominium* enjoys the true possession of the thing, and exercises real rights over it. Those owning ecclesiastical goods must make sure that *dominium*, as understood by the Church, is reflected in secure civil legal structures.

Dominium means that a person acquires, retains, administers, and alienates a temporal good (see canon 1254). If one cannot exercise all four of these actions, one does not have full ownership. This

---

[112] JOHN J. MYERS, "The Temporal Goods of the Church" in *The Code of Canon Law: Text and Commentary*, commissioned by the CLSA, James A. Coriden, Thomas J. Green, and Donald E. Heintschel (eds.), New York, Paulist, 1985, pp. 862-863 (=MYERS, "Temporal Goods").

[113] WILLIAM J. KING, "Mandated Diocesan Centralized Financial Service," in *CLSA AO3*, p. 332.

occurs when the Church receives goods in *trust* (see canon 1302): the Church acquires, retains, and administers the goods but is unable to alienate them since the Church is holding them for a long-term purpose agreed upon when the trust relationship was established. "The test of full ownership (*dominium*), then, consists in determining whether all four rights can be exercised."[114]

The discipline of canon 1256 means, for example, that goods of a parish (which is a public juridic person established *a iure:* see canon 515 §3) are owned by the parish. Its administrator, who represents it in all juridic affairs, is its pastor (canon 532; see canon 1279 §1), no one else. The ordinary is to exercise careful vigilance over the pastor's administrative function (canon 1276 §1) but the ordinary is neither the administrator of the parish nor the owner of its goods. Since these goods are not personal goods, neither the ordinary nor the pastor may dispose of them as either may wish. This must be reflected properly in diocesan practice and in civil legal structures.

The canon speaks of goods acquired "legitimately." This is to be understood as acquired "validly." In other words, if a temporal good has been acquired invalidly, it still belongs to its original owner. Invalid methods cannot be employed. "Any type of forcing or undue pressure would be contrary to the law and to the respect owed to persons; the goods thus received would not be legitimately acquired... and would have to be returned to their rightful owners."[115] If a temporal good is acquired through a method valid (though somehow illicit), however, it is considered nonetheless to have been acquired "legitimately" as that term is used in canon 1256.

CORRESPONDING CANON OF THE EASTERN CODE: CANON 1008 §2. The Eastern canon is practically identical to Latin canon 1256. The first paragraph of the Eastern canon 1008 corresponds to Latin canon 1273 but without reference to papal primacy of governance: "The Roman Pontiff is the supreme administrator and steward of all goods of the Church."

---

[114] FRANCIS G. MORRISEY, "Acquiring Temporal Goods for the Church's Mission," in *The Jurist*, 56 (1966), p. 592 (=MORRISEY, "Acquiring Temporal Goods").

[115] Ibid., p. 599.

TECHNICAL TERM: "ECCLESIASTICAL GOODS"

Can. 1257 – §1. All temporal goods which belong to the universal Church, the Apostolic See, or other public juridic persons in the Church are ecclesiastical goods and are governed by the following canons and their own statutes.

§2. The temporal goods of a private juridic person are governed by its own statutes but not by these canons unless other provision is expressly made.

Canon 1257 defines what is meant by the term *ecclesiastical goods*. The term designates the temporal goods which belong to the universal Church, the Apostolic See, and other public juridic persons in the Church. Excluded from the meaning of *ecclesiastical goods* (as that term is used in *Book V*) are temporal goods which belong to private juridic persons in the Church, even though private juridic persons have the capacity to acquire, retain, administer, and alienate temporal goods (canon 1255).[116]

In the 1917 code, the temporal goods of all juridic (moral) persons were considered ecclesiastical goods (CIC/1917, canon 1497 §1). The same is true of the Eastern code which makes no distinction between private and public juridic persons: all the goods of all juridic persons are considered ecclesiastical goods (CCEO canon 1009 §2). The 1983 code (which distinguishes two kinds of juridic persons, public and private) is more restrictive inasmuch as it designates as *ecclesiastical goods* only those belonging to public juridic persons. From this it follows that, when the revised code became operative, some juridic (moral) persons are now understood to be private juridic persons and their goods, previously considered *ecclesiastical goods*, are no longer so designated.

---

[116] In a broad sense, of course, the temporal goods of private juridical persons are ecclesial since they are owned by juridical persons established by the Church to assist in the mission furthering its proper purposes (see canon 114 §§1-2); it is only in a strict, legal sense that the term *ecclesiastical goods* is not assigned to the temporal goods of private juridic persons. Some canonists use the term *ecclesial goods* when referring to temporal goods owned by private juridic persons. See MARIANO LÓPEZ ALARCÓN, "Book V: The Temporal Goods of the Church, Introduction (cc. 1254-1258)," in *Exegetical Comm*, vol. 4, pp. 36-38; DE PAOLIS, *I beni temporali*, pp. 92-94; SCHOUPPE, pp. 44-48.

Public juridic persons "fulfill in the name of the Church, according to the norm of the prescripts of the law, the proper function entrusted to them in view of the public good" (canon 116 §1). The same is not said of private juridic persons – i.e., the law does not understand them to be performing their function *nomine Ecclesiae*; instead, they act in their own name.[117] For this reason, their temporal

---

[117] On May 26, 1969, the *coetus De iure patrimoniali Ecclesiae*, aware that the *coetus De personis* had distinguished public and private juridic persons, decided that the temporal goods of only *public* juridic persons are to be termed "ecclesiastical goods." The *coetus* reasoned that private juridic persons (e.g., associations of the faithful, hospitals, orphanages, personalized patrimonial funds promoting worship or charity by the free activity of the Christian faithful) act in their own names, not in the name of the Church. The *coetus* understood, however, that the governance of the goods of private juridic persons is subject to the vigilance and visitation of the local ordinary, that private juridic persons must have their own permanently appointed administrator, and that they must make provisions about other things in their legitimately approved statutes and particular law. *Communicationes*, 37 (2005), p. 208.
On May 30, 1969, four days later, the *coetus* unanimously voted that the temporal goods of private juridic persons are to be counted among ecclesiastical goods, but that these goods should not be subject to the common governance of ecclesiastical goods. Instead, they should be governed by special and proper norms. *Communicationes*, 37 (2005), pp. 220-221.
On December 15-18, 1969, the *coetus* revisited the canons it had already studied to determine whether or not these would pertain to private juridic persons. Multiple modifications were made. *Communicationes,* 37 (2005), pp. 223-237.
On December 19, 1969, the *coetus* voted in favor of legislating that the goods of private juridic persons are not subject to the common norms on temporal goods unless they are expressly included. As a result of this vote, the *coetus* again revisited all the modifications it had made during the previous days. It then drafted a new canon which stated:
§1. Ecclesiastical goods which belong to public canonical persons are governed by the canons which follow.
§2. The ecclesiastical goods which belong to private canonical persons, however, are governed by particular law or their own statutes, unless other provision has been made in these canons.
Communicationes, 37 (2005), p. 238.
On April 21, 1970, the *coetus* proposed yet another canon: "The subject capable of acquiring, retaining, and administering temporal goods is any moral person, whether public or private, which has been erected either by a prescript of the law itself or by special concession of competent ecclesiastical authority." *Communicationes*, 37 (2005), p. 261. This is the introduction of the term "temporal goods" (rather than "ecclesiastical goods") into the law; private juridic persons own "temporal goods" but not "ecclesiastical goods." Consequently, the 1977 *Schema* indicated that public and private juridic persons are subjects capable of owning temporal goods (canon 13) but that the canons govern only the temporal goods of public juridic persons unless otherwise indicated (canon 15).
The 1980 *Schema* limited the application of the term "ecclesiastical goods" to the temporal goods of the universal Church, the Apostolic See, and public juridic persons (canon 1208).

goods remain private goods and the technical term *ecclesiastical goods* is not applied to them, although the Church clearly recognizes that private juridic persons are persons in the Church who have the right to own temporal goods (canon 1255).[118] The ownership of the goods of a private juridic person is governed only by the statutes of private juridic persons, unless the law says otherwise.

To say that public juridic persons act in the name of the Church is to acknowledge that the temporal goods of these persons, called *ecclesiastical goods*, are used to assist in fulfilling the mission of the Church, not a private mission. "This concept of *ecclesiastical goods* opens to the theological values underlying the mission of the Church. Ecclesiastical goods are subordinated to achieving that goal. Temporal goods then are, in this way of understanding, transformed from being merely secular realities to being means of achieving the divine mission of the Church."[119]

"Ecclesiastical goods" are governed by both the canons of *Book V* and the statutes of the public juridic person which owns them. Canon 117 requires that juridic persons, both public and private, have their own statutes which are to be approved by the competent ecclesiastical authority. The temporal goods of private juridic persons are governed by their own statutes and not by the canons of *Book V*, unless other provision is made. Such "other provision" is made in a number of canons in *Book V*:

1. Canon 1263: private juridic persons can be subject to an extraordinary diocesan tax[120]

2. Canon 1265 §5: private juridic persons are forbidden to beg for alms without the written permission of their own ordinary and the local ordinary

3. Canon 1266: the local ordinary can order special collections

---

[118] The preface to the 1997 *Schema* had said that private juridic persons "do not act in the name of the Church, and therefore their goods cannot be called *ecclesiastical* in the strict sense like the goods of public juridic persons." In *Schema*, 1977, Preface, p. 4.

[119] Fox, "Introductory Thoughts," p. 252.

[120] See also canon 264 §2, which allows the diocesan bishop to impose the seminary tax on private juridic persons.

     in the oratories (see canons 1223-1225) of private juridic persons

4.   Canon 1267 §1: offerings given to the administrator of a private juridic person are presumed to be given to the private juridic person itself

5.   Canon 1269: private juridic persons can own and acquire sacred objects through prescription if such objects previously had been owned privately

6.   Canon 1280: private juridic persons must have a finance council or at least two financial counselors[121]

Should the statutes of private juridic persons be silent on an issue involving its temporal goods, it may be reasonable to apply norms governing public juridic persons to address that issue.

    Although the temporal goods of physical persons are not ecclesiastical goods, it may be noted that *Book V* makes several references to *physical persons*:

1.   Canon 1260: the Church has an innate right to require from the Christian faithful (physical persons) those things necessary for its proper purposes

2.   Canon 1261: the Christian faithful are free to give their temporal goods to the Church, and the diocesan bishop is to admonish them on this obligation

3.   Canon 1262: the Christian faithful are to give their support by responding to appeals

4.   Canon 1263: the diocesan bishop is permitted to impose an extraordinary and moderate exaction on physical persons in cases of grave necessity

5.   Canon 1265 §1: private persons, except mendicants, are forbidden to beg for alms for any pious or ecclesiastical purpose without the written permission of their own ordinary and the local ordinary

---

[121] In addition, canon 1480 §1 acknowledges the right of private juridic persons to stand trial through their legitimate representatives.

6. Canon 1267 §1: offerings given to physical persons who are administrators or superiors of (public or private) juridic persons are presumed to be given to the juridic person

7. Canon 1267 §3: offerings given by the faithful for a certain purpose can be applied only for that same purpose

8. Canon 1269: private persons can acquire privately owned sacred objects through prescription, but these can be used for profane purposes only if they have lost their dedication or blessing

9. Canon 1274 §3: insofar as necessary, each diocese is to establish a common fund whereby bishops are able to satisfy obligations toward persons who serve the Church

10. Canons 1278-1289: norms on administrators (who are physical persons)

11. Canon 1296: action may be taken against persons who alienate ecclesiastical goods in ways which are canonically invalid but civilly valid

12. Canon 1298: ecclesiastical goods are not to be sold or leased to administrators and their close relatives

13. Canon 1299: persons who are free in natural law and canon law to dispose their goods can bestow them for pious causes; civil formalities in depositions *inter vivos* and *mortis causa* should be observed, and heirs must be admonished to fulfill the intentions of the donors

14. Canon 1300: the legitimately accepted wills of the faithful for pious causes are to be fulfilled most diligently

15. Canon 1301 §2: persons who serve as executors of pious wills must render an account of their function to the ordinary

16. Canon 1302: physical persons can accept goods in trust for pious causes

17. Canon 1308 §3: founders can expressly give the ordinary the ability to reduce foundation Mass obligations because of diminished revenues

18. Canon 1310 §1: founders can expressly entrust to the ordinary

the power to reduce, moderate, or commute the wills of the faithful for pious causes (other than Masses)

CORRESPONDING CANON OF THE EASTERN CODE: CANON 1009 §2. Inasmuch as the Eastern code, like the 1917 Latin code, does not distinguish private and public juridic persons, Eastern canon 1009 §2 simply says, "All temporal goods which belong to juridic persons are ecclesiastical goods."

TECHNICAL TERM: "CHURCH"

Can. 1258 – In the following canons, the term Church signifies not only the universal Church or the Apostolic See but also any public juridic person in the Church unless it is otherwise apparent from the context or the nature of the matter.

Canon 1258 defines what is meant by the term *Church* in the canons of *Book V.* In this section of the code, *Church* refers the universal Church, the Apostolic See, and all other public juridic persons in the Church,[122] unless it is otherwise apparent from the context or from the nature of the matter.[123]

Defining the term *Church* with legal precision is important, since oftentimes one would not otherwise apply the term to public juridic persons, although they perform their role *nomine Ecclesiae* (canon 116 §1).

Excluded from the meaning of *Church* in *Book V* are private juridic persons (unless it is otherwise apparent from the context or the nature of the matter), just as canon 1257 says that their temporal goods are excluded from the meaning of *ecclesiastical goods* in *Book V* (unless other provision is expressly made).

Canon 1258 reflects the same doctrine as canon 1498 of the 1917 code, which applied the term *Church* to the universal Church,

---

[122] See canons 1259; 1261 §1; 1262; 1268; 1282; 1284 §2, 3°; 1284 §2, 9°; 1287; 1289; 1292 §2; 1293 §2; 1296; 1297; and 1299 §2.

[123] See canons 1254; 1255; 1257 §1; 1260; 1274 §3; 1286, 1°; 1290; and 1294 §2.

the Apostolic See, and any moral person in the Church (unless it was otherwise apparent from the context or the nature of the matter). The canon had not appeared in the 1977 *Schema* but was later restored since those drafting the proposed new legislation wished to avoid ambiguity by the use of a legal technical term.[124]

CORRESPONDING CANON OF THE EASTERN CODE: None.

---

[124] *Communicationes*, 12 (1980), p. 399.

CHAPTER THREE

THE ACQUISITION OF GOODS
(Title I: Canons 1259-1272)

Title I of *Book V* contains fourteen canons relating to the Church's acquisition of temporal goods. Canon 1259 asserts the Church's ability to acquire temporal goods by every just means of natural and positive law permitted by others. Canon 1260 affirms the Church's innate right to require temporal goods from the Christian faithful, and canon 1261 identifies the corresponding freedom and obligation of the Christian faithful to give offerings to the Church. The following canons identify a number of means whereby temporal goods are obtained by the Church: appeals (canon 1262); ordinary and extraordinary diocesan taxation (canon 1263); fees for acts of executive power granting favors and for executing rescripts (canon 1264); begging for alms (canon 1265); special collections for parochial, diocesan, national, or universal projects (canon 1266); offerings given to superiors or administrators of ecclesiastical juridic persons (canon 1267); and prescription (canons 1268-1270). Title I concludes with a canon requiring diocesan bishops to assist the needs of the Apostolic See (canon 1271), and a canon requiring the episcopal conference to issue norms, to be approved by the Apostolic See, governing benefices (canon 1272).

Other norms in *Book V* on the acquisition of temporal goods are contained in Title IV.

These canons reflect the discipline of the 1917 *Code of Canon Law* in its canons 1496; 1499 §1; 1503-1506; 1507 §1; 1508-1511; 1513; 1536 §§1-2; and 1624. Several canons have no predecessor in the first code: canons 1261 §1; 1262; 1267 §3; and 1271-1272.

Corresponding canons in the 1990 *Code of Canons of the Eastern Churches* are canons 1010-1012; 1013 §1; and 1014-1019. Several Latin canons have no corresponding canon in the Eastern code: canons 1261-1262; 1265 §2; and 1271-1272.

ACQUISITION OF TEMPORAL GOODS BY EVERY JUST MEANS

Can. 1259 – The Church can acquire temporal goods by every just means of natural or positive law permitted to others.

Canon 1254 §1 had already expressed the Church's innate right to acquire temporal goods independently from civil power in order to pursue the Church's proper ends. Canon 1259 expresses the principle that the Church is able to acquire temporal goods by every just means of natural or positive law (civil and canon) which are available to others. Both these canons confront those who deny or restrict the doctrine conveyed by them.

There are several methods of acquiring property based in the natural law, all of which apply for the Church.[1]

1.   Occupancy – the taking of something which has no owner with the intention of making it one's own
2.   Accession – the acquisition of ownership by gaining something produced by what one already owns
3.   Contract – the transfer of ownership by consent between two or more persons who are naturally capable to make the transfer
4.   Testament – the disposition of one's goods at the moment of death
5.   Labor – the acquiring of ownership of a good in return for work rendered to one who heretofore owns that good

The positive law, both civil and canonical, also identifies methods of acquiring property by the Church.[2] The civil law has

---

[1]   See BOUSCAREN-ELLIS-KORTH, p. 804.

[2]   See FRANCIS G. MORRISEY, "The Temporal Goods of the Church," in *The Canon Law: Letter and Spirit: A Practical Guide to the Code of Canon Law*, Gerard Sheehy, et al. (eds.), prepared by the CANON LAW SOCIETY OF GREAT BRITAIN AND IRELAND in association with the CANADIAN CANON LAW SOCIETY, Collegeville, The Liturgical Press, 1995, p. 711 (=MORRISEY, "Temporal Goods").

added certain requirements to many of the methods identified in the natural law (e.g., stipulations for the validity of a contract, requirements for the validity of a last will and testament, specifics concerning labor laws, etc.) and has developed other recognized means of acquiring property (e.g., prescription, etc.). The positive law of the Church, contained in the canons of this title, identify a number of "just means" whereby the Church is able to acquire temporal goods: free-will offerings (canon 1261), general appeals (canon 1262), diocesan taxation (canon 1263), prescribed fees and "stole fees" (canon 1264), begging for alms (canon 1265), special collections (canon 1266), and prescription (canon 1268-1270).[3] Mention is also made of episcopal support for the Apostolic See (canon 1271) and revenue accruing from benefices (canon 1272).[4] *Book V* also contains legislation on ways the Church may acquire temporal goods in Title IV – i.e., through pious wills (canons 1299-1301), pious trusts (canon 1302), and pious foundations (1303-1307). Sometimes, however, the goods received by pious wills, trusts, and foundations do not become ecclesiastical goods – i.e., when they are acquired

---

[3] CIC/1917, canon 1502 had made reference to local statutes and customs regarding tithing (*decimae*) and first fruits (*primitiae*) as a means to acquire temporal goods: "Particular statutes and laudable customs regarding tithes and first fruits are to be observed in every region." Giving one-tenth (i.e., a tithe) of the produce of the land to God (Deuteronomy 14:22), and giving the first fruits of the soil and animals to God (Numbers 18:19), both come from the Mosaic Law. STANISLAUS WOYWOOD commented on this canon: "The *decimae* (tithes or tenth part) of the fruits of one's property or income were demanded in ancient times by the law of the Church as an annual tax to the Church. Pope Gregory VII condemns in severe terms those who refused to pay the *decimae*, saying that they should know that they are guilty of the crime of sacrilege and incur the danger of eternal damnation [*Decetum Gratiani*, c. 1, C. XVI, q. 7]. The Council of Trent insists on the payment of these tithes [Sessio XXV, cap. 12, *De Reform.*]...The *primitiae* (or first fruits of fields, vineyards, orchards, gardens, etc.) originally referred to the first crop that was obtained from new fields or gardens, the first offspring of animals, etc. Following the example of the Old Testament, the Christians in many places introduced the custom of offering first fruits" (vol. 2, p. 191).
The 1983 code makes no mention of tithes and first fruits. Likewise the revised code does not make reference to the *cathedraticum* (CIC/1917, canon 1504), the "charitable subsidy" (CIC/1917, canon 1505) and the "foundation tax" (CIC/1917, canon 1506), but these canons are replaced by the revised legislation of canon 1263 (on the ordinary and extraordinary diocesan tax). See the commentary on canon 1263, below.

[4] Benefices were a principal source of revenue in the 1917 code: see CIC/1917, canons 1355-1356; 1409-1488; 1505-1506.

by private juridic persons or physical persons (e.g., trusts acquired by private individuals for pious causes). Therefore, a special title is assigned to these pious wills, trusts, and foundations – as if in an appendix[5] to *Book V.*

Other means for the Church to acquire goods not mentioned in *Book V* are by the merger (canon 121), division (canon 122) and extinction (canon 123) of public juridic persons; by the seminary collection and tax (canon 264); by the missions collection (canon 791, 4°); by fees for tribunal services (canon 1649); by fines (canon 1488 §1; 1489); by insurance claims; by civil court settlements; by grants, etc.[6]

Canon 1259 proclaims that the Church has the *ability* to acquire temporal goods; implicit in this statement is that the Church also has the right to *use* the goods legitimately acquired. Canon 1375 provides that a "just penalty" may be imposed upon those "who impede... the legitimate use of sacred goods or other ecclesiastical goods."[7]

CORRESPONDING CANON OF THE EASTERN CODE: CANON 1010. The Eastern legislation says that juridic persons (rather than the "Church," as defined in Latin canon 1258 which has no corresponding canon in the Eastern law) "can acquire temporal goods by any just means permitted to others." No reference is made to "natural or positive law."

INNATE RIGHT OF THE CHURCH TO REQUIRE
SUPPORT FROM THE FAITHFUL

> **Can. 1260 – The Church has an innate right to require from the Christian faithful those things which are necessary for the purposes proper to it.**

---

[5] See *Communicationes,* 5 (1973), p. 101; 37 (2005), pp. 267-268.

[6] MARIANO LÓPEZ ALARCÓN comments: "Special reference should be made, within the scope of public law, to income *iure imperiti,* which is not a means of acquiring goods, strictly speaking, but of requesting goods and collecting them in order to apply them to the fulfillment of the objectives of the Church." In "Book V," p. 968.

[7] This penal law is facultative (see canon 1315 §3) and indeterminate (see canon 1315 §2).

Canon 1254 §1 had identified the "innate right" (*ius nativum*) of the Church to own temporal goods independently from civil authority, and canon 1259 had said that the Church can acquire temporal goods by every just means of natural or positive law permitted to others. Canon 1260 claims the "innate right" (*ius nativum*) of the Church to require (*exigendi*) from the Christian faithful those things which are necessary for the purposes proper to the Church.[8] These "proper purposes" had already been identified in canon 1254 §2 as principally three: to order divine worship; to care for the decent support of the clergy and other ministers; and to exercise works of the sacred apostolate and of charity, especially toward the needy.

Canon 1260 explains that the Church has the innate right to require (*ius exigendi*) temporal assistance from the Christian faithful. During the consultation process on the 1977 *Schema,* some had suggested replacing *ius exigendi* with another term: the right to ask (*ius petendi*), the right to collect (*ius colligendi*), or the right to seek (*ius exquirendi*) assistance. Although the *coetus De bonis Ecclesiae temporalibus* agreed unanimously that this canon should state that the Church has the right to require (*ius exigendi*) the means necessary to achieve its principle purposes, the consultors also unanimously agreed that the legal text should use the term *ius exquirendi.*[9] Both the 1980 *Schema*[10] and the 1982 *Schema*[11] had employed *ius exquirendi*. The promulgated law, however, uses *ius exigendi,* as had the 1917 code (CIC/1917, canon 1496). The original term was restored during the private papal consultation process. Thus, the code clearly

---

[8] ROBERT T. KENNEDY remarks that the term "church" is not used here in the technical sense of canon 1258, which identifies the term with juridic persons (and the two moral persons: the Catholic Church and the Apostolic See). Since canon 1260 speaks of "innate rights," it cannot be referring to juridic persons which, as constructs of positive law, cannot be said to have "innate rights." In "Temporal Goods," p. 1460. One may observe, however, that the canon speaks of an "innate right" (i.e., a right with which an entity is born), not of a natural right (i.e., a right given by God); in light of this reasoning, one may conclude that juridic persons are "born" in the Church with the right mentioned in canon 1260: the right is given them by the Church when they are established by the Church, whether *a iure* or *ab homine.*

[9] *Communicationes,* 12 (1980), p. 400.

[10] 1980 *Schema*, p. 270.

[11] 1982 *Schema*, p. 219.

teaches that the Church has a right to require (rather than simply to ask, collect, or seek) the financial support of the faithful in order to achieve its proper purposes.

Canon 204 §1 defines the meaning of the term "Christian faithful" (*Christifidelis*): "The Christian faithful are those who, inasmuch as they have been incorporated in Christ through baptism, have been constituted as the people of God." All the baptized, in other words, are properly called the Christian faithful. In most canons of the code, however, the term refers only to Catholics (see canon 205)[12] who alone among all of the baptized are bound to merely ecclesiastical laws (see canon 11).

Related to canon 1260 are the norms of canon 222 §1 (obliging the Christian faithful to assist the needs of the Church) and canon 1261 §2 (reminding the diocesan bishop to admonish the faithful of the obligation of canon 222 §1).

The legislation of the 1917 code had included the phrase "independently of civil authority" in this canon (CIC/1917, canon 1496). This was omitted in the 1983 code, which nonetheless underscores the independent right of the Church to acquire temporal goods in canon 1254 §1. Also, to underscore the Church's independence from civil authority in this matter, canon 1260 speaks of its "innate right" to require support from the faithful, a phrase not found in the 1917 code.[13] It must be recalled, however, that sometimes the Church co-

---

[12] Those drafting the *Schema De populo Dei* explained that the term "Christian faithful" theologically refers to all the baptized, even non-Catholics, but that the term is used everywhere in the code as a reference to Catholics only: *Communicationes*, 14 (1982), p. 157. See DE PAOLIS, *De bonis Ecclesiae temporalibus*, p. 62; ROBERT KASLYN, "The Christian Faithful," in *New Commentary on the Code of Canon Law*, commissioned by the CLSA, John P. Beal, James A. Coriden, and Thomas J. Green (eds.), New York, Paulist, 2000, p. 204.

[13] CIC/1917, canon 1496 spoke only of the "right" (*ius*) without the modifier "innate." FRANCIS G. MORRISEY comments: "Of course, the *use* of this right might be restricted in some fashion by civil legislation or, in some countries, it might even be enhanced by public taxation laws (the well-known *Kirchensteuer* is an example). As regards the limitation of the use of the right, in some areas there are mortmain laws which have for their object the control of possessions of religious corporations or trusts: no lands are to be given to charities unless certain requisites are observed. Other places have restrictions concerning donations which are to be given to recognised charitable organizations if they are to qualify for taxation exemptions." In "Temporal Goods," p. 711.

operates actively with the secular government to exercise its innate right (e.g., in Germany through the *Kirchensteuer*).

The code contains no penal sanction for those among the Christian faithful who refuse to provide temporal goods to the Church, but it does provide that a "just penalty" may be imposed upon those "who impede... the legitimate use of sacred goods or other ecclesiastical goods" (canon 1375).

CORRESPONDING CANON OF THE EASTERN CODE: CANON 1011. Eastern legislation replaces "Church" with "competent authority," who has a "right" (not identified as an "innate" right) to require from the Christian faithful those things which are necessary for the purposes proper to the Church.

FREEDOM AND OBLIGATION OF THE CHRISTIAN FAITHFUL TO GIVE TEMPORAL GOODS

Can. 1261 – §1. The Christian faithful are free to give temporal goods for the benefit of the Church.

§2. The diocesan bishop is bound to admonish the faithful of the obligation mentioned in can. 222, §1 and in an appropriate manner to urge its observance.

Canon 1261 §1 is the corollary of the preceding canon. Just as the Church has the innate right to require temporal assistance from the Christian faithful (canon 1260), so the faithful have the freedom to donate their temporal goods to the Church. In a related fashion, canon 1299 §1 says that individual persons, who are able freely to dispose of their goods by natural law and canon law, can bestow their goods for pious causes through an act *inter vivos* and an act *mortis causa*. Reflected in these canons is the Church's recognition of the God-given capacity of the faithful to make donations to the Church. These canons contradict the views of those who hold that the secular government or any individual can restrict or eliminate this right.

A donation (i.e., a "free-will offering") is a voluntary transfer of ownership of property. Typically, a donation is irrevocable. The code says that donations to which are attached modal obligations or conditions can be accepted only with the permission of the ordinary (canon 1267 §2).[14] Donations given for a specific purpose can be used only for that purpose (canon 1267 §3; see canon 1300).

Further, as stated in canon 222 §1, all[15] the Christian faithful have the obligation "to assist the needs of the Church so that the Church has what is necessary for divine worship, for the works of the apostolate and of charity, and for the decent support of its ministers." Canon 1261 §2 explains that, just as the faithful have an obligation to assist the needs of the Church,[16] so the diocesan bishop (but not the other local ordinaries, i.e., the vicars general and episcopal vicars: see canon 134 §2) has the correlative duty to admonish (*monere tenetur*) the faithful about this obligation and, in an appropriate manner, to urge them to observe it.[17] This obligation is related to the episcopal obligation "to insist upon the duty which binds the faithful to exercise the apostolate according to each one's condition and ability and ... to exhort them to participate in and assist the various works of the apostolate according to the needs of place and time" (canon 394 §2).[18] The diocesan bishop's obligation is also mentioned in the *Directory for the Pastoral Ministry of Bishops*:

> In an appropriate manner, the Bishop will see to it that the faithful are educated to play their part in the support of the Church as active and responsible members. In this way, all will feel personally involved in the Church's activity and its charitable works and will gladly cooperate in the just administration of goods.... In this regard, so as not to overburden the faithful with excessive financial

---

[14] FRANCIS MORRISEY observes that a donation "can take the form of a donative trust, to the effect namely that unless the donation is used for the purpose specified, it must be returned to the donor. In this context also it is important to ensure that any such gift has a 'clean title,' i.e., that the donor is free to make it without any legal incumbrances." In "Temporal Goods," p. 711.

[15] Canon 222 §1 is among the canons identifying the obligations and rights of *all* the Christian faithful, not only those of the laity.

[16] See JOSEPH N. PERRY, "Support for the Church," in *CFH*, pp. 63-76.

[17] See *Presbyterorum ordinis*, n. 20.

[18] See also canon 392 §1 which reminds the diocesan bishop that he is bound to promote common ecclesiastical discipline and to urge the observance of all ecclesiastical laws.

appeals, the Bishop should carefully consider in each case whether there is a real necessity to raise funds.[19]

The discipline of canon 1261 is especially applicable in generating revenue through the so-called "regular church support" (e.g., "Sunday collections"), specific reference to which is not made in any other canon in *Book V.*

CORRESPONDING CANON OF THE EASTERN CODE: None.

APPEALS

Can. 1262 – The faithful are to give support to the Church by responding to appeals and according to the norms issued by the conference of bishops.

Canon 1262 explains that the faithful are to give their support to the Church (as that term is understood in canon 1258) by responding to appeals according to the norms issued by the conference of bishops.

The code does not address the fund-raising appeals of private juridic persons; nonetheless, they may rely upon the spirit and norms of guidelines issued by the episcopal conference for appeals made by public juridic persons.

The canon concerns "appeals" (*subventiones rogatas*) for free-will offerings. Although "appeals" certainly can include the so-called "regular Church support,"[20] the discipline of canon 1262

---

[19] *DPBM*, n. 191.

[20] ROBERT T. KENNEDY says that collections in churches are the subject matter of canon 1266, not canon 1262. In "Temporal Goods," p. 1461. One observes, however, that canon 1266 is about *special* collections, not those given on a regular basis.

The particular law for the United States related to canon 1262 and promulgated by the USCCB on June 8, 2007 concerns fund-raising appeals. The new law does not concern appeals for so-called "regular church support," as had the earlier NCCB norms developed in November, 1984, which gave to diocesan bishops responsibility to establish norms for church support in each diocese.

The particular law for Canada related to canon 1262 and issued by the CCCB on June 28, 1989 concerns collections and financial contributions. The Canadian particular law says that norms shall be determined by each diocesan bishop in order that local customs and even secular laws, federal and provincial, can be taken into consideration.

especially connotes special fund-raising requests made according to norms issued by the conference of bishops. Those preparing the legislation made a deliberate choice to place canon 1262 (on appeals to the faithful) before canon 1263 (on taxes) as means for the Church to acquire temporal goods. Appeals for voluntary offerings thus appear as preferred to taxation.[21]

PARTICULAR LAW FOR THE UNITED STATES.[22] On June 8, 2007, the USCCB issued a decree following *recognitio*[23] by the Apostolic See, promulgating the particular law for the United States on the fund-raising appeals to the faithful for Church support. The decree does not address the so-called "regular Church support" (e.g., "Sunday collections") as the first particular law[24] implementing canon 1262 in the United States had done. The revised decree instead only addresses special "fund-raising appeals." The decree follows:

Diocesan norms, presumably, would address "regular church support." (The Canadian law also addresses special collections and collections for cultural and philanthropical purposes gathered on the occasion of liturgical services which require the prior authorization of the local ordinary.)

Seemingly, the 1983 code addresses "regular church support" in the general provision on free-will offerings contained in canon 1261.

[21] *Communicationes*, 12 (1980), p. 402; 16 (1984), pp. 28-30.

[22] http://www.usccb.org/norms/1262.htm (December 1, 2008) The development of the particular law for the United States is explained by THOMAS J. PAPROCKI in "Recent Developments Concerning Temporal Goods, Including Complementary USCCB Norms," in *CLSA Proceedings*, 70 (2008), pp. 261-264 (=PAPROCKI, "Recent Developments"). See also: LEGAL RESOURCE CENTER FOR RELIGIOUS, "Commentary on USCCB Complementary Norms Implementing Canon 1262 on Fundraising Appeals" (August 14, 2007), manuscript, 6 pp.

[23] An explanatory note concerning the juridic importance of the *recognitio* was issued by the PONTIFICAL COUNCIL FOR LEGISLATIVE TEXTS, *Nota*, La natura giuridica e l'estensione della 'recognitio' della Sancta Sede (April 28, 2006), in *Communicationes*, 38 (2006), pp. 10-17.

[24] At its November, 1984 meeting, the NCCB had approved a simple norm implementing canon 1262: "The National Conference of Catholic Bishops authorizes diocesan bishops to establish norms for church support by the faithful for their own dioceses." In *The Jurist*, 53 (1993), p. 410; NCCB, *Implementation of the 1983 Code of Canon Law: Complementary Norms*, Washington, NCCB, 1991, p. 20. This norm implies that diocesan regulations be established for "regular church support."

Also, in 1977 fund-raising guidelines had been developed jointly by the NCCB, the Leadership Conference of Women Religious and the Conference of Major Superiors of Men. These were approved by the NCCB at its November 14-17, 1977 meeting. In *Origins,* 7 (1977-1978), pp. 378-380; *CLD*, vol. 8, pp. 415-421.

DECREE OF PROMULGATION
CANON 1262

On November 13, 2002, the members of the United States Conference of Catholic Bishops legitimately approved complementary legislation for the implementation of canon 1262 of the Code of Canon Law for the dioceses of the United States. The action was granted *recognitio* by the Congregation for Bishops in accord with article 82 of the Apostolic Constitution *Pastor Bonus* and issued by Decree N. 778/2005 of the Congregation for Bishops signed by His Eminence Giovanni Battista Cardinal Re, Prefect, and His Excellency Most Reverend Francesco Monterisi, Secretary, and dated May 2, 2007.

Wherefore, and in accord with the prescripts of canon 1262, the United States Conference of Catholic Bishops decrees that the following norms shall govern fund-raising appeals to the faithful for Church support:

Motivation

1. Fund-raising appeals are to be truthful and forthright, theologically sound, and should strive to motivate the faithful to a greater love of God and neighbor.
2. Fund-raising efforts are to be for defined needs.
3. The relationship of trust between donor and fund-raiser requires that
   a. funds collected be used for their intended purposes;
   b. funds collected are not absorbed by excessive fund-raising costs.
4. Donors are to be informed regarding the use of donated funds and assured that any restrictions on the use of the funds by the donor will be honored.

Competent Ecclesiastical Authority

5. Institutes of consecrated life and societies of apostolic life require approval of the respective competent major superiors and the diocesan bishop to solicit funds; diocesan entities require approval of the diocesan bishop to solicit funds; other Catholic entities and organizations require the approval of the diocesan bishop to solicit funds.

6. Approval for fund-raising by the competent authority is to be given in writing with reference to the purpose for which the funds are being raised, the time frame, and the methods to be used in raising them.

7. Oversight of fund-raising programs is to be maintained by competent authority through periodic review and, where necessary, appropriate sanction.

8. Competent major superiors of institutes of consecrated life and societies of apostolic life are to submit to the diocesan bishop of the place where the fund-raising originates periodic reports on the fund-raising programs and the apostolic activities they support.

Accountability

9. Fund-raisers are to provide regular reports to competent authority on the extent to which promises expressed or implied in the solicitation of funds have been fulfilled.

10. Fund-raising reports are to be prepared in scope and design to meet the particular concerns of those to whom the reports are due:
    c. the governing body and membership of the fund-raising organization;
    d. the competent authorities who approved and monitor the fund-raising effort;
    e. the donors to the organization;
    f. the beneficiaries of the funds raised.

11. Annual fund-raising reports are to provide both financial information and a review of the apostolic work for which the funds were raised. They are to set forth, at the least, the amount of money collected, the cost of conducting the fund-raising effort, and the amount and use of the funds disbursed.

Procedures

12. Funds beyond operating expenses are not to be accumulated or invested by a fund-raising office, but are to be turned over to the appropriate office for allocation and investment.

13. Special care is to be taken to see that ethical business relationships are maintained by fund-raisers with suppliers of goods and services.

14. Contracts between a religious fund-raiser and commercial suppliers and consultants are to insure that control over materials, designs, money and general operations remain in the hands of the religious fund-raiser.

15. Agreements are not to be made which directly or indirectly base payment either to the commercial firm or to the religious fund-raiser on a percentage basis.

Oversight

16. Competent authority is to ensure that fund-raising organizations:
    g. make available fund-raising reports to benefactors on a regular basis or upon reasonable request:
    h. provide their governing bodies with an annual financial statement prepared in accordance with generally accepted accounting principles and, where size warrants, by a certified public accountant.

17. In response to formal complaints, competent authority is to promptly investigate charges, remedy abuses and, when necessary, terminate the fund-raising program.

As President of the United States Conference of Catholic Bishops, I hereby decree that the effective date of this decree for all the dioceses of the United States Conference of Catholic Bishops will be August 15, 2007.

Given at the offices of the United States Conference of Catholic Bishops in the city of Washington, the District of Columbia, on the 8th day of June, in the year of our Lord 2007.

Most Reverend William S. Skylstad
Bishop of Spokane President, USCCB
Reverend Monsignor David J. Malloy
General Secretary, USCCB

These new norms for the implementation of canon 1262 reflect much of the discipline of *Book V*, particularly the ordinary's role of vigilance (canon 1276), respect for the intentions of donors (canon 1267 §3), reports to donors (canon 1287 §1), etc. The "diocesan bishop" to which Norm 5 refers is obviously the diocesan bishop where the fund-raising originates (see Norm 8).[25]

PARTICULAR LAW FOR CANADA.[26] On June 28, 1989 the CCCB promulgated the following as particular law implementing canon 1262 in Canada. This legislation had been approved by the CCCB at its plenary meeting on October 17-21, 1988 and reviewed by the Congregation for Bishops on February 3, 1989 (Prot. N. 6/84):

Decree No. 33 – In accordance with the prescripts of c. 1262 regarding collections and financial contributions, the Canadian Conference of Catholic Bishops hereby decrees that:

1. norms shall be determined in each diocese by the diocesan bishop;

2. in each parish, the faithful shall be informed about the purpose of each special collection and, in due time, given an account of the results, in accordance with the prescriptions of c. 1287 §2;

3. collections for cultural or philanthropic purposes shall not be taken up on the occasion of a liturgical service in churches or oratories without the prior authorization of the local ordinary.

The commentary[27] on this decree states:

1. According to canon 1262, the faithful are to give their support to the Church in response to appeals and in accordance with the norms laid down by the Episcopal Conference. The Canadian Conference of Catholic Bishops did not judge it opportune to

---

[25] THOMAS J. PAPROCKI observes that sometimes the fundraising may go beyond diocesan boundaries, in which situation the competent diocesan bishop to approve the fund-raising is the bishop of the diocese where the initiative originates, not all the bishops involved. He says, "The purpose of canon 1262 and its complementary norms is to provide episcopal oversight and accountability for fundraising by Catholic entities. Such oversight is best exercised by an individual overseer with a direct local relationship rather than by several different authorities in diverse geographic areas. If there is some problem that emerges in another locality, the bishop of that locale could make his concerns known to the appropriate bishop where the institution is located." In "Recent Developments," p. 272.

[26] CCCB, *Official Document No.* 611 in *Studia canonica*, 24 (1990), pp. 470-471; CCCB, *Complementary Norms to the 1983 Code of Canon Law*, Ottawa, CCCB Publications, 1996, pp. 102-105.

[27] *Studia canonica*, 24 (1990), pp. 470-473.

establish general rules for the whole country. In fact, various civil laws, both federal and provincial, as well as existing local customs concerning financial contributions by the faithful, make it impractical to establish norms which would apply to the whole of Canada.

2. Recourse was therefore had to canon 1261 which states that the diocesan bishop is bound to remind the faithful of the obligation they have to provide for the needs of the Church (canon 222, §1), and in an appropriate manner to urge it.

   The *Directory on the Pastoral Ministry of Bishops* invites the chief pastors to take "suitable measures that the faithful may be educated to a sense of participation and cooperation also as regards the temporal goods which the Church needs to fulfill her purpose, so that all according to their individual capacities consider themselves co-responsible... in the economic support of the Church community and of its works and charities..." (no. 133).

3. According to canon 1287, §2, administrators are to render accounts to the faithful concerning the use of the goods they have given to the Church, in accordance with the norms to be laid down by particular law. The decree of the Conference requires that the faithful shall be informed about the purpose of each *special* collection and the amount collected. However, the decree does not intend to limit application of canon 1287, §2 to these collections only.

4. Number 3 of the decree prohibits:
   - collections for cultural or philanthropic purposes, i.e., for means other than those described in canon 1254, §2;
   - on the occasion of liturgical celebrations;
   - in churches and oratories;
   - without prior authorization of the local Ordinary.
     This prohibition applies only in cases where the four conditions are met at the same time.

One notes that the Canadian decree identifies special collections (considered in canon 1266) as an aspect of special appeals to the faithful.[28]

Corresponding Canon of the Eastern Code. None.

DIOCESAN TAXES: ORDINARY AND EXTRAORDINARY

Can. 1263 – After the diocesan bishop has heard the finance council and the presbyteral council, he has the right to impose a moderate tax for the needs of the diocese upon public juridic persons subject to his governance; this tax is to be proportionate to their income. He is permitted only to impose an extraordinary and moderate exaction upon other physical and juridic persons in case of grave necessity and under the same conditions, without prejudice to particular laws and customs which attribute greater rights to him.

The code identifies three diocesan taxes which the diocesan bishop may impose upon persons subject to him: an ordinary tax, an extraordinary tax, and the seminary tax. (The seminary tax is discussed briefly in the following commentary.)

Canon 1263 concerns the ordinary and extraordinary taxes. It identifies two rights belonging to the diocesan bishop which he may exercise only after he has received the counsel (but not the consent: see canon 127)[29] of both the diocesan finance council and the presbyteral council:

1. the right to impose a moderate tax (*tributum*) for diocesan needs upon public juridic persons subject to his governance; this tax is to be proportionate to the income of the public juridic person

2. the right to impose an extraordinary and moderate exaction (*exactio*) in case of grave necessity and under the same condi-

---

[28]   The special collections authorized in Canada and the United States are listed in the commentary on canon 1266.

[29]   The *coetus De bonis Ecclesiae temporalibus* explicitly rejected a proposal requiring the consent of the presbyteral council on June 7, 1967: see *Communicationes*, 36 (2004), p. 261.

tions upon other physical and juridic persons, without prejudice to particular laws and customs which give him greater rights.

The canon gives him the *right* to impose these taxes, but not the *obligation*. He is entirely free not to impose any tax. Should he choose to impose the tax, however, he will issue the appropriate general decree.[30]

It must be understood clearly that, if a diocesan bishop imposes a mandatory financial "goal" on a public juridic person, he in fact is imposing the tax identified in canon 1263, whose requirements must be observed.[31]

The right to impose a tax is, put quite simply, "the right to take away someone's property."[32] Canon 1263 explains that the diocesan taxes may only come from *income*. Canons 1267 §3 and 1300 require administrators to respect and to protect the intentions of donors,[33] which intentions would likely not include the donations being subject to a tax.[34] Therefore, any tax imposed by the diocesan bishop cannot take a portion of the stable patrimony of a juridic person, nor donations made to the juridic persons for a particular intention

---

[30] Canon 29 defines general decrees: "General decrees, by which a competent legislator issues common prescripts for a community capable of receiving law, are laws properly speaking and are governed by the prescripts of the canons on laws."
MARIANO LÓPEZ ALARCÓN comments that this decree is subject to administrative recourse (canons 1732-1739), including subsequent recourse lodged before the Apostolic Signatura (*Pastor Bonus*, 123). In "Book V," p. 971. The same is said by PHILIPPE GREINER, "Les biens des paroisses dans le contexte des diocèses français," in *L'année canonique*, 47 (2005), p. 49, fn. 32.

[31] See JOHN A. RENKEN, "Canon 1263: Parish Financial Goals," in CLSA, *Roman Replies and Advisory Opinions*, Joseph J. Koury and Shiobhan Verbeek (eds.), Washington, CLSA, 2008, pp. 122-124.

[32] DONALD J FRUGÉ, "The Bishop's Power to Tax All Parish Funds" in *CLSA AO2*, p. 414.

[33] The intention of the donor is highlighted in a number of canons: 121; 122; 123; 326 §2; 531; 616 §1; 706, 3°; 954; 1267 §3; 1284 §2, 3°; 1300; 1302 §1; 1303 §2; 1304 §1; 1307 §1; and 1310 §2.

[34] NICHOLAS CAFARDI [and] DONALD J. FRUGÉ, "The Bishop's Power to Tax All Parish Funds" in *CLSA AO2*, pp. 410-416. Cafardi observes that the administrator of a public juridic person (e.g., a pastor) may designate free capital as part of stable patrimony, but doing so would be an act of extraordinary administration requiring the ordinary's written faculty (see canon 1281 §1).

specified by the donors.[35] A donation intended by its donor for the "general purposes" of a juridic person, without further specification, however, would be subject to diocesan taxation, since such a donation is simply part of the juridic person's income, which income is subject to taxation.

HISTORY OF THE DEVELOPMENT OF CANON 1263. Although the preferred means of generating revenue is the donations of the faithful given in response to appeals (canon 1262), inasmuch as canon 1263 allows the diocesan bishop to impose ordinary and extraordinary taxes on juridic and physical persons, special consideration is properly given to its development. The discipline of canon 1263 had not existed in the 1917 code, and its development reflects significant dialogue and controversy. Robert L. Kealy remarks that canon 1263 "is the most significant and most controversial canon in Book V."[36]

Early Discussions. The *coetus De iure patrimoniali Ecclesiae* proposed its first reflections in early 1967 on what was to develop into canon 1263.[37] According to a report published in 1973, the initial proposal of the *coetus* gave local ordinaries the right to impose taxes (*tributa*) on ecclesiastical persons, physical and moral, for the good of the diocese. The local ordinary *must* have heard the presbyteral council before imposing the tax, which would be done according to norms established by the conference of bishops. The 1973 report added that the prohibition on taxing Mass offerings should be placed in a more appropriate place in the new law, and explained that the

---

[35] See NICHOLAS CAFARDI, "L'autorità di imporre le tasse da parte del vescovo diocesano secondo quanto previsto dal canone 1263," in *Attuali problemi di interpretazione del Codice di diritto canonico*, Bruno Esposito (ed.), Rome: Millenium, 1977, pp. 135-138. Cafardi also mentions that the restriction on taxing Mass offerings, omitted from canon 1263 when promulgated but present in the drafts of that canon prior to promulgation, is unnecessary in light of the restrictions identified in canons 1267 §3 and 1300: Mass offerings are given with a specific intention of a donor, so not subject to taxation.

[36] ROBERT L. KEALY, *Diocesan Financial Support: Its History and Canonical Status*, Rome, Pontifical Gregorian University, 1986, p. 330 (=KEALY, *Diocesan Financial Support*).

[37] The earliest recorded consideration of what became canon 1263 took place on January 27, 1967: *Communicationes*, 36 (2004), p. 247. The initial draft was again discussed on June 6-7, 1967: *Communicationes* 26 (2004), pp. 258-262, 274.

faithful are to be induced more by persuasion than by coercion (*suasione magis quam coactione*) to contribute to the support of the Church by revenues sought and according to norms approved by the episcopal conference.[38]

The 1977 Schema. The 1977 *Schema* issued by the *coetus* had given the local ordinary the right to impose a tax (*tributum*) on physical persons and juridic persons (private and public) insofar as it is necessary for the good of the diocese, after hearing the presbyteral council. The episcopal conference was to establish norms to govern these taxes. The faithful are to support the Church by responding to appeals and according to norms issued by the episcopal conference. Bishops are to induce the faithful to fulfill this obligation (*obligatio*) more by persuasion than by coercion.[39] The proposed canon stated:

> **Canon 5 – §1. The local ordinary has the right to impose taxes (*tributa*) on ecclesiastical persons, both physical and juridic, whether public and private, insofar as they are necessary for the good of the diocese. Taxes are not to be imposed unless the presbyteral council has been heard.**
>
> **§2. Conferences of bishops must establish norms to govern the ordering of taxes for their respective territories.**
>
> **§3. The faithful are to contribute their support to the Church by responding to appeals (*subventiones rogatas*) and according to the norms approved by the conferences of bishops. Bishops, nevertheless, are to induce the faithful to fulfill this obligation more by persuasion than by coercion.[40]**

Those offering remarks on the *Schema* suggested that the proposed canon gave the bishop unlimited power as regards both the persons

---

[38] *Communicationes*, 5 (1973), p. 95.

[39] *Communicationes*, 12 (1980), p. 401.

[40] 1977 *Schema*, canon 5, p. 9. Canon 5 §3 of the 1977 canon developed into canon 1262 of the promulgated law, preceding canon 1263 in order to illustrate that free-will offerings are the preferred means to generate diocesan revenue.

subject to the tax and the goods which can be taxed; further, the
phrase "insofar as they are necessary for the good of the diocese"
appeared too vague. In light of comments received and its own discussions, the *coetus* decided to eliminate reference to the conference
of bishops since the various needs of individual dioceses prevent
uniform norms for the scope of the entire episcopal conference. It
also concluded that any diocesan tax on juridic persons (public or
private) should be extraordinary (not routine) and moderate, and
should be imposed by the diocesan bishop (not the local ordinary)
only in cases of grave necessity (not insofar as necessary for the good
of the diocese). The diocesan finance council and the presbyteral
council must be heard before the tax is imposed, and no tax may be
placed on Mass offerings.[41]

The 1980 Schema. As a result of discussion on the canon proposed in the 1977 *Schema*, the 1980 *Schema* offered the following
legislation:

> **Canon 1213. The diocesan bishop has the right, in
> case of grave necessity, to impose an extraordinary and
> moderate tax (*tributum*) on the Christian faithful and
> on juridic persons, public and private; he is not do this,
> however, unless he has heard the finance council and the
> presbyteral council; indeed, no tax can be imposed upon
> Mass offerings.**[42]

Several objections were raised to the proposed canon of the
1980 *Schema*.[43] Emmet Cardinal Carter of Toronto had recommended that a time limit be imposed on the taxation, lest it be perpetual;
the secretariat replied that this specification is unnecessary since the
tax is "extraordinary" and therefore not perpetual.[44]

Four prelates (Basil Cardinal Hume of Westminster, James
Cardinal Freeman of Sydney, Joseph Cardinal Ratzinger of the
CDF, and Auxiliary Bishop O'Connell of Melbourne) proposed an
alternate canon:

---

[41]   *Communicationes*, 12 (1980), pp. 401-403.
[42]   1980 *Schema*, p. 270.
[43]   The responses to the 1980 revision are reported in *Relatio*, pp. 280-290.
[44]   *Relatio*, p. 281.

Inasmuch as the needs of the Church require it, the diocesan bishop has the right to impose a moderate tax (*tributum*) on the Christian faithful and on juridic persons, public and private, equity being observed; he is not to do this, however, unless he has heard the finance council and the presbyteral council; indeed, no tax can be imposed upon Mass offerings.[45]

Cardinal Ratzinger proposed an additional paragraph: "The conference of bishops is able (*valet*) to establish norms for its territory to govern the ordering of taxes."[46] He also reflected that the proposed 1980 norm did not make sense in those areas where the *Kirchensteuersystem* is used and preferred, but which would no longer be able to be used if the proposed law became effective.[47]

Cardinals Freeman and Hume commented that the term "extraordinary" prevents the diocesan bishop from taxing for ordinary diocesan needs.[48]

The Secretariat rejected all these proposals. It commented that the 1980 *Schema* reflected world-wide concerns that the 1977 *Schema* had given the bishop too much power to tax, and that the 1980 *Schema* was more closely aligned to the 1917 code. Concerns over the *Kirchensteuersystem* are not pertinent since this is a secular tax not imposed by the Church. The Secretariat also underscored that the 1980 *Schema* preferred appeals (*subventiones rogatas*) for voluntary contributions over the imposition of taxes, so taxation should be an extraordinary means of generating diocesan income. In places where civil laws do not impose Church taxes, the Church likewise has no power to do so.[49] Nonetheless, the Secretariat agreed to place this canon after the canon on appeals (*subventiones rogatas*) which it had heretofore preceded; the Secretariat explained that this

---

[45] *Relatio*, p. 281.

[46] *Relatio*, p. 281. Note that canon 5 §2 of the 1977 *Schema* had said that the conference of bishops must (*debet*) establish territorial norms, but Cardinal Ratzinger suggested that the conference of bishops simply can (*valet*) do so.

[47] *Relatio*, p. 281.

[48] *Relatio*, p. 281.

[49] *Relatio*, p. 281.

inversion would show that appeals are the ordinary way to obtain ecclesiastical goods, and the taxation is the extraordinary way.[50]

Julio Cardinal Rosales of Cebu proposed that certain restrictions be added in the canon to limit the bishop's power to tax: those taxed must be subject to the jurisdiction of the diocesan bishop (i.e., excluded would be institutes of pontifical right), and no tax should be imposed on priests not receiving their stipend from the diocese. The Secretariat replied that the proposed canon was adequate because the tax is envisioned as being "extraordinary."[51]

Archbishop Joseph Bernardin of Cincinnati proposed yet another formulation for the diocesan tax:

> In order to fulfill the administration of the diocese, the diocesan bishop has the right to impose an ordinary and moderate tax (*tributum*) upon public juridic persons; nevertheless, he is not to do this unless he has the consent of the finance council and the presbyteral council, and in accord with the norms of the conference of bishops.[52]

The Secretariat replied by referring to its earlier remarks and added that the involvement of the conference of bishops was suppressed because it could lead to excessive and undesirable centralization; nonetheless, an episcopal conference may select to give itself a centralized role in diocesan taxation by establishing particular law (in accord with what became canon 455 of the Latin code).[53]

The 1981 Plenary Session. The text of the canon was again discussed during the 1981 plenary session. The secretariat of the commission had proposed six questions for discussion, and another forty questions were put forth by commission members, each having been proposed by at least ten prelates. Question 11 focused on canon 1213 of the 1980 *Schema*, the diocesan tax. It had been proposed by ten members: Basil Cardinal Hume of Westminster; John Car-

---

[50] *Relatio,* p. 282.
[51] *Relatio*, pp. 281-282.
[52] *Relatio*, pp. 282-283.
[53] *Relatio*, p. 283.

dinal Krol of Philadelphia; Maurice Cardinal Roy of Quebec; John Cardinal Willebrands of Utrecht; Archbishop Joseph Bernardin of Cincinnati; Archbishop Joseph MacNeil of Edmonton; Archbishop Simon Pimenta of Bombay; Bishop Thomas Stewart of Ch'unch'on, Korea; Bishop Paul Verschuren of Helsinki; and Auxiliary Bishop John O'Connell of Melbourne.[54]

John Cardinal Krol of Philadelphia urged that the revised law not limit the taxing power of the diocesan bishop to extraordinary situations of grave necessity. He explained that taxation is not alien to religion; that dioceses do not have sufficient support from foundations, benefices, or other sources; and that voluntary offerings from the faithful are insufficient to operate a diocese. He recommended that the law allow a proportionate tax to be imposed upon parishes to meet diocesan needs. He reported that in many dioceses in the United States and elsewhere there exists a legitimate custom of a moderate and proportionate diocesan tax.[55]

Archbishop Joseph Bernardin supported the proposal of Cardinal Krol, and added that a tax is necessary for many dioceses, that taxation enables all to participate in diocesan works, and that the required consultations would monitor potential abuse.[56]

As a result, Archbishop Rosalio Castillo Lara, secretary of the Pontifical Commission, proposed the following formulation:

> The diocesan bishop has the right, after hearing the finance council and the presbyteral council, to impose a moderate tax (*tributum*), proportionate to their income, upon public juridic persons subject to his governance, for the needs of the diocese; he can impose an extraordinary and moderate tax (*exactio*) upon other physical and juridic persons only in case of grave necessity and under the same conditions. No tax (*tributum*), however, can be imposed upon Mass offerings.[57]

---

[54] *Congregatio plenaria*, pp. 486-493.
[55] *Congregatio plenaria*, p. 486-488.
[56] *Congregatio plenaria*, p. 490.
[57] *Congregatio plenaria*, p. 493.

The vast majority of those present at the plenary session (41 out of 48 members) favored the proposal drafted by Archbishop Castillo Lara.[58] A minority (17 out of 48 members) favored eliminating reference to taxation of physical persons.[59]

The 1982 Schema. The new formulation[60] was then forwarded to Pope John Paul II, who discussed the proposed new code with a small group of canonists. The finally promulgated law omits reference to the impossibility of taxing Mass offerings (though this had been mentioned in earlier drafts[61]) and adds the phrase "without prejudice to particular laws and customs which attribute greater rights to him."

ORDINARY TAX. The first tax may be called "ordinary" (though it is not so entitled in canon 1263)[62] in comparison to the extraordi-

---

58 *Congregatio plenaria*, p. 493.

59 *Congregatio plenaria*, p. 492.

60 1982 *Schema*, p. 220. Canon 1263 of the 1982 *Schema* is the exact proposal of Archbishop Castillo Lara.

61 Mass offerings are not subject to taxation. This is stated explicitly in canon 1012 of the Eastern code, and had also been stated in CIC/1917, canon 1506. See PONTIFICAL COUNCIL FOR LEGISLATIVE TEXTS, *Decretum* De recursu super congrugentia inter legem particularem et normam codicalem [Recourse against a general decree which establishes a diocesan *tributum*] (February 8, 2000), in *Communicationes,* 32 (2000), p. 23 (= PCLT, *Decretum* Diocesan *Tributum*); JEAN PASSICOS, "Rapports droit général et particulier: Une contribution diocésaine imposée aux processus confiées à des religieux," in *L'année canonique*, 47 (2005), pp. 114-117.

The acts of the 1981 plenary assembly report that Archbishop Castillo Lara, when he had first read his proposed draft of the text before the members were to vote on it, had omitted the last sentence about Mass offerings and apologized for the omission. The assembly voted on the text with the last sentence included. See *Congregatio plenaria*, pp. 492-493.

ROBERT L. KEALY suggests that the omission of the prohibition on taxing Mass offerings is the result of an apparent oversight. Very early in the process of drafting the proposed new legislation, the *coetus De iure patrimoniali Ecclesiae* had recommended that the prohibition be mentioned in a more appropriate place elsewhere in the code (see *Communicationes*, 5 [1973] 95); Kealy opines that the Secretariat simply forgot to do so. He concludes his analysis: "Thus no explicit prohibition of Mass offerings appears in the code. Nevertheless, it [is] clear that there was no intention of introducing a tax on Mass offerings and the only safe interpretation is that such a tax continues to be prohibited." In *Diocesan Financial Support*, pp. 339-340. See also MORRISEY, "Temporal Goods," p. 713.

62 The PCLT comments that canon 1263 refers to two kinds of tributes: "ordinary" and "extraordinary." In *Decretum* Diocesan *Tributum*, p. 17.

Also, the *DPMB* refers to two types of taxes which a diocesan bishop may impose: "ordinary or extraordinary" (n. 216).

nary tax also mentioned in this canon. It is imposed on the public juridic persons subject to the diocesan bishop's governance.[63] It cannot be imposed on physical persons, private juridic persons, or public juridic persons not subject to the authority of the diocesan bishop.

The ordinary tax is "for the needs of the diocese." The canon does not specify the exact nature of these needs, but reference can certainly be made to the proper purposes for which the Church has ecclesiastical goods mentioned elsewhere in the code (canon 1254 §1; see canons 114 §2 and 222 §1). Included obviously among these needs are the recurring costs of operating diocesan agencies and institutions. Excluded from these needs are "extraordinary" endeavors for which an extraordinary tax may be imposed (e.g., renovation of the cathedral, establishment of a clergy retirement center, erection of a seminary, etc.).

The ordinary tax is to be "moderate."[64] "Moderate" indicates that the tax must be reasonable in relation to the economic situation of the juridic persons and not so extreme as to deprive those taxed from their means of livelihood. It also implies that the tax is to meet diocesan operational expenses, not to provide surplus revenue for diocesan investment.[65] The diocesan finance council and the presby-

---

[63] That only public juridic persons subject to the governance of the diocesan bishop are taxable is underscored in PCLT, *Decretum* Diocesan *Tributum*, p. 22.

[64] The PCLT comments that "moderate" and "proportionate" must take into account the particular circumstances of the locale. Concrete determinations are reserved to the diocesan bishop, although in an individual instance recourse is possible when one judges that the taxation is unjust. PCLT, *Decretum* Diocesan *Tributum*, p. 22.

[65] NICHOLAS CAFARDI says: "...the tax of canon 1263 is meant to cover expenses only. This is an objective limit. The diocesan expenses that this tax is meant to cover should be determinable to a certain degree of exactitude. If the tax does more than that, in other words, if it piles up diocesan surpluses, beyond needs, at the expense of the taxpaying parishes, then it is no longer a moderate tax, but an immoderate one, and hence illegal." In "Assessment of Parish Income for Diocesan Needs" in *CLSA AO2*, p. 401.

L.L. MCCREAVY had noted that the term "moderate" allows an elasticity to reflect diocesan needs. In "The Limits of Diocesan Taxation," in *Clergy Review*, 52 (1967) 985.

JOHN J. MYERS, referring specifically to the extraordinary tax which also must be moderate, comments: "'Moderate' is not so easily determined. Canon 1356 of the 1917 code used a maximum amount of five percent in reference to the seminary tax, but the base for figuring that is open to interpretation. Moreover, that is a tax for a very

teral council, from both of whom the diocesan bishop must receive counsel before imposing the tax, will no doubt assist in determining whether or not a proposed taxation formula is "moderate."

The ordinary tax is to be "proportionate" to the income of the juridic person. This indicates that a percentage of income is taxable, perhaps as that income is "adjusted" by various factors.[66] Also, theoretically, the formula could be a different percentage for public juridic persons having various levels of income: e.g., 7% for persons with an "adjusted" income of $100,000 or less; 7.5% for those with an "adjusted" income between $100,000 and $250,000, etc.[67] The formula could also take into account the indebtedness of the public juridic person. Once the bishop has set the formula following the required consultation, it can continue to be used regularly (e.g., annually). Further consultation would be required by law only to change the formula.[68] It is appropriate, however, that the diocesan bishop,

---

specific purpose as opposed to the more general purpose specified in the first part of canon 1263. One suspects that specific traditions and the degrees of centralization of certain functions and services in each diocese will help provide the context in which 'moderate' will be interpreted." In "Temporal Goods," p. 866.

[66] Some may consider basing the ordinary tax upon the number of parishioners. Francis G. Morrisey comments that this is not allowed: "The canon provided that the ordinary tax is to be imposed on juridic persons, not physical ones. Thus any form of 'head tax' based on the number of registered parishioners is no longer allowed as an ordinary means of taxation of parishes." In "Acquiring Temporal Goods for the Church's Mission," in *The Jurist,* 56 (1966) 595-596. One may consider to the contrary, however, that a formula of the ordinary tax based upon the number of parishioners would, in fact, be a tax nonetheless levied upon the juridic person of the parish, not directly onto physical persons. In addition, canon 1263 allows the extraordinary tax to be imposed upon physical persons. See also Morrisey, "Temporal Goods," p. 713; Robert L. Kealy, "Taxation, Assessments and Extraordinary Collections" in *CFH,* p. 82 (=Kealy, "Taxation").

[67] See Matthew J. Barrett, "The Theological Case for Progressive Taxation as Applied to Diocesan Taxes or Assessments under Canon Law in the United States," in *The Jurist,* 63 (2003), pp. 313, 330-331. Barrett contends "that Catholic social thought, including the U.S. Bishops' pastoral letter on the U.S. economy, as well as the economic policies supporting progressive taxes, urge diocesan bishops in the United States to use progressive rates whenever they impose diocesan taxes and assessments under canon 1263." Pp. 313-314.

[68] This position reflects common practice in many, if not most, dioceses. See James H. Provost, "Right of the Diocesan Bishop to Levy a Tax on a Juridic Person Subject to Him," *CLSA AOI,* p. 409; López Alarcón, "Temporal Goods," p. 971.
Robert T. Kennedy expresses a contrary view and says that consultation should be repeated prior to each renewal of a recurring tax. In "Temporal Goods," p. 1463.

when consulting the presbyteral council and the diocesan finance council to set the taxation formula, explains that the formula will be used repeatedly (e.g., annually) until such time as the formula is changed. To modify the formula validly, the diocesan bishop must have a new consultation with the two councils.

Canon 1263 gives the diocesan bishop the right to impose this ordinary tax upon public juridic persons subject to his authority. If he imposes it upon *some* such persons, the law does not require that he impose it upon *all* of them. He may, for example, impose it only upon parishes but not upon other public juridic persons subject to his authority (e.g., universities, hospitals, etc.). Likewise, he may also select to exclude some juridic (both public and private) and physical persons from the extraordinary tax.

The ordinary tax is levied by the diocesan bishop, following the required consultations, upon "public juridic persons subject to his governance." Exempt from his governance are institutes of consecrated life so designated by the Supreme Pontiff (canon 591; see canons 588; 594). Although members of religious institutes and societies of apostolic life are subject to the diocesan bishop regarding the care of souls, the exercise of divine worship, and works of the apostolate (canons 678 §1; 738 §1), they possess a just autonomy of life (see canons 586; 738 §1). They are not otherwise subject to episcopal governance and, therefore, are not subject to the ordinary diocesan tax.[69]

Some may question whether or not an institute of consecrated life of diocesan right is subject to the ordinary tax. Canon 586 assures that all institutes of consecrated life, both of pontifical and diocesan right, possess a "just autonomy of life" which the local ordinary is "to preserve and safeguard." It seems, therefore, that diocesan institutes are *not* subject to the taxing power of the diocesan bishop.[70]

In its only response to a *dubium* proposed about *Book V*, the Pontifical Council for the Interpretation of Legislative Texts on May 20, 1989 responded that excluded from ordinary taxation are the

---

[69] See KEALY, "Taxation," pp. 81-82.
[70] See KEALY, *Diocesan Financial Support*, p. 333.

external schools of religious institutes of pontifical right.[71] This is
because these schools are not subject to the full jurisdiction of the
diocesan bishop. They are subject to the visitation of the diocesan
bishop; he cannot, however claim the right to visit those "schools
which are open exclusively to the institute's own students," i.e., the
institute's "internal schools" (canon 683 §1). Further, the diocesan
bishop has the right to exercise vigilance over "the Catholic schools
in his territory, even those which members of religious institutes have
founded or direct... without prejudice, however, to their autonomy
regarding the internal direction of their schools" (canon 806 §1).
Even though the diocesan bishop has the right to visit, and to exercise
vigilance over, the external schools of religious in his territory, these
are not subject to the imposition of the diocesan ordinary tax. These
schools are apostolates of religious institutes which, as mentioned
above, enjoy a "just autonomy of life" which the local ordinary must
"preserve and safeguard" (canon 586) even in the case of religious
institutes of diocesan right (canon 594). These religious institutes
are not public juridic persons subject to the governing authority of
the diocesan bishop (see canon 591). At the same time, however, if a
Catholic school has been established as a public juridic person subject
to the diocesan bishop, even if the school is staffed by members of
a religious institute, it would be subject to the ordinary diocesan tax
mentioned in canon 1263.[72] It is then no longer an external school of
a religious institute, but a public juridic person in the diocese.

Moreover, the Pontifical Council for Legislative Texts issued
on February 8, 2000 a *Decretum* which addressed the imposition

---

[71] PONTIFICAL COUNCIL FOR THE INTERPRETATION OF LEGISLATIVE TEXTS, *Responsiones ad proposita dubia* (May 20, 1989), *AAS*, 81 (1989), p. 991. See PCLT, *Decretum* Diocesan *Tributum*, p. 20.

[72] See LAWRENCE G. WRENN, *Authentic Interpretations on the 1983 Code*, Washington, CLSA, 1993, pp. 57-58. ROBERT T. KENNEDY, however, in light of the authentic interpretation, reasons that "schools which, though established as public juridic persons in their own right, continue to be sponsored and governed by religious institutes of pontifical right, would not, according to the authentic interpretation, be subject to the authority of the diocesan bishop for purposes of a tax imposed in accord with the first part of canon 1263." In "Temporal Goods," p. 1464. See also VELASIO DE PAOLIS, "Adnotatione ad responsum authenticum circa canonem 1263," in *Periodica*, 80 (1991), pp. 108-127.

of diocesan taxes upon parishes entrusted to, and upon churches and chapels connected with, a religious institute or a society of apostolic life.[73] The decree recalls that parishes are distinct public juridic persons (see canon 515 §2) fully subject to the diocesan tax, even if they have been entrusted to a clerical religious institute or a clerical society of apostolic life by a written agreement between the diocesan bishop and the competent superior of the institute or society (see canon 520). This written agreement should distinguish the juridic personality of the parish and that of the institute or society.[74] Churches and chapels attached to the house of a religious institute are not subject to the diocesan bishop since they are not distinct public juridic persons subject to the diocesan bishop; therefore, the diocesan bishop may impose a tax only upon (1) public juridic persons subject to him which have churches and oratories, and (2) chapels and oratories established as juridic persons subject to him.

This ordinary tax is not to be confused with the *cathedraticum* which had been mentioned in canon 1504 of the 1917 code: "All churches or benefices subject to the jurisdiction of the bishop, even lay confraternities, as a sign of their subjection, must annually pay to the bishop a *cathedraticum* or moderate tax determined according to the norm of canon 1507 §1, unless it has already been determined by ancient custom."[75] The obligation to give the *cathedraticum* ceased

---

[73] PCLT, *Decretum* Diocesan *Tributum*, pp. 20-22.

[74] The *Decretum* notes that some parishes had been united *pleno iure* to a religious institute in accord with CIC/1917, canon 1425. It recalls the response of the PONTIFICAL COMMISSION FOR THE INTERPRETATION OF THE DECREES OF VATICAN COUNCIL II that, in light of *Ecclesiae sanctae*, I, n. 33, the local ordinary can sever this union, thereby separating parishes from religious houses to which they had been united *pleno iure*. Should the separation occur, however, attention must be given to acquired rights of the religious institute (e.g., its continuing pastoral care of the parish with which it had been united *pleno iure*).

The *Decree* adds that, generally, even parishes considered united *pleno iure* to a religious institute, inasmuch as they are parishes, are subject to the diocesan bishop and, consequently, to the diocesan tax, unless specific documents or acquired rights indicate otherwise. In the case of dispute in a concrete case, recourse can be made to the competent congregations which will decide the matter conjointly. PCLT, *Decretum* Diocesan *Tributum*, pp. 20-21.

[75] Commonly, though mistakenly, the *cathedraticum* was used in reference to a tax imposed upon parishes to meet diocesan operational costs. In the United States,

when the diocese was vacant.[76] The *cathedraticum* was to be a uniform tax imposed upon all churches and benefices; it was not to be proportionate to the number of parishioners, the income, or other factors.[77] The *cathedraticum* is not mentioned in the 1983 code.[78]

The *cathedraticum* was a mandatory annual tax for the bishop imposed by law. Unlike the *cathedraticum*, the ordinary tax in canon 1263 of the revised code is not mandatory (the diocesan bishop need never impose it); it need not be annual (although it can occur each year by deliberate design of the diocesan bishop); it is not for the bishop (it is for the needs of the diocese); and it can be imposed only

---

the Second Plenary Council of Baltimore had approved that a definite portion of parochial income would be given annually to the ordinary to support him and the diocesan curia; the portion of income was to be determined by the diocesan synod and promulgated by the ordinary as diocesan law (n. 100). The Sacred Congregation for the Propagation of the Faith approved this plenary legislation. Such taxation of parishes for diocesan needs was not envisioned by the 1917 code but was tolerated by the Apostolic See as an effective means to operate the diocese. See BOUSCAREN-ELLIS-KORTH, pp. 807-808; KEALY, "Taxation," p. 89, fn. 20.

[76] See SACRED CONGREGATION FOR THE COUNCIL, *Resolutio* "Civitatis Castelli et Alatrina," (August 20, 1917), in *AAS*, 9 (1917), pp. 497-502; *CLD*, vol. 1, p. 719.

[77] See the *Resolutio* of the Sacred Congregation for the Council, "Dioecesis N. et aliarum in Gallia," (March 13, 1920) in *AAS*, 12 (1920), pp. 444-447; *CLD*, vol. 1, pp. 719-720. A number of French bishops had sought to generate substantial revenues through the *cathedraticum* and to make it proportionate to the revenue or population of parishes or institutions. The Congregation refused permission to do so for a number of reasons: the proposals intended to generate revenue (something contrary to the *cathedraticum* which is meant to be a token of subjection, not a tax); the amounts of taxation proposed were considered excessive; the proposed tax was to be imposed on parish churches only (not on all churches, oratories, chapels, and moral persons as the *cathedraticum* is to be imposed); and the tax was not envisioned as uniform (but the *cathedraticum* was to be uniform and not reflecting either parish revenue or size). For more discussion, see DONALD J. FRUGÉ, "Taxes in the Proposed Law," in *CLSA Proceedings*, 44 (1982), pp. 275-276 (=FRUGÉ, "Taxes").

[78] Also suppressed in the 1983 code are the "charitable subsidy" (CIC/1917, canon 1505) and the "foundation tax" (CIC/1917, canon 1506).

The charitable subsidy was an extraordinary and moderate exaction (besides the seminary tax mentioned in CIC/1917, canons 1355-1356, and the benefice pension mentioned in CIC/1917, canon 1429) imposed by the local ordinary on all beneficiaries, both secular and religious, in light of special diocesan needs.

The foundation tax was imposed by the ordinary, for the good of the diocese or for patrons, upon churches, benefices, and other ecclesiastical institutes subject to him at the time of their foundation or consecration. The canon on the foundation tax says there can be no taxation of Mass offerings, whether manual or foundational.

after the diocesan bishop has heard the diocesan finance council and the presbyteral council (it is not imposed *a iure*).[79]

EXTRAORDINARY TAX. The extraordinary tax can be imposed only "in case of grave necessity." It is not expected that the exaction be for routine expenditures, nor that the tax be imposed regularly to provide for recurring diocesan needs.[80] At the same time, the canon does not require a necessity of "an exceptionally serious nature."[81] The extraordinary tax is imposed by the diocesan bishop upon other physical[82] and other (public and private) juridic persons (*ceteris personis physicis et iuridicis*[83]) in the diocese. Like the ordinary tax, it is to be moderate, i.e., not so great as to so harm those taxed as to deprive them of the means necessary to fulfill their own purposes. It is imposed "under the same conditions" as the ordinary tax, i.e., proportionate to the income of the persons, and following the diocesan bishop's consultations with the diocesan finance council and the presbyteral council. Also, as in the case of the ordinary tax, the diocesan bishop is not required to impose the extraordinary tax on *all* physical and juridic persons; he may choose to impose it upon

---

[79] Prior to the 1983 code, many dioceses in the United States imposed a diocesan tax upon parishes; it was sometimes considered to be the *cathedraticum*. DONALD J. FRUGÉ concludes that such diocesan practices were not authorized by the 1917 code. In *The Taxation Practices of United States Bishops in Relation to the Authority of Bishops to Tax According to the Code of Canon Law and Proposed Revisions*, Washington, The Catholic University of America, 1982, pp. 138-139, 190.

[80] The extraordinary tax is not to be a "permanent" one. *Relatio*, p. 281.

[81] MORRISEY, "Temporal Goods," p. 713.

[82] The Archbishop of Munster imposed a 10% tax on the income of diocesan priests: 5% for the priest serving in the so-called "Diaspora" regions and for retired priests; 3% for the "pension fund;" and 2% for the subsistence of housekeepers serving priests. This tax was approved for five years on January 15, 1960 by the SACRED CONGREGATION FOR THE COUNCIL (Prot. N. 48651/A), and renewed for another five years on October 6, 1964 (Prot. N. 93863/A): *CLD*, vol. 7, pp. 894-895.

[83] ROBERT F. KEALY addresses the adjective "other" (*ceteris*): "'Other juridic persons': Does this mean that public juridic persons, who are subject to the first tax, are not also subject to the second tax? Common sense says, No. 'Other juridic persons' is meant to include private juridic persons, not to exclude public juridic persons." In *Diocesan Financial Support*, p. 339. In a related fashion, DANIEL TIRAPU observes: "It is not clear whether this tax may also be imposed upon public juridical persons; the literal meaning of the canon appears to exclude them (*ceteris*)." In "The Acquisition of Goods" in *Exegetical Comm*, vol. 4, p. 57.

some but not upon others. Those persons taxed, however, must be within the bishop's diocese.[84]

The canon requires the extraordinary tax to be imposed with the same restrictions as the ordinary tax "without prejudice to particular laws and customs which attribute greater rights to him."[85] This phrase was added during the 1982 private papal consultation with select canonists after the final text of proposed legislation was presented to him.[86] A literal reading of this canon indicates that particular laws and customs may permit the diocesan bishop to impose extraordinary taxes without the restrictions otherwise placed upon him.[87] Robert L. Kealy, however, suggests that the canon does not permit new particular legislation giving bishops greater powers than are permitted by the text itself of the canon, "for to do so would make the restrictions of the canon meaningless. It seems that this

---

[84] ROBERT T. KENNEDY, while not presuming to reach a definite conclusion, raises the question whether or not the diocesan bishop can tax public juridic persons not subject to him. He notes that canon 264 (on the seminary tax) allows the diocesan bishop to impose a tax on juridic persons, private and public, which have a seat in the diocese (unless they live on alms alone or also have a college of students or teachers to promote the common good), seemingly even if they are not otherwise subject to the diocesan bishop. This may be taken as an indication that canon 1263 also allows the diocesan bishop to exact the "extraordinary tax" from juridic persons in the diocese who are not otherwise his subjects. In "Temporal Goods," p. 1464. JEAN-CLAUD PÉRISSET, p. 87, also raises the possibility that the diocesan bishop can impose the extraordinary tax on public juridic persons not subject to him. JOHN J. MYERS clearly concludes that "individuals and private and public juridic persons not subject to the diocesan bishop, therefore, could be burdened with this extraordinary tax." In "Temporal Goods," p. 865. See also KEALY, *Diocesan Financial Support*, p. 337; DANIEL TIRAPU, p. 57.

[85] The Latin construction of canon 1263 shows that this clause concerns only the extraordinary tax.

[86] During this same private papal consultation, omitted from the text was the last sentence of the proposed canon: "No tax can be imposed, however, upon Mass offerings." See 1982 *Schema*, canon 1263.

[87] JOHN J. MYERS opines that this phrase would allow the diocesan bishop to continue to impose the *cathedraticum*. In "Temporal Goods," p. 866.
ROBERT L. KEALY, however, disagrees, and argues that both the *cathedraticum* (and foundation tax) have been eliminated in the 1983 code: "Both taxes have been eliminated by virtue of the fact that they are not provided for in the new code. Under the 1917 code, they were universal law and canon 6, §1, 1° states that the 1917 code was abrogated when the new code went into effect. Since they were a matter of universal law, one cannot argue for their continued existence under the rubric of custom or particular law by virtue of the final clause of canon 1263." In *Diocesan Financial Support*, pp. 345-346.

exception was introduced particularly with Germany and Austria in mind because, at least in some regions where there is a Church tax collected by the State, the State is acting as an agent for the Church and not in its own name and the particular dioceses have to empower the civil finance ministry to collect a tax. Thus, without this clause in canon 1263, they would be unable to do so."[88]

The canon says that the extraordinary tax may be imposed only for cases of "grave necessity" (unlike the ordinary tax, which may be imposed simply "for the needs of the diocese.") Such cases of grave necessity may include exceptional diocesan needs (e.g., to renovate the cathedral, to build a retirement facility for clergy, to erect a seminary, etc.) or other serious needs (e.g., to assist the placement of immigrants, to provide disaster assistance, etc.).[89]

SEMINARY TAX. Canon 264 speaks of a tax which may be imposed by a bishop to provide for the needs of the seminary:

> **Canon 264 – §1. In addition to the offering mentioned in can. 1266, a bishop can impose a tax (*tributum*) in the diocese to provide for the needs of the seminary.**
>
> **§2. All ecclesiastical juridic persons, even private ones, which have a seat in the diocese are subject to the tax for the seminary unless they are sustained by alms alone or**

---

[88] KEALY, "Taxation," p. 85.

ROBERT T. KENNEDY observes that any particular law giving the diocesan bishop greater rights would have to be a supradiocesan law, requiring *recognitio* by the Apostolic See (canons 446, 455). In "Temporal Goods," p. 1465.

STEFANO MESTER opines that the clause allows the diocesan bishop to impose the ordinary tax on physical persons, and the extraordinary tax outside cases of grave necessity. In "I beni temporali della Chiesa (le novità apportate dal nuovo codice)," in *Apollinaris*, 57 (1984), p. 51.

[89] The extraordinary tax succeeds the foundation tax of CIC/1917, canon 1506 which was a tax for the benefit of the diocese or in favor of a patron imposed by the ordinary on churches, benefices, or other ecclesiastical institutions subject to him at the time of foundation or consecration. As such, it was an extraordinary tax. See KEALY, *Diocesan Financial Support*, p. 191.

Further, inasmuch as canon 1263 allows the imposition of an extraordinary and moderate exaction (*exactio*) upon physical persons, the canon also reflects the discipline of CIC/1917, canon 1505 which permitted the local ordinary to impose an extraordinary and moderate exaction (*exactio*) on all beneficiaries (*omnibus beneficiariis*), both secular and religious (but *not* upon the benefices themselves), if a special diocesan need compelled.

**in fact have a college of students or teachers to promote
the common good of the Church. A tax of this type must
be general, in proportion to the revenues of those who
are subject to it, and determined according to the needs
of the seminary.**

The canon envisions a special collection for the seminary (see canon
1266). In addition, the bishop has the ability (but not the *obligation*)
to impose the seminary tax explained in canon 264. Subject to the
seminary tax are all public and private juridic persons having a seat
in the diocese; excluded are juridic persons sustained by alms (e.g.,
certain religious institutes), juridic persons who have a college of
students or teachers to promote the common good of the Church (e.g.,
a house of religious formation), and physical persons. The seminary
tax is to be general, proportionate to the revenue of the juridic person
being taxed, and reflecting the needs of the seminary.[90] Inasmuch

---

[90]   Canon 264 succeeds CIC/1917, canon 1356 which provided detailed legislation concerning the seminary tribute. It said that, any contrary custom having been reprobated,
any contrary privilege having been abrogated, and no appeal being admitted, subject
to the seminary tax were: the *mensa episcopalis*; all benefices (even of regulars or
those over which one has the right of patronage); parishes and quasi-parishes (even
if they have no other revenue than the offerings of the faithful); hospitals erected by
ecclesiastical authority; sodalities canonically erected; church buildings that have
their own income; and every religious house (even exempt), unless it exists solely on
alms or has in it a college for students or teachers to promote the common good of
the Church. The tribute was to be general and of the same proportion for all; it was
to be larger or smaller according to the needs of the seminary but not to exceed five
percent (5%) of the annual income, and to be lessened as the revenue of the seminary
increased.

Interestingly, the 1917 code defined *taxable income* as that which remained at the
end of the year after all the obligations and necessary expenses had been paid;
daily distributions from a benefice were not computed in the income but, if all the
income of the benefice consists in distributions, one third of them was not counted;
the offerings of the faithful also were not counted but, if all the income of the parish
consisted of offerings of the faithful, one third of these offerings was not counted.

Both codes envision the possibility of the mandating of a special collection for the
seminary. Both codes give the diocesan bishop the option of imposing a tax to further meet the needs of the seminary. The tax is to be general, proportionate to the
income of the entity being taxed, and reflecting the needs of the seminary. Exempt
from the tax are those who live from alms or have a college for students or teachers.
Unlike its predecessor in the 1917 code, canon 264 does not define what constitutes
the "taxable income" of the juridic person, nor does it place a percentage limit on
the taxation of its income. See FRUGÉ, "Taxes," pp. 274-275, 279-280.

as the tax is to based upon revenue, the stable patrimony of a juridic person is not subject to this tax, just as the stable patrimony is also not subject to the diocesan tax mentioned in canon 1263.

CONSULTATION AND CONSENT. Canon 1263 requires the diocesan bishop to consult the diocesan finance council and the presbyteral council before he imposes any diocesan tax. Other canons in *Book V* also require that consultation (or consent) be given by a group or by individuals before the diocesan bishop performs specific acts. Velasio De Paolis reflects that such participation of others "is a real involvement and coresponsibility; this must not be reduced to a mere formality. As a matter of fact, law must never be pure formality."[91]

Canon 127 discusses the specifics of the dialogue between a superior, including the diocesan bishop, and groups who are required by law to give their counsel or consent:

1. Concerning consultation or consent from a college or group of persons:
   a. The superior must convoke the college or group according to the norm of canon 166 (unless, in the case of counsel only, particular or proper law provides otherwise [canon 127 §1]).
   b. For consent to be valid, an absolute majority of those present must concur (canon 127 §1).
   c. For consultation to be valid, the advice of all must be sought (canon 127 §1).
2. Concerning consultation or consent of certain persons as individuals:
   a. In the case of *consent*, if the superior fails to seek their consent, or fails to follow the opinion of any or all, the superior's action is *invalid* (canon 127 §2, 1°).
   b. In the case of *consultation*, if the superior fails to seek their consent, the superior's action is *invalid*. Further, even though not required to follow their opinion, even if it is unanimous, the superior "is nonetheless not to act contrary to that opin-

---

91   DE PAOLIS, "Temporal Goods… Consecrated Life," p. 353.

ion, especially if unanimous, without a reason which is overriding in the superior's judgment" (canon 127 §2, 2°). Without an overriding contrary reason, the superior's action is *illicit* if the superior disregards completely the advice offered.[92]

3. Those who give their counsel or consent have the obligation to offer their opinion sincerely. In addition, if the gravity of the matter so requires, they are to maintain secrecy, something upon which the superior may insist (canon 127 §3).

Furthermore, the code says that, whenever counsel or consent is mandated before the diocesan bishop alienates diocesan goods or gives permission to alienate the goods of public juridic persons subject to him (if such goods belong to stable patrimony and their value exceeds a minimum amount determined by the conference of bishops: see canon 1291), those giving counsel or consent must first be thoroughly informed both about the economic state of the public juridic person whose goods are proposed for alienation and about any previous alienations (canon 1292 §4). Indeed, there is every reason to expect "full disclosure" of appropriate information whenever any superior needs the counsel or consent *for any reason*.

Receiving the required counsel or consent enables the diocesan bishop to act validly. Nonetheless, even after he receives the counsel or consent, he is not *required* to act at all.

---

[92] FRANCIS G. MORRISEY comments that if a superior who must receive counsel from a group acts contrary to the group's unanimous opinion without an overriding reason, the superior's action is *illicit* if he completely disregards the advice offered. In "Temporal Goods," p. 723.

The *DPMB*, speaking of the bishop's consultation with the presbyteral council, makes a statement which is also true of the bishop's collaboration with the diocesan finance council: "After obtaining the opinion of the council, the Bishop is free to make the decisions he thinks are appropriate, evaluating and deciding the matter *'coram Domino'*, except when universal or particular law requires the consent of the council in certain questions. However, the Bishop should not act contrary to the unanimous opinion of his councillors without a serious and overriding reason, which he must weigh carefully according to his prudent judgment" (n. 182).

For a more detailed discussion of the application of canon 127, particularly in relation to ecclesiastical goods, see: THOMAS J. GREEN, "Shepherding the Patrimony of the Poor: Diocesan and Parish Structures of Financial Administration," in *The Jurist*, 56 (1997), pp. 710-713. (=GREEN, "Shepherding the Patrimony").

DIOCESAN FINANCE COUNCIL.[93] Canon 1263 requires the diocesan bishop to consult the diocesan finance council before he imposes an ordinary or extraordinary diocesan tax.

The code explains that a diocese is a juridic person *a iure* (canon 373) which is represented in all juridic affairs by its diocesan bishop. The same code requires that each diocese have its own finance council. This is an application of the discipline of canon 1280 for dioceses. Two canons discuss the establishment, composition, and general functions of the diocesan finance council:

> **Can. 492 – §1. In every diocese a finance council is to be established, over which the diocesan bishop himself or his delegate presides and which consists of at least three members of the Christian faithful truly expert in financial affairs and civil law, outstanding in integrity, and appointed by the bishop.**
>
> **§2. Members of the finance council are to be appointed for five years, but at the end of this period they can be appointed for other five year terms.**
>
> **§3. Persons who are related to the bishop up to the fourth degree of consanguinity or affinity are excluded from the finance council.**
>
> **Can. 493 – In addition to the functions entrusted to it in Book V, *The Temporal Goods of the Church*, the finance council prepares each year, according to the directions of the diocesan bishop, a budget of the income and expen-**

---

[93] The 1917 code did not contain legislation for a diocesan finance council. It did, however, provide for a "council of administration" which assisted the ordinary in fulfilling properly his vigilance of temporal goods. It was to be situated in the see city with the ordinary as its president and two or three suitable men (*viri*) as members chosen by the ordinary after he heard the college of consultors. These men were to have expertise in civil and canon law, insofar as possible, and not to be related to the ordinary in the first or second degree of affinity or consanguinity. They were to take an oath in the presence of the ordinary that they would fulfill their roles faithfully. The local ordinary was to hear the council of administration, which had only a consultative vote, in "administrative matters of greater importance" (canon 1504). The wording of the canon does *not* exclude *lay* males from being members of the council of administration.

> ditures which are foreseen for the entire governance of the diocese in the coming year and at the end of the year examines an account of the revenues and expenses.

Several important observations are to be made regarding these two canons.[94]

First, the diocesan finance council is required by law; it is not optional. Since this is a constitutive law, the diocesan bishop cannot dispense from it (see canon 86). Functions of the diocesan finance council are determined by universal law,[95] but particular law can establish other functions for it. The diocesan bishop himself or his

---

[94] See ADRIAN FARRELLY, "The Diocesan Finance Council: Functions and Duties According to the *Code of Canon Law*," in *Studia canonica,* 23 (1989), pp. 149-166 (=FARRELLY, "Diocesan Finance Council"); KEVIN E. MCDONOUGH, "The Diocesan and Pastoral Finance Council," in *CFH,* pp. 135-149.

[95] The bishops of the United States passed a resolution on diocesan financial reporting which is operative through the year 2011: "Annually, at the end of the fiscal year, each suffragan bishop is asked to send a letter to his metropolitan archbishop containing: (1) the names and professional titles of the members of the diocesan finance council; (2) the dates on which the finance council has met during the preceding fiscal year and since the end of that fiscal year; (3) a statement signed by the finance council members and the finance officer stating that they have met, reviewed, and discussed the [audited] financial statements of the diocese and the management letter, if any, for that fiscal year and have reviewed the management letter and the recommendations made by the auditors. The metropolitan archbishop will provide this same letter to the senior suffragan bishop in the province." This resolution was effective January 1, 2001, and was renewed by action of the body of bishops in November 2004 to be effective through 2006. In November 2006, the resolution was again renewed by an action of the body of bishops to be effective through 2011. This resolution was recommended by the NCCB Committee on Budget and Finance as a means of "helping bishops pay attention to the law of the Church and confirming that each is doing so." http://www.usccb.org/finance/dfr.shtml (December 1, 2008)
In light of several serious acts of financial malfeasance in parishes recently, a similar practice for parishes in the United States was recommended by Bishop Dennis Schnurr, treasurer of the USCCB on March 23, 2007. He explained that the USCCB Accounting Practices Committee (APC) had recommended a series of best practices to enhance the financial administration of parishes; these were reviewed and supported by the USCCB Committee on Budget and Finance. The recommendations ask that annually each parish send a letter to the diocesan bishop containing:
  – the names and professional titles of the members of the parish finance council;
  – the dates on which the parish finance council had met during the preceding fiscal year;
  – the date(s) on which the approved (i.e., by the parish finance council) parish financial statements/budgets had been made available to the parishioners during the preceding

delegate presides. He is *not* a member of the council. It is comprised of at least three members of the Christian faithful who are appointed to a renewable five-year term by the diocesan bishop. They must be truly expert in financial affairs and civil law, outstanding in integrity, and not related to the diocesan bishop up to the fourth degree of consanguinity or affinity.[96] Inasmuch as members of the diocesan finance council involve themselves in the administration of ecclesiastical goods, they "are bound to fulfill their functions in the name of the Church according to the norm of law (canon 1282).

The code does not say that the diocesan finance council "possesses a consultative vote only," as canon 514 §1 does say about the

---

fiscal year and since the end of the fiscal year; a copy of these published financial statements/budgets should be provided to the bishop;

– a statement signed by the parish priest and the finance council members that they have met, and developed and discussed the financial statements and budget of the parish.

Other short-term recommendations of the APC are: "that thorough diocesan training be provided to the parish finance council members regarding their roles and responsibilities; that diocesan policies exist for conflicts of interest, whistle blower, and fraud (including prosecution in all cases); that each parish complete an annual internal control questionnaire and that a proper review and follow-up be made by qualified diocesan personnel." Its long-term recommendations are: "that a parish best practices manual be developed, similar to *Diocesan Financial Issues* which has been developed for the dioceses; and that financial training be integrated into current seminarian programs (and/or ongoing faith formation programs) such that students will be prepared to handle these eventualities." See MOST REVEREND DENNIS M. SCHNURR, Memorandum "Parish Financial Governance," sent to all bishops on March 23, 2007. http://www.usccb.org/finance/parishfinancialgovernance.pdf (December 1, 2008)

96 The *DPMB* reminds bishops that a finance council must exist for each diocese, parish, and other juridic person. It adds that "[t]he members of these councils should be chosen from among those faithful who are knowledgeable in financial affairs and civil law, renowned for their honesty and love for the Church and its apostolates. In those places where the permanent diaconate has been instituted, steps should be taken to arrange the participation of the deacons in finance councils, according to the charism of their order.

"Together with the diocesan finance council, the Bishop examines work proposals, budgets, and plans for financing them, and he makes the necessary decisions in conformity with the law. Moreover, the diocesan finance council, jointly with the college of consultors, *must be consulted* for acts of administration which, given the economic situation of the diocese, are of *greater importance*; for acts of *extraordinary administration* (established by the Episcopal Conference), the Bishop needs the *consent* of the college of consultors and the diocesan finance council" (n. 192).

diocesan pastoral council,[97] which is not required by universal law (see canon 511). As its name indicates, the diocesan finance council assists the diocesan bishop in matters of finances and temporalities. In practice, the diocesan finance council performs a variety of important functions beyond the few mandatory functions assigned to it by universal law. In collaborating with the diocesan finance council, the diocesan bishop sometimes must receive its *counsel* or *consent* before he can act validly (see canon 127).

The code identifies the following as the mandatory functions to the diocesan finance council:[98]

1. to prepare an annual diocesan budget of foreseen income and expenditures (canon 493)[99]

2. to examine the annual diocesan report of revenue and expenses (canon 493; see canon 494 §4)

3. to review the annual financial reports presented by administrators of any ecclesiastical goods whatsoever which have not been legitimately exempted from the power of governance of the diocesan bishop, after the administrators have submitted these to the local ordinary (canon 1287 §1)[100]

---

[97] The optional diocesan pastoral council is concerned with "pastoral planning," i.e., with identifying pastoral needs, studying them, and proposing practical conclusions about them (canon 511). Its primary focus is not financial affairs. Yet, inasmuch as pastoral planning has obvious financial implications and inasmuch as pastoral planning is irresponsible without considering these implications, it will be important that the diocesan pastoral council has some rapport with the diocesan finance council. The same can be said about the relationship between the optional parish pastoral council (canon 536) and the mandated parish finance council (canon 537). See GREEN, "Shepherding the Patrimony," pp. 721-723, 729-731; JOHN A. RENKEN, "Pastoral Councils: Pastoral Planning and Dialogue Among the People of God," in *The Jurist*, 53 (1993), pp. 152-154.

[98] Nothing prevents the diocesan bishop from establishing by particular law other mandatory general functions of the diocesan finance council (e.g., to propose modifications in salaries and benefits for diocesan employees, to offer recommendations on investment of diocesan funds, to review investment portfolios, etc.).

[99] An annual budget is required for dioceses by canon 493. Annual budgets for other juridic persons is only *strongly recommended*, though particular law can require them (canon 1284 §2).

[100] This means that the diocesan finance council must review the annual financial reports of parishes, since parishes are public juridic persons *a iure* (canon 515 §3) which have not been exempted from the power of governance of the diocesan bishop.

4. to elect a temporary diocesan finance officer if the diocesan finance officer is elected the diocesan administrator *sede vacante* (canon 423 §2)[101]

The code requires the diocesan bishop to receive the *consent* of the diocesan finance council before he performs the following three acts:

1. to place acts of extraordinary diocesan administration as defined by the conference of bishops (canon 1277; the college of consultors must also give its consent)

2. to give permission to alienate goods of public juridic persons subject to his authority, and to alienate diocesan goods, which belong to stable patrimony and whose value is beyond the minimum amount established by the conference of bishops (canon 1292 §2; the college of consultors and "those concerned" must also give their consent)

3. to give permission to administrators to perform any contractual transaction which can worsen the patrimonial condition of a public juridic person subject to his authority, or to perform the transaction himself if it involves diocesan goods (canon 1295; the college of consultors and "those concerned" must also give their consent; see canon 1292 §2)

In these instances, the diocesan bishop acts *invalidly* if he does not receive, or acts against, the consent of the diocesan finance council (and of the others mentioned in the individual canons).

The code requires the diocesan bishop to receive the *counsel* of the diocesan finance council before he performs the following seven acts:

---

[101] *Sede vacante*, the law forbids the "superior" of the diocese (i.e., the diocesan administrator) from being also the "administrator" of diocesan goods (i.e., the diocesan finance officer). These offices are "incompatible" (see canon 152).

The provision of canon 423 §2 enabling the diocesan finance council (a group which may be comprised entirely of lay persons) to confer an ecclesiastical office (see canons 145-183) gives remarkable and exceptional power to the council. As a rule, offices in a particular church are freely conferred by the diocesan bishop (canon 157).

The appointment of the temporary finance officer must be done in writing (canon 156).

1. to appoint and to remove the diocesan finance officer (canon 494 §§2-3; the college of consultors must also give its counsel)[102]
2. to impose a moderate tax upon public juridic persons subject to his authority (canon 1263; the presbyteral council must also give its counsel)
3. to impose an extraordinary tax upon other juridic persons and upon physical persons subject to his authority (canon 1263; the presbyteral council must also give its counsel)
4. to place "non-routine" acts of ordinary diocesan administration which are more important in light of the economic condition of the diocese (canon 1277; the college of consultors must also give its counsel)
5. to determine acts of extraordinary administration placed by public juridic persons subject to him (canon 1281 §1)
6. to make a prudent judgment on the investment of money and movable goods assigned to an endowment for the benefit of a foundation (canon 1305)
7. to lessen equitably the obligations attached to a foundation (but not foundation Masses) if, through no fault of the administrators, the fulfillment of these obligations becomes impossible because of diminished revenue or some other cause (canon 1310 §2; "those concerned" must also give their counsel)

In these instances, the diocesan bishop acts *invalidly* if he does not receive the counsel of the diocesan finance council (and of the others mentioned in the individual canons).

Given the immensity of a diocesan bishop's responsibilities concerning ecclesiastical goods, and given the complexity of various civil laws and economic factors affecting those responsibilities, the diocesan bishop may rely upon the expertise of the diocesan

---

[102] The Eastern law makes the eparchial finance officer *ipso iure* a member of the eparchial finance council (CCEO, canon 263 §2). The Latin code does not. Given that the finance council must give its counsel for the appointment and removal of the finance officer, and given that the finance officer must render an annual report of receipts and expenditures to the finance council, it seems preferable not to appoint the finance officer to the finance council upon which he depends for his appointment and continuation in office and to which he must submit an annual report of his function, lest there be even the appearance of impropriety.

finance council in countless matters beyond the few mentioned in the code. A spirit of transparency and prudence will wisely guide him in determining those matters.

To perform the "minimum" general functions entrusted to it by universal law, the diocesan finance council must logically meet at least twice a year: i.e., to prepare a budget for the coming fiscal year, and to review income and expenditures from the past fiscal year both for the diocese and for public juridic persons subject to the diocesan bishop. Still, it seems that in practice the service of the diocesan finance council would require more frequent meetings if it is truly to assist the diocesan bishop in his tasks, which involve significantly more than the annual budget and the annual financial statements. Therefore, diocesan particular law may specify that the diocesan finance council meet more frequently.

PRESBYTERAL COUNCIL. Canon 1263 requires the diocesan bishop to receive the counsel of the presbyteral council before he imposes a diocesan tax. Canon 495 §1 discusses the establishment and general function of the presbyteral council:

> **Can. 495 – §1. In each diocese a presbyteral council is to be established, that is, a group of priests which, representing the presbyterate, is to be like a senate of the bishop and which assists the bishop in the governance of the diocese according to the norm of law to promote as much as possible the pastoral good of the portion of the people of God entrusted to him.**[103]

The code identifies several situations in which the diocesan bishop must receive the *counsel*[104] of the presbyteral council before he acts:

---

[103] Canon 495 §2 requires an apostolic prefect or apostolic vicar to establish a council of at least three missionary presbyters whose opinion he is to hear in more serious matters, even by letter, in lieu of a presbyteral council. Canons 496-501 treat various aspects of the presbyteral council.

[104] "The presbyteral council possesses only a consultative vote; the diocesan bishop is to hear it in affairs of greater importance but needs its consent only in cases expressly defined by law" (canon 500 §2). The universal law in fact identifies no situations in which the diocesan bishop must receive the consent of the presbyteral council to perform an episcopal function.

1. to convoke a diocesan synod (canon 461 §1)
2. to establish, suppress, or notably alter parishes (canon 515 §2)
3. to allocate offerings made by the faithful for parochial services and to remunerate the clerics who perform them (canon 531; see canon 551)
4. to mandate a pastoral council in each parish (canon 536 §1)
5. to erect a new church building (canon 1215 §2)
6. to relegate a church to profane but not sordid use (canon 1222 §2)
7. to impose the ordinary and extraordinary diocesan tax (canon 1263)
8. to establish a group of priests whom the diocesan bishop will consult in removing[105] or transferring an unwilling pastor (canons 1742 §1, 1745, 2°, 1750)

One observes that the majority of these situations involve ecclesiastical goods. The *Directory for the Pastoral Ministry of Bishops* says that the diocesan bishop should involve the presbyteral council in important financial decisions:

> The Bishop should involve the diocesan clergy, through the presbyteral council, in the important financial decisions that he wishes to make, and he should seek their opinion in such matters. In certain cases, it may also be helpful to consult the diocesan pastoral council.[106]

COLLEGE OF CONSULTORS. The college of consultors is a group of six to twelve priests freely chosen by the diocesan bishop from among the members of the presbyteral council for a period of five years[107]; the college performs "the functions determined by

---

[105] One of the legitimate causes for which a pastor can be removed administratively from office is "poor administration of temporal affairs with grave damage to the Church whenever another remedy to this harm cannot be found" (canon 1741, 5°).

[106] *DPMB*, n. 189 b).

[107] Lest a diocese have no college of consultors, canon 502 §1 says that the college continues to exercise its proper functions when the five years have lapsed until a new college is established (see canon 186).

law" (canon 502 §1).[108] Members of the college of consultors retain membership in the college even if their terms of membership on the presbyteral council have expired.[109] Clearly, significant functions of the college of consultors involve various aspects of central diocesan administration, particularly when the see is vacant or impeded; such functions include:[110]

1. to elect a diocesan administrator within eight days when the see becomes vacant (canon 421 §1), and to witness his profession of faith (canon 833, 4°)
2. to inform the Apostolic See of the death of the diocesan bishop, if there is no auxiliary bishop (canon 422)
3. to assume diocesan governance when the see is vacant before the election of the diocesan administrator, if there is no auxiliary bishop (canon 419)
4. to see the apostolic letter of appointment of the diocesan bishop, in the presence of the chancellor, when he takes canonical possession of the diocese (canon 382 §2)
5. to see the apostolic letter of appointment of the coadjutor bishop, together with the diocesan bishop and in the presence of the chancellor, when he takes possession of his office (canon 404 §1)
6. to see the apostolic letter of appointment of both the coadjutor bishop and the auxiliary bishop, in the presence of the chancellor, when they take possession of their office, if the diocesan bishop is completely impeded (canon 404 §3)
7. to select a priest to govern an impeded see, if there is no coadjutor bishop (or if he also is impeded) and if the diocesan bishop

---

[108] Canon 502 §4 says that in an apostolic vicariate and prefecture, the council of the mission (mentioned in canon 495 §2) has the functions of the college of consultors, unless the law determines otherwise.

[109] See Pontifical Commission for the Authentic Interpretation of the Code of Canon Law, "Responsum ad propositum dubium" in *AAS*, 76 (1984), p. 747. The authentic interpretation adds that the diocesan bishop must replace a consultor who ceases his function during the five-year appointment to the college of consultors only if his absence would result in a college of fewer than the required six counselors.

[110] In addition to these functions which belong to the college of consultors as a group, members of the college *as individuals* are to be heard by the pontifical legate whenever a diocesan bishop or a coadjutor bishop is to be appointed (canon 377 §3).

has not composed a secret document identifying priests, listed in order of preference, to govern the impeded see (canon 413 §3)

8. to fulfill the functions of the presbyteral council when the see is vacant and until, within a year, the new diocesan bishop reestablishes the presbyteral council (canon 501 §2)

The code identifies three instances when the college of consultors must give its *consent* before the diocesan administrator is able to perform certain functions:

1. to grant excardination or incardination of clergy, after the see has been vacant for a year (canon 272)
2. to remove the chancellor and other notaries (canon 485)
3. to issue dimissorial letters (canon 1018 §1, 2°)

Although the college of consultors obviously assumes a special role in the exceptional circumstances identified above, its more routine function is to assist the diocesan bishop in significant aspects of his care for ecclesiastical goods. The diocesan bishop must receive the *counsel* of the college of consultors:

1. to appoint the diocesan finance officer (canon 494 §1)
2. to remove the diocesan finance officer during his or her five year term (canon 494 §2)
3. to place "non-routine" acts of administration of diocesan ecclesiastical goods which are more important in light of the economic condition of the diocese (canon 1277)

He must receive its *consent*:

1. to place acts of extraordinary administration as defined by the conference of bishops (canon 1277; the diocesan finance council must also give its consent)
2. to give permission to alienate goods of public juridic persons subject to his authority, and to alienate diocesan goods, which belong to stable patrimony and whose value is beyond the minimum amount established by the conference of bishops (canon 1292 §2; the diocesan finance council and "those concerned" must also give their consent)

3. to give permission to administrators to perform any contractual transaction which can worsen the patrimonial condition of a public juridic person subject to his authority, or to perform the transaction himself if it involves diocesan goods (canon 1295; the diocesan finance council and "those concerned" must also give their consent; see canon 1292 §2)

"THOSE CONCERNED." As is evident from the above, sometimes the diocesan bishop must be in dialogue with "those concerned." Two canons require their *consent* before the diocesan bishop is able:

1. to give permission to alienate goods of public juridic persons subject to his authority, and to alienate diocesan goods, which belong to stable patrimony and whose value is beyond the minimum amount established by the conference of bishops (canon 1292 §2; the diocesan finance council and the college of consultors must also give their consent)

2. to give permission to administrators to perform any contractual transaction which can worsen the patrimonial condition of a public juridic person subject to his authority, or to perform the transaction himself if it involves diocesan goods (canon 1295; the diocesan finance council and the college of consultors must also give their consent; see canon 1292 §2)

Two other canons require their *counsel* before the ordinary (which includes the diocesan bishop) is able:

1. to render a prudent judgment on the investment of money and movable goods assigned to the endowment of a pious foundation (canon 1305 §1; his finance council must also be heard)

2. to lessen equitably the obligations attached to a foundation (but not foundation Masses) if, through no fault of the administrators, the fulfillment of these obligations becomes impossible because of diminished revenue or some other cause (canon 1310 §2; his finance council must also be heard)

"Those concerned" may be those who lawfully hold rights over the ecclesiastical good being considered. Francis Morrisey observes that "in the case of parochial property, the parish priest [pastor] would certainly be [one concerned] (see can. 532); in other cases, each to be examined in its own circumstances, it might well be the original donor or the lawful representative thereof, or anyone who might retain an acknowledged legal interest in the property in question."[111]

PASTORAL COUNCILS. The code provides the option of establishing a diocesan pastoral council (canon 511-514) and parish pastoral councils (canon 536).[112]

The diocesan pastoral council, under the authority of the bishop, "investigates, considers, and proposes practical conclusions about those things which pertain to pastoral works in the diocese." Put another way, the purpose of the pastoral council is "pastoral planning." If the diocesan bishop should decide to establish it, the diocesan pastoral council is to be convoked at least once a year and enjoys a consultative vote. The diocesan bishop is the president of the pastoral council; he convokes its gatherings and publicizes its workings. Members are to be Catholics with firm faith, good morals, and prudence. They are selected to be representative of the diversity of persons in the diocese: they are to be clerics, members of institutes of consecrated life, and especially lay persons. The *Directory for the Pastoral Ministry of Bishops* suggests that in certain important financial decisions "it may also be helpful [for the diocesan bishop] to consult the diocesan pastoral council."[113]

The parish pastoral council may be mandated for each parish by diocesan particular law, after he has heard the presbyteral council (canon 536).[114] Its purpose is to "assist in fostering pastoral activity" (this, in effect, is the same purpose as the diocesan pastoral council: "pastoral planning"). The pastor is the president of the pastoral council. The parish pastoral council is to have only a consultative vote; norms governing it are to be established by the diocesan bishop.

---

[111] See MORRISEY, "Temporal Goods," p. 734.

[112] For a study of the development of legislation on pastoral councils, diocesan and parochial, see RENKEN, "Pastoral Councils," pp. 132-154.

[113] *DPMB*, n. 189 b). See SIGNIÉ, pp. 137-138.

[114] If the diocesan bishop has not legitimately mandated the establishment of parish pastoral councils, pastors may nonetheless freely select to establish them in their parishes. Such non-mandated parish pastoral councils, however, should comply with the provisions of canon 536.

Members include those who share in pastoral care by virtue of their office in the parish.

Both of these pastoral councils focus on the pastoral works of the Church, and in a special way try to discern ways whereby the pastoral needs of the Church may be met effectively. In much, if not all, of this discernment, economic concerns eventually arise. Responsible planning involves an analysis of the availability of temporal goods to achieve any proposed initiative. This indicates, therefore, that ecclesiastical goods are also the concern of pastoral councils, even if no canon formally relates pastoral councils to the code's discipline in *Book V*.[115] Dioceses and parishes will wisely discern ways for those engaged in pastoral planning in the Church to be in candid and transparent dialogue with those administering the temporal goods of the Church.

CORRESPONDING CANON OF THE EASTERN CODE: CANON 1012. The Eastern code contains significant differences from Latin canon 1263. It simply speaks of a "tax" (*tributum*) without distinguishing ordinary and extraordinary ones. It allows the eparchial bishop to impose a tax upon juridic persons subject to him "insofar as it is necessary for the good of the eparchy" after he has received the *consent* (not the *counsel*) of the eparchial finance council (with no reference to the presbyteral council). The tax is to be proportionate to the income of the juridic person. The canon specifically excludes taxes "on the offerings received on the occasion of the celebration of the Divine Liturgy," something not mentioned in the Latin law. It allows the imposition of taxes (*tributa*) on physical persons "only according to the norm of particular law of their own Church *sui iuris*."[116]

---

[115] Interestingly, when Francis Cardinal König had suggested that the proposed law provide some connection or relationship between the parish pastoral council and the parish finance council, the secretariat responded that no connection is foreseen since the councils are diverse entities. *Relatio*, p. 127.

[116] See ANNA FAVERGIOTTI, "Il fondamento dell'obbligazione tributaria nello stato moderno e nel diritto canonico ed orientale: Note comparative," in *Atti del Congresso Internazionale: Incontro fra canoni d'oriente e d'occidente*, Raffaele Coppola (ed.), 3 vols., Bari, Cacucci editore, 1994, vol. 2, pp. 571-582.

PROVINCIAL FEES AND OFFERINGS

> **Can. 1264 – Unless the law has provided otherwise, it is for a meeting of the bishops of a province:**
> **1° to fix the fees for acts of executive power granting a favor or for the execution of rescripts of the Apostolic See, to be approved by the Apostolic See itself;**
> **2° to set a limit on the offerings on the occasion of the administration of sacraments and sacramentals.**

Canon 1264 explains that, unless the law provides otherwise, the bishops of a province[117] have two obligations regarding the acquisition of ecclesiastical goods:

1. to fix the fees (*taxa*) for acts of executive power granting a favor or for the execution of rescripts of the Apostolic See, to be approved by the Apostolic See itself
2. to set a limit on the offerings (*oblata*) given on the occasion of the administration of sacraments and sacramentals.

Canon 952 §3 identifies a third obligation of the provincial bishops: to define by decree for the entire province a uniform offering (*stips*) to be given for the celebration and application of Mass.

These norms need not be determined during a provincial council (canon 440), but can be established simply during a meeting of the bishops of the province. The law assigns a deliberative vote in the provincial council to the coadjutor and auxiliary bishops of the province (canon 443 §1, 2°); it does not exclude their deliberative vote in the less formal gathering.

Excluded from canon 1264 are judicial expenses, which are to be determined by "the bishop who directs the tribunal" (canon 1649; see canons 1419, 1423).

TAXES FOR FAVORS AND RESCRIPTS. Canon 1264, 1° requires the provincial bishops to establish uniform *taxes*[118] for acts of executive

---

[117] Canon 431 §1 explains that the purposes of ecclesiastical provinces are: "[t]o promote the common pastoral action of different neighboring dioceses according to the circumstances of persons and places and to foster more suitably the relations of the diocesan bishops among themselves."

[118] The SACRED CONGREGATION FOR THE COUNCIL issued a *Resolutio* on December 11, 1920, clarifying that the provincial bishops must set a *definite* amount for these taxes

power (see canons 135 §4, 136-144) granting favors (e.g, dispensations, privileges, etc.), and for the execution of rescripts (see canons 59-75) of the Apostolic See within the ecclesiastical province. These amounts of all these *taxa* are to be approved (*approbanda*) by the Holy See.[119]

The 1917 code had included a separate canon providing legislation for the granting of marriage dispensations (CIC/1917, canon 1056). Such legislation is not found in the 1983 code. Therefore, any determination of fees for the granting of marriage dispensations must be established in the method described in canon 1264, 1°.

SACRAMENTAL OFFERINGS OR "STOLE FEES." Canon 1264, 2° requires the provincial bishops to establish the maximum limit on *offerings*[120] given on the occasion of the administration of sacraments

---

and offerings, observing "a certain discretion." They may not establish minimum and maximum amounts within which each ordinary can establish the fees for his diocese. The congregation contrasted this canon with the legislation allowing the ordinary to set the amount for funeral taxes (CIC/1917, canon 1234). The *Resolutio* makes reference to the Bull of Pope Innocent XI, *Essendo avuto* (October 8, 1678) and the Decree of the Sacred Congregation for the Council (June 10, 1896). In *AAS*, 13 (1921), p. 350; *CLD*, vol. 1, pp. 720-721.

[119] It was suggested during consultation on the 1977 *Schema* that the revised law add the requirement that the fees set for these taxes by the provincial bishops be approved by the Apostolic See, as had been required by CIC/1917, canon 1507 §1. The *coetus De bonis Ecclesiae temporalibus* accepted the recommendation. *Communicationes,* 12 (1980), p. 403.

Canon 1264, 1° requires the approval (*approbatio*) of the Apostolic See; in many other instances, the universal law requires simply the review (*recognitio*): see canons 451, 455 §2, 456, 838 §§2-3, 1120.

Also, ROBERT T. KENNEDY observes about canon 1264, 1°: "The syntax of the Latin text makes clear that approval of the Apostolic See must be obtained for all such fees, not just those for execution of rescripts of the Apostolic See itself." In "Temporal Goods," p. 1466.

[120] The *coetus De bonis Ecclesiae temporalibus* replaced the word "*taxae*" in the 1977 *Schema* with the word "*oblatio*" in reference to sacraments and sacramentals, but retained the former term in relation to acts of executive power and the execution of rescripts of the Apostolic See. Some suggestions had been received during the consultation process to eliminate a monetary exchange on the occasion of the administration of sacraments and sacramentals in order to reflect the statement of the 1971 Synod of Bishops that priests' income should be separated from their acts of ministry, especially sacramental ones. The consultors, however, aware that in many regions of the world priests rely on these offerings, decided to retain the norm on monetary exchange but not to refer to it as taxation. *Communicationes,* 12 (1980), p. 403.

It will be recalled that the directive of the 1971 Synod of Bishops is reflected in canons 531 and 551, which require that sacramental offerings be given to the parish.

and sacramentals; these are commonly called "stole fees." These offerings are not taxes, nor should legislating them be considered simony.[121] They are instead simply offerings whereby the faithful contribute to the support of the Church on the occasion of the administration of sacraments and sacramentals. Commonly, these offerings are given on the occasion of baptisms, weddings, and funerals. The amount of these offerings is to be established by the bishops of the province; their determination needs neither the review nor the approval of the Apostolic See.

Nothing prevents the recipient of a sacrament or sacramental from giving an amount larger or smaller than the determined offering. Canon 848, however, forbids the minister of the sacraments to require a higher offering and requires the minister to make sure that the sacraments are available to the needy:

> **Can. 848 – The minister is to seek nothing for the administration of the sacraments beyond the offerings defined by the competent authority, always taking care that the needy are not deprived of the assistance of the sacraments because of poverty.**

Canon 1181 makes reference to canon 1264 in discussing the offerings to be given for funerals:

> **Can. 1181 – Regarding offerings on the occasion of funeral rites, the prescripts of can. 1264 are to be observed, with the caution, however, that there is to be no favoritism toward persons in funerals and that the poor are not deprived of fitting funerals.**

This canon expects the provincial bishops to set the maximum limit for funeral offerings. It also admonishes against favoritism toward the wealthy and discrimination against the poor.

---

[121] Canon 1380 establishes a penalty for simony: "A person who celebrates or receives a sacrament through simony is to be punished with an interdict or suspension." This penal law is preceptive (see canon 1344) and determinate (see canon 1315 §2). Further, canon 1385 prohibits making an unlawful profit from Mass offerings: "A person who illegitimately makes a profit from Mass offerings is to be punished with a censure or another just penalty." (See also canon 947.) This penal law is also preceptive and determinate.

Canon 1264, 2° is to be read in conjunction with canon 531:

> **Can. 531** – **Although another person has performed a certain parochial function, that person is to put the offerings received from the Christian faithful on that occasion into the parochial account, unless in the case of voluntary offerings the contrary intention of the donor is certain. The diocesan bishop, after having heard the presbyteral council, is competent to establish prescripts which provide for the allocation of these offerings and the remuneration of clerics fulfilling the same function.**

The discipline of canon 531 applies the presumption in canon 1267 §1 (that the offerings given to superiors or administrators of any ecclesiastical juridic person are presumed to have been given to the juridic person itself unless the contrary is established) to parishes. The "administrator" of a parish (which is a juridic person *a iure*: see canon 515 §3) is its pastor (canon 532); therefore, sacramental offerings given to the pastor are presumed to be given to the parish. Canon 551 applies canon 531 to parochial vicars (see canon 545). Indeed, the maximum offerings, set by the provincial bishops and received in a parish on the occasion of the administration of a sacrament or sacramental, belong to the parish, even if someone not assigned to the parish performs these functions.

Canons 1267 §1, 531, and 551 allow the overturning of this presumption when, in the case of voluntary offerings, the intention of the donor to give a gift to the cleric is certain.

Canon 531 says that, after the diocesan bishop hears the presbyteral council,[122] he is competent to establish norms (1) for the allocation of these offerings and (2) for the remuneration of the clerics who perform the related functions. There are no restrictions in the universal law on either the allocation of the offerings or the remuneration of the clerics. Regarding the allocation of the offerings, some dioceses simply retain them as part of ordinary parish

---

[122] The diocesan bishop's consultation with the presbyteral council is required before he can act validly (see canon 127 §1).

revenue[123] or assign them to one of the institutes mentioned in canon 1274. Regarding the remuneration of the clerics, the code does not specify that the diocesan norms apply only to visiting clergy: the norms also apply to those clergy assigned to the parish (see canon 551). Nonetheless, in keeping with the spirit of the code, clerics are not to rely on sacramental offerings for their sustenance; instead, they should receive sufficient remuneration to provide for their needs otherwise (see canon 281 §1; *Presbyterorum ordinis*, n. 20).

MASS OFFERINGS. Neither canon 1264 nor canon 531 address the offerings given for the celebration of Mass, commonly called "Mass stipends," which are treated in canons 945-958 of the code. Several of these canons merit special mention here.

Canon 952 says that the provincial bishops are to set by decree the offering to be given on the occasion of the celebration of Masses throughout the province; this particular law is to be observed also by religious:

> **Can. 952 – §1. It is for the provincial council or a meeting of the bishops of the province to define by decree for the entire province the offering to be given for the celebration and application of Mass, and a priest is not permitted to seek a larger sum. Nevertheless, he is permitted to accept for the application of a Mass a voluntary offering which is larger or even smaller than the one defined.**
>
> **§2. Where there is no such decree, the custom in force in the diocese is to be observed.**
>
> **§3. Members of all religious institutes must also observe the same decree or local custom mentioned in §§1 and 2.**

Canon 945 §1 says that a priest is able to receive Mass offerings, in accord with the approved practice of the Church. Put simply, the Mass offering belongs to the priest who celebrates or concelebrates the Mass, and is unable to be treated like the sacramental offerings

---

[123] In this case, the offerings may be subject to the ordinary diocesan tax mentioned in canon 1263, depending on the formula set by the diocesan bishop after he has heard the presbyteral council and the diocesan finance council.

treated in canon 1264, 2°. It is not subject to the ordinary or extraordinary diocesan tax.[124]

Canon 950 states that if a sum of money is given for the celebration of Masses without specifying the number, the number of Masses is to be determined based on the Mass offering of the place where the donor resides, unless the intention of the donor is legitimately presumed otherwise.[125]

Some dioceses give priests the option to contribute freely their Mass offerings to the general parochial account in return for an increased remuneration from the parish. It appears this volun-

---

[124] See the commentary on canon 1263; EUGENE J. FITZSIMMONS, "Mass Offerings and Stole Fees," in *CFH*, pp. 63-76.

[125] FRANCIS G. MORRISEY discusses "money left to parishes in a will for the celebration of Masses. In order to provide for respect of the intentions of the donors, yet at the same time take into account our theology relating to the infinite value of the Mass, in some dioceses bishops have established a policy to the effect that if the number of Masses is not specified in the will, and if the amount available for the celebration of Masses is more than thirty times the diocesan offering, then the sum is to be divided by thirty (in line with the former 'month's mind Masses'); the celebrant receives the ordinary offering in the diocese, and the rest goes to the parish or institution that was the beneficiary. Such a policy would have to be issued before a will is received and the executors notified accordingly when they present the request for Masses. If the number of Masses is indicated in the will and the bequest is accepted, then, of course, the intention has to be honored. At times, a percentage of what remains is taxed to provide for the continuing education of priests, and so forth." In "Acquiring Temporal Goods," p. 595.
Canon 950 requires that money offered for Masses without specifying their number is to be computed on the basis of the offering established for the place where the donor resides "unless the intention of the donor must be presumed legitimately to have been different," and canon 952 §1 requires the provincial bishops to determine Mass offerings for the province. Morrisey's proposal seems to suggest that the donor's intention would be different if the diocesan bishop had promulgated a policy which explains that a pre-determined number of Masses (e.g., thirty) will be offered when the number of Masses is not specified in a will and a significant sum has been inherited. Inasmuch as the provincial bishops establish Mass offerings, perhaps it would be "canonically more prudent" for the provincial bishops, rather than an individual bishop, to establish such a policy. Obvious concerns with such a policy, whether issued by the provincial bishops or a diocesan bishop, are that one cannot presume with certainty that a donor had been aware of the policy, and that the ordinary must assure fulfillment of a donor's intention (see canons 1300-1301). Further, the discipline on calculating Mass offerings not otherwise specified in canon 950 is clear.
See also JOHN M. HUELS, "Indeterminate Mass Obligations," in CLSA, *Roman Replies and Advisory Opinions*, Joseph J. Koury and Shiobhan M. Verbeek (eds.), Washington, CLSA, 2007, pp. 79-80.

tary practice seeks to parallel the legislation of canons 531 and 551 mandating that offerings for certain parochial functions be given to the parish. This practice would seem permitted provided the priest has the *option* to choose either (1) to surrender voluntarily the Mass offerings in return for the increased remuneration, or (2) to retain the Mass offerings and not receive the increased remuneration.[126] If the priest selects the first option, in effect he would be freely giving his Mass offerings to the parish and in return receiving an adjusted remuneration. Nonetheless, even in this setting, the Mass offering must be given to any priest (e.g., a visiting priest) who is not among those receiving the option of increased remuneration in lieu of in-dividual offerings voluntarily surrendered to the parish. Given the complexity of customizing this arrangement for each priest, one may question its practical advantage.

Canon 951 allows a priest to retain only one Mass offering per day (except on Christmas, when he may retain as many as three). By its decree entitled *Mos igitur*, dated February 22, 1992, however, the Congregation for the Clergy allows a priest to offer one Mass for which he has received several Mass offerings but under very strict conditions: i.e., the faithful making the individual offerings must agree to a Mass for their intention being celebrated with other intentions; the priest may retain only the amount for a single Mass

---

[126] In 1981, before the promulgation of the 1983 code, an American archbishop sought an indult from the Holy See whereby stole fees and stipends would be assigned to a parish or institution rather than to the priest directly. This had been proposed by the archdiocesan priests' senate in an effort to provide a just and equitable remuneration to priests. The Congregation for the Clergy replied:

"We have no objection as far as the stole fees are concerned, according to the spirit of the Motu Proprio *Ecclesiae sanctae*, n. 8 (*AAS* 58 [1966] 757-787).

"We cannot, however, grant the requested indult to assign Mass stipends to the parish or institution where the Sacraments are celebrated, since it is part of the letter and the spirit of the law, to give the Mass stipend directly to the celebrant (can. 824 and can. 1506 C.I.C., confirmed by the rather recent Motu Proprio *Firma in Traditione* (*AAS* 66 [1974] 308-311)."

In CLSA, *Roman Replies and Advisory Opinions*, Washington, CLSA, 1984, pp. 1-2.

One notes that the requested indult would not have given the priests an option to surrender the Mass stipends in lieu of adjusted remuneration or not. See James I. Donlon, "Priests' Remuneration and Mass Stipends," in *CLSA AO3*, pp. 254-256.

set by the provincial bishops and must remit the excess money to the purposes prescribed by ordinary, as required by canon 951 §1 (see canon 946); and the faithful are to be informed of the time and place of a Mass celebrated with "collective" intentions, which is not to occur more than twice a week. Priests are to keep in mind that this practice is an exception to the norm of canon 948, which states clearly: "Separate Masses are to be applied for the intentions of those for whom a single offering, although small, has been given and accepted." Priests with surplus offerings are to forward them to other priests (see canon 955) or to their own ordinary (canon 956).[127] Diocesan bishops are to see to the observance of the norms of *Mos igitur* by all priests, secular and religious.

Interest accrued on Mass offerings need not be used for Masses. The interest may be applied for any purpose determined by the recipient of the offerings.[128]

TRIBUNAL FEES. In addition to the fees and offerings discussed in canon 1264 and the Mass offerings discussed in canon 952 §3 (all of which are established by the provincial bishops), the code also provides for the establishment of fees for judicial expenses. These tribunal fees, however, are established by the bishop who directs the tribunal (see canons 1419 §1, 1423). He may freely select to set these fees after he has freely consulted the bishops who direct neighboring tribunals. The pertinent canon says:

> **Can. 1649 – §1. The bishop who directs the tribunal is to establish norms concerning:**
> **1° the requirement of the parties to pay or compensate judicial expenses;**
> **2° the fees for procurators, advocates, experts, and**

---

[127] See CONGREGATION FOR THE CLERGY, Decree, *Mos igitur* (February 22, 1991), in *AAS*, 83 (1991), pp. 443-446; English translation in *Origins,* 20 (1990-1991), pp. 705-706. For an extensive commentary on *Mos igitur* see: GILBERTO AGUSTONI, Commentary on the Decree, in *Origins*, 20 (1990-1991), pp. 706-707; JULIO MANZANARES, "De stipendio pro missis ad intentionem 'collectivam' celebratis iuxta decretum 'Mos igitur,'" in *Periodica*, 80 (1991), pp. 579-608.

[128] See PAUL GOLDEN, "Mass Offerings Held in an Interest Bearing Account," in CLSA, *Roman Replies and Advisory Opinions*, Joseph J. Koury and Shiobhan M. Verbeek (eds.), Washington, CLSA, 2007, p. 78.

interpreters and the indemnity for the witnesses;

3° the grant of gratuitous legal assistance or reduction of expenses;

4° the recovery of damages owed by a person who not only lost the trial but also entered into the litigation rashly;

5° the deposit of money or the provision furnished for the payment of expenses and recovery of damages.

§2. There is to be no separate appeal from the determination of expenses, fees, and recovery of damages, but the party can make recourse within fifteen days to the same judge who can adjust the assessment.[129]

CORRESPONDING CANON OF THE EASTERN CODE: CANON 1013. The corresponding canon of the Eastern code entrusts to the eparchial bishop, within limits established by his particular Church *sui iuris*, the determination of fees "for the various acts of the power of governance" and for "the offerings on the occasion of the celebration of the Divine Liturgy, sacraments, sacramentals or any other liturgical celebrations, unless common law provides otherwise." It asks patriarchs and eparchial bishops of various Churches *sui iuris* exercising their power in the same territory to take care, after mutual consultation, to establish the same norms for fees and offerings.

BEGGING FOR ALMS

Can. 1265 – §1. Without prejudice to the right of religious mendicants, any private person, whether physical or juridic, is forbidden to beg for alms for any pious or ecclesiastical institute or purpose without the written permission of that person's own ordinary and of the local ordinary.

§2. The conference of bishops can establish norms for begging for alms which all must observe, including those who by their foundation are called and are mendicants.

---

[129] See also PONTIFICAL COUNCIL FOR LEGISLATIVE TEXTS, instruction *Dignitas connubii,* Vatican City, Libreria editrice Vaticana, 2005, arts. 302-308.

Canon 1265 §1 forbids private persons, both physical and juridic, to beg for alms (*stipem cogere*) for any pious or ecclesiastical institute or purpose without the prior written permission of two ordinaries: the person's own ordinary, and the ordinary of the place where the begging would occur.[130] Should the ordinaries decide to grant this written permission, they will also be aware of the discipline of canon 1262 (on "appeals") and canon 1266 (on "special collections") whereby the faithful are approached for special financial assistance.

The canon does *not* forbid public juridic persons from begging for alms.[131] If the canon did so, it would be contradicting the "innate right" of the "Church" (a technical term which signifies public juridic persons: canon 1257 §1) to require necessary support from the Christian faithful (canon 1260).

The canon does *not* forbid religious mendicants from begging for alms. Mendicants (from the Latin, *mendicare*, to beg) are those religious who live from alms: e.g., Dominicans, Franciscans, Capuchins, Augustinians, Carmelites.[132] If the diocesan bishop consents to a group of mendicants to establish a house in the diocese, he understands that he is giving them the right to lead a life in accord with the character and proper purpose of their institute (canon 611, 1°).

Canon 1265 §2 says that the conference of bishops can (*potest*) establish norms for begging (*stipe quaeritanda*) which must be observed by all, even by mendicants. Thus, the begging by mendicants must be done within approved limits. The norms established by the episcopal conference help coordinate fund-raising efforts beyond diocesan boundaries and protect those begging from arbitrary refusal by a local ordinary.[133] The canon does *not* say that the conference

---

[130] CIC/1917, canon 1503, had required the permission of the Apostolic See *or* that of the two ordinaries.

[131] The 1977 *Schema* had permitted all members of institutes of consecrated life to beg for alms. Those making recommendations on the draft legislation, however, believed this could lead to abuses. As a result the *coetus De bonis Ecclesiae temporalibus* gave permission to beg for alms only to mendicants. *Communicationes,* 12 (1980), p. 404.

[132] JAMES A. CORIDEN, *An Introduction to Canon Law,* New York, Paulist Press, 1991, p. 166.

[133] See DANIEL J. WARD, "Religious Institute Raising Funds in Diocese," in *CLSA AO2,* p. 404.

of bishops *must* set norms. Diocesan norms would govern begging
for alms if the conference of bishops selects not to establish norms
for the scope of the conference.

Strictly speaking, "to beg for alms" means to go indiscrimi-
nately from door to door to seek alms for some pious purpose. This
would involve identifying potential donors and calling upon them
in person (not through letters) for financial assistance. Generally
considered to be excluded from "begging for alms" are such acts as:
asking discretely for financial assistance from persons known to the
one seeking the funds; collecting alms in a church or at an ecclesial
gathering; going to private homes when invited; or visiting donors
to thank them for previous generosity.[134]

Canon 1265 reflects the discipline of *Ecclesiae sanctae*, I, n.
27, which implements *Christus Dominus*, nn. 33-35 on the rapport
between bishops and religious, although the conciliar decree does
not mention fund-raising by religious. *Ecclesiae sanctae* states:

(1) The Episcopal Conference of any country can, with the interested religious Superiors, make regulations on seeking alms,
which must be observed by all religious orders, including those
who in their Institute are called mendicants and really are such,
but without prejudice to their right to beg.

(2) Similarly, religious should not proceed to collect funds by way
of public prescription without the consent of the Ordinaries of
the places where such collections are being made.[135]

PARTICULAR LAW FOR THE UNITED STATES AND CANADA. The
conferences of bishops in the United States and in Canada have not
established norms for begging for alms.

---

[134] BOUSCAREN-ELLIS-KORTH, p. 808. These authors add: "*What about begging letters?*
Strictly speaking, begging letters do not come under the law, since in such begging
there is no personal, oral request for alms. Custom, which is the best interpreter of
law… allows them. Besides, there is less danger of abuse and embarrassment in a
letter requesting alms than there is in a personal request for them. One can always
toss letters into the wastebasket. If the receiver of a circular letter, which describes
the usefulness of a certain good work that is being promoted, decides to send an
alms, his gift is considered to be a free-will offering" (p. 808).
   See the rather extensive norms regulating begging by religious in CIC/1917, canons
621-624.
[135] In *CLD*, vol. 6, p. 279.

CORRESPONDING CANON OF THE EASTERN CODE: CANON 1015. The Eastern code forbids any person, physical or juridic, from collecting alms without the *permission* of the authority to whom they are subject and the written *consent* of the local hierarch where the alms are collected. It makes no reference to mendicants nor to supraeparchial authorities who may establish norms for begging.

SPECIAL COLLECTIONS

> **Can. 1266 – In all churches and oratories which are, in fact, habitually open to the Christian faithful, including those which belong to religious institutes, the local ordinary can order the taking up of a special collection for specific parochial, diocesan, national, or universal projects; this collection must be diligently sent afterwards to the diocesan curia.**

Canon 1266 allows the local ordinary to order the taking up of a special collection for specific parochial, diocesan, national, or universal projects (*incepta*) in all churches and oratories which are, in fact, habitually open to the Christian faithful, including those churches and oratories which belong to religious institutes. After it has been gathered, the special collection must be diligently sent to the diocesan curia, which will convey it to the designated recipient.[136] To refuse to transmit the entire amount gathered would be to violate the intention of the donor (see canon 1267 §3).

This canon concerns "special" collections, not routine ones (i.e., this canon is not about "regular church support"). It is expected that these special collections be moderately proposed.[137] Nothing prevents a single collection from being designated for several dis-

---

[136] It would seem that, if a special collection is designated by the local ordinary for a given parish, there would be no need to send it to the diocesan curia merely to have it immediately returned to the parish. Revenue for the parish generated by the special collection would be reported with the annual parish financial report (see canon 1287 §1). The special collections to be sent to the diocesan curia, therefore, would be those for diocesan, national, and universal projects.

[137] See *Communicationes*, 12 (1980), p. 405.

tinct projects; in such a situation, however, it is important to respect the wishes of the donor who may select to contribute only to *some* of the projects in a joint-project collection. Canon 1267 §3 is clear: "Offerings given by the faithful for a certain purpose can be applied only for that same purpose."

The special collections of canon 1266 are distinct from the appeals of canon 1262. Were the subject matter of these two canons the same, there would be no need for two canons. Norms for appeals are to be issued by the conference of bishops; norms for special collections are not set by the conference of bishops. Nonetheless, the conference of bishops will often propose special collections which the local ordinary then can order to be gathered in his diocese.

The special collections of canon 1266 are also distinct from the taxes of canon 1263. The diocesan bishop alone can impose the taxes, but the local ordinary can order the special collections. The diocesan bishop cannot impose the taxes validly unless he has first received the counsel of the diocesan finance council and the presbyteral council; the local ordinary can order the special collections without any prior consultation. The tax determines a mandatory amount to be surrendered; the special collection has no such mandatory goal (but, if it does have such a goal, it is not a "special collection" governed by canon 1266, but instead a "tax" governed by canon 1263); in other words, the special collection is a free-willing offering, and the tax is not. Finally, the tax is "for the needs of the diocese" (the ordinary tax) or for cases of "grave necessity" (the extraordinary tax) presumably in the diocese; the special collection can be for parochial, diocesan, national, or universal projects.

The *Directory for the Pastoral Ministry of Bishops* mentions the appeals, the diocesan taxes, and the special collections which may be gathered in the diocese for a variety of diocesan needs:

> Invoking the spirit of faith of the people of God, the Bishop will appeal to the generosity of the faithful by asking them to contribute financially to the needs of the Church and to the support of the clergy, and also to the

establishment of new parishes and other places of worship. For these diocesan projects, the Bishop may order a *special collection* in all the churches and oratories open to the faithful (including those belonging to religious institutes and societies of apostolic life), in the form of special "appeal days" or in some other appropriate manner. With the same end in view, he may also impose a moderate *tax*, whether ordinary or extraordinary.

For promoting financial appeals among the faithful and for raising funds, unless the Episcopal Conference has determined otherwise, it can be helpful to establish a special *canonical association or foundation* directed by members of the lay faithful.

In this area, the Bishop must never allow financial concerns to take precedence over pastoral concerns since, in the eyes of the world, that spirit of faith and detachment from material goods, which is proper to the Church, must shine forth. [138]

Canon 791, 4° requires in each diocese an annual collection for the missions, the proceeds of which are to be forwarded to the Holy See.[139] Canon 264 §1 provides for a special collection to be gathered for the seminary (in addition to which the diocesan bishop can impose the "seminary tax").[140] No other special collection is identified in the universal law.

---

[138] *DPMB*, n. 216.

[139] See the SACRED CONGREGATION FOR THE PROPAGATION OF THE FAITH, "Instructio de apto modo pro missionibus stipem corrogandi," (June 29, 1952), pp. 549-551; *CLD*, vol. 3, pp. 254-256.

[140] CIC/1917, canon 1355, 1° had permitted the diocesan bishop to order pastors and rectors of churches, even exempt ones, to gather a collection (*stips*) for the seminary at stated times. CIC/1917, canon 1355, 2° had allowed him to impose a tribute (*tributum*) or tax (*taxa*) in the diocese to support the seminary. If the tax and the collection were insufficient, CIC/1917, canon 1355, 3° permitted the bishop to attribute some simple benefices to the seminary.

Canon 1266 has no direct predecessor in the 1917 code.[141]

CHURCHES AND ORATORIES. The special collections may be gathered in churches and oratories which are de facto habitually open to the Christian faithful, including those which belong to religious. Canon 1214 says that a church is "a sacred building designated for divine worship to which the faithful have the right of entry for the exercise, especially the public exercise, of public worship." Canon 1223 says that an oratory is "a place for divine worship designated by permission of the ordinary for the benefit of some community or group of the faithful who gather in it and to which other members of the faithful can also come with the consent of the competent superior."[142]

Canon 611, 3° says that the consent of the diocesan bishop to erect a religious house of any clerical institute carries with it the right to have a church (although the institute "must obtain his permission before building a church in a certain and determined place": canon 1215 §3). Canon 608 requires every religious house "to have at least an oratory in which the Eucharist is to be celebrated and reserved."

When the local ordinary orders a special collection, he can require it in *some* churches and oratories, but he does not need to require it in *all* of them. This may occur, for example, when the local ordinary permits several parishes to have a special collection for a designated special purpose (e.g., the operation of a school serving several parishes).

SPECIAL COLLECTIONS IN THE UNITED STATES. The discipline of this canon and the particular legislation for the United States find practical application in the thirteen annual special collections

---

[141] DE PAOLIS, *De bonis Ecclesiae temporalibus,* p. 68. The edition of the 1983 code containing its sources, however, says that canon 1266 developed from canon 1505. That canon had permitted the local ordinary to impose an extraordinary and moderate exaction (besides the seminary tax) and the benefice pension upon all *beneficiaries* (not benefices), both secular and religious, in light of special diocesan needs.

[142] The code lists a third place for divine worship: the *private chapel,* which is "designated by permission of the local ordinary for the benefit of one or more physical persons" (canon 1226).

endorsed by the USCCB, which the local ordinary would order for the diocese:[143]

- Aid to the Church in Central and Eastern Europe
- Black and Indian Missions
- Catholic Campaign for Human Development
- Catholic Communication Campaign
- Catholic Home Mission Appeal
- Catholic Relief Services
- The Catholic University of America
- Church in Latin America
- Holy Land
- Operation Rice Bowl
- Peter's Pence
- Retirement Fund for Religious
- World Mission Sunday

SPECIAL COLLECTIONS IN CANADA. The CCCB endorses five national special collections in Canada, which the local ordinary would order for the diocese:[144]

- Development and Peace
- Needs of the Church in the Holy Land
- The Pope's Pastoral Works
- Needs of the Church in Canada
- World Mission Sunday

CORRESPONDING CANON OF THE EASTERN CODE: CANON 1014. The Eastern code states very simply that the eparchial bishop can order special collections for the Church in all churches habitually open to the Christian faithful. It makes no reference to oratories, churches belonging to religious, the more specific designation of the offering (for specific parochial, diocesan, national, or universal projects), or to the involvement of the eparchial curia.

---

[143] http://www.usccb.org/finance/2008-2009%20COLLECTION%20SCHEDULE.pdf (December 1, 2008)

[144] CANADIAN CONFERENCE OF CATHOLIC BISHOPS, *Ordo, 2008-2009*, Ottawa, CCCB Publications, 2008, p. 392.

OFFERINGS TO ADMINISTRATORS; OFFERINGS REFUSED;
OFFERINGS REQUIRING PERMISSION;
APPLYING INTENTIONS OF DONORS

> **Can. 1267 – §1. Unless the contrary is established, offerings given to superiors or administrators of any ecclesiastical juridic person, even a private one, are presumed given to the juridic person itself.**
>
> **§2. The offerings mentioned in §1 cannot be refused except for a just cause and, in matters of greater importance if it concerns a public juridic person, with the permission of the ordinary; the permission of the same ordinary is required to accept offerings burdened by a modal obligation or condition, without prejudice to the prescript of can. 1295.**
>
> **§3. Offerings given by the faithful for a certain purpose can be applied only for that same purpose.**

Canon 1267 concerns the receiving of offerings by juridic persons who must use them properly. It is important to understand that a juridic person is *never* required to accept a gift of any kind; gifts can be refused.[145] At the same time, however, the presumption is that an offering will be accepted. This is why the canon requires a just cause to refuse a gift and, if the gift is of greater importance, also the permission of the ordinary.

Canon 1267 §1 explains that offerings given to superiors or administrators of any ecclesiastical juridic person (public or private) are presumed to be given to the juridic person itself, unless the contrary is established.[146] Like any presumption, this can be overturned

---

[145] Note that canon 1302 §1 requires the refusal of a pious trust if the donor expressly and enirely prohibits the involvement of the ordinary.

[146] Several changes were made in this canon as a result of recommendations on the 1977 *Schema*. The *Schema* had said, "Unless the contrary is proven (*probetur*)," which was replaced with "Unless the contrary is established (*constet*)." The revision added the clarification that §1 of the canon also applies to *private* juridic persons, but deleted reference to gifts given to "the assistants" of administrators and superiors of juridic persons. Very importantly, added to the draft legislation was the requirement of a "just cause" to refuse an offering, and of the permission of the ordinary to refuse a gift to which is attached a modal obligation or a condition. (The specification that the involvement of the ordinary only pertains to refusals of gifts by *public* juridic persons was added only after the 1982 draft – i.e., during the private papal study of the proposed legislative text.) Finally, also as a result of consultation on the 1977 *Schema*, §3 was inserted into the canon. *Communicationes,* 12 (1980), pp. 405-406.

by contrary proof (see canons 1584-1586).[147] Related to this norm is canon 531, which says that offerings received when performing a certain parochial function are to be placed in the parochial account, unless in the case of *voluntary offerings* the contrary intention of the donor is certain. The prescripts of canon 531 are to be applied also to parochial vicars (canon 551).[148] Thus, if a pastor, parochial vicar, or visiting cleric assists at a wedding in a parish, the *wedding offering* is to be placed in the parish account; he may retain an additional *voluntary offering* if the donor certainly intends it as a personal gift. Also related to this norm is canon 510 §4, which legislates that offerings (*eleemosynae*) given to a church which is both parochial and capitular are presumed to be given to the parish and not to the chapter, unless it is otherwise evident.

Canon 1267 §2 says that the offerings given to superiors or administrators of juridic persons can be refused only for a just cause.[149] In matters of great importance,[150] an offering given to the superior or administrator of a *public* juridic person can be refused

---

[147] On April 6, 1920, the APOSTOLIC SIGNATURA declared that the presumption of CIC/1917, canon 1536 §1, the predecessor of canon 1267, applies also in the case of goods given before the promulgation of the 1917 code. *AAS*, 12 (1921), p. 252.

[148] See JAMES H. PROVOST and RICHARD A. HILL, "Stole Fees," in *The Jurist*, 85 (1985), pp. 321-324.

[149] A "just cause" for refusing a gift may be that the gift is given with perpetual conditions attached. The *coetus De bonis Ecclesiae temporalibus* questioned the advisability of establishing perpetual non-autonomous pious foundations (canon 1303 §1, 2°), so the law only provides that these be established "for a long period of time, to be determined by particular law." This differs from CIC/1917, canon 1544 §1 which said that they can be established "perpetually or for a long period of time." See the commentary on canon 1303.

[150] The code does not define what is meant by a gift of "great importance." Reference may be made to a similar phrase in canon 1277, which requires the counsel of the diocesan finance council and the college of consultors before the diocesan bishop places "non-routine" acts of ordinary diocesan administration "which are more important in light of the economic condition of the diocese," but where the meaning of the phrase "more important" is also not explained. It may be reasonable to hold as a rule of thumb that the "matters of greater importance" in canon 1267 would involve gifts whose value surpasses the minimum amount set by the conference of bishops for the alienation of ecclesiastical goods (see canon 1292 §1). In addition, it may also happen that a gift is considered to be of greater importance if a certain notoriety is attached to it or its donor. In the final analysis, the decision on the meaning of the term rests with the person wishing to refuse the gift, unless its meaning has been certainly defined by a higher authority.

only for a just cause *and* with the permission of the ordinary.[151] This permission of the ordinary is not required if a private juridic person wishes to refuse an offering; presumably, the statutes would govern such a refusal. Nor is the permission of the local ordinary required for a public juridic person to refuse a gift of lesser importance (only a just cause is required).

The canon adds that same ordinary is also to give his permission to accept offerings burdened by a modal obligation or condition. A "modal obligation" is a particular responsibility undertaken by the recipient of a gift; the failure to fulfill the obligation *does not* result in returning the gift to its donor. A "condition" is a requirement attached to a gift upon the fulfillment of which depends the retention of the gift; the failure to fulfill the condition *does* result in returning the gift to its donor.[152] Further, if the acceptance of such a gift may worsen the patrimonial condition of the public juridic person subject to the diocesan bishop (see canon 1295), the diocesan bishop would need the counsel of the diocesan finance council, the college of consultors, and those concerned (see canon 1292 §1). The patrimonial condition may be threatened when the public juridic person has less discretion or independence after accepting the gift.

Canon 1267 §3 requires that offerings given by the faithful for a certain purpose be applied only for that same purpose. Offerings given for a specific purpose are "contractual" upon acceptance (see canon 1290, on the code's general acceptance of civil law provisions on contracts). If there is some doubt about the donor's intention,[153]

---

[151] CIC/1917, canon 1536 §2 had required the permission of the local ordinary to refuse any offering, not only those "of greater importance." CIC/1917, canon 1536 §3 indicated an action for damages from the illegitimate refusal of a gift; this is omitted from the revised law.

[152] ROBERT T. KENNEDY distinguishes a gift with a "modal obligation" attached from a gift with a "condition" attached: "A modal obligation, according to Roman law whence the term is derived, is an obligation undertaken at the time of accepting a gift which is enforceable against the donee but the breach of which does not result in reversion of the gift to the donor. A conditional gift, on the other hand, conditions transfer of ownership upon fulfillment of the condition; breach results in a reversion of ownership to the donor." In "Temporal Goods," p. 1469.

[153] The intention of the donor is highlighted in a number of canons: 121; 122; 123; 326 §2; 531; 616 §1; 706, 3°; 954; 1267 §3; 1284 §2, 3°; 1300; 1302 §1; 1303 §2; 1304 §1; 1307 §1; and 1310 §2.

recourse should be made to the donor; if this is not possible, recourse would be made to the ordinary since he is the "executor of all pious wills," both *mortis causa* and *inter vivos* (canon 1301 §1). Advance dialogue between the potential donor and the intended recipient will provide clarification and prevent eventual confusion concerning the donor's intention. In a related vein, canon 1287 §2 requires administrators to render an account to the faithful concerning the goods offered by them to the Church; this will show that administrators have complied with donors' intentions.

If harm comes to the juridic person because its superior or administrator refused the offering without the permission of the ordinary, the superior or administrator is obliged to repair the damage (see canon 128).[154]

CORRESPONDING CANON OF THE EASTERN CODE: CANON 1016. The Eastern law contains the same basic legislation as Latin canon 1267 but modifies the sequence of the paragraphs, placing first what corresponds to Latin canon 1267 §3. Since the Eastern code does not distinguish public and private juridic persons, the permission of the hierarch and a just cause are required in matters of greater importance in order for any juridic person to refuse an offering.

PRESCRIPTION (IN GENERAL)

Can. 1268 – The Church recognizes prescription as a means of acquiring temporal goods and freeing oneself from them, according to the norm of cann. 197-199.

Canon 1268 recognizes prescription as a means of acquiring the ownership of temporal goods and of losing the ownership of temporal goods, in accord with legal norms, by the passing of a

---

[154] CIC/1917, canon 1536 §3 had said that the unlawful refusal of an offering by a superior gives rise to an action for a *restitutio in integrum* or to indemnity, according to the losses sustained by the refusal. This retaliatory action is not mentioned in the 1983 code.

period of time. Specific norms applying canon 1268 are found in canons 1269 and 1270.[155]

Canon 197 defines prescription as "a means of acquiring or losing a subjective right as well as of freeing oneself from obligations"; it adds that "[t]he Church receives prescription as it is in civil legislation of the nation in question, without prejudice to the exceptions which are established in the canons of this Code." In other words, canon 197 "canonizes" the civil legislation on prescription, except when civil law contradicts canon law. Canons 1269 and 1270 identify situations where canon law takes precedence over civil law.

It is important for administrators of ecclesiastical goods to be aware of secular legislation on prescription. It is possible that canon law contains provisions beyond, or contrary to, the secular legislation.

Four conditions are necessary for prescription to occur: (1) the object must actually be held;[156] (2) the object must be held in good faith for the entire time;[157] (3) the object must be subject to prescription;[158] and (4) the time required by law must have passed.

Prescription is a means to acquire temporal goods, but it is also a means whereby ecclesiastical goods may be lost through lack of oversight. Administrators have a special obligation to exercise vigilance so that ecclesiastical goods are not lost (canon 1284 §2, 1°), so they must take care that such goods are not lost carelessly by prescription.

---

[155] The 1917 code had placed all the canons on prescription among the canons governing temporal goods: CIC/1917, canons 1508-1512. The *coetus De bonis Ecclesiae temporalibus* on June 5, 1967 recommended that the revised code place the common norms about prescription among the general norms of the code, and place particular norms concerning prescription among the related specific canons. *Communicationes,* 36 (2004), pp. 251-252. As a result, the 1983 code places general norms on prescription (which pertains to more than only temporal goods) in *Book I: General Norms* (canons 197-199). See 1977 *Schema,* Preface, p. 4.

[156] This reflects *Regula iuris* 3: "Sine possessione praescriptio non procedit."

[157] This reflects *Regula iuris* 2: "Possessor malae fidei ullo tempore non praescribit."

[158] The 1983 code indicates that Mass offerings and obligations are not subject to prescription (see canon 199, 5°). CIC/1917, canon 1509 had indicated three temporal goods not subject to prescription: (1) stipends and offerings for Masses; (2) ecclesiastical benefices without title; and (3) payment of the *cathedraticum.*

CORRESPONDING CANON OF THE EASTERN CODE: CANON 1017. The Eastern code omits the words "as a means of acquiring temporal goods and freeing oneself from them" and simply explains that temporal goods are subject to prescription according to Eastern canons 1540-1547. Eastern canon 1540 (which corresponds to Latin canon 197) recognizes prescription as it is in civil law "unless common law establishes otherwise." Eastern canon 1542 (which corresponds to Latin canon 199) adds that "rights that directly regard the spiritual life of the Christian faithful" are not subject to prescription.

PRESCRIPTION OF SACRED OBJECTS

> **Can. 1269 – If sacred objects are privately owned, private persons can acquire them through prescription, but it is not permitted to employ them for profane uses unless they have lost their dedication or blessing; if they belong to a public ecclesiastical juridic person, however, only another public ecclesiastical juridic person can acquire them.**

Canon 1269 concerns sacred objects[159] acquired through prescription by both private persons and public ecclesiastical juridic persons. Sacred objects are "designated for divine worship by dedication or blessing;" they are to be treated with reverence and "are not to be employed for profane or inappropriate use even if they are owned by private persons" (canon 1171). Persons who profane a sacred object, movable or immovable, are to be punished with a just penalty (canon 1376).[160] Sacred objects owned by a public juridic person are ecclesiastical goods; those owned by a private juridic person or a physical person are not ecclesiastical goods (see canon 1257 §1).

The code identifies several sacred objects: sacred images (canon 1188), sacred relics (canon 1190), sacred places (i.e., "those which are designated for divine worship or for the burial of the faith-

---

[159] For further reflections on sacred objects, see SCHOUPPE, pp. 55-60.

[160] This penal law is preceptive (see canon 1343) and indeterminate (see canon 1315 §2).

ful by a dedication or blessing which the liturgical books prescribe for this purpose" (canon 1205). In its treatment of sacred places, the code mentions churches (canons 1214-1222), oratories (canons 1223-1225, 1229), private chapels (canons 1226-1229), shrines (canons 1230-1234), altars (canons 1235-1239), and cemeteries (canons 1240-1243).

Sacred places can be secularized. Canon 1212 legislates: "Sacred places lose their dedication or blessing if they have been destroyed in large part, or if they have been turned over permanently to profane use by decree of the competent ordinary or in fact." Canon 1222 contains norms specifically for the relegation of churches "to profane but not sordid use." The code contains no norms for the secularization of other sacred objects.

If sacred objects are owned by a public juridic person, only another public ecclesiastical juridic person can acquire them through prescription, even if the civil law were to determine the contrary. The sacred objects owned by a public juridic person are *ecclesiastical goods* in the sense of canon 1257 §1 and, as such, can be acquired through prescription only by another public juridic person. If the sacred object is immovable property or precious movable property which belongs to the Apostolic See, the period of prescription is 100 years; if the sacred object is immovable property or precious movable property which belongs to another public juridic person, the prescription period is 30 years (canon 1270). Otherwise, the period of time for the prescription of a sacred object is determined by the civil law (see canon 197).

If sacred objects are owned privately (whether by physical persons or private juridic persons), private (physical and juridic) persons can acquire them by prescription but they cannot be used for profane purposes unless they have lost their dedication or blessing.[161] Of course, privately owned sacred objects can also be acquired by public juridic persons. The time period for prescription of sacred objects owned by private (physical and juridic) persons is determined by the civil law (see canon 197).

---

[161] This reflects *Regula iuris* 51: "Semel Deo dicatum non est ad usus humanos ulterius transferendum."

CORRESPONDING CANON OF THE EASTERN CODE: CANON 1018.
The Eastern law basically repeats the discipline of Latin canon 1269
but inserts a definition of sacred objects: they are objects "which have
been destined for divine worship by dedication or blessing."

PRESCRIPTION PERIODS

**Can. 1270 – If they belong to the Apostolic See, immov-
able property, precious movable objects, and personal
or real rights and actions are prescribed by a period of
a hundred years; if they belong to another public ecclesiastical juridic person, they are prescribed by a period
of thirty years.**

Canon 1270 identifies the time periods required for acquiring
immovable property, precious movable objects (some of which may
be sacred objects), and personal or real rights and legal actions by
means of prescription. There is no canonically prescribed time period for the prescription of "non-precious" movable goods (including
non-precious movable "sacred" goods).

If the goods identified in canon 1270 belong to the Apostolic
See,[162] the prescription period is 100 years. If they belong to another
public juridic person, the prescription period is 30 years.[163] These
time periods exist in the universal law of the Church; they are not
necessarily the periods for prescription which exist in the civil law.
If there is a conflict between canon law and civil law, the canon law

---

[162] The "Apostolic See" is defined in canon 361: "In this Code, the term Apostolic See
or Holy See refers not only to the Roman Pontiff but also to the Secretariat of State,
the Council for the Public Affairs of the Church, and other institutes of the Roman
Curia, unless it is otherwise apparent from the nature of the matter or the context
of the words." In canon 1270, the Apostolic See includes all these institutes of the
Roman Curia. In canon 113 §1, however, the Apostolic See means only the Roman
Pontiff. See the commentary on canon 1255.

[163] See canons 200-203 on the computation of time. FRANCIS G. MORRISEY comments:
"The canons on prescription might easily apply in the case of a diocese that was
divided. Thus, for instance, until the period of thirty years has elapsed, the new
diocese could remain subject to claims arising from the former diocese for the period
before the division took place unless other provisions were made at the time of the
reorganization." In "Acquiring Temporal Goods," p. 598. Obviously, the same applies
in the case of dividing other public juridic persons.

prevails from the standpoint of the Church (see canon 197), but the civil law will likely prevail in secular society.

The prescription period for other ecclesiastical goods (i.e., those which are not immovable property, precious movable objects, and personal or real rights and actions) are determined by civil law (canon 197),[164] even if these goods belong to the Apostolic See or a public juridic person. The civil law also determines the prescription period for *all* temporal goods belonging to private juridic persons which, by reason of canon 1257 §1, are not termed "ecclesiastical goods."

PRECIOUS OBJECTS. This canon does not define precisely what is meant by precious objects, perhaps in order to allow its meaning to surface with more precision in practice and to allow local applications.[165] Yet, the code does describe "precious images" as "those distinguished by age, art, or veneration" (canon 1189).

The code requires that mention of precious (and culturally

---

[164] MARIANO LÓPEZ ALARCÓN mentions other periods of prescription still operative: "According to the authors, the privilege of one hundred years prescription periods on behalf of the Friars Minor, the Capuchins, and the Cistercians, and a sixty year prescription period for the Benedictines and the mendicants, were still in effect according to canon 4 of the *CIC*/17. The same criterion applies in virtue of canon 4 of the *CIC*/83." In "Temporal Goods," p. 717, fn. 3.

During the consultation process on the 1977 *Schema*, some had suggested that the revised law lessen the prescription periods from 100 years and 30 years (which repeats the prescription periods of CIC/1917, canon 1511). The *coetus De bonis Ecclesiae temporalibus* saw no reason to make any reduction in these time periods. The *coetus* also rejected the recommendation to forbid prescription of any good owned by the Apostolic See. The *coetus* likewise rejected the recommendation that canon law follow the civil law on the prescription of objects mentioned in this canon and owned by public juridic persons; the group reasoned that this would cause too much disparity. *Communicationes*, 12 (1980), p. 407.

[165] On April 11, 1971, the SACRED CONGREGATION FOR THE CLERGY issued a letter to the presidents of episcopal conferences on the care of the historico-artistic heritage of the Church. It asks that "[a]ncient works of sacred art should always and everywhere be taken care of so that they will richly contribute to divine worship and support of the active participation of the People of God in the sacred liturgy." It calls upon diocesan curias to be vigilant, in accord with norms issued by the ordinary, that an inventory be made of sacred edifices and things which are noteworthy artistically and historically; a copy of the inventory, with eventual changes, should be preserved in the church and the diocesan curia. Changes made in sacred places to reflect the liturgical reform should follow the vote of the commission for sacred art, the commission for sacred liturgy, perhaps the commission for sacred music, and the advice of experts. Attention should also be given to civil law for the protection of more notable artistic works. In *AAS*, 63 (1971), pp. 315-318; *CLD*, vol. 7, pp. 821-824.

valuable) movable goods must be made in the inventory of ecclesiastical goods (canon 1283, 2°). It legislates that the permission of the Apostolic See is required for the valid alienation of "goods precious for artistic or historical reasons" (canon 1292 §2; see canon 638 §4). It may be helpful to recall the discipline of the 1917 code which defined "precious temporal goods" as those "which have a notable worth by reason of artistic value, historical value, or material value" (CIC/1917, canon 1497 §2),[166] much as the 1983 code describes "precious images."

It is obvious that precious objects are not to be identified necessarily with sacred objects (i.e., those "designated for divine worship by dedication or blessing," canon 1171); not all sacred objects are precious objects, though some sacred objects are also precious objects. It is equally obvious that precious objects are not so designated based on their financial value, since the code requires the permission of the Apostolic See to alienate any precious goods of any value (see canon 1292 §2). Although some goods may have small financial value, they may still be considered precious objects by the law of the Church.

CORRESPONDING CANON OF THE EASTERN CODE: CANON 1019. The Eastern canon reflects the discipline of Latin canon 1270 but makes two additions. First, it defines precious movable property as "those things which are of great importance on account of art, history, or subject matter." Second, it adds that immovable property, precious movable property, and personal or real rights and actions

---

[166] The Pontifical Commission for Preserving the Patrimony of Art and History exists within the Congregation for the Clergy. It "has the duty of acting as curator for the artistic and historical patrimony of the whole Church." (*Pastor bonus*, art. 99; see arts. 100-104) See DANTE BALBONI, "La conservazione e la tutela dei monumenti e dei beni artistici," in *Monitor ecclesiasticus*, 111 (1986), pp. 109-121; CONCEPCIÓN PRESAS BARROSA, "El patrimonio artístico de la Iglesia en el 'Codex iuris canonici' y en el 'Codex canonum Ecclesiarum orientalium:' Aproximaciones al respecto," in *Ius in vita et in missione Ecclesiae*, Vatican City, Libreria editrice Vaticana, 1994, pp. 791-801; GIORGIO FELICIANI, "La notion de bien culturel en droit canonique," in *L'année canonique*, 47 (2005), 63-74; GIORGIO FELICIANI, "La nozione di bene culturale nell'ordinamento canonico," in *Iustitia in caritate: Miscellanea di studi in onore di Velasio de Paolis*, James J. Conn and Luigi Sabbarese (eds.), Rome, Urbaniana University Press, 2005, pp. 445-455; SCHOUPPE, pp. 60-63.

are prescribed by a period of 50 years "if they belong to some Church
sui iuris or eparchy." It maintains for such goods the prescription
periods of 100 years (if they belong to the Apostolic See) and of 30
years (if they belong to other juridic persons).

DIOCESAN ASSISTANCE TO THE APOSTOLIC SEE

> **Can. 1271 – By reason of the bond of unity and charity
> and according to the resources of their dioceses, bishops
> are to assist in procuring those means which the Apos-
> tolic See needs, according to the conditions of the times,
> so that it is able to offer service properly to the universal
> Church.**

This canon has no predecessor in the 1917 code, nor was it
included in the 1977 *Schema*. It was developed after many of those
consulted on the 1977 *Schema* had suggested that the revised law
mention the moral obligation of dioceses to make contributions to assist the Apostolic See in fulfilling its function.[167] Canon 1271 reminds
diocesan bishops of their bond of unity and charity[168] by which they
are to assist the needs of the Apostolic See (see canon 361), according to contemporary conditions, so that it can offer proper service to
the universal Church. This assistance is not a tax; it is voluntary. It
comes directly from the juridic person of the diocese, not from the
physical person of the diocesan bishop.

Canon 1266 gives local ordinaries the right to order a special
collection for "universal" initiatives. The support of the Apostolic
See envisioned in canon 1271 is more than any special collection
gathered in accord with canon 1266, though the revenue gathered

---

[167] *Communicationes,* 12 (1980), pp. 411-412. When there was some discussion concerning whether the canon should mention "ordinaries" or "bishops" in order to include
religious ordinaries, the *coetus* selected "bishops" since they have the ability to order
a special collection (in all churches, even those of religious). This may reveal that, at
the time, the consultors envisioned assistance to the Holy See being achieved through
a special collection rather than in some other fashion.

[168] See *Lumen gentium,* n. 23; *Christus Dominus,* n. 3; *Ecclesiae sanctae,* I, n. 5. See E.
MIRAGOLI, "L'obolo di San Pietro, tra le esigenze della carità e dell'amministrazone
(c. 1271)," in *Quaderni di diritto ecclesiale,* 5 (1992), pp. 67-77.

through such a collection may also assist the service of the Apostolic See. Dioceses in the United States have the annual "Peter's Pence" collection, and dioceses in Canada have the annual collection for "The Pope's Pastoral Works." These collections, no doubt, help the faithful recall that they are "members of the diocese and of the universal Church," something which every pastor must make a special effort to emphasize (canon 529 §2).

This canon was invoked by the Secretary of State in a letter dated March 25, 1987 when he asked diocesan bishops to come to the assistance of the Apostolic See in the midst of a budget deficit. Similarly, canon 640 was invoked in a letter dated June 29, 1987 to religious institutes.[169] Later, at a Vatican meeting of the presidents of the world's conferences of bishops on April 8-9, 1991 to address the financial crisis of the Holy See, Archbishop Angelo Sodano, pro-Secretary of State, implored the world's bishops to provide economic assistance. Invoking the norm of canon 1271, the presidents of the conferences of bishops thereafter issued an open letter to their brother bishops throughout the world, inviting them to offer financial help to assist the services which the Holy See renders to the universal Church.[170]

Just as canon 1271 invites voluntary assistance to be provided by bishops to support the mission of the Apostolic See, so canon 1274 §3 invites bishops to establish a common fund through which voluntary assistance can be given by richer dioceses to poorer ones.

CORRESPONDING CANON OF THE EASTERN CODE. None.

BENEFICES TO BE ELIMINATED

Can. 1272 – In regions where benefices properly so called still exist, it is for the conference of bishops, through appropriate norms agreed to and approved by the Apostolic See, to direct the governance of such benefices in

---

[169] MORRISEY, "Temporal Goods," p. 717.

[170] The address of Archbishop Sodano and the open letter to the world's bishops from the presidents of the episcopal conferences are reported in *La documentation catholique,* 88 (1991), pp. 553-554.

> such a way that the income and even, insofar as possible,
> the endowment itself of the benefices are gradually trans-
> ferred to the institute mentioned in can. 1274, §1.

Canon 1272 concerns benefices.[171] A benefice was defined in
canon 1409 of the 1917 code as "a juridic entity, permanently constituted or erected by the competent ecclesiastical authority, and consisting of a sacred office and the right to receive the revenue accruing
from the endowment of such office." The 1917 code had devoted 80
canons to benefices (CIC/1917, canons 1409-1488), but the 1983 code
mentions benefices only in canon 1272. Vatican II in *Presbyterorum
ordinis*, n. 20 had said that priests are entitled to a just remuneration
and called for the gradual elimination of benefices:

> Completely devoted as they are to the service of God in
> the fulfillment of the office entrusted to them, priests are
> entitled to receive a just remuneration. For "laborers de-
> serve their wages" (Lk 10:7) and "the Lord commanded
> that they who proclaim the Gospel should get their living
> from the Gospel" (1 Cor 9:14). For this reason, insofar
> as provision is not made from some other source for the
> just remuneration of priests, the faithful are bound by a
> real obligation of seeing to it that the necessary provision
> for a decent and fitting livelihood for the priests is avail-
> able. This obligation arises from the fact that it is for the
> benefit of the faithful that priests are working. Bishops
> are bound to warn the faithful of their obligation in this
> connection. They should also, either individually for their
> own dioceses or better still by acting together for a com-
> mon territory, see to it that rules are drawn up by which
> due provision is made for the decent support of those who
> hold or have held any office in the serving of God.

---

[171] Interestingly, canon 1272 is placed in *Title I: The Acquisition of Goods*, although
the discipline of the canon focuses on how to administer already existing benefices
and to transfer their earnings and even the corpus to the institute of canon 1274 §1.
Inasmuch as canon 1272 invites, insofar as possible, the elimination of benefices, it
is about administration of existing goods, not the acquisition of new goods.

Taking into consideration the conditions of different places and times as well as the nature of the office they hold, the remuneration to be received by each of the priests should be fundamentally the same for all living in the same circumstances. It should be in keeping with their status and in addition should give priests the means not only of providing properly for the salary of those who devote themselves to their service but also of personally assisting in some way those who are in need. The Church has always from its very beginnings held this ministry to the poor in great honor. Moreover, priests' remuneration should be such as to allow the priest a proper holiday each year. The bishop should see to it that priests are able to have a holiday.

It is, however, to the office that sacred ministers fulfill that the greatest importance must be attached. For this reason the so-called system of benefices is to be abandoned or else reformed in such a way that the part that has to do with the benefice – that is, the right to the revenues attached to an endowment of the office – shall be regarded as secondary and the principal emphasis in law given to the ecclesiastical office itself. This should in the future be understood as any office conferred in a permanent fashion and to be exercised for a spiritual purpose.[172]

The implementation of this conciliar directive on benefices is treated in *Ecclesiae sanctae*, I, n.8 which mandated:

Patriarchal Synods and Episcopal Conferences should see to it that norms be established, either for individual dioceses, or for several of them together, or for the whole

---

[172] FLANNERY I, pp. 898-899. See also *Presbyterorum ordinis*, n. 21 (which is the source of the discipline found in canon 1274); and *Christus Dominus*, n. 28 (which invites priests to be mindful that their worldly goods are closely connected with their sacred office, so they should contribute liberally to the material needs of the diocese as directed by the bishop).

territory, by which suitable provision is made for the sustenance of all clerics who exercise or have exercised an office for the service of the People of God. The remuneration to be given to clerics should in the first place be the same for all those who work under the same conditions, taking into account both the nature of the work and the circumstances of time and place; and the remuneration should be sufficient so that clerics can lead a decent life and be in a position to help the poor.

The reform of the system of benefices is entrusted to the Commission for the Revision of the Code of Canon Law. In the meantime the Bishops, after having sought the advice of their councils of priests, should see to it that a fair distribution of goods is provided for, including the income from benefices.[173]

In addition, the 1967 Synod of Bishops also addressed the topic of the remuneration of priests, and indicated that their income should be separated from their acts of ministry, especially their sacramental ones:

The remuneration of priests, to be determined certainly in a spirit of evangelical poverty, but as far as possible equitable and sufficient, is a duty of justice and ought to include social security. Excessive differences in this matter must be removed, especially among priests of the same diocese or jurisdiction, account also being taken of the average condition of the people of the region.

It seems greatly to be desired that the Christian people be gradually instructed in such a way that priests' incomes may be separated from the acts of their ministry, especially sacramental ones.[174]

---

[173] *CLD*, vol. 6, p. 269. See also *Ecclesiae sanctae*, I, n. 18 (on the implementation of *Christus Dominus*, n. 28).

[174] SYNOD OF BISHOPS, document on the Ministerial Priesthood *Ultimis temporibus* (November 30, 1967), in *AAS*, 63 (1971), pp. 920-921; English translation in FLANNERY 2, pp. 692-693 (=1967 SYNOD OF BISHOPS).

The *coetus De iure patrimoniali Ecclesiae* began its work of revising the code with lengthy discussion about eliminating extensive legislation about benefices.[175]

Canon 1272 reflects the conciliar directive that benefices gradually be eliminated or at least reformed.[176] It does not, however, legislate that existing benefices must be suppressed immediately. Rather, it calls upon the conference of bishops to direct the governance of any existing benefices, such that the income and, insofar as possible, even the corpus of the endowment of each benefice are transferred gradually to a diocesan "institute for clergy support" (canon 1274 §1). The law presumes that this diocesan institute will succeed benefices in providing clergy remuneration. The norms of the conference of bishops by which benefices are to be eliminated are to be agreed to and approved by the Apostolic See. If such norms are not developed by the conference of bishops and approved, the existing practices on benefices, operative under the 1917 code, will necessarily remain in effect.[177]

Given the conciliar mandate to suppress benefices and the legislation of canon 1272, it is not envisioned that any new benefices may be established.

Also reflecting *Presbyterorum ordinis*, n. 20, the 1983 code says that clerics are to receive remuneration (*remuneratio*) sufficient to provide their own needs and to pay those providing necessary services. They are also to receive social security to assist in case of illness, incapacity, or old age. Special consideration is to be given to permanent deacons.[178] The pertinent canon states:

Can. 281 – §1. When clerics dedicate themselves to ecclesiastical ministry, they deserve remuneration which is consistent with their condition, taking into account the

---

[175] *Communicationes,* 36 (2004), pp. 236-240.

[176] POPE PAUL VI reserved to himself the conferral of benefices in the Diocese of Rome following Vatican Council II: *motu proprio Romae dioecesis* On the Conferral of Ecclesiastical Benefices in Rome (June 30,1968), in *AAS*, 60 (1968), pp. 377-381; *CLD*, vol. 7, pp. 890-894.

[177] DE PAOLIS, *De bonis Ecclesiae temporalibus*, p. 73; see SCHOUPPE, pp. 145-151.

[178] Presumably, the norm of 281 §3 would also apply to celibate permanent deacons, *mutatis mutandis*.

nature of their function and the conditions of places and times, and by which they can provide for the necessities of their life as well as for the equitable payment of those whose services they need.

§2. Provision must also be made so that they possess that social assistance which provides for their needs suitably if they suffer from illness, incapacity, or old age.

§3. Married deacons who devote themselves completely to ecclesiastical ministry deserve remuneration by which they are able to provide for the support of themselves and their families. Those who receive remuneration by reason of a civil profession which they exercise or have exercised, however, are to take care of the needs of themselves and their families from the income derived from it.

Canon 1274 §§1-2 proposes the establishment of a diocesan "institute for clergy support" and the establishment of another (diocesan or super-diocesan) "institute for clergy social security."[179]

Clearly, the discipline of canons 281 and 1274 is intended to succeed the benefice system of support enshrined in the 1917 code.

PARTICULAR LAW FOR THE UNITED STATES AND CANADA. Benefices do not exist in the United States or Canada.[180] Therefore, no action has been taken by the conferences of bishops to implement canon 1272.

CORRESPONDING CANON OF THE EASTERN CODE. None.

---

[179] It was certainly the intention of the *coetus De bonis Ecclesiae temporalibus* that funds from benefices be transferred to the "institute for clergy support" in canon 1274 §1. The *coetus* envisioned that the revised code would place focus on ecclesiastical offices, not benefices. See the preface to the 1977 *Schema*, p. 5.

[180] Nonetheless, on September 26, 1921, PIETRO CARDINAL GASPARRI, president of the Pontifical Commission for the Authentic Interpretation of the Canons of the Code, wrote to the Apostolic Delegate in the United States that "a parish is always an ecclesiastical benefice according to c. 1411, 5°, whether it has the proper endowment (resources or revenue) as described and defined in c. 1410, or even if lacking such endowment (resources or revenue) it be erected according to the provisions of c. 1415, 3°."

In a letter dated November 10, 1922, the Apostolic Delegate communicated Cardinal Gasparri's conclusions to the bishops of the United States with his own comments: "It is evident from this official answer that all the parishes of the United States having the three necessary qualifications, viz., (1) a resident pastor; (2) endowment (resources or revenue according to the provisions of canons 1410 or 1415, §3); and (3) boundaries, are not only parishes in the strict canonical sense, but are also ecclesiastical benefices." In *CLD*, vol. 1, pp. 150-151.

Nonetheless, parishes in the United States have not been regarded as benefices.

CHAPTER FOUR

THE ADMINISTRATION OF GOODS
(Title II: Canons 1273-1289)

Title II of *Book V* contains seventeen canons relating to the Church's administration of ecclesiastical goods. Canon 1273 asserts that the Roman Pontiff, in virtue of his primacy of governance, is the supreme administrator and steward of all ecclesiastical goods. Canon 1274 calls for dioceses to establish three special funds: for clergy support, for clergy social security, and for other purposes (i.e., to fulfill obligations to other Church ministers, to meet diocesan needs, and to assist poorer dioceses), unless these purposes are being fulfilled in another way. Canon 1275 says that any inter-diocesan aggregate of goods is to be administered according to norms approved by the participating bishops. Canon 1276 requires ordinaries to exercise vigilance over ecclesiastical goods of public juridic persons subject to them, and to issue special instructions ordering their administration. Canon 1277 requires the diocesan bishop to receive the advice of the diocesan finance council and the college of consultors before placing "non-routine" acts of ordinary diocesan administration which are more important in light of the local economy, and to receive the consent of the same two bodies to place acts of extraordinary diocesan administration (as such extraordinary acts are defined by the episcopal conference). Canon 1278 gives the diocesan bishop the option of entrusting certain acts concerning administration to his diocesan finance officer. Canon 1279 explains that the administration of ecclesiastical goods pertains to the one who immediately governs the juridic person which owns them; if a juridic person does not have its own administrator, the ordinary is to appoint suitable persons to perform the administrator's role. Canon 1280 mandates each juridic person to have its own finance council, or at least two financial consultants. The remaining nine canons of Title II identify several specific responsibilities of administrators: to obtain a special written faculty before placing acts of extraordinary administration (canon 1281); to follow the norm of law in fulfilling their function in the name of the Church (canon 1282); to take an oath and to make an inventory before beginning their function (canon 1283); to fulfill their function with all the diligence of a good householder in very specific ways (canon 1284); to avoid making donations for piety or charity except from movable goods not belonging to the stable patrimony and within the limits of ordinary administration (canon 1285); to observe meticulously civil labor laws and social policies according to the teaching of the Church, and to pay a just and decent wage (canon 1286); to render appropriate financial reports (canon 1287); to obtain written permission from the ordinary to initiate or contest civil litigation (canon 1288); and to avoid relinquishing their administrative function on their own initiative (canon 1289).

Other norms in *Book V* on the administration of temporal goods are contained in Title IV.

These canons reflect the discipline of the 1917 *Code of Canon Law* in its canons 1182 §2; 1518-1519; 1520 §3; 1521-1528; and 1535. Several canons have no predecessor in the first code: canons 1274-1275; 1278; 1280; 1281 §2; 1284 §2, 2°, 5°, 8°; and 1284 §3.

Corresponding canons in the 1991 *Code of Canons of the Eastern Churches* are canons 263 §4; 1008 §1; 1021-1026; and 1028-1033. Several Latin canons have no corresponding canon in the Eastern code: canons 1274 §§4-5; 1275; 1278; 1279 §2; 1280; and 1282.

ROMAN PONTIFF AS SUPREME ADMINISTRATOR AND STEWARD OF ALL ECCLESIASTICAL GOODS

Can. 1273 – By virtue of his primacy of governance, the Roman Pontiff is the supreme administrator and steward of all ecclesiastical goods.

Canon 1254 §1 had already expressed the Church's innate right to administer its acquired temporal goods independently from civil power in order to pursue the Church's proper ends. Administration involves three activities: (1) to preserve the goods owned; (2) to help them bear fruit; and (3) to apply these fruits to the purpose(s) for which the goods are owned.[1] Often it pertains to the function of governance (*munus regendi*) in the Church.[2] Administration is not the same as acquiring the goods, but focuses on the useful maintenance of these goods once they have been acquired. Nor is administration the same as alienation, which involves passing ownership of a good to another.

DISTINCT ROLES: LEGAL REPRESENTATIVE, ADMINISTRATOR, SUPERIOR.[3] To understand administration of ecclesiastical goods properly, several considerations must be kept in mind.[4] Ecclesiastical goods (canon 1257 §1) are owned by the public juridic person which has acquired them legitimately (canon 1256). Every public juridic person has a legal representative, an administrator, and a superior(s).[5] These functions are distinct but related.

1. Every public juridic person has its proper legal representative (canon 118). The legal representative acts on behalf of the public

---

[1] DE PAOLIS, *I beni temporali*, pp. 144-145. JOHN J. MYERS says that administration in *Book V* "refers to those actions or sets of actions which are directed to preserving church property; improving property or resources; managing the collections and distribution of income from a variety of sources, including offerings of the faithful and return on investments. It also includes keeping accurate records and properly reporting income and expenses." In "Temporal Goods," p. 870. See also PCLT, *Nota, La funzione dell'autorità*, p. 26.

[2] SIGNIÉ, p. 103; see note 8, below.

[3] See PCLT, *Nota, La funzione dell'autorità*, p. 27, fn. 14.

[4] DE PAOLIS, *I beni temporali*, pp. 148-151; DE PAOLIS, *De bonis Ecclesiae temporalibus*, pp. 78-81. See VINCENZO MOSCA, "Il ruolo della gierarchia nell'ammnistrazione communiale dei beni della Chiesa," in *Iustitia in caritate: Miscellanea di studi in onore di Velasio De Paolis*, James J. Conn and Luigi Sabbarese (eds.), Rome, Urbaniana University Press, 2005, pp. 396-397.

[5] For an extensive consideration of the distinctions among the legal representative, administrator, and superior of a juridic person, see: VELASIO DE PAOLIS, "L'amministrazione dei beni: Soggetti cui è demandata in via immediata e loro funzioni (cc. 1279-1289)," in *I beni temporali della Chiesa*, Studi Giuridici, 50, Vatican City, Libreria editrice Vaticana, 1999, pp. 59-82.

juridic person whom he or she represents in the legal forum, civil and canonical.[6]

Sometimes, the legal representative is also the administrator of the public juridic person.[7]

2. Every public juridic person has its proper administrator (canon 1279).[8] Administration indicates an executive function which an administrator fulfills in the name of the Church and according to canon law and the directives of superiors.[9] Administration

---

[6] "Juridic persons stand trial through their legitimate representatives" (canon 1480 §1; see canon 1419, which requires the appellate tribunal to act as the first instance court in cases concerning the temporal goods of a juridic person represented by the diocesan bishop). The legal representative of a diocese is the diocesan bishop (canon 393), and of a parish is the pastor (canon 532).

[7] The legal representative of a diocese is its diocesan bishop, but the routine administrator of diocesan goods, under the authority of the diocesan bishop, is the diocesan finance officer. The legal representative of the parish is its pastor, who also is the administrator of parochial goods (canon 532). See PCLT, *Nota, La funzione* dell'autorità, p. 27, fn. 14.

[8] The PONTIFICAL COUNCIL FOR LEGISLATIVE TEXTS observes that the term "administration" has two meanings in the law. Some times (e.g., in *Book I* of the Code), it refers to a function proper to ecclesiastical authority whereby acts of governance are placed. Other times (e.g., in *Book V* of the Code: see canon 1279), it refers to economic administration intended to preserve patrimony, to make it bear fruit, and to use it. The Pontifical Council says that one must keep these two senses of "administration" in mind when reading *Book V*, especially its Title II, where the term is used in both senses. Canon 1273, for example, refers to papal power of governance in the Church and over ecclesiastical goods of public juridic persons *rather than* to his economic administration of them. See PCLT, *Nota, La funzione* dell'autorità, p. 26.

[9] See KENNEDY, "Temporal Goods," p. 1474.

VELASIO DE PAOLIS comments: "The administration must be carried out under the supervision of the ordinary or superior. The one who administers church goods has only an executive function which he or she must fulfill according to canon law and the directives of superiors. The latter have supervision over church goods, not their administration. Supervision implies the right to visit, to demand reports, and to prescribe a correct and orderly system of administration in accord with universal, particular, and proper laws. In some cases, supervision is expressed also by authorizations given by a superior authority to carry out administrative acts of a certain gravity or importance (see cc. 1276, 1277, 1281, 1285, 1292)." In "Temporal Goods... Consecrated Life," p. 352.

The "routine" ordinary administration of the diocesan ecclesiastical goods is done by the diocesan finance officer, under the authority of the diocesan bishop (canon 494 §3). See PCLT, *Nota, La funzione* dell'autorità, p. 27, fn. 14.

In religious institutes and their provinces, the administrator of ecclesiastical goods is the finance officer who must be distinct from the respective superior under whose direction the finance officer functions; insofar as possible, even local communities should have a finance officer distinct from the local superior (canon 636 §1). The

does not imply the capacity to dispose of goods on one's own authority. Administrators perform the functions outlined in canons 1284-1289 (see also canon 1283).

Sometimes, the administrator is also the superior of the public juridic person (see canon 1279 §1).[10]

3. Every administrator of a public juridic person has a superior, who ultimately is the Roman Pontiff (see canons 1256, 1273). Superiors are those who oversee the administration of ecclesiastical goods. They exercise vigilance (see canon 1278). Supervision reflects the public nature of ecclesiastical goods owned by public juridic persons, and is done to guarantee the autonomy of public juridic person (even as regards any eventual conflict of interest between the juridic person and its administrator and/or legal representative).[11]

Superiors perform acts of administration which transcend the limit and manner of ordinary administration (see canons 638 §1, 1277, 1281 §§1-2), including acts which may worsen the economic condition of the juridic person (canon 1295). Superiors also give permission for the validity of certain acts of alienation (canons 638, §3, 1291-1294).[12]

---

administration of parochial ecclesiastical goods is done by the pastor (canon 532) who serves under the direction of the diocesan bishop (canon 515 §1). Thus, superiors direct the administrators of ecclesiastical goods belonging to the diocese, the parish, the religious institute, the province, and the canonically erected houses.

[10] For a religious institute, canon 636 §1 permits, but does not recommend, that the local superior may be the finance officer of the local community, and canon 638 §2 says that superiors perform acts of ordinary administration. Canon 741 applies these norms to societies of apostolic life. Canon 718 allows proper law to apply these norms to secular institutes.

[11] PCLT, *Nota,* La funzione dell'autorità, pp. 26-27.

[12] While the diocesan finance officer is the "routine" administrator of diocesan ecclesiastical goods, his or her power is limited to acts of ordinary diocesan administration which are "routine" (i.e., to those which are not more important in light of the economic condition of the diocese). The diocesan bishop (not the diocesan finance officer) alone is able to perform "non-routine" acts of ordinary diocesan administration more important in light of diocesan economic conditions and acts of extraordinary administration (canon 1277). Further, the diocesan bishop alone may alienate diocesan goods (canon 1292 §1) or enter transactions which may worsen the patrimonial condition of the diocese (canon 1295). Admittedly, in all these situations, the diocesan bishop needs the counsel/consent of the others identified in the respective canons.

ROMAN PONTIFF AS SUPREME ADMINISTRATOR AND STEWARD.
Canon 1273 legislates that the Roman Pontiff, who "possesses supreme, full, immediate and universal ordinary power in the Church,
which he is always able to exercise freely" (canon 331; see canons
134 §1; 333) from the moment he accepts his legitimate election
(canon 332), is the supreme administrator (*administrator*) and
steward (*dispensator*)[13] of all ecclesiastical goods (i.e., those which
belong to public juridic persons).[14] His supreme administration and
stewardship is based in his supreme and universal power of governance.[15] He exercises this power of governance in order to protect

---

Likewise, the law assigns the acts of ordinary administration of the goods of a
religious institute to its superior and others identified in proper law (canon 638 §2).
The same proper law is to define acts of extraordinary administration and who can
perform them validly (canon 638 §1). The code requires the written permission of
the competent superior and the consent of the council to perform acts of alienation
and transactions which may worsen the patrimonial condition of a juridic person
(canon 638 §3). See VELASIO DE PAOLIS, "Alcune osservazioni sulla nozione di amministrazione dei beni temporali della Chiesa," in *Periodica*, 88 (1999), pp. 120-123
(=DE PAOLIS, "Alcune osservazioni"); SIGNIÉ, pp. 112-116.

13   JORDAN HITE observes: "Canon 1273 describes the pope as administrator and steward.
Although the term 'steward' is not used in the remainder of the canons in regard to
the administration of church property it is a concept which is useful for explaining
the concept of administration since it refers to all those actions which are intended for
the preservation, development, management, reception, and use of church property.
In a sense an administrator receives church property in trust for the Church and its
works." In "Church Law on Property and Contracts," in *The Jurist*, 44 (1984), p. 120
(=HITE, "Church Law").

14   Canon 1273 speaks of "ecclesiastical goods" which, according to canon 1257 §1, do
not belong to private juridic persons. Therefore, strictly thinking, one concludes that
canon 1273 does not address the relation of the Roman Pontiff to temporal goods
owned by private juridic persons. Yet, inasmuch as private juridic persons are also
persons in the Church (*personae in Ecclesia*), and inasmuch as canon 1256 says the
all juridic persons own goods "[u]nder the supreme authority of the Roman Pontiff,"
it is not unreasonable to suggest that the Roman Pontiff is also the supreme administrator and steward of the temporal goods of private juridic persons. He possesses
supreme, full, immediate, and universal ordinary power in the Church (canon 331)
over all persons, including juridic ones, private and public.
See HUGO A. VON USTINOV, "El régimen canónico de los bienes de propriedad de
las personas juridicas privadas," in *Anuario Argentino de Derecho Canónico*, 13
(2006), p. 210.

15   When reviewing comments on the 1977 *Schema*, the *coetus De bonis Ecclesiae
temporalibus* changed reference to the Roman Pontiff's "jurisdiction" to his "power
of governance." *Communicationes*, 12 (1980), p. 413. See also PCLT, *Nota*, La funzione dell'autorità, pp. 29-31; FRANCESCO SALERNO, "L'amministrazione dei beni: la
funzione primaziale del Romano Pontifice," in *I beni temporali della Chiesa*, Studi
Giuridici, 50, Vatican City, Libreria editrice Vaticana, 1999, pp. 103-140.

ecclesiastical goods so that they achieve their proper purposes. In cases of abuse by an administrator of a public juridic person, he is able to intervene, even directly.[16]

To say that the Roman Pontiff is the supreme administrator and steward of all ecclesiastical goods is *not* to say that he is their owner. He does not have *dominium* over them.[17] Rather, ecclesiastical goods belong to the juridic person which lawfully owns them: "Under the supreme authority of the Roman Pontiff, ownership of goods belongs to that person which has acquired them legitimately" (canon 1256). The relation of the Roman Pontiff to the temporal goods of the Church is an exercise of his universal jurisdiction (see canon 331).[18] Saint Thomas Aquinas had said: "The things of the Church are his as the principal steward; they are not his, however, as lord and possessor."[19]

---

[16] PCLT, *Nota,* La funzione dell'autorità, p. 31.

[17] PCLT, *Nota,* La funzione dell'autorità, p. 30.
On November 22, 1967, the secretary of the *coetus De bonis Ecclesiae temporalibus* recalled the letter of Pope Benedict XIV, *Cum encyclicas,* in which the Roman Pontiff said that, in their common estimation, theologians conclude the pope does not have *dominium* over all ecclesiastical goods, but canonists conclude the opposite. *Communicationes* 36 (2004), p. 288. See also *Communicationes,* 12 (1980), pp. 397-399; DE PAOLIS, "Alcune osservazioni," pp. 104-105; JESUS MIÑAMBRES, "Il Romano Pontifice garante ultimo della destinazione dei beni ecclesiastici," in *Iustitia in caritate: Miscellanea di studi in onore di Velasio de Paolis,* James J. Conn and Luigi Sabbarese (eds.), Rome, Urbaniana University Press, 2005, pp. 431-443.

[18] JOHN A. ABBO and JEROME D. HANNON comment that the right of the Roman Pontiff is similar to the secular right of eminent domain: "In virtue of his position as supreme dispenser of all ecclesiastical property, the Roman Pontiff enjoys a right analogous to the right of eminent domain in reference to the property of subordinate ecclesiastical bodies. He can, in virtue of this power, condone usurpations by the secular authority of the property of all these subordinate ecclesiastical bodies or transfer the property of one of them to another. But in doing so he is required to observe the conditions requisite in the case of the exercise of the right of eminent domain on the part of the secular power, i.e., he must be moved by a proportionately serious reason and he must provide for adequate compensation. No one else in the Church enjoys this power over subordinate bodies subject to their jurisdiction. Religious superiors general cannot transfer the property of one province to another, and bishops cannot transfer the property of one parish to another, no matter how serious a reason they may have for doing so and even though they are willing to provide adequate compensation. Even should secular law recognize such an act on the part of the bishop, as it would if it had granted him incorporation as a corporation sole, his act, in the absence of an apostolic indult, would be canonically invalid and unjust." In *The Sacred Canons,* rev. ed., Saint Louis, B. Herder Book Co., 1957, vol. 2, pp. 710-711.

[19] "Quamvis enim res Ecclesiae sunt eius ut principalis dispensatoris, non tamen sunt eius ut domini et possessoris." *Summa* 2-2ae, q. 100, art. 1, ad sept.

Further, to say that the Roman Pontiff is the supreme administrator of all ecclesiastical goods is *not* to say he is their personal administrator. Each ecclesiastical good has its own administrator, identified by universal law or the statutes of the public juridic person owning them; if the statutes are silent, the ordinary is to appoint an administrator for a three year term, renewable (canon 1279). If the administrator is negligent (canon 1279 §1), the Roman Pontiff (who is also an ordinary: canon 134 §1) has the right to intervene, as does any other appropriate ordinary. Should the Roman Pontiff intervene directly in the administration of some ecclesiastical good, it follows that, depending upon the nature of the papal intervention, the function of the usual administrator may be suspended for the duration of the special papal intervention.[20] Also, like any other ordinary, the Roman Pontiff exercises vigilance over all ecclesiastical goods (canon 1276 §1) and may issue instructions to order the entire matter of their administration (canon 1276 §2).

The Roman Pontiff exercises his role as supreme administrator and steward of all ecclesiastical goods in a number of ways. He promulgates laws (e.g., the *Code of Canon Law*, the *Code of Canons of the Eastern Churches*, the apostolic constitution *Pastor Bonus*). He reserves to himself certain executive activities concerning ecclesiastical goods (e.g., canons 1292 §2; 1308 §1; 1310 §3). He also reserves to himself approval of certain norms regarding ecclesiastical goods (e.g., canons 1264, 1°; 1272). In practice, several dicasteries of the

---

[20] RENÉ METZ comments: "In extraordinary circumstances... particularly in unresolved controversies and in cases of appeal, [the Roman Pontiff] may intervene in view of the good of the persons concerned or of a higher good, and as supreme steward, also himself perform all the acts of administration over these goods which normally belong to the owner. Such an intervention by the Roman Pontiff can then substitute or supercede all action by the owner over these goods...." In "The Temporal Goods of the Church," in *A Guide to the Eastern Code*, George Nedungatt (ed.), Kanonika, 10, Rome, Pontificio Istituto Orientale, p. 692.

JOHN J. MYERS adds that, in light of the doctrine of canon 1273, "the Supreme Pontiff could personally direct the administration of goods of juridic persons in the Church should the well-being of the Church so dictate. He might be called upon to correct abuses or to require sacrifice on the part of some for the greater good." In "Temporal Goods," p. 871.

Apostolic See are involved with the administration of temporal goods in the name of the Roman Pontiff:[21]

1. Congregation for the Clergy – "This Congregation carries out everything that pertains to the Holy See regarding the regulation of ecclesiastical goods, and especially their correct administration; it grants the necessary approvals and *recognitiones*, and it further sees to it that serious thought is given to the support and social security of the clergy." (*Pastor bonus*, art. 98)
   "The congregation deals with those matters that are within the competence of the Holy See... concerning Mass obligations as well as pious wills in general and pious foundations." (*Pastor bonus*, art. 97, 2°)

2. Congregation for Institutes of Consecrated Life and Societies of Apostolic Life – "It deals with everything which, in accordance with the law, belongs to the Holy See concerning... administration of goods" of institutes of consecrated life and societies of apostolic life. (*Pastor bonus*, art. 108 §1)

3. Congregation for the Evangelization of Peoples – "the Congregation administers its own funds and other resources destined for the missions...." (*Pastor bonus*, art. 92)

4. Congregation for the Oriental Churches – "The Congregation for the Oriental Churches considers those matters, whether concerning persons or things, affecting the Catholic Oriental Churches." (*Pastor bonus*, art. 56)

5. Pontifical Commission for Preserving the Patrimony of Art and History – "At the Congregation for the Clergy there exists the Pontifical Commission for Preserving the Patrimony of Art and History that has the duty of acting as curator for the artistic and historical patrimony of the whole Church." (*Pastor bonus*, art. 99)

6. Administration of the Patrimony of the Apostolic See – "It is the function of the Administration of the Patrimony of the Apostolic See to administer the properties owned by the Holy See in order to underwrite the expenses for the Roman Curia to function." (*Pastor bonus*, art. 172; see arts. 173-175)

---

[21] See PCLT, *Nota, La funzione dell'autorità*, pp. 31-32; SCHOUPPE, pp. 179-183,187-191.

7. Prefecture for the Economic Affairs of the Holy See – "The
    Prefecture for the Economic Affairs of the Holy See has the
    function of supervising and governing the temporal goods of
    the administrations that are dependent on the Holy See, or of
    which the Holy See has charge, whatever the autonomy of these
    administrations may happen to be." (*Pastor bonus*, art. 176; see
    arts. 177-179)

In addition to the dicasteries above which serve in the name
of the Roman Pontiff in caring for ecclesiastical goods, mention
should also be made of the Apostolic Camera which functions *sede
Romana vacante*:

> When the Apostolic See falls vacant, it is the right and
> the duty of the cardinal camerlengo of the Holy Roman
> Church, personally or through his delegate, to request,
> from all administrations dependent on the Holy See,
> reports on their patrimonial and economic status as well
> as any information on any extraordinary business that
> may at that time be underway, and, from the Prefecture
> for the Economic Affairs of the Holy See he shall request
> a financial statement on income and expenditures of the
> previous year and the budgetary estimates for the fol-
> lowing year. He is in duty bound to submit these reports
> and estimates to the College of Cardinals. (*Pastor bonus*,
> art. 171 §2)[22]

The Apostolic Camera is involved with oversight of ecclesiastical goods but, inasmuch as it functions when the Petrine see is
vacant, it does not serve in the name of the Roman Pontiff.

CORRESPONDING CANON OF THE EASTERN CODE: CANON 1008
§1. The corresponding Eastern law is situated as the first paragraph
of the second "preliminary canon" on temporal goods. It excludes
the phrase of Latin canon 1273, "By virtue of his primacy of governance."

---

[22] See SECRETARIAT OF STATE, "Regolamento della Camera Apostolica" (March 3,
2008), in *Communicationes*, 40 (2008), pp. 62-80.

INSTITUTES FOR CLERGY; COMMON FUND FOR EMPLOYEES, DIOCESAN NEEDS, ASSISTING POORER DIOCESES

Can. 1274 – §1. Each diocese is to have a special institute which is to collect goods or offerings for the purpose of providing, according to the norm of can. 281, for the support of clerics who offer service for the benefit of the diocese, unless provision is made for them in another way.

§2. Where social provision for the benefit of clergy has not yet been suitably arranged, the conference of bishops is to take care that there is an institute which provides sufficiently for the social security of clerics.

§3. Insofar as necessary, each diocese is to establish a common fund through which bishops are able to satisfy obligations towards other persons who serve the Church and meet the various needs of the diocese and through which the richer dioceses can also assist the poorer ones.

§4. According to different local circumstances, the purposes mentioned in §2 and §3 can be obtained more suitably through a federation of diocesan institutes, through a cooperative endeavor, or even through an appropriate association established for various dioceses or for the entire territory of the conference of bishops.

§5. If possible, these institutes are to be established in such a way that they also have recognition in civil law.

Canon 1274 provides for the establishment of three[23] entities for special purposes: (1) an "institute for clergy support," (2) an "institute for social security of clergy," and (3) a "common fund" intended to assist in fulfilling obligations toward persons other than clerics who serve the Church, to meet diocesan needs, and to assist

---

[23] Interestingly, the *DPMB*, n. 190 makes mention of only two of these institutes: the "institute for clergy support" and the "common fund." It specifically mentions that the "common fund" may be formed "by means of special agreements and institutes on an interdiocesan or national level" and recommends that both institutes be established with civil legal recognition.

poorer dioceses. Every effort must be made to assure that these entities have civil legal recognition. These institutes reflect the "proper
purposes of the Church" mentioned in canon 1254 §1 on account of
which the Church has temporal goods. Canon 1274 did not have a
predecessor in the 1917 code wherein the benefice system was the
ordinary means to support clergy.[24] This canon finds it origin in the
conciliar decree *Presbyterorum ordinis,* n. 21:

> The example of the faithful in the primitive Church of
> Jerusalem should be always kept in mind. There "they
> had everything in common" (Acts 4:32), and "distribu-
> tion was made to each as any had need" (Acts 4:35). It is
> then an excellent arrangement, at least in places where the
> support of clergy depends completely or to a great extent
> on the offerings of the faithful, that the money offered in
> this way should be collected by some kind of diocesan
> agency. The bishop would administer this agency with
> the help of priests appointed for this purpose and also lay
> experts in financial matters, where the advantage of such
> appointment may make it advisable.
>
> It is also desirable that as far as possible there should
> be set up in each diocese or region a common fund to
> enable bishops to satisfy obligations to people employed
> in the service of the Church and to meet the various needs
> of the diocese. From this fund too, richer dioceses would
> be able to help poorer ones, so that the abundance of the
> one may supply for the want of the other. This common
> fund also should be made up mainly of moneys from the
> offerings of the faithful as well as from those coming
> from other sources to be determined by law.
>
> Moreover, in countries where social security has not
> yet been adequately organized for the benefit of clergy,

---

[24] For a discussion of the Church's teaching on temporal goods and clergy during the
period between Vatican II and the 1983 code, see: MARCO CISTERNINO, *L'uso dei
beni temporali da parte dei chierici dal Concilio Vaticano II al CJC 1983,* Rome,
Pontifica Università Lateranense, Pontificii Instituti Utriusque Juris, 1999.

episcopal conferences are to make provision, in harmony with ecclesiastical and civil law, for the setting up of diocesan organizations (even federated with one another), or organizations for different dioceses grouped together, or an association catering to the whole territory: the purpose of these being that under the supervision of the hierarchy satisfactory provision should be made both for suitable insurance and what is called health assistance, and for the proper support of priests who suffer from sickness, ill health or old age.

Priests should assist this organization when it has been set up, moved by a spirit of solidarity with their brother priests, sharing their hardships, and at the same time realizing that in this way they can, without anxiety for their future, practice poverty with a readier appreciation of the Gospel and devote themselves completely to the salvation of souls. Those responsible should do their utmost to have such organizations combined on an international scale, so as to give them more stability and strength and promote their wider diffusion.[25]

Norms for the implementation of this conciliar directive were provided in *Ecclesiae sanctae*, I, n. 8, which makes reference to the revision of the Code of Canon Law:

The Conferences should take care that, at least in regions where the support of clergy depends entirely or in great part on the offerings of the faithful, a special institute be set up in every diocese to collect offerings for this purpose. The administrator of this institution shall be the Bishop of the diocese himself, assisted by delegated priests and, if it seems desirable, also by laymen who are familiar with business matters.

Finally, these Episcopal Conferences should see to it

---

[25] FLANNERY I, pp. 899-900; see SCHOUPPE, pp. 204-209.

that, always with due regard for ecclesiastical and civil laws, there be in each country either diocesan institutions, which may also be affiliated with one another, or institutions established for several dioceses, or an association established for the whole country, by which, under the vigilance of the entire Hierarchy, adequate provision is made for proper security and health insurance, and for the proper support of clerics who are sick, incapacitated, or aged.

It will be the concern of the Code of Canon Law now being revised, to determine the manner in which another common fund is to be established in individual dioceses or regions, by which the Bishops will be able to satisfy other obligations to persons serving the Church, and to meet various needs of the diocese, and by which the richer dioceses will be able to help the poorer ones.[26]

One will also recall the statement of the 1967 Synod of Bishops which calls for the remuneration of priests to be equitable and sufficient, to include social security, and to be more uniform for priests of the same diocese. The synod also explained that priests' incomes should be separated from their ministry, especially from their sacramental ministry.[27]

A careful reading of canon 1274 shows that its provisions are requirements *only* if some or all of the issues identified are not already being met in some other fashion. If these concerns are already being addressed adequately in another way, there is no canonical requirement that the institute(s) be established. At the same time, even if these purposes are being met by some other means, the diocesan bishop may nonetheless decide to establish some or all of these three institutes to enhance what is being provided in another way.

The funding for the institutes will primarily come from gifts of the faithful. The diocesan bishop may seek their funding through

---

[26] *CLD*, 6, pp. 269-270.
[27] 1967 SYNOD OF BISHOPS, pp. 692-693.

a special appeal (canon 1262), the imposition of a tax (canon 1263), or a special collection (canon 1266). The code itself indicates two specific sources for funding the "institute for clergy support" mentioned in canon 1274 §1: (1) canon 1272 says that the income and endowment of benefices, where they still exist, should gradually be placed into this institute, and (2) canon 1303 §2 requires that the goods of a non-autonomous pious foundation subject to the diocesan bishop, when time for the foundation is completed, are to be placed into it unless the donor expressly manifested a different intention. Interestingly, the code does not indicate the placement of revenue from these sources (canons 1272 and 1303 §2) in dioceses where the "institute for clergy support" (which is not mandatory) does not exist. In such a situation, the spirit of the law would expect that these revenues be directed to clergy support in some similar fashion.

"INSTITUTE FOR CLERGY SUPPORT." Canon 1274 §1 requires each diocese to have a special institute (*speciale institutum*) gathering goods or offerings to support the clergy who serve the diocese, unless this support is provided some other way.[28] The Pontifical Council for Legislative Texts explains the purpose of this institute:

> The *diocesan institute or fund* has the task, in those cases in which the designated level of remuneration for the individual cleric is not met, of supplementing the partial remuneration received from ecclesiastical entities or the stipend received from other sources. Nothing prohibits the entities subject to the Diocesan Bishop, or

---

[28] The PONTIFICAL COUNCIL FOR LEGISLATIVE TEXTS identifies three possible sources for clergy *remuneratio*:
  a. ecclesiastical entities for which the priests exercise their ministry, whether full-time or part-time;
  b. subjects from which the priests receive what corresponds to a true and proper stipend, or a pension, according to the norms in force of the relevant juridical order;
  c. the diocesan institute or fund [of canon 1274 §1].
In *Decretum* De recursu super congrugentia inter legem particularem et normam codicalem [Recourse against diocesan norms on the clergy remuneration fund] (April 29, 2000), in *Communicationes*, 32 (2000), p. 165 (=PCLT, *Decretum* Clergy Remuneration).

having contracted with him, from paying directly to the
diocesan institute the contribution owed to the individual
priest, if the fiscal system in use would make that advantageous.[29]

This institute reflects the norm of canon 281 which refers to
clergy remuneration (*remuneratio*).[30] It also reflects the unity of the
bishop and his presbyterate and, perhaps for this reason, its funds are
not to be commingled with those of other dioceses in inter-diocesan
institutes (as is permitted by canon 1274 §4 for the funds of the other
two institutes mentioned in canon 1274 §2 and canon 1274 §3).[31]

The canon indicates that the support of the clergy is *primarily* a
diocesan obligation.[32] It is not immediately an obligation of a parish
or other institution (although in most settings clergy are remuner-
ated by the parish or institution they serve). Canon 1274 §1 requires

---

[29] PCLT, *Decretum* Clergy Remuneration, p. 165. The *Decretum* explains that the
    ecclesiastical entity which a priest serves "may be at the diocesan level or at a broader
    level. All of these entities are bound, by virtue of the service requested, to make their
    proper contribution, according to particular law." It also explains that a *stipend* is
    "compensation for work performed, agreed upon and measured in relationship to
    either the quantity or the quality of the services rendered" which may come from
    "either ecclesiastical entities (imagine, for example, a Catholic school, etc.) or civil
    entities – whether private or public – for which the priests exercise a task, by virtue
    of an express or tacit mandate of their own ordinary." Ibid., pp. 164-165.

[30] Canon 281 §2 refers to clergy *social assistance* (providing for priests who suffer ill-
    ness, incapacity, or old age). *Social assistance* is the specific focus of the "institute
    for social security of clergy" in canon 1274 §2. Therefore, one can conclude that the
    institute of canon 1274 §1 has for its specific focus only clergy remuneration (and
    not other means of clergy support).
    Canon 281 §3 mentions a special provision for married deacons: "Married deacons
    who devote themselves completely to ecclesiastical ministry deserve remuneration
    (*remuneratio*) by which they are able to provide for the support of themselves and
    their families. Those who receive remuneration by reason of a civil profession which
    they exercise or have exercised, however, are to take care of the needs of themselves
    and their families from the income derived from it." It seems the same practice would
    apply to permanent deacons who are not married.

[31] Initially, the *coetus De iure patrimoniali Ecclesiae* had envisioned an inter-diocesan
    federation also to collaborate in the "institute for clergy support" (canon 1274 §1);
    one consultor, however, suggested that the purposes of such an institute are often
    more suitably obtained by a diocesan institute, and after more discussion the other
    consultors agreed. *Communicationes,* 37 (2005), p. 218; see also *Communicationes,*
    12 (1980), p. 409.

[32] See DE PAOLIS, *De bonis Ecclesiae temporalibus*, p. 84.

that the diocesan "institute for clergy support" is only mandatory if remuneration is not provided in some other fashion. To the measure that clergy receive suitable remuneration from parishes or institutions, there is no obligation to establish this institute.

The institute is intended to provide support for clerics who offer their service to benefit the diocese, even if they are incardinated elsewhere (see canon 265).

The 1977 *Schema* had assigned a role in clergy remuneration to the conference of bishops, but upon further reflection the *coetus De bonis Ecclesiae temporalibus* omitted reference to the conference since its inclusion could cause confusion on the appropriate relation of the conference of bishops and individual bishops.[33]

"INSTITUTE FOR SOCIAL SECURITY OF CLERGY." Canon 1274 §2 requires that the conference of bishops sees that an "institute (*institutum*) for social security of clergy" is established wherever social provision for clergy is not otherwise sufficiently assured (i.e., either where there is no secular social security provision at all, or where that provision, though existing, is inadequate).[34] The social security of clergy is an obligation which immediately rests with the diocesan bishop (see canon 281 §2). Canon 1274 §4 allows the possibility of establishing inter-diocesan endeavors to achieve this purpose.[35]

---

[33] *Communicationes,* 12 (1980), p. 409.

[34] DE PAOLIS, *De bonis Ecclesiae temporalibus,* p. 86.

[35] The PONTIFICAL COUNCIL FOR LEGISLATIVE TEXTS explains that *pensions* may be calculated in clergy *remuneration*: "With respect to the inclusion of pensions collected, *or which could be collected* (inasmuch as they are owed, if requested, by the State), one notes that, taking into account the state of the economic resources of the diocese and of the specific context of the general principles set forth above, they could be included in the calculation of remuneration. If one considers the necessary equality that should exist among the priests of a diocese, it may be appropriate or necessary to include in the pool of resources to be distributed all those incomes that are able to be objectively quantified. It is not only licit but also appropriate to take into account – whether partially or totally, depending on the circumstances – the income received by the individual, as long as it does not come from strictly personal savings. There have been some objections that pensions should be considered as income from personal resources and not be figured into the accounting. However, other than the practical difficulty involved in a system of remuneration that seeks to encompass even personal income derived from inheritances or from capital, one cannot forget that a pension 'owed' by the State and income from personal goods are economic goods that are quite different." PCLT, *Decretum* Clergy Remuneration, p. 166.

The conference of bishops would fulfill the role mandated by canon 1274 §2 if it simply assures that each diocese makes appropriate provisions for the social security of clergy.

"COMMON FUND." Canon 1274 §3 also invites each diocese to establish, if necessary, a "common fund" (*massa communis*) allowing the diocesan bishop:

1. to satisfy obligations to others who serve the Church,[36]
2. to meet various diocesan needs, and
3. to assist poorer dioceses.

Unlike the institutes (*instituta*) considered in the previous two paragraphs, canon 1274 §3 envisions the creation of a common fund (*massa communis*) to meet various needs. During the process of drafting the proposed new law, there was some consideration given to uniting this fund with the "institute for clergy support."[37] In the end, however, this proposal was rejected, especially because a fund for clergy support had already been established in a number of dioceses.[38] Canon 1274 §4 allows the possibility of inter-diocesan endeavors to achieve the purposes of the "common fund."

OPTIONAL INTER-DIOCESAN COLLABORATION.[39] Canon 1274 §4 allows that the purposes mentioned in canon 1274 §2 and canon 1274 §3 may achieved in three possible ways, depending on local circumstances, in addition to individual diocesan management:

1. through a federation of diocesan institutes,
2. through a cooperative endeavor, or
3. through an appropriate association established for various dioceses or for all the dioceses of the conference of bishops.

---

[36] These church employees "have the right to decent remuneration (*remuneratio*) appropriate to their condition so that they are able to provide decently for their own needs and those of their family. They also have a right for their social provision, social security, and health benefits to be duly provided" (canon 231 §2).

[37] See BRENDAN DALY, "Use of Clergy Trust Fund to Pay Lay Pastoral Workers," in CLSA, *Roman Replies and Advisory Opinions*, Joseph J. Koury and Shiobhan M. Verbeek (eds.), Washington, CLSA, 2007, pp. 94-97.

[38] *Communicationes*, 12 (1980), p. 408.

[39] The code also admits the possibility of inter-diocesan collaboration in the establishment of an inter-diocesan seminary (canon 237) and an inter-diocesan tribunal (canon 1423).

The canon does not suggest that the institute mentioned in canon 1274 §1 be part of an inter-diocesan cooperation. As mentioned above, the "institute for clergy support" reflects the unity of the diocesan bishop with his presbyterate and this explains why it is not envisioned as being commingled with any institute addressing other purposes.

CIVIL LEGAL RECOGNITION. Canon 1274 §5 says that, if possible, the two "institutes" and the "common fund" are to be so established that they are recognized by the pertinent civil law. Some suggest that these entities be established as public juridic persons by the competent authority (e.g., as autonomous pious foundations: canon 1303 §1, 1°).[40] Others suggest that establishment as public juridic persons is unnecessary and that the entities can be non-autonomous pious foundations (canon 1303 §1, 2°) entrusted to the diocese. In any event, canon 1274 §5 expects that the institutes and the common fund be recognized by civil law. The civilly recognized method will depend upon both the options available in the locale and the preference of the diocesan bishop(s).[41] Further, it will be very important that clear norms governing any inter-diocesan endeavor be developed in accord with canon law and in a manner agreed upon by the diocesan bishops concerned (see canon 1275).

---

[40] On May 29, 1969, the *coetus De iure patrimoniali Ecclesiae* made a deliberate choice not to assign juridic personality to the institutes mentioned in canon 1272; rather, such a determination would be made by particular law in light of different local circumstances: *Communicationes,* 37 (2005), p. 218. See also MORRISEY, "Temporal Goods," p. 720.
  MARIANO LÓPEZ ALCARÓN, however, recommends quite directly: "These funds [of the "institute for clergy support"] would have to be structured as public juridic persons of the *universitates rerum* type, and they should act on behalf of the Church, with duly approved statutes...." He expresses, however, that the "common fund" need not be established as a separate juridic person. In "Book V," pp. 720-721. VELASIO DE PAOLIS also explains that the "institute for clergy support" has the nature of a public juridic person (a *universitas rerum*: canon 115 §1); he does not conclude the same about the other two institutes mentioned in canon 1274.

[41] NICHOLAS P. CAFARDI and JORDAN HITE suggest that the preferred civil law device to protect the funds in these institutes is the "irrevocable trust" which, they say, "has been used because it dedicates the funds irrevocably, it insulates the funds from liability, and it provides an ease of administration not present in other legal structures." In "Civil and Canonical Requirements of a Clergy Retirement Fund," in *CLSA AO1,* p. 419.

OTHER DIOCESAN INSTITUTES. The institutes proposed in canon 1274 are not exhaustive. The diocesan bishop can establish other institutes for other purposes. Such an institute may allow inter-diocesan collaboration (see canons 1274 §4, 1275), and should be established in a manner recognized by civil law (see canon 1275 §5). A diocese, for example, may establish a fund into which excess capital of parishes may be placed, and from which funds may be borrowed by other parishes. Such an institute may be considered a kind of "inter-parochial cooperative" whereby funds may be made available to needy parishes at a lower rate of interest, without the requirement of excessive collateral, etc. Should such a fund be established, however, care must be taken to monitor carefully the amounts of investments and earnings or indebtedness of each participating parish.

CORRESPONDING CANON OF THE EASTERN CODE: CANON 1021. The corresponding Eastern canon is situated as the last canon in "Chapter I: The Acquisition of Temporal Goods."[42] The canon omits the content of Latin canon 1274 §§4-5.[43] Concerning the "institute for clergy support," it adds that this institute (*institutum*) is to be established "according to the norm of the particular Church *sui iuris.*" Its purpose is to provide "suitably for the appropriate and fundamentally equal support of all clerics who offer service for the benefit of the eparchy." Concerning the "institute (*institutum*) for social security of clergy," the Eastern law says that "the particular law of each Church *sui iuris* is to provide for the erection of institutes which protect these benefits under the vigilance of the local hierarch." Concerning the eparchial "common fund" (*massa communis*) for the other purposes, it is to be established "in a manner determined by the particular law of its own Church *sui iuris.*" Like the Latin law, the Eastern code does not require the establishment of these entities if their purposes are being achieved adequately in another way.

---

[42] Latin canon 1274 is placed in *Title II: The Administration of Goods*, thereby giving emphasis on how the financial institutions are to be administered. Eastern canon 1021 is placed in *Chapter I: The Acquisition of Temporal Goods*, thereby placing focus on how the financial institutions are funded.

[43] But see CCEO, canon 1020, which addresses the concern of CIC, canon 1274 §5.

ADMINISTRATION OF INTER-DIOCESAN
AGGREGATES OF GOODS

**Can. 1275 – An aggregate of goods which come from
different dioceses is administered according to the norms
appropriately agreed upon by the bishops concerned.**

Canon 1275 requires that any aggregate of goods (*massa bonorum*) from different dioceses is to be administered by norms agreed
upon by the participating diocesan bishops. When such an aggregate
has been established, it is an example of inter-diocesan cooperation.
Since its funds come from different dioceses, it follows that its governing statutes be agreed upon by the participating diocesan bishops.
This canon had no predecessor in the 1917 code.

The ecclesiastical goods from different dioceses which comprise this aggregate may be destined for a number of purposes (e.g.,
Catholic education, social outreach ministry, etc.). Two obvious
purposes for such an aggregate are those mentioned in canon 1274
§2 (the "institute for social support of clergy") and canon 1274 §3
(the "common fund"). Since the "institute for clergy support" must
be a strictly diocesan fund by mandate of canon 1274 §1, its goods
do not pertain to the option of canon 1275.

Any instrument of inter-diocesan cooperation will have statutes (see canon 94) governing obvious details (e.g., administration
of the fund, how dioceses enter and exit participation, the means of
determining particular policies, the manner of revising the statutes,
the policy on the distribution of assets according to the level of
contributions by individual participating dioceses, the investment
strategies, the powers reserved to all participating dioceses, the
manner to dissolve the fund, the allocation of assets and liabilities
upon dissolution, etc.).

As mentioned in the commentary on canon 1274 §5, it will also
be particularly advisable that an aggregate of goods be so established
by the competent ecclesiastical authorities that it has recognition in
civil law. Also, nothing prevents it from being established as a public
juridic person.

In the 1977 *Schema*, this canon had entrusted the establishment of the norms of this aggregate to the conference of bishops.[44] Opponents of this proposed draft had suggested that the work of the conference of bishops would restrict the ministry of diocesan bishops.[45] Therefore, reference to the episcopal conference was omitted from the 1980 *Schema*.

CORRESPONDING CANON OF THE EASTERN CODE. None.

VIGILANCE AND INSTRUCTIONS OF ORDINARIES

Can. 1276 – §1. It is for the ordinary to exercise careful vigilance over the administration of all the goods which belong to public juridic persons subject to him, without prejudice to legitimate titles which attribute more significant rights to him.

§2. With due regard for rights, legitimate customs, and circumstances, ordinaries are to take care of the ordering of the entire matter of the administration of ecclesiastical goods by issuing special instructions within the limits of universal and particular law.

Other canons in *Book V* assign more specific powers to the ordinary,[46] but this canon speaks of his general vigilance over the ecclesiastical goods owned by public juridic persons subject to him. Unlike the Roman Pontiff (who is the supreme administrator and steward of all ecclesiastical goods [canon 1273] and also an ordinary [canon 134 §1]), other ordinaries are not identified in the 1983 code as the administrators and stewards of ecclesiastical goods belonging to public juridic persons subject to them. Instead, other ordinaries exercise a general canonical vigilance over such goods. The ordinary is not their immediate administrator; each such juridic person has its own administrator, assigned by universal law, particular law, statutes, legitimate custom (canon 1279 §1), or by

---

[44]   1977 *Schema*, canon 19, p. 13.

[45]   *Relatio*, pp. 284-285.

[46]   See Appendix III.

special provision of the ordinary (canon 1279 §2).[47]

Canon 1273 had said that the Supreme Pontiff is the "supreme administrator" of all ecclesiastical goods. The ordinary in canon 1276 may be called the "investigator" or "supervisor"[48] of the goods of public juridic persons subject to him. His role is one of vigilance, and this will entail his issuing special instructions on administration. He cannot, however, interfere illegitimately in administration as long as it is done within the norms of the law.

Canon 1276 §1 requires the ordinary to exercise careful vigilance (*sedulo advigilare*) over the administration of all ecclesiastical goods of public juridic persons subject to him, and acknowledges that he may enjoy even more rights by some other legal title (e.g., universal law,[49] particular law, statutes, concordats, custom, papal delegation, etc.).[50] Canon 1276 §1 reflects the norm of canon 392 §2 which says that diocesan bishops (who are ordinaries: see canon 134 §1) are "to exercise vigilance so that abuses do not creep into ecclesiastical discipline, especially regarding... the administration

---

[47] See DE PAOLIS, "Alcune osservazioni," pp. 105-110. The diocesan bishop must appoint a diocesan finance officer to perform "routine" acts of ordinary diocesan administration. The diocesan finance officer functions under the authority of the diocesan bishop, in accord with the budget determined by the diocesan finance council (canon 494 §3), and "in the name of the Church according to the norm of law" (canon 1282). The diocesan bishop, however, is the sole competent agent in the diocese to perform "non-routine" acts of ordinary diocesan administration (i.e., acts of ordinary administration which are more important in light of the economic condition of the diocese) and acts of extraordinary diocesan administration (canon 1277).

[48] See WOYWOOD, vol. 2, p. 203. JOSÉ T. MARTÍN DE AGAR calls the ordinary the "mediate administrator" of ecclesiastical goods subject to him. In "Bienes temporales y misión de la Iglesia" in *Manual de Derecho Canónico*, 2nd ed., Pamplona, 1991, p. 708.
A rotal decision on February 28, 1919, called the bishop the "supreme administrator of ecclesiastical property in his diocese." *AAS,* 12 (1920), p. 85; *CLD*, vol. 1, pp. 726-727. This terminology is inconsistent with the discipline of the code.

[49] Canon 637, for example, gives the local ordinary the right to receive an annual account of administration from autonomous monasteries (see canon 617) and the right to be informed about the financial conditions of a religious house of diocesan right.
Canon 1741, 5° identifies as a legitimate cause for which the diocesan bishop may remove a pastor from office his "poor administration of temporal affairs with grave damage to the Church whenever another remedy to this harm cannot be found."

[50] See PCLT, *Nota,* La funzione dell'autorità, p. 28.

of goods." The code permits the diocesan bishop to entrust vigilance over the administration of public juridic persons subject to him to the diocesan finance officer (canon 1278).

Book V mentions several specific instances when the ordinary, exercising his role of vigilance, is to become *immediately* involved in the function of administrators of public juridic persons:

1. Canon 1279 §1: the ordinary has the right to intervene when an administrator is negligent.
2. Canon 1279 §2: the ordinary is to appoint administrators for public juridic persons subject to him which do not have administrators.
3. Canon 1281 §1: the ordinary is to give the written faculty for administrators to place acts of extraordinary administration, without prejudice to the statutes.
4. Canon 1281 §2: the diocesan bishop (an ordinary[51]) is to define acts of extraordinary administration for juridic persons subject to him, if its statutes are silent, after he hears the diocesan finance council.
5. Canon 1283, 1°: the ordinary (or his delegate) is to receive from administrators their oath to be efficient and faithful in their function.
6. Canon 1287 §1: the local ordinary is to receive annual financial reports from administrators of ecclesiastical goods subject to the diocesan bishop; these reports are to be presented for examination to the diocesan finance council.
7. Canon 1288: their own ordinary is to give administrators written permission to initiate or contest civil litigation.

Indeed, the ordinary is to exercise vigilance over all aspects of the administration of goods belonging to juridic persons subject to him (see, e.g., canons 1280; 1282; 1283, 2°; 1283, 3°; 1284; 1285; 1286).

In addition, canon 1301 says that the ordinary, inasmuch as he

---

[51] Other ordinaries are excluded from canon 1281 §2.

is the executor of all pious wills, exercises vigilance (even through visitation, should he so choose or should it be necessary) to make sure that pious wills are fulfilled. Other executors must render him an account when they have completed their function. Stipulations contrary to the rights of the ordinary over pious wills are to be considered as non-existent (*non appositae*).

The ordinary's vigilance does not make him the owner of the ecclesiastical goods of public juridic persons, but it does require him "to exercise a reasonable standard of care in providing for and reviewing (subject to the principle of subsidiarity) the fiscal operations or temporal governance of ... public juridic persons subject to him within the diocese. It must be emphasized repeatedly that this general oversight does not permit, however, any invasion of the assets or property of a juridic person other than the diocese itself by the diocesan bishop. Rather, the exercise of vigilance is expressed, not in a right of control, but in a right to legislate policy and particular law regarding ... fiscal administration, a right to specify how universal and particular law are to be implemented within the diocese, and a right to intervene through a defined process of law in the case of suspected malfeasance or mismanagement by the ... proper administrator of a public juridic person."[52] In exercising this vigilance role, "he can ensure greater financial accountability and involvement by lay faithful in diocesan governance."[53]

Canon 1276 §2 says ordinaries are to issue special instructions (*instructiones*), within the limits of universal and particular law (e.g., laws issued by the conference of bishops, the provincial bishops, or the diocesan bishop),[54] on the ordering of all aspects of the administration of ecclesiastical goods (with due regard for various rights, legitimate customs, and circumstances). The issuing of special instructions by the ordinary is an application of the principle of

[52] WILLIAM J. KING, "Mandated Diocesan Centralized Financial Service" in *CLSA AO3*, p. 332.

[53] ROBERT KASLYN, "Accountability of Diocesan Bishops: A Significant Aspect of Ecclesial Communion," in *The Jurist*, 67 (2007), p. 138.

[54] PCLT, *Nota,* La funzione dell'autorità, p. 28.

subsidiarity operative in *Book V.*[55] Instructions "clarify the prescripts
of law and elaborate on and determine the methods to be observed
in fulfilling them. They are given for the use of those whose duty
it is to see that laws are executed and oblige them in the execution
of the laws" (canon 34 §1). "The ordinances of instructions do not
derogate from laws. If these ordinances cannot be reconciled with
the prescripts of laws, they lack all force" (canon 34 §2). When the
ordinary issues the instructions proposed in canon 1276 §2, he is
not making new laws; instead, he is clarifying the prescripts of laws
and providing ways to fulfill them. The *Directory for the Pastoral
Ministry of Bishops* discusses the instructions which a diocesan
bishop issues:

> As the one who presides over the particular Church, it
> falls to the Bishop to *organize* the administration of eccle-
> siastical goods. He does this through suitable norms and
> instructions, in harmony with the directives of the Apos-
> tolic See, and he may also make use of any guidelines and
> resources supplied by the Episcopal Conference.[56]

For parishes, the financial instructions of the diocesan bishop
may be issued in the form of a "parish finance handbook" or a "parish finance directory."[57] A similar instrument is common in religious
institutes (see canon 635 §2).

The diocesan bishop (exercising his legislative authority:
see canon 391) may enact particular laws (see canon 8 §2) for his

---

[55] PCLT, *Nota,* La funzione dell'autorità, p. 28.

[56] *DPMB*, n. 188.

[57] MARY JUDITH O'BRIEN suggests possible issues to be included in a parochial instruction concerning ecclesiastical goods of a parish. She comments about the practical
value of instructions, especially as compared to the statutes of a parish: *"Instructions* provide a less formal and austere document than *statutes*; this is especially
beneficial given the communication occurring directly between the diocesan bishop
and priests. An added benefit is that *instructions* are provided at one time; statutes
are more cumbersome as these would be replicated for each parish. The flexibility
and convenience of *instructions* are especially noteworthy for revisions which may
occur in the future" ("Instructions for Parochial Temporal Administrators," *Catholic
Lawyer* 41 [2001], p. 114, fn. 1).

diocese, within the perimeters of universal law, in order to govern the ecclesiastical goods of public juridic persons subject to him. He may, for example, set minimum and maximum limits for alienation of parochial goods belonging to a stable patrimony, between which amounts the pastor needs the involvement of the parish finance council, of the local ordinary, and, if appropriate, of those concerned. Or, he may require surplus operating funds of public juridic persons subject to his governance be deposited into a common account.[58] He or his vicar general (both of whom are ordinaries) may issue special instructions on the process to be followed in complying with particular diocesan law.

The agent of vigilance and special instructions is the *ordinary* (not only the local ordinary). This includes diocesan bishops and their legal equivalents; vicars general; episcopal vicars (if the administration of temporal goods is within their competence); and, for their own members, major superiors of clerical institutes of pontifical right and of clerical societies of apostolic life of pontifical right (see canon 134 §1).

INTERNAL AUDITS OF PARISHES (AND OTHER PUBLIC JURIDIC PERSONS). In many dioceses, a program for regular internal audits of parishes has been established as a practical application of canon 1276. Nothing prevents similar internal audits from being mandated for other public juridic persons subject to the vigilance of the ordinary.

On November 12, 2007, Bishop Daniel F. Walsh, chair of the USCCB Ad Hoc Committee on Diocesan Audits, discussed such audits.[59] A year earlier, this committee had been asked "to consider how the use of either internal or external audits of parishes would enhance the transparency and accountability of Church finances

---

[58]　If this is done, very careful attention must be given to assure that the assets of each public juridic person remain distinct. See KING, "Mandated Diocesan Centralized Financial Service," pp. 334-336.

[59]　[USCCB] Ad Hoc Committee on Diocesan Audits, "Report to the Body of Bishops [by] Most Rev. Daniel F. Walsh, Chairman," (November 12, 2007). Available at http://www.usccb.org/finance/Report%20to%20Bishops%20Nov%2007.pdf (December 1, 2008)

and the good stewardship of pastors and administrators."[60] The committee enlisted the assistance of the Diocesan Fiscal Management Conference (DFMC) which offered several recommendations to the Ad Hoc Committee on Diocesan Audits, six of which Bishop Walsh underscored:

- Parishes contain the most significant assets within any (arch) diocese. Strong systems of internal controls will reduce the risk of fraud, misuse, waste or embezzlement. An internal audit department would help ensure parishes are following appropriate business practices, civil regulation and diocesan requirements and procedures. The DFMC strongly supports the value and need for regular internal audits of parishes.

- An internal audit program would be a vital aid to the bishop in fulfilling his responsibility under canons 1276 and 1284.

- Scarcity of resources may limit funds available for accounting, reporting and financial management. Inadequate staffing can make separation of duties impossible and lead to ineffective internal controls. Organizations with ineffective internal controls are particularly vulnerable to costly mistakes and the illicit actions of the unscrupulous.

- Recognizing that most people employed by the Church consider their work as ministry, it is easy to place excessive trust in the individual. Parishes may view the imposition of internal controls as somehow impugning the integrity of the staff. This trusting environment is exactly what a dishonest employee exploits.

---

[60] DAVID GIBSON comments on the importance of accountability and transparency in financial matters in the Church: "Catholics are now focusing on fiscal accountability as a priority in restoring trust in the Church. Polls consistently show that eight in ten Catholics rate Church financial reform as a top concern. Just as important, both conservatives and liberals agree on this issue, making it one of the rare areas of convergence in a polarized church....

"Opening the church's books involves no change in doctrine or theology, and the bishop or pastor would still have the final say on how diocesan or parish funds are spent. The priority right now is for simple transparency, so that everyone can know what is coming in and what is going out, and where it is going." In "The Bottom Line: Will Church Finances Be the Next Scandal?" in *Commonweal*, 131 (February 13, 2004), pp. 10, 13. See KASLYN, "Accountability of Diocesan Bishops," pp. 135-138.

- Supervision, separation of duties and internal controls are ways to help honorable people remain honest. An effective internal audit program does not guarantee thefts will not occur. However, it will increase the opportunity for detection and thus serve as a significant deterrent. It will also encourage the development of stronger parish financial management, monitor adherence to federal and state laws and create a reporting mechanism to identify parishes with greater risk.

- The primary role of the internal audit function is to aid pastors in fulfilling their canonical and legal responsibilities. An effective internal audit will help safeguard the assets of a parish, ensure that record keeping, accounting, and reporting comply with the policies of the diocese, identify areas of improvement and report findings and observations to the pastor, parish finance council and the audit or accounting committee of the diocese.

Bishop Walsh explained that the heart of the DFMC recommendations can be summarized as follows:

> The DFMC correlates the need for internal audits of parishes as integral to the canonical requirement that parishes report to the diocesan bishop. The DFMC therefore recommends that all parishes submit an annual report to the diocesan bishop. The report should be accompanied by the parish financial statements for the fiscal year and the budget for the prospective year. The DFMC recommends that such reports be signed by the pastor, key employees and members of the parish finance council. The report should include the names and professional titles of the parish finance council members, the dates the parish finance council met during the preceding fiscal year and the date(s) when the parish financial statements and budget were made available to the parishioners. The report should include an attestation that the signers affirm that the financial statements, to the best of their knowledge, accurately reflect the financial condition of

the parish; that the parish finance council has reviewed
and approved the financial statements and budget; that
the signers have not received any credible report that has
not been reported to the diocesan bishop or his delegate
of fraud, abuse or misappropriation and that the signers
have not engaged in any activity with the parish from
which they or their family could personally benefit and
could be considered a conflict of interest without fully
disclosing the conflict of interest to the pastor and parish
finance council and such conflict has been reviewed by
the parish finance council.

Aware that not every diocese can staff and fund an internal audit
department in its curia, the DFMC offered three models to illustrate
how a diocese may implement an internal audit program:

1. It is recommended as a best practice that dioceses hire internal
    audit staff that report directly to an independent accounting/
    auditing committee and the diocesan bishop or his delegate.
    The internal audit staff should routinely visit parishes to as-
    sess financial management, internal controls and adherence to
    diocesan policy and directives.

2. As an alternative, a diocese could use part-time staff or out-
    source internal audits to independent CPAs who would report
    jointly to the pastor, parish finance council and the bishop.
    These could be performed every two to three years or when a
    pastor changes.

3. At a minimum, consider recruiting retired or volunteer CPAs,
    accountants or auditors to visit parishes and conduct reviews
    of finances. In the absence of qualified volunteers, the parish
    finance councils could be utilized to perform basic internal
    control review in order to gather assurance that these policies
    and procedures are in place and functioning.

In the end, Bishop Walsh reported that his committee "strongly encouraged" internal or external audits of parishes, but added that "it
is unlikely audits could be mandated by the [episcopal] conference.

Their importance can be stressed and more detailed models might be developed as a logical extension of the canonical requirement that the bishop provide the parish financial reports to the finance council in each diocese."

Even if financial audits are not mandated by the conference of bishops, however, a diocesan bishop may mandate regular internal audits of parishes (and of other public juridic persons subject to him) by means of particular diocesan law. This would be a practical application of the letter and spirit of canon 1276.

CORRESPONDING CANON OF THE EASTERN CODE: CANON 1022. The Eastern canon assigns the role of vigilance to the "eparchial bishop" (not the ordinary). It says that the "opportune" (rather than "special") instructions of the hierarch are to be issued "within the limits of common law and the particular law of their own Church *sui iuris*, that the entire administration of ecclesiastical goods is suitably ordered."

ACTS OF ORDINARY AND EXTRAORDINARY DIOCESAN ADMINISTRATION

Can. 1277 – The diocesan bishop must hear the finance council and college of consultors to place acts of administration which are more important in light of the economic condition of the diocese. In addition to the cases specially expressed in universal law or the charter of a foundation, however, he needs the consent of the finance council and of the college of consultors to place acts of extraordinary administration. It is for the conference of bishops to define which acts are to be considered of extraordinary administration.

This canon distinguishes three kinds of acts of administration[61] of diocesan ecclesiastical goods:

---

[61] It is important to recall that acts of administration are not to be confused with acts of alienation. These acts are distinguished in the 1983 code, but in the 1917 code the distinction was not so clear (see CIC/1917, canons 1495 §1; 1533). For this reason, some documents, especially those issued prior to the revised code, treat acts of

(1) acts of ordinary administration (which we may wish to designate as "routine" acts in order to distinguish them from acts of ordinary diocesan administration which are more important in light of the economic condition of the diocese, and which we may designate as "non-routine" acts)

(2) acts of ordinary administration which are more important in light of the economic condition of the diocese, and

(3) acts of extraordinary administration.[62]

The canon requires that, before placing either of the latter two acts of diocesan administration, the diocesan bishop must be in dialogue with the diocesan finance council and the college of consultors for the *validity* of his act. These groups must give their *counsel* before the bishop performs the "non-routine" acts of ordinary administration which are more important in light of the diocesan economic setting. They must give their *consent* before he places acts of *extraordinary* administration. Once he has received the required counsel or consent, the diocesan bishop (not the diocesan finance officer) performs these acts.[63]

ACTS OF ORDINARY DIOCESAN ADMINISTRATION. Ordinary administration involves whatever is done routinely to maintain ecclesiastical goods. Canon 1284 §2 offers examples of activities involved in acts of ordinary administration, including diocesan. Commentators commonly identify as acts of ordinary administration such tasks as: "the collection of debts, rents, interests or dividends; contracts and payments necessary for the ordinary maintenance of the church and its personnel; the opening of checking accounts to facilitate

---

administration and alienation together. This is the case, for example, in the 1856 *Instruction* of the SACRED CONGREGATION FOR THE PROPAGATION OF THE FAITH and the 1986 norms to implement canon 1277 norms of the NCCB, both of which are included in this commentary on canon 1277. The universal law governing acts of alienation is found in canons 1291-1294 for diocesan goods and for the goods of public juridic persons subject to the diocesan bishop, and in canon 638 §3 for goods of religious institutes (see canons 718 and 741 §1).

[62] See DE PAOLIS, *De bonis Ecclesiae temporalibus*, p. 88; FRANCESCO GRAZIAN, *La nozione di amministrazione e di alienazione nel Codice di Diritto Canonico*, Tesi Gregoriani, 55, Rome, Editrice Pontificia Università Gregoriana, 2002, pp. 200-232.

[63] See DE PAOLIS, "Alcune osservazioni," pp. 129-130, 139.

these payments; and the acceptance of ordinary donations."[64] Put quite simply, acts of ordinary administration involve "the normal transaction of business by the canonical stewards of a public juridic person, i.e., things done routinely or regularly."[65]

"Routine" acts of ordinary diocesan administration are performed by the diocesan finance officer, who administers diocesan goods under the supervision of the diocesan bishop (canon 494 §3).[66] The code makes it clear that the diocesan bishop alone is the agent to perform "non-routine" acts of ordinary administration which are more important in light of diocesan economic conditions (canon 1277), acts of extraordinary administration (canon 1277), and transactions which can worsen the patrimonial condition of the diocese (canon 1295; see canon 1292 §1).[67]

Acts of ordinary administration are also mentioned in canon 638 §§1-2 (concerning religious institutes[68]), canon 1281 §§1-2 (concerning juridic persons subject to an ordinary: e.g., a parish) and canon 1524 §2 (which requires that, in order to renounce a trial, guardians and administrators of juridic persons obtain the counsel or consent of those whose involvement is necessary to place acts which exceed the limits of ordinary administration).

---

[64] ABBO-HANNON, vol. 2, p. 731. BOUSCAREN-ELLIS-KORTH offer a similar reflection: "*Ordinary administration* includes whatever is necessary for the preservation of church property and whatever actions are required to collect the income from such property; also the payment of current bills and taxes, the making of ordinary repairs, and keeping an ordinary bank account. Ordinary acts of administration also include such acts as are to be done at fixed intervals (monthly, quarterly, annually) as well as those which are necessary for the customary transaction of business" (pp. 829-830). See also VROMANT, p. 161.

[65] MAIDA-CAFARDI, *Church Property*, pp. 301-302. The authors give the following examples: "maintaining property and checking accounts, receiving rent or interest income, accepting nominal gifts, paying bills, and making routine sales and purchases" (p. 302). See SIGNIÉ, pp. 104-107.

[66] In a religious institute, acts of ordinary administration are performed by the superior and other officials designated in proper law (canon 638 §2); the finance officer of a religious institute manages the administration of religious goods under the direction of the superior (canon 636 §1). In a parish, acts of ordinary administration are performed by the pastor (see canon 532).

[67] The transactions of canon 1295 are not acts of alienation. Furthermore, canon 1292 §1 makes it clear that the diocesan bishop alone is the agent of acts of alienation of diocesan property.

[68] Canon 741 §1 applies the norm of canon 638 §§1-2 to societies of apostolic life. Canon 718 allows proper law to apply the norm to secular institutes.

ACTS OF ORDINARY DIOCESAN ADMINISTRATION WHICH ARE
"MORE IMPORTANT IN LIGHT OF THE ECONOMIC CONDITION OF THE
DIOCESE." Within each diocese, some acts of ordinary administration
are considered *more important in light of its economic condition.*[69]
Such acts are to be performed by the diocesan bishop, not the dioc-
esan finance officer.

Before the diocesan bishop may perform such acts, he must
receive the counsel of both the college of consultors and the diocesan
finance council. These important acts of ordinary administration
may have adverse impact on the ecclesiastical goods owned by the
diocese. For this reason, the legislator requires the diocesan bishop
to receive the counsel of the diocesan finance council and the college
of consultors in order to place the acts validly.

The determination of these acts must be made by the diocesan
bishop, which he may prudently decide to identify in collaboration
with the diocesan finance council, the college of consultors, and
perhaps others.[70] The determination may be made on a case-by-case
basis. Perhaps preferably, however, the determination may be made
in a more general fashion (i.e., for this diocese, at this time, certain
specific acts of ordinary diocesan administration are considered
more important in light of the economic condition of the diocese).
Such a general determination may be identified in diocesan statutes[71]

---

[69] CIC/1917, canon 1520 §3 had required the local ordinary to hear the diocesan council
of administration in acts of administration of "greater importance," but did not further
specify. The revised code gives more clarity by indicating that the criterion whereby
to judge if the actions are of "greater importance" is *the economic condition of the
diocese.* See SIGNIÉ, pp. 107-108.

[70] See PAPROCKI, "Recent Developments," p. 281.

[71] Since a diocese is *ipso iure* a juridic person (canon 373), it is required to have statutes
(see canon 117). The diocesan statutes would wisely define acts of ordinary administration more important in light of the economic condition of the diocese.

THOMAS J. PAPROCKI suggests that consideration be given to identifying the following
as acts of administration more important in light of the economic condition of the
diocese: (1) approving an unbalanced operating budget; (2) any financial transaction that involves an amount in excess of the minimum amount set in accord with
canon 1292 §1, including, but not limited to, purchasing real estate; construction,
alteration, or demolition of a building; making a loan, secured or unsecured; long-
term (over 2 years) investments; acting as a guarantor or surety for the obligation of
another juridic person; (3) initiating a capital campaign; (4) accepting or refusing
a donation or bequest of real estate; (5) accepting or refusing a donation or bequest

or particular law. Obviously, the determinations will vary among dioceses, depending on the economic condition of each.

Specific acts of ordinary administration more important in light of economic conditions of other juridic persons are not mentioned in the universal law, though nothing prevents particular law from making such designations.

ACTS OF EXTRAORDINARY DIOCESAN ADMINISTRATION. Acts of extraordinary administration are acts which do not routinely occur, that is, "acts which exceed the limits and manner of ordinary administration" (canon 1281 §1). Jordan Hite says that acts of extraordinary administration "are those which because of the nature or importance of the action or its financial value require the permission of a higher authority. Examples would include ... acceptance or refusal of major bequests or gifts, purchase of land, construction of new buildings or extensive repair of old buildings, initial investment of capital, other expenditures of an amount over a certain limit. Establishing a hospital or school is usually considered an act of extraordinary administration because of its nature or importance."[72] Velasio De Paolis concludes that "designating some good as stable patrimony is an act of extraordinary administration."[73]

The legislator requires the conference of bishops[74] to identify acts of extraordinary diocesan administration. Given the obviously great importance of these acts of administration for all the dioceses belonging to the conference, the legislator requires the diocesan bishop to receive the consent of the diocesan finance council and

---

with accompanying financial obligations that could last for more than five years; (6) erection of a diocesan cemetery; and (7) conferral by decree of public or private juridic personality. He says, "These are only suggestions. The diocesan finance council and college of consultors could suggest others. When adopted, it would be wise to list them in the diocesan statutes (canon 94), *pagella*, listing of policies and procedures or by whatever mechanism the diocesan bishop uses to promulgate particular law for the diocese." In "Recent Developments," p. 282.

[72] HITE, "Church Law," p. 121.

[73] DE PAOLIS, *De bonis Ecclesiae temporalibus*, p. 101.

[74] In commenting on the 1980 *Schema*, Archbishop Joseph Bernardin recommended that the law assign designating acts of extraordinary administration to the conference of bishops. The secretariat rejected this recommendation; nonetheless, the 1982 *Schema* included Archbishop Bernardin's recommendation. *Relatio*, p. 286.

the college of consultors in order to place the acts validly. Only the diocesan bishop can perform acts of extraordinary diocesan administration.

For religious institutes, acts of extraordinary administration are to be determined by proper law (canon 638 §1).[75] For other juridic persons, these acts are to be determined by their statutes; if the statutes are silent, the diocesan bishop determines acts of extraordinary administration for juridic persons subject to him after he had heard the finance council (canon 1281 §1).

Inasmuch as acts of extraordinary administration must be identified in a legitimate way, it is clear that they are not identified "accidentally." Acts of administration not defined as extraordinary are ordinary. In determining acts which exceed the limits and manner of ordinary administration, attention will be given to a number of factors, such as:

- the quantity involved
- the risk of loss
- the effect that the act can have on the substance of the temporal good
- the effect that the act can have on the revenue of the temporal good
- the endangerment of the stable patrimony
- the modality and complexity of the transaction
- the predicted financial return
- the value of the thing
- the duration of the time of execution
- the certitude of economic results

---

[75] Canon 638 §1 says that, with due regard for the prescriptions of universal law, the proper law of each religious institute is "to determine acts which exceed the limit and manner of extraordinary administration and what is necessary to place an act of extraordinary administration validly." In other words, the proper law of each religious institute must define what constitutes acts of extraordinary administration *and* what processes (including consultations and consents) are required for valid acts of extraordinary administration. Canon 741 §1 specifically applies the requisites of canon 638 §1 to societies of apostolic life. Canon 718 allows proper law to apply the norm to secular institutes.

- the patrimonial and economic impact on the juridic person in question, etc.[76]

The Sacred Congregation for the Propagation of the Faith issued an *Instruction* on July 21, 1856 identifying acts of extraordinary administration for the dioceses of Holland.[77] The *Instruction* identifies the following as acts which exceed the limits of ordinary administration:

1. To accept or to renounce an inheritance, legacy, donation, or foundation;
2. To purchase immovable property;
3. To sell, exchange, mortgage, or pawn immovable Church property; or to subject it to any other servitude or burden, or to lease it for a period of more than three years;
4. To sell, exchange, mortgage, or divert in any other way from the place for which they are destined, objects of art, historical documents, or other movable property of *great importance*;
5. To borrow large sums of money as a loan, or to make agreements and other onerous contracts;
6. To build, pull down, or rebuild in a new form any church building or to make extraordinary repairs upon them;
7. To establish a cemetery;
8. To start or to suppress parochial institutions which are parish property;
9. To impose a *per capita* tax, to put on a drive (*collectas inducere*), or to give to others things belonging to a church;
10. To enter upon a lawsuit either as litigant or as defender.

---

[76] See SIGNIÉ, pp. 108-110; DE PAOLIS, *I beni temporali,* p. 147.

[77] SACRED CONGREGATION FOR THE PROPAGATION OF THE FAITH, *Collectanea Sacrae Congregationis de propaganda fide,* 2nd ed. vol. 1, "Congregatio generalis" (July 21, 1856), Vatican City, Ex Typographia polyglotta, 1907, n. 1127, art. 20, p. 603. This is cited as a source for CIC/1917, canon 1527 §1, which is the source for canon 1281 §1 of the 1983 code.
See SUGAWARA, "Amministrazione e alienazione dei beni temporali," p. 255, fn. 4; DAVID J. WALKOWIAK, "Ordinary and Extraordinary Administration" in *CFH,* pp. 186-187.

As is evident, some of these would not be considered acts of administration in the 1983 code; rather, some are acts of acquisition or acts of alienation in the revised law. Nonetheless, the list may be helpful in guiding those who must determine acts of extraordinary administration.

PARTICULAR LAW FOR THE UNITED STATES. A formal decree on acts of extraordinary administration has not been issued by the USCCB. At its general meeting in November, 1985, the NCCB issued provisions on the application of canon 1277; these were publicized on June 27, 1986.[78] The provisions state:

CANON 1277 -
ORDINARY AND EXTRAORDINARY ADMINISTRATION
BY A DIOCESAN BISHOP

The diocesan bishop must hear the finance council and the college of consultors in order to perform the more important acts of administration in light of the economic situation of the diocese; he needs the consent of this council and that of the college of consultors in order to perform acts of extraordinary administration besides cases specifically mentioned in universal law or in the charter of a foundation. It is for the conference of bishops to define what is meant by acts of extraordinary administration.

Complementary Norm: In accord with the norms of canon 1277, the National Conference of Catholic Bishops determines that the following are to be considered acts of extraordinary administration and therefore subject to the limits of canons that regulate such acts.

1. To alienate (in the strict sense, convey or transfer ownership) goods of the stable patrimony when the value exceeds the minimum limit (canon. 1292 §1).

2. To alienate goods donated to the Church through a vow, or to alienate goods that are especially valuable due to their artistic or historical value regardless of the appraised value (canon 1292 §2).

---

[78] NCCB, *Implementation of the 1983 Code of Canon Law. Complementary Norms*, Washington, NCCB, 1991, p. 21. These provisions never received the *recognitio* of the Apostolic See.

3. To incur indebtedness (without corresponding increase in the assets of the diocese) that exceeds the minimum limit (canon 1295).

4. To encumber stable patrimony the value of which exceeds the minimum limit (canon 1295).

5. To lease Church property when the annual lease income exceeds the minimum limit (canon 1297).

6. To lease Church property when the value of the leased property exceeds the minimum and the lease is for more than nine (9) years (canon 1297).

   Approved: General Meeting, November 1985
   Promulgated: Memorandum to All Bishops, June 27, 1986

A careful reading of these norms reveals several concerns. Norms 1 and 2 concern acts of alienation (not administration). Norms 5 and 6 concern leasing, about which canon 1297 requires distinct particular law established by the conference of bishops (which, in fact, were promulgated by the USCCB on June 8, 2007). Thus, only Norms 3 and 4 would concern acts of extraordinary administration (i.e., acts which can worsen the patrimonial condition of a juridic person).[79]

At its November 12-15, 2007 meeting, the USCCB voted favorably on establishing the following five actions as acts of extraordinary administration for dioceses:

1. Initiating a program of financing the issuance of instruments such as bonds, annuities, mortgages or bank debt in excess of the minimum set in accord with canon 1292 §1.

2. Resolving an individual or aggregate claim(s) by financial settlement in excess of the minimum amount set in accord with canon 1292 §1.

3. Engaging in the regular management or operation of a trade or business that is not substantially related to the performance of the religious, spiritual, educational or charitable purposes of the Church, for the purpose of generating income to carry on such activities.

---

[79] See DE PAOLIS, *De bonis Ecclesiae temporalibus*, p. 101.

4. Entering into any financial transaction or contractual agreement, the terms of which address matters involving an actual or potential conflict of interest for the diocesan bishop, vicar(s) general, episcopal vicar(s), auxiliary bishop(s) or diocesan finance officer.

5. Filing a petition of relief under Title 11 of the United States Code (commonly referred to as the United States Bankruptcy Code).[80]

This proposal has been forwarded to the Holy See for *recognitio*, which is pending.

Inasmuch as no particular law yet exists in the United States defining acts of diocesan administration, all acts of administration must be considered "ordinary" (since acts of extraordinary administration must be clearly defined). It may be especially prudent for a diocesan bishop, therefore, to identify certain acts which, while they cannot be considered acts of extraordinary diocesan administration (which only the conference of bishops can designate), are "non-routine" acts of more important ordinary administration in light of the economic condition of the diocese. This would be a temporary measure, pending the implementation of particular law identifying acts of extraordinary diocesan administration. This measure would reflect the spirit of canon 1277, which expects the diocesan bishop to be involved with the diocesan finance council and the college of consultors in significant acts of diocesan administration.

PARTICULAR LAW FOR CANADA.[81] On February 10, 1994, the CCCB issued particular law for the implementation of canon 1277 in Canada:

---

[80] Reported by the USCCB Office of Media Relations www.usccb.org/com/archives/2002/07-172.shtml (December 1, 2008). See PAPROCKI, "Recent Developments," pp. 278-279.

[81] CCCB, *Official Document No. 536-1* in CANADIAN CANON LAW SOCIETY, *Newsletter*, 20 (June, 1994); CCCB, *Complementary Norms to the 1983 Code of Canon Law*, Ottawa, CCCB, 1996, pp. 104-109. This is a revision of the Decree No. 9 originally published as *Official Document No. 536* on October 23, 1984; it had been reviewed by the Apostolic See (see letter of the apostolic nunciature, Prot. N. 20506, March 8, 1985): in *Studia canonica*, 19 (1985), p. 185. This earlier decree was corrected (as mentioned in commentary on the revised decree) since it had included some acts

Decree No. 9 – In accordance with the prescripts of c. 1277, the Canadian Conference of Catholic Bishops hereby decrees that the following as acts of extraordinary administration and therefore will be subject to the limitations of canons which regulate such acts:

1. non-cumulative acts over five per cent (5%) of the maximum amount approved by the Episcopal Conference and recognized by the Apostolic See for the alienation of Church property;
2. acceptance or refusal of an inheritance, a bequest, a donation or foundation because of long-term obligations;
3. erection of a cemetery;
4. court action;
5. purchasing of real estate.

The commentary on the revised decree states:

> Following some practical difficulties in the implementation of the decree [of October 23, 1984], it was revised by the Conference on March 20, 1992, and submitted to the Holy See. The Congregation of Bishops has now authorized the promulgation of the amended decree (Letter of Apostolic Nunciature, Prot. No. 4211/93, September 8, 1993).

> 1. The Code distinguishes three categories of acts: acts of *ordinary* administration (recurring expenses), acts which in view of the particular circumstances of the diocese are of *major importance* (these acts are to be determined by each bishop in his diocese), and acts of *extraordinary* administration. Canon 1277 provides that the Conference of Bishops is to determine which acts of temporal administration constitute acts of *extraordinary* administration.
> 2. When it is question of goods belonging to the diocese (and not to other juridical persons), the bishop must *consult* the

---

which were not acts of administration: "Acts which, according to the prescriptions of the *Code of Canon Law*, require the approval or the advice of certain groups or advisors." "Acts of alienation of property (these acts are also subject to the limitations of canon 1292 ss)." "Acts which endanger the patrimony of a juridical person (these acts are also subject to the limitations of canon 1292 ss)."

Finance Committee and the College of Consultors in carrying out acts of administration of *major importance*. However, acts of *extraordinary* administration require the *consent* of both the Finance Committee and the College of Consultors before they can be validly carried out by the diocesan bishop (Canon 1277).

Goods belonging to parishes are administered by the parish priest in accordance with Canons 1281-1288, under the supervision of the Ordinary (Canon 1276, §1). For this purpose, the parish priest is aided by the parish finance committee (see Canon 537; also Canon 1280). It is for the diocesan bishop, after consulting the diocesan finance committee, to determine what acts are to be considered "extraordinary" for the juridical persons subject to him (Canon 1281, §2).

3. According to paragraph 1 of the revised decree, non-cumulative acts involving the sum of more than $175,000 are acts of *extraordinary* administration (that is, 5% of the approved maximum amount for Canada which is $3,500,000 CDN, indexed to January 1, 1993 – see Decree No. 38).

4. If a bequest contains long-term obligations (generally considered to be more than 25 years), the diocesan bishop needs the *consent* of both the Finance Committee and the College of Consultors either to accept the bequest or to refuse it.

5. Lawsuits are governed by the prescriptions of Canon 1288.

6. Any purchase of real estate requires the *consent* of both the Finance Committee and the College of Consultors before the transaction can be completed validly.

7. In the case of religious institutes or societies of apostolic life who have to seek permission, etc., from the diocesan Ordinary or render an account to him (see Canons 637, 638, §4 and 741, §1), "it is for an institute's own law, within the limits of universal law, to define the acts which exceed the purpose and the manner of ordinary administration, and to establish what is needed for the validity of an act of extraordinary administration" (Canon 638, §1).

8. The original Decree No. 9 had included other acts which are no longer listed as acts of extraordinary administration. In particular, acts which by law require the *advice* of certain groups of persons had been listed as acts of extraordinary administration in Canada. This, for all practical purposes, had eliminated the category of *acts of major importance*. In virtue of the amended decree, then, while these acts remain subject to the prescriptions of Canon 1277, they no longer require the *consent* of the college of consultors and the finance committee (the *advice* of these bodies is sufficient).

9. Acts of *alienation* of property (both in the strict sense – conveyance, sales, etc. – and in the broad sense of the term – acts which could jeopardize the patrimonial condition of a juridical person) had also been listed previously under the category of *extraordinary administration*. However, since the 1983 Code distinguishes clearly between acts of administration and acts of alienation, the latter should not be listed under the category of *extraordinary administration*. Obviously, the prescriptions of the Code relating to alienation (Canons 1292-1295) are to be applied. The *consent* of the finance committee and of the college of consultors is required for acts of alienation above the indexed sum of $350,000 CDN (that is, above 10% of the maximum amount approved by the Conference – see Decree No. 10), and, if the value exceeds $3,500,000 CDN, the consent of the Apostolic See is also required (see Decree No. 38).

CORRESPONDING CANON OF THE EASTERN CODE: None. There is no canon in the Eastern code corresponding exactly to Latin canon 1277. Yet, Eastern canon 263 §4 says that the eparchial bishop is not to fail to hear the eparchial finance council "in the more important acts concerning financial matters." It clarifies additionally: "The members of this council have only a consultative vote, unless their consent is required by common law in cases specifically mentioned or by the founding document."

OPTIONAL FUNCTIONS OF THE DIOCESAN FINANCE OFFICER

Can. 1278 – In addition to the functions mentioned in can. 494, §§3 and 4, the diocesan bishop can entrust to the finance officer the functions mentioned in cann. 1276, §1 and 1279, §2.

Canon 1278 recalls functions (*munera*) of the diocesan finance officer assigned elsewhere in the code, to which the diocesan bishop can entrust two additional duties.[82] The mandatory functions entrusted by universal law to the diocesan finance officer are:

1. To administer the goods of the diocese under the authority of the diocesan bishop, in accord with the budget determined by the diocesan finance council (canon 494 §3)

2. To meet out of diocesan income the expenses authorized by the diocesan bishop or others designated by him (canon 494 §3)

3. To render an account of income and expenditures to the diocesan finance council at the end of the fiscal year (canon 494 §4)

To these functions common to every diocesan finance officer, canon 1278 enables the diocesan bishop to add two others:

1. To exercise careful vigilance over the administration of public juridic persons subject to the diocesan bishop (canon 1276 §1)

2. To appoint administrators of the goods of a public juridic person which is subject to the ordinary and which does not have its own administrators designated by law, the charter of the foundation, or its own statutes (canon 1279 §2).[83]

---

[82] See FREDERICK C. EASTON, "The Diocesan Finance Officer," in *CFH*, pp. 125-134.

[83] FRANCIS G. MORRISEY concludes that in this situation the diocesan bishop would not be delegating the diocesan finance officer to *appoint* these administrators, but rather that the diocesan bishop would appoint the diocesan finance officer to *serve as* the administrator. In "Temporal Goods," pp. 724-725. This same position is taken by other canonists: MARIANO LÓPEZ ALARCÓN, in "Book V," p. 986; VELASIO DE PAOLIS, in *De bonis Ecclesiae temporalibus*, p. 89; LUIGI MISTÒ, "I beni temporali della Chiesa," in *Scuola cattolica*, 119 (1991), p. 325. According to this interpretation of canon 1278, the diocesan finance officer would not be exercising delegated power of the diocesan bishop, but would simply be the administrator of a public juridic person.

The diocesan finance officer is the "routine" administrator of the ecclesiastical goods of the diocese, a function he performs under the authority of the diocesan bishop. The Code says he or she must be "truly expert in financial affairs and absolutely distinguished for honesty" (canon 424 §1). As one who holds an ecclesiastical office, he or she must also be "in the communion of the Church" and be "endowed with those qualifications which are required for the office" (canon 149 §1). The *Directory for the Pastoral Ministry of Bishops* repeats the discipline of canon 494 §3 (that the diocesan finance officer "must administer the goods of the diocese according to the parameters approved by the finance council and according to the approved budget")[84] and offers a more detailed description of his or her qualifications:

> The finance officer, who may be a permanent deacon or
> a lay person, must possess extensive experience in the
> administration of financial affairs. He must have a good
> knowledge of civil and canonical legislation concerning

ROBERT T. KENNEDY, however, contends that canon 1278 empowers the diocesan bishop to delegate the diocesan finance officer with the power to appoint the administrators mentioned in canon 1279 §2. In "Temporal Goods," p. 1480. JOHN HUELS concurs and offers a suggested faculty which the diocesan bishop may give to the diocesan finance officer: "If a public juridic person does not have its own administrator, whether by law, custom, the charter of foundation, or its statutes, you may appoint a suitable administrator for a three-year term and reappoint the same person for another term (c. 1279 §2)." In *Empowerment for Ministry*, New York, Paulist Press, 2003, p. 197; see p. 195.

The Kennedy position seems preferable to that which claims canon 1278 empowers the diocesan bishop merely to appoint the diocesan finance officer to serve as the administrator in canon 1279 §2. Were the latter so, there would be no need for the special provision of canon 1278, since the diocesan bishop could appoint the diocesan finance officer, *just as he could appoint anyone else qualified*, to perform the role mentioned in canon 1279 §2. Further, it would appear inappropriate for the diocesan finance officer also to be the "specially appointed" administrator of goods of public juridic persons (canon 1279 §2) over whose administrator he or she may also be exercising vigilance by special concession of the diocesan bishop (canon 1276 §1). See DE PAOLIS, "Alcune osservazioni," p. 118. Nonetheless, one must observe that Eastern canon 262 §2 gives by common law to the eparchial finance officer the function of administering goods that lack an administrator designated by the law.

[84] *DPMB*, n. 192.

temporal goods and of any legal agreements with the civil authority concerning ecclesiastical goods.[85]

The universal law also mandates that a finance officer, commonly called the treasurer or bursar, be established in each religious institute. Canon 636 §1 states: "In each institute and likewise in each province which is governed by a major superior, there is to be a finance officer, distinct from the major superior and constituted according to the norm of proper law, who is to administer goods under the direction of the respective superior. Insofar as possible, a finance officer distinct from the local superior is also to be designated even in local communities." Just as each diocese must have a diocesan finance officer who functions under the authority of the diocesan bishop (canon 494 §3), so each religious institute and province is to have a finance officer who functions under the direction of the superior. Canon 638 §2 says that the superior and other persons designated by proper law (which may include the finance officer) are able to perform acts of ordinary administration, something which in a diocese is done routinely by its finance officer under the authority of the diocesan bishop.[86]

CORRESPONDING CANON OF THE EASTERN CODE. None.[87]

---

[85] *DPMB*, n. 192.

[86] VELASIO DE PAOLIS observes: "[C]anon 636, which refers to administration of the temporal goods of religious, deserves special attention. After stating that the general or provincial econome must be different from the major superior, the code says that he or she is to administer the goods under the direction of the respective superior. In this case the superior has not only supervision but the direction itself, which evidently is something more, since direction also implies a real right to dispose of the goods themselves. As a matter of fact, canon 638, §2 states that 'besides the superiors, even the other officials appointed for that purpose in their proper law can, within the purview of their office, validly make expenditures and perform juridical acts of ordinary administration.' The religious superiors, therefore, have not only supervision but can also perform administrative acts that are proper to economes. In their own purview, religious superiors have more power than local ordinaries in their diocesan purview. The reason is very simple if we understand the typical setup of religious institutes and the religious vows. The diocesan ordinary, even with regard to *diocesan* church goods, cannot dispose of them. But every juridical person has its own competent organs." In "Temporal Goods... Consecrated Life," pp. 352-353. Nonetheless, one must recall that the diocesan bishop "has all ordinary, proper, and immediate power which is required for the exercise of his pastoral function except

ADMINISTRATORS OF ECCLESIASTICAL GOODS

Can. 1279 – §1. The administration of ecclesiastical goods pertains to the one who immediately governs the person to which the goods belong unless particular law, statutes, or legitimate custom determine otherwise and without prejudice to the right of the ordinary to intervene in case of negligence by an administrator.

§2. In the administration of the goods of a public juridic person which does not have its own administrators by law, the charter of the foundation, or its own statutes, the ordinary to whom it is subject is to appoint suitable persons for three years; the same persons can be reappointed by the ordinary.

Canon 1279 §1 defines the person competent to administer ecclesiastical goods.[88] The administration of such goods belongs to

---

for cases which the law or a decree of the Supreme Pontiff reserves to the supreme authority or to another ecclesiastical authority" (canon 381 §1). The code does not say that the diocesan bishop *cannot* perform routine acts of ordinary diocesan administration; it simply says that such acts are performed by the diocesan finance officer under the authority of the diocesan bishop (canon 494 §3). The code also explains that the diocesan bishop (not the diocesan finance officer) is the agent to perform acts of ordinary diocesan administration which are more important in light of the economic condition of the diocese (canon 1277), acts of extraordinary diocesan administration (canon 1277), acts of diocesan administration which can worsen the patrimonial condition of the diocese (canon 1292), and acts of alienation of diocesan goods belonging to stable patrimony and valued beyond the minimum amount established by the conference of bishops (canon 1292 §2).

[87] Note, however, that CCEO canon 262 §3 gives by common law to the eparchial finance officer the functions, among others, of overseeing the administration of ecclesiastical goods through the eparchy and of administering goods which lack an administrator designated by the law.

[88] Commentators offer various interpretations on the purpose of this canon. Among other things, some conclude it intends to define the function of administrators, and others conclude it intends to assure that every public juridic person has an administrator and that the ordinary, in his vigilance role, intervenes in cases of negligence. See DE PAOLIS, "Alcune osservazioni," pp. 110-114. In fact, the canon addresses all these issues.

CIC/1917, canon 1521 §1 allowed the local ordinary to appoint only suitable men (*viros idoneos*) to serve as administrators; their reappointment was discouraged. The 1977 *Schema* had also made reference to *viros idoneos* (canon 24). During the consultation process, it was suggested to change the language to *personas idoneas* so that women would be included. The consultors agreed: *Communicationes,* 12 (1980), p. 416.

the one who immediately governs the juridic person to which they belong,[89] unless a different determination is made by particular law, statutes, or legitimate custom. For example, the administrator of the ecclesiastical goods of a parish is its pastor (canon 532) who governs the parish under the authority of the diocesan bishop (canon 515 §1).[90]

The canon adds that the ordinary has the right to intervene in case of the negligence of an administrator. This is consistent with his exercising careful vigilance over the administration of all the goods which belong to public juridic persons subject to him (canon 1276 §1). Even though the diocesan bishop may entrust this careful vigilance to the diocesan finance officer (see canon 1278), canon 1279 §1 does not indicate that the diocesan finance officer may intervene in the case of an administrator's negligence. Rather, the diocesan finance officer would inform the diocesan bishop about an administrator's negligence, and the diocesan bishop himself would then make the intervention.

Canon 1279 §2 is suppletive law. If a public juridic person subject to the ordinary does not have its own administrator (as identified by law, the charter of the foundation, or its own statutes), then the ordinary is to appoint a suitable person to serve as administrator for a term of three years, renewable. If the ordinary involved is the diocesan bishop, he may delegate the diocesan finance officer to appoint administrators of the goods of public juridic persons subject to himself (canon 1278). Canon 1279 §2 wants to make sure that each

---

[89] Inasmuch as this canon identifies the administrator of the goods of a juridic person as the one who immediately governs it, those revising the code eliminated as superfluous CIC/1917, canons 1182-1184 which had identified the administrators of the goods of various types of churches. See 1977 *Schema*, Preface, p. 5.

[90] THOMAS J. GREEN raises the interesting possibility of the appointment of a *parish finance officer* to *assist* in the administration of parochial ecclesiastical goods, in "Shepherding the Patrimony," pp. 709, 710, 732-734. It must be understood, however, that such a figure would not diminish the role of the pastor who by universal law must remain the legal representative of the parish and the administrator of parochial goods (canon 532). See also PHILIPPE GREINER, "Les biens des paroisses dans le contexte des diocèses français," in *L'année canonique*, 47 (2005), pp. 41-42; SIGNIÉ, pp. 116, 133.

public juridic person *always* has an administrator.[91]

CORRESPONDING CANON OF THE EASTERN CODE: CANON 1023. The Eastern canon corresponding to Latin canon 1279 §1 is quite succinct. It states that the administration of ecclesiastical goods of a juridic person pertains to the one who immediately governs it, unless the law provides otherwise. It contains no reference to the right of the ordinary to intervene in the case of negligence or to appoint administrators who are lacking. No canon corresponding to Latin canon 1279 §2 exists in the Eastern code.[92]

MANDATORY FINANCE COUNCILS OR FINANCIAL COUNSELORS

Can. 1280 – Each juridic person is to have its own finance council or at least two counselors who, according to the norm of the statutes, are to assist the administrator in fulfilling his or her function.

Canon 1280 requires each juridic person[93] to have its own finance council or at least two counselors who, according to its stat-

---

91   For reflection on the responsibility of the ordinary to appoint administrators of public juridic persons, see PCLT, *Nota,* La funzione dell'autorità, pp. 28-29. This document also explains that the ordinary *cannot* supply administrators for *private* juridic persons unless this power is given to him by the statutes or decree of establishment of the private juridic person. It mentions, however, the norm of canon 1480 §2 whereby, in a trial when the legal representative of a *private* or *public* juridic person is lacking or negligent, the ordinary can stand trial personally or through another in the name of a juridic person subject to him. PCLT, *Nota,* La funzione dell'autorità, p. 27, fn. 14.
One notes that canon 1279 §2 is about the appointment of an *administrator* by the ordinary, but canon 1480 §2 is about the appointment of a *legal representative* by the ordinary.

92   Eastern canon 262 §2, however, says that eparchial finance officer is "to administer the temporal goods that lack an administrator designated by law." See the commentary on Latin canon 1278.

93   Canon 1257 §2 says that the temporal goods of private juridic persons are not governed by the norms of *Book V* "unless other provision is expressly made." The words of canon 1280, "each juridic person," appear to be such an expressly made "other provision." See DE PAOLIS, *I beni temporali*, p. 163; DE PAOLIS, *De bonis Ecclesiae temporalibus*, p. 90; MORRISEY, "Temporal Goods," p. 725.
ROBERT T. KENNEDY, however, concludes that the discipline of canon 1280 only applies to *public* juridic persons. He reaches this conclusion based on text (the canon

utes, assist the administrator in his or her function (*munus*). This
is an example of the code engaging others in the administration of
ecclesiastical goods. This canon did not have a predecessor in the
1917 code.[94]

Elsewhere, the universal law requires the establishment of finance councils in each diocese (canons 492-493) and in each parish
(canon 537), each of which is a public juridic person. These juridic
persons cannot select to have two financial counselors instead of a
finance council.

The Sacred Congregation for Religious issued a decree, *Inter
ea*, on September 15, 1909 which required religious institutes to
establish a council of vigilance over temporal goods where a general
council did not exist. Implicit in this is that the general council can
take on the functions of a finance council in a religious institute. "It
would seem that, all things considered, the same would apply at the
provincial level and at the local level also."[95] Nonetheless, the 1983
code requires that religious institutes, as public juridic persons, follow the discipline of canon 1280 (see canon 635 §1).

DIOCESAN FINANCE COUNCIL. The code's discipline on the
diocesan finance council is treated in the commentary on canon
1263, where it is mentioned for the first time in *Book V*.

PARISH FINANCE COUNCIL. The code explains that a parish is a
juridic person *a iure* (canon 515 §3) which is represented in all juridic

---

does not include reference to private juridic persons, as canon 1267 §1 does) and
context (canon 1280 is situated between canons 1279 §2 and 1281, which may be
taken as a "cluster" of canons all dealing with public juridic persons) (see canon 17).
In "Temporal Goods," p. 1482.

In the end, whether canon 1280 does or does not bind them, private juridic persons
nonetheless will wisely welcome the effective service of a finance council or at least
two counselors to assist their administrators. The statutes of the private juridic person
would make this provision.

[94] This canon was added after the *coetus* drafting the proposed new law received comments on the 1977 *Schema* which had not included it. *Communicationes,* 12 (1980)
415-416.

[95] FRANCIS G. MORRISEY, "Religious Institute's Finance Council" in *CLSA AO2*, pp.
409-410.

affairs by its pastor[96] who "is to take care that the goods of the parish are administered according to the norm of cann. 1281-1288" (canon 532). The code also requires that each parish have its own finance council (and not merely two financial counselors) whose members assist the pastor in his parochial administration:

> Can. 537 – In each parish there is to be a finance council which is governed, in addition to universal law, by norms issued by the diocesan bishop and in which the Christian faithful, selected according to these norms, are to assist the pastor in the administration of the goods of the parish, without prejudice to the prescript of can. 532.

Several important observations are to be made about this canon.[97] The parish finance council is required by law; it is not optional. Since this is a constitutive law, the diocesan bishop cannot dispense from it (see canon 86). Its purpose is to assist the pastor in his administration of parochial goods according to the norms of canons 1281-1288; this assistance is offered in such a way, however, that the pastor remains responsible for taking care that parochial

---

[96] The same responsibilities of the pastor (canon 519) rest with the parochial administrator (canon 540), the "moderator" of the group of priests to whom a parish is entrusted *in solidum* (canon 534 §2, 3°), and the priest having the powers and faculties of a pastor who directs the pastoral care of a parish where a participation in the exercise of pastoral care has been entrusted to other than a priest (canon 517 §2). See JOHN A. RENKEN, "Parishes, Pastors, and Parochial Vicars," in *New Commentary on the Code of Canon Law*, commissioned by the CLSA, John P. Beal, James A. Coriden, and Thomas J. Green (eds.), New York, Paulist, 2000, pp. 684-688.

[97] This canon had not existed in the 1977 *Schema Canonum Libri II: De Populo Dei*, but was inserted thereafter by the *coetus De populo Dei*. The draft legislation, initially proposed on May 14, 1980 by the *coetus De populo Dei*, had mentioned finance councils for parishes, quasi-parishes, and "supra-parishes." Archbishop Rosalio José Castillo Lara observed that an extensive treatment of parish, quasi-parish, and supra-parish finance councils is unnecessary since *Book V* would require a council of administration for all juridic persons. He therefore proposed a less extensive canon, which became canon 537 of the promulgated law. *Communicationes*, 13 (1981), pp. 307-308.

The sources for canon 537 are CIC/1917, canons 1183-1184 (concerning the "council of maintenance" of church property), 1520 §§1-2 and 1521 §1 (the diocesan council of administration), and 1525 §1 (requiring an annual report of administrators to be presented to the local ordinary).

goods are administered properly (see canon 532).[98] Its functions are
determined by universal law and by the particular law established
by the diocesan bishop.[99] It is comprised of members of the Christian faithful. Canon 537 does not say that the parish finance council
"possesses a consultative vote only,"[100] as canon 536 §2 does say
about the parish pastoral council, which is not required by universal
law but may be required by the particular law of the diocese (canon
536 §1).[101]

The specific functions of the parish finance council are to be
determined by universal law and especially by diocesan particular
law. As a matter of fact, the universal law assigns to the parish finance
council only the general function of assisting the pastor in the administration of parish goods. No more specific functions are identified.
It would appear appropriate that particular law assign to the parish

---

[98] THOMAS J. GREEN reflects on the parish finance council: "Each parish as a public
juridic person is to be governed by its own statutes, which are to be approved by
the bishop (canons 94, 117). Its statutes are to define the purpose, constitution, government, and operation of the parish. In this connection the statutes should define
clearly the precise relationship of the finance council to the pastor, whose primary
administrative leadership position is to be respected (canon 532) and whom the
council is to assist in exercising the various facets of his administrative role (e.g.,
canons 1281-1288). The finance council does not have an autonomous executive
role but needs to be reviewed constantly in relationship to the pastor as the primary
administrative figure in the parish. The finance council is to collaborate with him
in making the most effective use of parish financial resources for the good of the
Church." In "Shepherding the Patrimony," p. 729. See also AGOSTINO DE ANGELIS,
"I consigli per gli affari economici: Statuti e indicazioni applicative," in *Monitor
ecclesiasticus*, 111 (1986), pp. 57-68; SIGNIÉ, pp. 116-138.

[99] In commenting on the 1980 *Schema*, Archbishop Joseph Bernardin had recommended
that particular law for parish finance councils be established by both the diocesan
bishop and the conference of bishops. The secretariat rejected his recommendation
since it judged that the legislative intervention of the conference in this matter is
unnecessary. Instead, diocesan bishops should issue particular laws in accord with
the universal law. *Relatio*, p. 128.

[100] Nonetheless, from the wording of canon 537 ("to assist the pastor in the administration of the goods of the parish"), it is clear that the parish finance council is not an
"administrative council." The administration of the parish rests with the pastor alone
(canon 532). Canon 537 does not compromise the pastor's administrative role. See
FRANCESCO COCCOPALERMO, "Quaestiones de parochia in novo codice," in *Periodica*,
73 (1984), pp. 403-404.

[101] In a similar fashion, the code does not say that the diocesan finance council (canons
492-493) "possesses only a consultative vote" as canon 514 §1 does say about the
diocesan pastoral council. Likewise, the diocesan finance council is required by
universal law (canon 492) but the diocesan pastoral council is not (canon 511).

finance council at least two basic or routine functions mandated by universal law for the diocesan finance council – i.e.

1. to prepare an annual budget (which is required for dioceses in canon 493, but only *strongly recommended* for other juridic persons by universal law, which provides that the annual parish budget may be *required* by particular law: see canon 1284 §3)
2. to examine the annual statement of income and expenditures (see canon 493).

If these documents are prepared by the pastor or a parish staff member, particular law may require that the parish finance council offer its *counsel* before they are presented to the local ordinary (see canon 1287 §1).

The particular law may also wisely require the *counsel* of the parish finance council before the pastor seeks to perform acts of extraordinary administration, as such acts are defined by the diocesan bishop with the counsel of the finance council (canon 1281 §2), or acts of alienation.

Canon 537 does not indicate the qualities to be possessed by the members of the parish finance council. It would seem appropriate, however, that particular law require they have at least the same qualifications as members of the diocesan finance council – i.e., that those serving on the parish finance council be "members of the Christian faithful truly expert in financial affairs and civil law [and] outstanding in integrity" but not related to the pastor (nor, perhaps, to the bishop) up to the fourth degree of consanguinity or affinity (see canon 492 §§1, 3). Particular law may also require that members of the parish finance council be parishioners.[102] In addition, it may indicate how they become members of the council (e.g., by

---

[102] The code identifies two kinds of parishes: territorial and personal (canon 518). One becomes a member of a territorial parish by having a domicile or quasi-domicile within its boundaries (see canons 102 §3, 107 §1). One becomes a member of a personal parish by belonging to the rite, language, or nationality for which it was established. See JOHN A. RENKEN, "Parishes, Pastors, and Parochial Vicars," pp. 688-689.

appointment, election, ex officio,[103] etc.), the length of their terms, and their number.

Particular law may also identify the minimum number of times that the parish finance council meets annually. If it is involved with the annual budget and the annual financial report, logically the parish finance council would need to meet at least twice a year. Inasmuch as it truly assists the pastor in parish administration, however, it seemingly would need to meet more frequently.[104] Therefore, the diocesan particular law may specify that the parish finance council meet a minimum number of times annually (e.g., quarterly).

CORRESPONDING CANON OF THE EASTERN CODE: None.

ACTS OF ORDINARY AND EXTRAORDINARY "NON-DIOCESAN" ADMINISTRATION; INVALID AND ILLICIT ADMINISTRATION

Can. 1281 – §1. Without prejudice to the prescripts of the statutes, administrators invalidly place acts which exceed the limits and manner of ordinary administration unless they have first obtained a written faculty from the ordinary.

§2. The statutes are to define the acts which exceed the

---

[103] It may be appropriate, for example, that the parish's appointed lay trustees, where they exist in a civil law, serve as ex officio members of the parish finance council.

[104] PATRICK J. SHEA identifies a number of functions with which the parish financial council may be involved: "personnel policies; internal control policies and procedures; review of contracts, investments, insurance, banking arrangements; construction and renovation and review of proposals for maintenance of buildings and grounds; litigation; technology; employee benefits; inventory of assets; approval of non-budgeted expenses over a certain amount and approval of all matters that require the consent of the diocesan bishop; review leasing arrangements; monitor performance and implementation of budget; review budgets of parish organizations." In "Parish Finance Councils," *CLSA Proceedings*, 68 (2006), pp. 180-181.
Another listing is proposed by JOHN HUELS: "The precise duties of the finance council should be listed in diocesan statutes. The competence of the council could extend to the preparing or reviewing of budgets and reports; advising on all acts of extraordinary administration and alienation, on contracts, salaries and benefits of parish employees, insurance, investments, loans, mortgages, leases, rents, fund raising, land and buildings and, overall, on any financial and legal matters within the council's competence as specified by particular law or as brought to its attention by the pastor." In *The Pastoral Companion: A Canon Law Handbook for Catholic Ministry*, 3rd rev. ed., Quincy, Franciscan Herald Press, 1995, p. 356.

limit and manner of ordinary administration; if the statutes are silent in this regard, however, the diocesan bishop
is competent to determine such acts for the persons subject
to him, after having heard the finance council.

§3. Unless and to the extent that it is to its own advantage, a juridic person is not bound to answer for acts
invalidly placed by its administrators. A juridic person
itself, however, will answer for acts illegitimately but
validly placed by its administrators, without prejudice to
its right of action or recourse against the administrators
who have damaged it.

Canon 1277 had legislated that certain acts of *diocesan* administration are invalid if the diocesan bishop fails to receive from the
diocesan finance council and the college of consultors either their
counsel (for the case of acts of ordinary administration which are
more important in light of the economic condition of the diocese)
or their consent (for the case of acts of extraordinary administration, as these are defined by the conference of bishops). Canon 1281
legislates on the validity and liceity of acts of administration placed
by administrators of public juridic persons *other than dioceses*.[105]
Acts of administration are invalid if canon law so states (see canon
10). If the law places requirements which are not identified as being for validity and those requirements are not observed, the act of
administration is valid but illicit.

Without prejudice to the pertinent statutes, administrators act
invalidly[106] when, without the prior written faculty[107] of the ordi-

---

[105] The local ordinary has a more remote relation to private juridic persons: canon 1276 speaks of the ordinary exercising vigilance over the goods of *public* (not private) juridic persons, which perform their function "in the name of the Church" (see canon 116 §1). One reasonably concludes that canon 1281, which refers to both the "ordinary" and the "diocesan bishop," concerns acts of extraordinary administration performed only by the administrators of *public* juridic persons. See HUGO A. VON USTINOV, "El régimen canónico de los bienes de propriedad de las personas juridicas privadas," in *Anuario Argentino de Derecho Canónico*, 13 (2006), p. 211.

[106] VELASIO DE PAOLIS says that the validity of the act of extraordinary administration requires that the permission be *requested* and *granted* in writing. In *I beni temporali*, p. 164.

[107] A faculty is more than a mere permission; it is a "power to act." It is governed by the code's prescriptions on delegated power of governance (see canon 132 §1). Canon

nary, they place acts of extraordinary administration – i.e., acts of administration which exceed the *limits*[108] and *manner* of ordinary administration.

The code itself does not define acts of extraordinary administration. The conference of bishops is to define acts of extraordinary administration for *dioceses* (canon 1277). For other public juridic persons, acts of extraordinary administration are to be defined in their statutes. If the statutes fail to do so,[109] the diocesan bishop is to determine the acts of extraordinary administration for the persons subject to him after he has heard his finance council.[110] In doing this, the diocesan bishop may wish to follow the norms issued by the conference of bishops for acts of extraordinary *diocesan* administration.

Within a diocese, there may be some wisdom in determining acts of extraordinary administration for select parishes or for parishes belonging to certain categories (e.g., those with a certain number of parishioners, those with a certain annual income, etc.), rather than having one determination for all parishes. What may be extraordinary for one parish may not be so for another. The precise

---

1281 §1 says that an administrator of ecclesiastical goods may be given a faculty to place validly acts beyond the limits and manner of ordinary administration. Since administrators of ecclesiastical goods may be lay persons, and since all administrators can be given the faculty in canon 1281 §1, the application of this canon is an instance of lay persons being given a faculty.

[108] One notes that canon 1281 §1 speaks of *limits* (*fines*, in the plural) but canon 1281 §2 speaks of *limit* (*finem*, in the singular). This difference has no obvious practical legal significance.

[109] Statutes (canon 94) are required for all juridic persons, and no aggregate intending to obtain juridic personality is to acquire it without statutes (canon 117).

[110] If the statutes of public juridic persons not subject to the diocesan bishop are silent, the determination of acts of extraordinary administration is made by the competent authority identified in universal, particular, or proper law. See DE PAOLIS, *De bonis Ecclesiae temporalibus*, p. 90.

The 1977 *Schema* had said that the diocesan bishop is to define acts of extraordinary administration following consultation with the diocesan finance council. The *coetus De bonis Ecclesiae temporalibus* changed the draft to clarify that the diocesan bishop, following consultation with the diocesan finance council, is to define acts of extraordinary administration *only* for juridic persons subject to him. *Communicationes*, 12 (1980), p. 417.

determination for each parish would be identified in its statutes.[111]

Many, if not most, public juridic persons are established with civil legal recognition (e.g., parishes, hospitals, universities, social service agencies, etc.). It will be helpful for the corresponding civil legal documents to define acts of extraordinary administration. This will assure that the same requirements to perform acts of extraordinary administration are expected in both the ecclesiastical forum and the secular forum. To have identical requirements in the civil forum and the canonical forum will be helpful especially if the Church pursues civil litigation against an administrator who had placed canonically invalid acts of extraordinary administration.[112]

If the acts of administration are both valid and licit, the juridic person is responsible for them. If the acts of administration are *invalid* (and, therefore, also illicit), the juridic person is not responsible[113] unless and to the extent that they are to the advantage of the juridic person. If the acts are *valid but illicit*, however, the juridic person is responsible, but it has the right of canonical action or recourse against the administrators who have caused it damage. The person placing invalid or illicit acts of administration may be subject to the penalty mentioned in canon 1389 on abuse of ecclesiastical power:

Canon 1389 – §1. A person who abuses an ecclesiastical power or function is to be punished according to the

---

[111] See O'BRIEN, pp. 119, 121-127.

[112] See canon 1296 which indicates that competent authority may decide to take action to vindicate the rights of the Church when ecclesiastical goods have been *alienated* in a manner which is valid civilly but invalid canonically.

[113] The PONTIFICAL COUNCIL FOR LEGISLATIVE TEXTS stated very clearly: "The diocesan bishop cannot be held juridically responsible for acts which a diocesan presbyter performs in transgression of universal and particular canonical norms." The diocesan bishop can be responsible for a diocesan presbyter's illegitimate acts only (1) if the bishop does not provide the presbyter with the necessary helps mandated by law (see canon 384), or (2) if the bishop does not provide adequate pastoral remedies when he is aware of the presbyter's misconduct (see canon 1341). In *Nota*, Elementi per configurare l'ambito di responsabilità canonica del vescovo diocesano nei riguardi dei presbiteri incardinati nella propria diocesi e che esercitano nella medesima il loro ministero (February 12, 2004), in *Communicationes*, 36 (2004), pp. 36-37 (=PCLT, *Nota*, Elementi per configurare l'ambito). (This *nota* addressed acts of pedophilia committed by a presbyter, and concluded that the diocesan bishop does not have juridic responsibility for the presbyter's action based on the canonical subordination of a diocesan presbyter to his bishop.)

gravity of the act or omission, not excluding privation of office, unless a law or precept has already established the penalty for this abuse.

§2. A person who through culpable negligence illegitimately places or omits an act of ecclesiastical power, ministry or function with harm to another is to be punished with a just penalty.[114]

Canon 1729 §1 provides for an injured party, during a penal trial, to bring a contentious action to repair damages incurred personally by one who commits this delict (see canon 1596). Indeed, even outside the penal process, administrators who place invalid acts must repair damages in light of canon 128:

Can. 128 – Whoever illegitimately inflicts damage upon someone by a juridic act or by any other act placed with malice or negligence is obliged to repair the damage inflicted.[115]

Attention must also be given to the norm of canon 639 §4[116]

---

[114] Canon 1389 §1 is preceptive (see canon 1344) and indeterminate (see canon 1315 §2), but does allow privation of office as a penalty.

Canon 1389 §2 is preceptive (see canon 1344) and indeterminate (see canon 1315 §2). Unlike the first paragraph, this second paragraph focuses on an abuse done with *culpa* (not *dolus*) – i.e., the violation of a law or precept through omission of necessary diligence (canon 1321 §2). The harm done to another must be demonstrable in order to illustrate that the penal law has been violated. No other penal law in *Book VI* identifies negligence (*culpa*) as the basis for a sanction; all the others require malice (*dolus*) (see canon 1321 §1). If a person places or omits an act of ecclesiastical power, ministry, or function by failing to exert due diligence and, as a result, harm comes to someone, the offender commits the delict of canon 1389 §2.

Another penalty is established in canon 1377, concerning *alienation*: "A person who alienates ecclesiastical goods without the prescribed permission is to be punished with a just penalty." The "permission" referred to in this canon is actually the requisite "consent," without with the alienation is invalid. This penal law is preceptive (see canon 1344) and indeterminate (see canon 1315 §2).

For a more comprehensive treatment of penal law and temporal goods, see ELIZABETH MCDONOUGH, "Addressing Irregularities in the Administration of Church Property," in *CFH*, pp. 223-243; JOHN A. RENKEN, "Penal Law and Financial Malfeasance," in *Studia canonica*, 42 (2008), pp. 5-57.

[115] See JOHN J. FOLMER, "The Canonization of Civil Law: The Law of Personal Injury," in *CLSA Proceedings*, 46 (1984), pp. 46-65.

[116] Canon 639 §2 explains that a member of a religious institute must answer for a

which says that "an action can always be brought against [a member of a religious institute] who has profited from the contract [illicitly] entered into." This legislation is extended to members of societies of apostolic life (canon 741 §1). The proper law of secular institutes may apply this discipline to its members (canon 718).

CORRESPONDING CANON OF THE EASTERN CODE: CANON 1024. The Eastern law requires the written "consent" (not the "faculty") of the "competent authority" to place validly acts of extraordinary administration. If the statutes do not determine acts of extraordinary administration, such acts are to be determined by "the authority to whom the juridic person is immediately subject... after having consulted the competent council." The Eastern code omits any reference to a juridic person answering for valid but illegitimate acts placed by administrators, or to any action or recourse against administrators who damage the juridic person.

OBLIGATION TO FULFILL ADMINISTRATIVE FUNCTION

Can. 1282 – All clerics or lay persons who take part in the administration of ecclesiastical goods by a legitimate title are bound to fulfill their functions in the name of the Church according to the norm of law.

Canon 1282 legislates that all persons who have a part in the administration of ecclesiastical goods by a legitimate title have the legal duty to fulfill their functions, which are performed in the name of the Church, according to the law. Ecclesiastical goods are owned by public juridic persons (canon 1257 §1) which always perform their function for the public good "in the name of the Church" (canon 116

---

contract entered into concerning his or her own goods with the permission of the superior, but if the business was conducted by mandate of the superior, the religious institute must answer. Canon 639 §3 says that the individual member is responsible, not the religious institute, for a contract entered without any permission of superiors. The discipline of canon 639 §§2-3 applies for members of societies of apostolic life (canon 741 §1). The proper law of secular institutes may apply this discipline to its members (canon 718).

§1).[117] From this it follows that their administrators also fulfill their function "in the name of the Church," i.e., in a spirit of ecclesial communion and under the vigilance of, and following the directives of, competent ecclesiastical authority.[118]

The reference to "clerics and lay persons" is a deliberate change from the former code, which had made mention only of "lay men" (*viri*: CIC/1917, canon 1521 §1).[119] The canon addresses not only the administrators of ecclesiastical goods, but also others "who take part in the administration of ecclesiastical goods" by a legitimate title (e.g., members of the diocesan finance council, the college of consultors, etc.).[120]

The administration of ecclesiastical goods is to be done "according to the norm of law." The law may be universal law, particular law, proper law, statutes, and any civil laws "canonized" by canon law. The universal law makes it clear that ecclesiastical goods are owned for the very specific purposes outlined in canon 1254 §2; the administrator of ecclesiastical goods performs his or her function to fulfill these purposes and for no other reason.

---

[117] ADAM J. MAIDA and NICHOLAS P. CAFARDI suggest that the canonical administrators of ecclesiastical goods be described in terms of stewardship: "The notion of stewardship is a good one to apply to canonical administrators because it contains three important and pertinent concepts. First, the notion of stewardship connotes the fiduciary relationship that the administrator has toward the public juridic person. A steward is one who stands in a confidential position, a position of trust, toward the object of his or her stewardship. Human agents who act on behalf of public juridic persons do so in a relationship of trust toward the juridic person. Second is the idea of property and goods being held by one for the benefit of others. Property held by the steward is not the steward's own. It belongs to others, but the steward will hold, manage, and make the best of it for the true owner. Finally, stewardship connotes that one has been charged by a higher authority to look after the affairs of someone who cannot do so for himself or herself. In this regard, we are reminded particularly of the many stories of the Lord regarding stewards, entrusted to look after the affairs of an absent master. To make a clear legal analogy, the notion of stewardship carries within it the concepts of fiduciary relationship (the trust placed in the administrator by the public juridic person), bailment (the holding of property and goods for the benefit of others), and guardianship (the duty to look after the affairs of persons who are themselves unable to do so)." In *Church Property*, p. 62.

[118] See DE PAOLIS, *De bonis Ecclesiae temporalibus*, p. 91.

[119] *Communicationes*, 12 (1980), p. 416.

[120] The persons bound by this canon are not only those who hold an ecclesiastical office as defined in canon 145 §1. The "legitimate" title referred to in canon 1282 is not necessarily an office. See DE PAOLIS, *De bonis Ecclesiae temporalibus*, p. 91.

The code does not include a listing of personal qualifications for most administrators of ecclesiastical goods. Such qualifications may be identified in the statutes of a juridic person. To establish them, analogous reference may be made to qualifications for being a member of the diocesan finance council (canon 492): being a member of the Christian faithful (see canon 204 §1), truly expert in financial affairs and civil law, outstanding in integrity, not related to the superior of the public juridic person by consanguinity or affinity through the fourth degree. Likewise, and also relying upon canon 492, the statutes of the public juridic person would determine who appoints the administrator, the length of the administrator's term, and whether the term is renewable.

CORRESPONDING CANON OF THE EASTERN CODE: None.

OATH OF ADMINISTRATORS; INVENTORY OF GOODS

Can. 1283 – Before administrators begin their function:

1° they must take an oath before the ordinary or his delegate that they will administer well and faithfully;

2° they are to prepare and sign an accurate and clear inventory of immovable property, movable objects, whether precious or of some cultural value, or other goods, with their description and appraisal; any inventory already done is to be reviewed;

3° one copy of this inventory is to be preserved in the archive of the administration and another in the archive of the curia; any change which the patrimony happens to undergo is to be noted in each copy.

Canon 1283 explains that administrators must perform two tasks before they begin their work:

1. they must take an *oath* before the ordinary (or his delegate) to perform their function well and faithfully;

2. they must prepare and sign an accurate and clear *inventory* of the immovable property, precious movable objects, movable objects

of cultural value, and other goods. The inventory is to describe
the ecclesiastical goods and to appraise them. Any previous
inventory must be reviewed. A copy of the new inventory is to
be placed in both the curia and the archive of the administration;
the copies are to note any eventual changes in the patrimony.

This canon obviously pertains only to administrators of public juridic
persons; the requirements of taking an oath before, and present-
ing an inventory to, the ordinary does not apply to private juridic
persons who are not said to perform their function "in the name
of the Church" (see canon 116). Private juridic persons act in their
own name, with a certain autonomy, although they are established
by decree of competent ecclesiastical authority (canon 114 §1) and
recognized as persons in the Church (see canon 113 §2).

OATH. An oath is "the invocation of the divine name in witness to the truth" which cannot be taken validly by a proxy (canon
1199).[121] An oath extorted by malice, force, or grave fear is null by
the law itself (canon 1200 §2). A promissory oath (such as the one
in this canon) specially obliges the person by virtue of religion to do
what is affirmed by the oath (canon 1200 §1). Canon 1283 requires
the administrator to take an oath before the ordinary (or his delegate)
attesting to his or her intention to perform the administrative role

---

[121] Several canons mention taking an oath: canons 380; 876; 1454; 1455 §3; 1532; 1562
§2; 1568; 1728 §2. An oath is different from a mere promise inasmuch as an oath
invokes God as a witness to the matter promised, thereby making an oath to be an
act of the virtue of religion. A mere promise does not invoke God. Several canons
mention making a simple promise: canons 153 §3; 471, 1°; 1062; 1125; 1126; 1489.
One suggestion concerning the draft of this canon in the 1977 *Schema* recommended
that it make mention of a promise (rather than an oath) to fulfill one's office faithfully.
Only one consultor agreed with this recommendation. *Communicationes*, 12 (1980),
p. 418.

In the 1981 *congregatio plenaria*, Thomas Cardinal O'Fiaich suggested that the canon
not require an oath since the oath would bind even pastors who are not required to
make an oath concerning their other obligations. He observed that the CIC/1917,
canon 1522, 1° obliged only some administrators (i.e., the laity: see CIC/1917, canon
1521) to take the oath. The secretariat chose to maintain the general norm requiring
an oath for all administrators since the faithful administration of ecclesiastical goods
is very important. *Relatio*, pp. 286-297.

well and faithfully. It is appropriate for the copy of the oath to be maintained in the curia.

On July 1, 1989, the Congregation for the Doctrine of the Faith issued the "Profession of Faith and Oath of Fidelity on Assuming an Office to be Exercised in the Name of the Church."[122] The oath of fidelity, which is to be taken by those mentioned in canon 833, 5°-8°, includes the following:

> I shall carry out with the greatest care and fidelity the duties incumbent on me toward both the universal Church and the particular church in which, according to the provisions of the law, I have been called to exercise my service....
>
> I shall follow and foster the common discipline of the whole Church and I shall observe all ecclesiastical laws, especially those which are contained in the Code of Canon Law.[123]

Taking this oath, together with the approved formula of the profession of faith contained in the same document from the Congregation for the Doctrine of the Faith, is required to be taken by: vicars general, episcopal vicars, and judicial vicars (canon 833, 5°); pastors, rectors of seminaries, teachers of theology and philosophy in seminaries, those to be promoted to the diaconate (canon 833, 6°); rectors of ecclesiastical or Catholic universities, and teachers in any universities who teach disciplines pertaining to faith and morals (canon 833, 7°); and superiors in clerical religious institutes and societies of apostolic life, according to their constitutions (canon 833, 8°).

---

[122] CONGREGATION FOR THE DOCTRINE OF THE FAITH, "Professio fidei et iuriurandum fidelitatis in suscipiendo officio nomine Ecclesiae exercendo" (July 1, 1989), in *AAS*, 81 (1989), pp. 106, 1169; see also CONGREGATION FOR THE DOCTRINE OF THE FAITH, "Professio fidei et iuriurandum fidelitatis in suscipiendo officio nomine Ecclesiae exercendo una cum nota doctrinali adnexa" (June 29, 1998), in *AAS*, 90 (1998), pp. 543-544.

[123] Translation contained in *New Commentary on the Code of Canon Law*, commissioned by the CLSA, John P. Beal, James A. Coriden, and Thomas J. Green (eds.), New York, Paulist, 2000, p. 1854.

Particular law may prudently require the oath of fidelity, or at least the elements mentioned above, to be taken by all administrators of ecclesiastical goods.

INVENTORY. A new inventory must be made by the administrator before beginning his or her function. The inventory envisioned is to be quite detailed. It must list everything owned by the public juridic person (i.e., immovable property, movable objects both precious and having cultural value, and "other goods"). In particular, the inventory will identify goods which constitute the *stable* patrimony (see canon 1285, 1291) of the public juridic person. This new inventory must be compared to any previous inventory; this is the occasion to note missing items and to identify new ones. In proper administration, however, the new and the immediately previous inventories should be identical since the inventory is meant to be a "living document"; all modifications should regularly be identified in it.

Ordinaries who exercise vigilance over the administration of ecclesiastical goods which belong to public juridic persons subject to them (see canon 1276 §1) may wish to develop common forms for the inventories and to establish regular intervals at which the existing inventory is reviewed, modified if necessary, and submitted to the archive of the administration and of the curia.[124] Particular law may require, for example, that an updated inventory be made annually and submitted to the local ordinary together with the annual report of administration (see canons 1284 §2, 8°, 1287 §1).

Canon 1283 envisions two copies of the inventory. One is to be placed in the archive of the administration, and the other is to be placed in the archive of the curia. The curia is that of the superior of the administrator of the public juridic person. Both copies should be modified as patrimony changes.

The purpose of a detailed inventory is to indicate the ecclesiastical goods which belong to the public juridic person. In a parish, it would certainly be easier for the inventory to indicate goods which do *not* belong to it (e.g., the goods which belong to the clergy

---

[124] For sample inventories, see LAWRENCE A. DiNARDO, "The Inventory of Property" in *CFH*, pp. 151-163.

serving the parish). Nonetheless, the inventory required by canon 1283, 2°-3° should be a clear and certain statement identifying those goods which *do* belong to the parish, with their appraised value. Therefore, an inventory identifying what does *not* belong to the parish is inadequate.

The *Directory for the Pastoral Ministry of Bishops* reminds the diocesan bishop that, in his responsibility as a good head of a household, "[h]e must see to the preparation and updating of *inventories,* including photographs, with the description and appraisal of immovable and movable goods which are precious or of some cultural value."[125]

MOVABLE GOODS WHICH ARE PRECIOUS OR WHICH HAVE CULTURAL VALUE. The inventory of ecclesiastical goods must mention both movable goods which are precious and movable goods which have cultural value, and must include their description and appraisal.

The meaning of "precious goods" is discussed in the commentary on canon 1270.[126]

Movable goods having "cultural value" are those with a particular connection to the local culture. A great deal of subjectivity is required in determining them. It may be quite difficult, if not impossible, to assign a monetary value to these goods. Certainly, goods having great cultural value may be, but need not be, also "precious" and "sacred."[127]

CORRESPONDING CANONS OF THE EASTERN CODE: CANONS 1025-1026. Eastern canon 1025, which corresponds to Latin canon

---

[125] *DPMB*, n. 189 e).

[126] Reference to movable goods having cultural value was added when Monsignor Santi, a *peritus* to Giovanni Cardinal Colombo of Milan, had suggested, in reflecting on the 1977 *Schema*, that these are "goods which in any way, ordinary or extraordinary, give witness to a culture inspired by faith." The secretariat accepted this recommendation in the 1980 *Schema*. *Relatio*, p. 287.

[127] See SACRED CONGREGATION OF THE COUNCIL, *In applicatione* (June 25, 1930), *AAS*, 22 (1930), pp. 410-417; PONTIFICAL COMMISSION FOR PRESERVING THE PATRIMONY OF ART AND HISTORY, circular letter *Les bibliothèques ecclésiastiques dans la mission de l'Église* (March 19, 1994, Prot. N. 179/91/35), in *La documentation catholique*, 91 (1994), pp. 510-516.

1283, 1°-2°, requires that the administrator make a "promise" (not an "oath") to fulfill the administrative "office" (not "function") "faithfully" (rather than "well and faithfully"). The administrator must "sign" (not "prepare and sign") an "accurate" (rather than "accurate and clear") inventory of "the ecclesiastical goods" (without further specification) which have been entrusted to him or her, to be reviewed by the hierarch; the canon does not require an appraisal of these goods, nor a review of any previous inventories.

Canon 1026 corresponds to canon 1283, 3° and specifies that a copy of the inventory is to be preserved in the archive of the "eparchial" curia; any changes in "stable patrimony"[128] (rather than merely "patrimony") are to be noted in both copies of the inventory.

ADDITIONAL CANON OF THE EASTERN CODE: CANON 1027. Following these canons, the Eastern code inserts canon 1027 which has no corresponding Latin canon.[129] It says: "Authorities are to take care that administrators of ecclesiastical goods give suitable guarantees valid in civil law so that the Church suffers no loss by reason of the death or cessation from office of the same administrators."

ADMINISTRATORS AS DILIGENT HOUSEHOLDERS; FUNCTIONS OF ADMINISTRATORS

Can. 1284 – §1. All administrators are bound to fulfill their function with the diligence of a good householder.

§2. Consequently they must:

1° exercise vigilance so that the goods entrusted to their care are in no way lost or damaged, taking out insurance policies for this purpose insofar as necessary;

2° take care that the ownership of ecclesiastical goods is protected by civilly valid methods;

---

[128] For a discussion of the meaning of "stable patrimony," a term not found in the 1917 Code, see the commentary on canon 1285. The term "stable patrimony" is used twice in the Latin Code (canons 1285 and 1291) but three times in the Eastern Code (canons 1026 [which corresponds to canon 1283], 1029 [which corresponds to Latin canon 1285], and 1035 §1 [which corresponds to Latin canon 1291]).

[129] But see Latin canon 1284 §2, 2° which says administrators are "to take care that the ownership of ecclesiastical goods is protected by civilly valid methods."

3° observe the prescripts of both canon and civil law or those imposed by a founder, a donor, or legitimate authority, and especially be on guard so that no damage comes to the Church from the non-observance of civil laws;

4° collect the return of goods and the income accurately and on time, protect what is collected, and use them according to the intention of the founder or legitimate norms;

5° pay at the stated time the interest due on a loan or mortgage and take care that the capital debt itself is repaid in a timely manner;

6° with the consent of the ordinary, invest the money which is left over after expenses and can be usefully set aside for the purposes of the juridic person;

7° keep well-organized books of receipts and expenditures;

8° draw up a report of the administration at the end of each year;

9° organize correctly and protect in a suitable and proper archive the documents and records on which the property rights of the Church or the institute are based, and deposit authentic copies of them in the archive of the curia when it can be done conveniently.

§3. It is strongly recommended that administrators prepare budgets of incomes and expenditures each year; it is left to particular law, however, to require them and to determine more precisely the ways in which they are to be presented.

Canon 1283 identifies two responsibilities of administrators *before* they begin their function. Canon 1284 identifies responsibilities of administrators *while* they perform their function. It legislates that administrators have the duty to fulfill their function with the diligence of a good householder (*diligentia boni patrisfamiliae*). Administrators have nine specific obligations listed in canon 1284 §2. Canon 1284 §3 says that particular law can require a tenth obligation: the preparation of an annual budget of projected income and expenditures.

These obligations listed in canon 1284 §2 reflect CIC/1917, canon 1523 with several additional obligations: (1°) to have insurance policies to protect against loss or damage; (2°) to take care that ownership is protected with civilly valid methods; (5°) to pay interest on time and to reduce debt in a timely fashion; and (8°) to draw up an annual report of administration. Reference to an annual budget (canon 1284 §3) was also not mentioned in the 1917 code. The additions made in the 1983 code obviously reflect wisdom which accrued since the promulgation of legislation earlier in the twentieth century.

The discipline of canon 1284 is directed to administrators of public juridic persons; this conclusion is based on the fact that, unless the contrary is indicated (as is done in canon 1267 §1), the canons of *Book V* regard only public juridic persons (canon 1257 §1).[130] Nonetheless, inasmuch as the issues addressed by canon 1284 propose wise administrative practices, there is every reason also for administrators of private juridic persons to perform those practices.[131]

Should the administrator fail to observe any of these norms, his or her action would be canonically valid but illicit, since there is nothing in the text of canon 1284 expressly indicating that the legislation binds for validity (see canon 10). Nonetheless, should the administrator, through culpable negligence, illegitimately place an act of administration with harm to another, the law requires that the administrator be punished with an indeterminate just penalty (canon 1389 §2). Further, an administrator who illegitimately inflicts damage upon someone by a juridic act or any other act placed with malice or negligence is obliged to repair the damage (canon 128).

Presbyterorum ordinis, n. 17 of Vatican II calls upon priests "to manage ecclesiastical property, properly so called, according to the nature of the case and the norm of ecclesiastical laws, and with the help, as far as possible, of skilled lay persons. They are to apply this property always to those purposes for the achievement of

---

[130] Note also that canon 1284 §2, 2° refers to "ecclesiastical goods," which are owned only by *public* juridic persons (see canon 1257 §1).

[131] See KENNEDY, "Temporal Goods," pp. 1483-1484.

which the Church is allowed to own temporal goods."[132] A cleric administers ecclesiastical goods for the sake of the Church and not for personal gain. The same spirit morally binds all administrators of ecclesiastical goods.

VIGILANCE AND INSURANCE. Just as canon 1276 §1 requires the ordinary to exercise vigilance over the administration of all ecclesiastical goods belonging to public juridic persons subject to him, so also canon 1284 §2, 1° requires administrators to exercise their own vigilance so that the goods entrusted to their care are in no way lost or damaged. This reflects the fact that administrators are not the owners of the ecclesiastical goods but rather persons who exercise a fiduciary role which must be performed with great care and diligence, lest harm come to the public juridic person who owns the ecclesiastical goods (see canon 1256). Insofar as necessary, administrators are to take out insurance policies to protect these ecclesiastical goods. These insurance policies should assure replacement in case of property loss, and should periodically be reviewed to keep pace with inflation.[133]

CIVIL LEGAL PROTECTION.[134] Canon 1284 §2, 2° requires administrators to protect the property of public juridic persons by employing methods which are recognized in the civil legal forum,

---

[132] FLANNERY I, p. 895.

[133] See MAIDA-CAFARDI, *Church Property,* p. 68; JOSEPH A. FRANK, "Insurance and Ecclesiastical Goods," in *CFH,* pp. 215-221. The *DPMB* says that the diocesan bishop "should instill in pastors and in those charged with the administration of goods a strong sense of responsibility for the *preservation* of goods, taking adequate security measures so as to avoid theft." (no. 189 e)

K.A. HALL identifies the following as kinds of insurance which may protect Church property: (1) general liability; (2) personal injury liability (libel, slander, defamation, etc.); (3) civil damages; (4) legal defense; (5) policy territory, on and off the premises; (6) advertising injury; (7) additional insured, including volunteers; (8) participants coverage (in recreation and sports); (9) medical expenses (no fault coverage); (10) non-owned coverage; (11) mental anguish rider; (12) counseling liability; (13) abuse and harassment (vicarious liability); (14) employers liability rider (bodily injury); (15) employee benefits liability (for errors or omissions); (16) pollution liability (environmental damage); (17) tenants legal liability; (18) directors and officers liability (wrongful and negligent acts); (19) umbrella or excess liability. In "Facing the Risk – Liability Insurance Checklist," *CCCC Bulletin,* 4 (1998), p. 5.

[134] This element of administration was added after consultation on the 1977 *Schema. Communicationes,* 12 (1980), p. 419.

notwithstanding the fact that canon 1254 §1 proclaims the right of the Church to retain temporal goods independently from civil authority. If public juridic persons themselves are civilly incorporated, the civil legal documents must reflect canon law. Property owned by public juridic persons must be properly registered in the civil forum as owned by them. Further, since canon law considers the apostolates of a public juridic person (e.g., hospitals, schools, social service agencies, etc.) as works of the public juridic person itself, if these apostolates are separately civilly incorporated, they must be so fashioned civilly that the juridic person retains canonical ownership and rights – minimally, by identifying in the civil documents certain powers reserved to the canonical owner of ecclesiastical goods.[135] Likewise, of course, civil legal documents must reflect the Church's commitment to respect the intentions of the donors of ecclesiastical goods (see canon 1299 §2).

OBSERVING LAWS AND PRESCRIPTS. Canon 1284 §2, 3° requires administrators to observe civil law, canon law, and prescripts imposed by a founder, donor, or legitimate authority, and to take special care that no damage results from ignoring civil laws. This

---

[135] See the commentary on canon 1255 concerning "reserved powers" of the owners of civilly incorporated ecclesiastical goods.

ADAM J. MAIDA and NICHOLAS P. CAFARDI comment: "The theory has been raised that such insistence on legislating canonical realities into the civil law structure of incorporated apostolates creates a danger that the sponsoring public juridic person as a whole will become liable for the acts or omissions of the incorporated apostolate (e.g., piercing the corporate veil). Stated another way, this concern is that the advantages of separate incorporation are lost by creating close ties between the religious or diocesan sponsor and the incorporated apostolate. Actually, the types of canonical control required to be maintained by the religious or diocesan sponsor over the affairs of incorporated apostolates are not so great as to create that type of civil control that results in a loss of the advantages of separate incorporation. Where properly carried out by competent attorneys who are familiar with canonical requirements and the flexibility of the civil law, such risks are minimized.

"The other side of this coin, namely, the failure of the canonical stewards of public juridic persons to insist on a civil law structure for the juridic person itself or for its incorporated apostolates that mirrors canonical requirements, does present a very real danger. Where such a civil law structure is not used, the public juridic person or its apostolates may be bound in the civil law to act in a way that violates the canons or that is not in the best interests of the Church or the individual public juridic person." In *Church Property*, p. 70.

requirement of administrators is identified, as is the one immediately above, with due regard for the claim of canon 1254 §1 regarding the separation of Church and State. The prescripts of canon law must always be observed. Civil laws must be observed provided they do not contradict divine law or canon law (see canon 22), and special care must be taken lest damage come to the public juridic person by disregarding civil legal norms. Further, administrators are to observe any prescripts imposed by a founder, donor, or legitimate authority. Several canons commit the Church to respecting and following the intentions of donors.[136]

GATHERING AND PROTECTING REVENUE. Canon 1284 §2, 4° requires administrators to collect income accurately and on time. When this income is collected, it is to be protected (e.g., deposited immediately in a financial institution, or placed in a secure place until it is soon deposited). It is to be used for the proper purposes of the Church and according to the intention of the founder or legitimate norms.

DEBT REDUCTION. Canon 1284 §2, 5° requires administrators to work to eliminate any debts incurred by the public juridic person in a timely fashion. Administrators must see to it that any interest due on a loan or mortgage is paid when the interest is due. A workable debt reduction schedule should be established so that the principal is eliminated in a reasonable amount of time.

Canon 639 §1, in legislation on religious institutes, says that a juridic person is responsible for debts and obligations entered with the permission of the superior. Canon 639 §5 admonishes religious superiors "to take care that they do not permit debts to be contracted unless it is certain that the interest on the debt can be paid off from ordinary income and that the capital sum can be paid off through legitimate amortization within a period that is not too long." Canon 741 §1 applies this to societies of apostolic life. Canon 718 allows proper law to apply this discipline to secular institutes.

---

[136] The intention of the donor is highlighted in a number of canons: 121; 122; 123; 326 §2; 531; 616 §1; 706, 3°; 954; 1267 §3; 1284 §2, 3°; 1300; 1302 §1; 1303 §2; 1304 §1; 1307 §1; and 1310 §2.

INVESTMENTS. Canon 1284 §2, 6° requires administrators to invest any money which remains after paying the expenses of the public juridic person. The investment of these funds, which are to be set aside to further the purposes of the public juridic person, requires the permission of the ordinary. These funds may become part of its stable patrimony if they are legitimately designated as such (see canon 1291); such possible designation, however, is an act of extraordinary administration.[137] Administrators do not need the ordinary's consent simply to deposit money into a bank account which accrues interest.[138] Canon 1294 §2 stipulates that money received from alienation is either to be spent according to the purposes of the alienation or "to be invested carefully for the advantage of the Church."

ACCURATE FINANCIAL RECORD KEEPING. Canon 1284 §2, 7° requires administrators to keep well organized records of income and expenses. This obligation reflects the norm of canon 1283, 2°-3° that administrators keep well organized and updated records of ecclesiastical goods of public juridic persons in an inventory which is periodically updated. If administrators have made a budget of projected income and expenditures (canon 1284 §3), the records of actual income and expenditures would be compared periodically to the projections (perhaps on a monthly basis). It would be especially helpful for the members of the finance council (or the two financial counselors) of the public juridic person (canon 1280) to receive these periodic comparisons.

Accurate record keeping is also required by canon 958 §1 which requires the pastor or rector of a church or other pious place where Mass offerings are received "to have a special book in which they note accurately the number of Masses to be celebrated, the intention, the offering, and their celebration." The financial records of Mass offerings are to be diligently maintained.[139]

---

[137] See DE PAOLIS, *De bonis Ecclesiae temporalibus*, p. 101.

[138] MORRISEY, "Temporal Goods," p. 728.

[139] PAUL GOLDEN comments that "[t]oday, the special book could be a computer program." In "Mass Offerings Held in an Interest Bearing Account," p. 78.

Accurate record keeping is likewise required by canon 1307 §2 which requires the pastor or rector having a foundation to maintain a book noting the individual obligations, their fulfillment, and the offerings.

Annual Reports of Administration. Canon 1284 §2, 8° requires administrators to prepare an annual report of the administration. These annual reports will minimally reflect other issues concerning the administration of public juridic persons which are addressed in canon 1284 §2: e.g., income and expenses, debts incurred or reduced, investments, insurance coverage, compliance with the intentions of donors, legal protections, etc. Competent authorities may develop a form for the annual reports of administration and identify when these reports must be submitted, and may require that an updated inventory (see canon 1283, 3°) be submitted with the annual report of administration.

The recipients of annual reports of administration are identified in the commentary on canon 1287.

Protection of Legal Documents. Canon 1284 §2, 9° requires administrators to organize and protect securely the documents and records which identify the property rights of the Church. Authentic copies of them are to be deposited in the curial archive, if this can be done conveniently. Clearly, the canon refers to both civil and canonical legal documents. Administrators must be careful to make sure these documents are kept current. The inventory of the ecclesiastical goods of a public juridic person, which is to be updated regularly, is a canonical legal document identifying ecclesiastical goods (see canon 1283, 2°-3°). Care should be taken that its content is reflected in corresponding civil legal documents and insurance policies.

Annual Budget. The universal law requires that each diocesan finance council establish an annual diocesan budget, according to the directives of the diocesan bishop (canon 493). Canon 1284 §3 says that it is earnestly recommended (*enixe commendatur*[140])

---

[140] This phrase is found in several other canons: 904; 945 §2; 1065 §2; 1152 §1; 1176 §3.

that particular law require administrators of other juridic persons to prepare an annual budget of projected income[141] and expenses. A budget, responsibly and reasonably made, can assist in planning, i.e., in identifying priorities and responding to the needs, both long-term and short-term, of every public juridic person. It can also assist in eliminating any debts (see canon 1284 §2, 5°).

Even if particular law does not mandate the creation of an annual budget, there are countless prudent reasons for administrators of juridic persons to make one freely.

Particular law can determine the details of the annual budget and the formulary to be employed. Many, if not most, dioceses require that parishes create annual budgets (which are to be submitted to the local ordinary or a competent curial official), provide the appropriate budget form to be completed (which typically parallels the form of the annual report of income and expenditures), and expect the members of the parish finance council to collaborate with the pastor in preparing it.

The budget of every juridic person should reflect the proper purposes of the Church, for which it owns temporal goods (see canon 1254 §2).

CORRESPONDING CANON OF THE EASTERN CODE: CANON 1028. The Eastern code corresponds almost exactly to Latin canon 1284 with one exception: it makes no reference to the administrator taking care that the ownership of ecclesiastical goods is protected by civilly valid methods (canon 1284 §2, 2°). Instead, this topic is addressed at length in Eastern canon 1020, which is placed among the canons of "Chapter I: The Acquisition of Temporal Goods" and which legislates:

> **Canon 1020 – §1. Each authority is bound by the grave obligation to take care that temporal goods acquired by the Church are registered in the name of the juridic person to whom they belong, after having observed all the prescripts of civil law which protect the rights of the Church.**

---

[141] This "income" will include money accruing from donations, investments, rent, etc.

**§2. However, if civil law does not allow temporal
goods to be registered in the name of a juridic person,
each authority is to take care that, after having heard
experts in civil law and the competent council, the rights
of the Church remain unharmed by using methods valid
in civil law.**

**§3. These prescripts are to be observed also with re-
spect to temporal goods legitimately possessed by a juridic
person, but whose acquisition has not yet been confirmed
by written records.**

**§4. The immediately higher authority is bound to urge
the observance of these prescripts.**

Also related to the discipline of Latin canon 1284 §2, 2° is Eastern
canon 1027, which is not found in the Latin code. Eastern canon 1027
is placed among the canons of "Chapter II: The Administration of
Ecclesiastical Goods" and says:

**Canon 1027 – Authorities are to take care that admin-
istrators of ecclesiastical goods give suitable guarantees
valid in civil law so that the Church suffers no loss by
reason of the death or cessation from office of the same
administrators.**

DONATIONS ONLY FROM MOVABLE GOODS
BELONGING TO A NON-STABLE PATRIMONY

**Can. 1285 – Within the limits of ordinary administra-
tion only, administrators are permitted to make donations
for purposes of piety or Christian charity from movable
goods which do not belong to the stable patrimony.**

Canon 1285 concerns donations made by public juridic persons
through their administrators. It permits (*fas est*)[142] administrators to

---

[142] ROBERT T. KENNEDY comments about the use of this phrase: "This is an instance
where the force of the Latin is lost in English translation. The Latin *fas est adminis-
tratoribus*, translated 'administrators are permitted,' is stronger than mere permission; *fas* connotes a religiously based right or responsibility. It can be translated 'it
is lawful,' but with the connotation of lawful by divine command as distinguished

make donations for purposes of piety or Christian charity from movable goods that do not belong to the stable patrimony of the juridic person, but only within the limits of ordinary administration.[143]

The donations made by the administrators must be for purposes of piety or Christian charity (i.e., for pious causes: see canon 1299 §1).[144] Such donations are made for one of the principal purposes of the Church for which it has temporal goods, identified in canon 1254 §2 where specific reference is made to works of charity, especially toward the needy (see also canons 114 §2; 222 §1).

Donations can be made only within the limits of ordinary administration. Acts of extraordinary administration are to be defined by the statutes of the public juridic person. If the statutes are silent, such acts are defined by the diocesan bishop for public juridic persons subject to him after he has received the counsel of the finance council (canon 1281). For dioceses, such acts are determined by the conference of bishops (canon 1277). Canon 1285 concerns only donative acts within the scope of the *ordinary* administration of ecclesiastical goods.

Donations may be made only from movable goods which are not part of a stable patrimony. Immovable goods, whether belonging to a stable patrimony or not, may never be donated.

STABLE PATRIMONY. Everything owned by a juridic person

---

from lawfulness by human command or right (*ius est*)." In "Temporal Goods," p. 1487.

The phrase *fas est* appears in ten canons: 45; 366, 2°; 396, 2°; 628 §3; 748 §2; 762; 952 §1; 1177 §2; 1285; and 1609 §4.

The opposite phrase is *nefas est*, which carries the connotation that something is forbidden by divine command. It appears in four canons: 927; 983 §1; 1026; 1190 §1.

[143] CIC/1917 canon 1535, which is the predecessor of canon 1285, prohibited prelates and rectors of churches from making donations from the movable goods of their churches beyond small and moderate ones according to the legitimate custom of the place, except for reasons of remuneration, piety, or Christian charity. Donations made in violation of this canon could be revoked by administrators' successors in office.

[144] Canon 640 reminds religious institutes that they are to contribute something from their own goods to provide for the needs of the Church and the support of the poor. In light of canon 1285, any such donation by religious institutes must be from movable goods not belonging to stable patrimony. See MESTER, p. 53.

is its *patrimony*, but only some of that patrimony is considered its *stable patrimony*. All its other goods are *non-stable patrimony*. It is critically important to note the distinction between these two fundamental categories of all ecclesiastical goods.

The code does not define *patrimonium stabile* but, by the very wording of the canons 1285 and 1291 (the only two places in the code where the term appears[145]), the law presumes that juridic persons possess it. The term had not appeared in the 1917 code,[146] and consideration had been given during the code revision process to eliminating it.[147]

A good becomes part of stable patrimony by *legitimate designation* (see canon 1291). Such designation is "legitimate" when it is done according to the norm of universal law, particular law, proper

---

[145] "Stable patrimony" is mentioned a third time in the Eastern code. CCEO canon 1027 says changes in the stable patrimony of a juridic person are to be noted in its regularly updated inventory.

[146] The term *stable patrimony* was introduced into the proposed legislation by the *coetus De bonis Ecclesiae temporalibus* in order to identify goods which are protected against irresponsible alienation by administrators. CIC/1917, canon 1530 §1, which is the predecessor of canon 1291, spoke of "immovable ecclesiastical goods and movable ecclesiastical goods which can be saved by preserving them" (*res ecclesiasticas immobiles et mobiles, quae servando servari possunt*). The term *stable patrimony* may be considered the successor to this phrase, in which case one understands that stable patrimony includes both immovable and movable goods. The Latin phrase is admittedly difficult to translate. The author is indebted to DR. PIERRE BELLEMARE, professor of Latin at Saint Paul University, Ottawa, for assistance. Obviously, the phrase "*quae servando servari possunt*" is a reference only to the *res mobiles*. This is consistent with authors, including: F. WERNZ and P. VIDAL, *Ius canonicum*, vol. 4: *De rebus*, Rome, Gregorian University, 1935, pp. 225-226; S. SIPOS, *Enchiridion iuris canonici*, Rome, Herder, 1954, pp. 697-698; STANISLAUS WOYWOOD and CALLISTUS SMITH, *A Practical Commentary on the Code of Canon Law*, vol. 2, New York, Joseph F. Wagner, 1948, pp. 207-208.

Some movable goods cannot be saved because they are not preserved: i.e., they are fungible, which means they are consumed in their very use.

See *Communicationes*, 37 (2005), pp. 120-121; SUGAWARA, "Amministrazione e alienazione dei beni temporali," p. 269.

[147] *Communicationes*, 12 (1980), p. 420. The *coetus De bonis Ecclesiae temporalibus* had received recommendations to eliminate the term "stable patrimony" from the 1977 *Schema*. The recommendations indicated that this phrase was more apt to conditions of an earlier time, but that it does not seem suitable for the modern age which experiences so much economic change. Nonetheless, the *coetus* retained the term in order to place some limit on the donations proscribed by this canon. The *coetus* considered the term to reflect the conventional notion of what this canon conveys.

law, or statutes. Legitimate designation cannot happen "accidentally"; rather, it requires a positive act by competent ecclesiastical
authority.[148] Authors propose that such action by competent authority
is an act of extraordinary administration (see canons 1277, 1281 §§1-
2).[149] It is important that such designation occur, lest there be confusion concerning whether or not an ecclesiastical good belongs to the
stable patrimony of a juridic person. Without legitimate designation
as stable patrimony, the presumption must prevail that an ecclesiastical good is non-stable patrimony (see canons 1584-1586).[150]

Robert T. Kennedy offers the following reflections on the
meaning of "stable patrimony" in the code:

> Stable patrimony is all property, real or personal, movable
> or immovable, tangible or intangible, that, either of its
> nature or by explicit designation, is destined to remain in
> the possession of its owner for a long or indefinite period
> of time to afford financial security for the future. It is the
> opposite of free or liquid capital which is intended to be
> used to meet operating expenses or otherwise disposed
> of within a reasonably short period of time (within one
> or, at most, two years).
>
> There are four general categories of stable patrimony:
> (1) real estate (land, buildings); (2) non-fungible person-
> alty (tangible movable property that is not consumed in its
> use, such as automobiles, furniture, books); (3) long-term
> (over two years) investments in securities (stocks, bonds,

---

[148] DANIEL J. WARD offers a practical reflection: "It is not possible to make a universal
determination on what is included in stable patrimony except for those properties
which have been so designated. Therefore, when a [public juridic person] decides to
alienate property, it is necessary to make factual determination whether or not the
property is part of its stable patrimony and subject to the norms of alienation. To
alleviate the dilemma, a [public juridic person] could establish canonical principles
setting forth what will not be considered part of the stable patrimony. Based on these
principles, the [public juridic person] would designate future-acquired property as
part of or not part of its stable patrimony." In "Temporal Goods," p. 201, fn. 10.

[149] DE PAOLIS, *De bonis Ecclesiae temporalibus*, p. 101; DE PAOLIS, *I beni temporali*, p.
187; SCHOUPPE, p. 156.

[150] See DOHENY, *Practical Problems*, p. 43.

treasury notes); (4) restricted funds, that is, funds, even if comprised of cash or short-term securities, that have been set aside for a specific purpose, such as pension funds or certain building or educational funds. As a general rule, these four categories of assets are intended to afford reliable security for the future, enabling a juridic person to continue to serve the purposes for which it was created. They are said to be immobilized, stabilized, frozen; they are what is meant by "stable patrimony." Cash and its equivalents (e.g., checking and regular savings accounts, short-term certificates of deposit, securities to be held only for a short term), on the other hand, are considered to be liquid or free capital; it is intended that they be consumed in their use within a relatively short period of time (e.g., to meet operating expenses) and, hence, they are not stable patrimony.[151]

Another description of stable patrimony is provided by Mariano López Alarcón:

> Stable patrimony is comprised of those goods that constitute the minimum secure financial basis to enable the juridical person to subsist autonomously and to attend to the purposes and services proper to it; there are no absolute rules, however, for establishing the stability of a patrimony, since this depends not only on the nature and the quality of the goods, but also on the financial requirements for the fulfillment of the objectives, as well as on the stationary or expansive situation of the institution when discharging its commitments.[152]

---

[151] KENNEDY, "Temporal Goods," pp. 1495-1496.

[152] LÓPEZ ALARCÓN, "Book V," p. 993; see also VELASIO DE PAOLIS, "De bonis Ecclesiae temporalibus in novo Codice iuris canonici," in *Periodica*, 73 (1984), p. 145; DE PAOLIS, *De bonis Ecclesiae temporalibus*, p. 100; ADRIAN FARRELLY, "Diocesan Finance Council," p. 160; FRANCESCO GRAZIAN, "Patrimonio stabile: istituto dimenticato?" in *Quaderni di diritto ecclesiale*, 16 (2003), pp. 282-296; SCHOUPPE, pp. 155-157.

Yet another definition, quite direct and simple, is proposed by Virginio Rovera:

> [Stable patrimony is] those goods which… are designated to form the permanent endowment of an entity which, directly or indirectly, allows the entity itself to achieve its proper ends.[153]

Further, Vittorio Palestro says:

> Stable patrimony is that complex of goods, movable or immovable, rights, active and passive relations (*rapporti*), which constitute the minimum but indispensable economic base in order that the juridic person can subsist autonomously and operate.[154]

Further, while not attempting to give a definition of stable patrimony, Velasio De Paolis offers several observations about the term:

> The concept of stable patrimony is a new notion introduced to answer the needs of our modern economy, which no longer rests prevalently on goods once defined as immovable. Jurisprudence needs to define the concept of stable patrimony further. One thing is certain: the new code presupposes that every juridical person has a stable patrimony which can be made up of either movable or immovable goods. The determination of these goods depends on the organs of the juridical person itself, inasmuch as a legitimate ascription is required for those goods to become a part of the stable patrimony. When we speak of legitimate ascription we mean that such an

---

[153] VIRGINIO ROVERA, *I beni temporali nella Chiesa* in *La Normative del nuovo Codice*, Rome: Queriniana, 1983, p. 277. [Author's translation.]

[154] VITTORIO PALESTRO, "La disciplina canonica in materia di alienzatione e di locazione (cann. 1291-1298)," in *I beni temporali della Chiesa*, Studi Giuridici, 50, Città del Vaticano, Libreria editrice Vaticana, 1999, p. 147. [Author's translation.]

ascription is done according to the norms of law and even according to particular law.[155]

The Italian Episcopal Conference issued in 2005 an instruction on administration of ecclesiastical goods which mentions stable patrimony and distinguishes it from ecclesiastical goods which are non-stable patrimony:

> In general, the following can be considered *stable patrimony*:
> - goods which are part of the foundational property of the entity;
> - goods coming to the entity itself, if the donor has so designated them;
> - goods assigned to stable patrimony by the administrative organ of the entity;
> - mobile goods given *ex voto* to the juridic person.
>
> On the contrary, not considered as *stable patrimony* – unless the entity has been legitimately designated as such – are the fruits of the earth, of work or of other contractual activity; revenue from capital and from immovable patrimony; funds temporarily invested to achieve a higher return; immovable funds designated by will of the donor to be immobilized for the immediate use of the proceeds.
>
> To be underscored is the importance of a "legitimate designation" (cfr. can. 1291) in order for a good to be part of the stable patrimony of a juridic person.
>
> Therefore, it is opportune that every juridic person prepare

---

[155] De Paolis, "Temporal Goods... Consecrated Life," p. 356. He also explains that the code wisely omits saying that stable patrimony is composed of immovable goods since, in the modern world, movable goods often also comprise part of stable patrimony. The distinguishing character of any ecclesiastical good belonging to the stable patrimony of a juridic person, is its having been lawfully assigned as stable patrimony by the competent ecclesiastical authority. In *De bonis Ecclesiae temporalibus*, p. 101.

A listing of rotal decisions revealing its jurisprudence on ecclesiastical goods is found in Begus, *Diritto patrimoniale canonico*, pp. 251-257.

a list of goods constituting its own stable patrimony.[156]

The goods which constitute the stable patrimony of a public juridic person have been frozen, stabilized, or immobilized.[157] Immobilization is a permanent designation of goods with the intention to preserve them so a juridic person can achieve its proper purposes. Although some goods may be considered part of stable patrimony due to custom (see canon 26), and although a presumption may exist that certain goods (e.g., land and buildings which obviously constitute the majority of immovable ecclesiastical goods[158]) are part of stable patrimony, legitimate designation must be made by competent authority in order to identify precisely those goods which constitute stable patrimony.

Ecclesiastical goods which are *non-stable patrimony* have not been immobilized. A very common example of non-stable patrimony is money[159] (which is intended, first of all, as a means of barter or exchange). It is a commodity to be used for ordinary operations. Sometimes, excess money of a public juridic person is kept as "cash on hand" or is invested for a short period of time in order to earn additional income without the intention of making it part of stable

---

[156] CONFERENZA EPISCOPALE ITALIANA, "Istruzione in materia amministrativa (2005)," testo approvato dalla 54a Assemblea Generale, Roma (May 30-31, 2005), art. 53. [Author's translation.]

[157] Commenting on the 1917 code, WILLIAM J. DOHENY defines *stable capital*: "Stable, invested, or fixed capital is that money which is not being used primarily as a means of barter or exchange, but which has been invested in property or holdings of some kind, whether these be in the form of corporeal or incorporeal property, either movable or immovable. Examples of such would be investments in bonds, stocks, mortgages, and the like." In *Practical Problems in Church Finance*, Milwaukee, Bruce Publishing Co., 1941, p. 43 (=DOHENY, *Practical Problems*).

[158] VELASIO DE PAOLIS says, "Nevertheless, there can be a presumption that immovable goods constitute stable patrimony." In *De bonis Ecclesiae temporalibus*, p. 101.
NICHOLAS CAFARDI concludes that the purpose or use of ecclesiastical goods also designates them as part of stable patrimony: "It has been consistent praxis of canon law that those assets that are necessary to a juridic person in order to accomplish the ends for which it was established are part of the stable patrimony of that juridic person and may not be freely alienated." In "Alienation of Church Property," in *CFH*, p. 252.

[159] DANIEL J. WARD remarks that "in canon law cash is not considered under property law unless it is formally designated by a competent authority or donor for a set purpose as fixed capital," i.e., as stable patrimony. In "Temporal Goods," p. 195.

patrimony.[160] Nonetheless, invested funds can be designated legitimately as stable patrimony.

Ecclesiastical goods belonging to stable patrimony of a public juridic person are not forever frozen. They can become non-stable patrimony. Indeed, the norms of canon 1291-1294 provide legislation whereby such goods are able to be alienated and, thereby, to become non-stable patrimony.

In the final analysis, we can say that stable patrimony is made up of those immovable and movable goods which, by legitimate designation of competent authority through an act of extraordinary administration, form the secure basis of a juridic person so that it can perform its works. Stable patrimony is a legally protected good. The distinction between stable and non-stable patrimony is the fundamental distinction of all ecclesiastical goods, and this distinction should be indicated on regularly updated inventories (see canon 1283, 2°-3°). Donations by administrators of ecclesiastical goods can never be made from goods belonging to stable patrimony (canon 1285). Permission of competent authority is needed for the valid alienation of the stable patrimony which belongs to a public juridic person and whose value exceeds the defined sum (canon 1291). The norms of canon 1291-1294 apply not only to alienation but also to any contractual transaction which can worsen the (stable) patrimonial

---

[160] Canon 1284 §2, 6° requires the permission of the ordinary for an administrator to invest surplus funds. Permission for such investment does not convert the funds into stable patrimony. Unless surplus funds have been clearly designated as stable patrimony, even if they have been invested with permission of the ordinary, they remain non-stable patrimony.

DOHENY proposes that the following are not considered immobilized assets: (a) Money placed in safe investments (i.e., bonds, stocks, etc.) until such times as auspicious opportunities or sufficient sums warrant the construction of ecclesiastical buildings; (b) Investments in stocks, bonds, bank notes, etc. that are transferred into money and put on deposit for some reasonable cause; (c) Money invested in stocks, bonds, bank notes, etc. that is transferred to other stocks, bonds, bank notes, etc. that are equally safe and lucrative; (d) Money placed in stocks, bonds, bank notes, mortgages, etc. that is withdrawn and changed to safer forms, even though the interest returns are not as lucrative; and (e) Money placed in stocks, bonds, bank notes, mortgages, etc. which is withdrawn and changed into more lucrative forms, provided that these latter forms are considered reasonably safe investments. In *Practical Problems*, pp. 51-53. In terminology consistent with the 1983 code, these goods would be non-stable patrimony unless they have been legitimately designated otherwise.

condition of a juridic person (canon 1295). Stable patrimony is not subject to taxation, though income produced by stable patrimony can be taxed (see canons 264 §2 and 1263). Put another way, the distinction between stable patrimony and non-stable patrimony is the basis for determinations in matters of alienation, contractual transactions which may threaten a public juridic person, charitable donations, and diocesan taxation.

CORRESPONDING CANON OF THE EASTERN CODE: CANON 1029. The Eastern law says an administrators are not to make (*ne faciat*) donations from movable goods that do not belong to the stable patrimony, except "within moderation according to legitimate custom" and unless for a "just cause" of piety or charity.

JUSTICE IN EMPLOYMENT

Can. 1286 – Administrators of goods
1° in the employment of workers are to observe meticulously also the civil laws concerning labor and social policy, according to the principles handed down by the Church;
2° are to pay a just and decent wage to employees so that they are able to provide fittingly for their own needs and those of their dependents.

Canon 1286 identifies two additional responsibilities which belong to the administrators of ecclesiastical goods:
1. to observe meticulously civil labor and social policy laws in employment, according to the principles laid down by the Church;
2. to pay a just and decent wage so employees can support themselves and their dependents.

Canon 1286, 1° requires administrators of ecclesiastical goods to observe civil laws in matters of employment and social policy (e.g., minimum wage, health insurance, workers' compensation, social security, unemployment insurance, employment contracts, vacations and holidays, etc.). Inasmuch as the code requires observance of these civil rights of employees, to be fulfilled by employers in justice, the same become ecclesiastical rights.[161] This "canonization" of civil law must be done "according to the principles handed down by the Church."[162] If there is a conflict between civil law and canon law (or divine law) concerning the rights of employees, obviously canon law (or divine law) must prevail for the Church (see canon 22). This would occur, for example, if civil labor policy requires employee benefits for those in same-sex unions, abortion, contraceptives, etc.

This canon does *not* demand that the Church follow the civil laws from which the Church is exempted by the secular government.[163] At the same time, the Church would be expected to promote labor and social matters which, although perhaps not required by secular law, are nonetheless encouraged by Church doctrine.

---

[161] Several canons make reference to justice: canons 222 §2; 287 §1; 528 §1; 695 §1; 797; 978 §1; 1148 §3; 1199 §1; 1341; 1435; 1445 §3, 1°; 1446 §1; 1453; 1670; 1722; 1727 §2.

[162] One is reminded of the many messages from Supreme Pontiffs over the past century and more which present the social teaching of the Church, particularly:

Leo XIII, encyclical letter *Rerum novarum* (May 15, 1891), in *AAS*, 23 (1890-1891), pp. 641-670;

Pius XI, encyclical letter *Quadragesimo anno* (May 15, 1931), in *AAS*, 23 (1931), pp. 177-228;

John XXIII, encyclical letter *Pacem in terris* (April 11, 1963), in *AAS*, 55 (1963), pp. 257-304;

Paul VI, encyclical letter *Populorum progressio* (March 26, 1967), in *AAS*, 59 (1967), pp. 257-299;

Paul VI, apostolic letter *Octogesimo adveniens* (May 24, 1971), in *AAS*, 63 (1971), pp. 401-441;

John Paul II, encyclical letter *Laborem exercens* (September 14, 1981), in *AAS*, 73 (1981), pp. 577-647;

John Paul II, encyclical letter *Sollicitudo rei socialis* (December 30, 1987), in *AAS*, 80 (1988), pp. 513-586;

John Paul II, encyclical letter *Centessimus annus* (May 1, 1991), in *AAS*, 83 (1991), pp. 793-867.

See also: Congregation for Catholic Education, circular letter *Guidelines for the Study and Teaching of the Church's Social Doctrine in the Formation of Priests* (June 27, 1989), Vatican City State, Typis polyglottis Vaticanis, 1989; Pontifical Council for Justice and Peace, *Compendium of the Social Doctrine of the Church* (October 25, 2004), Vatican City State, Typis polyglottis Vaticanis, 2004.

[163] See Myers, "Temporal Goods," p. 877.

A particular example of this is promotion of the right of Church employees to form unions or to organize themselves to protect their interests.[164]

Canon 1286, 2° requires the Church to provide employees with a just and decent wage sufficient to support themselves and their dependents; this reflects the Church's social teaching. The 1971 Synod of Bishops had said:

> If the Church must give witness to justice, she knows that whoever intends to speak to men of justice must first practice justice before them. Therefore, it is necessary above all to examine the Church's way of acting, her possessions, and her style of life.[165]

The code itself offers several norms related to employee compensation and benefits.[166] Clergy are to receive adequate remuneration (*remuneratio*) for their personal needs and services (canon 281 §1), social security (canon 281 §2), time for spiritual retreat (canon 276 §2, 4°), time for vacation (canons 283 §2, 533 §2, 550 §3), and

---

[164] TERENCE T. GRANT reflects: "Further, an interpretation of canon 1286, 1° in light of the Church's social teaching would direct that administrators recognize and honor the right of church personnel to form labor unions or otherwise organize themselves to protect their interests. This right was proclaimed by Leo XIII in 1891 in his encyclical letter *Rerum novarum*. The natural right of workers to associate was subsequently reaffirmed by Pius XI in 1931 and by John XXIII in 1961. The Second Vatican Council in turn gave unequivocal recognition to the right of workers to form labor unions.... Finally, John Paul II firmly restated this right, and referred to it as a right possessed by employees in 'each type of work... every profession.'
"In light of this social teaching and in view of the obligation imposed by canon 1286, 1°, it seems clear that church administrators may not interfere with the efforts of workers who exercise their right to organize." In "Social Justice in the 1983 Code of Canon Law: An Examination of Selected Canons," in *The Jurist*, 49 (1989), pp. 135-136.
See also: DONALD J. HERMANN, "The Code of Canon Law Provisions on Labor Relations," in *The Jurist*, 44 (1984), pp. 180-193; MAURO RIVELLA, "La remunerazione del lavoro ecclesiale," in *Quaderni di Diritto Ecclesiale,* 19 (2006), pp. 175-184.

[165] SYNOD OF BISHOPS, document *De iustitia in mundo* (November 30, 1971), in *AAS,* 63 (1971), p. 933; English translation in *Origins*, 1 (1971-1972), p. 394.

[166] For further discussion on compensation and benefits for those serving the Church, see WILLIAM P. DALY, "Remuneration for Church Employees" in *CFH*, pp. 53-59; HERMANN, pp. 153-193.

on-going ministerial formation (canon 279).[167] A written agreement is to be drawn up between diocesan bishops and competent religious superiors to address, among other things, economic matters (e.g., salary, benefits, allowances for housing and transportation, vacation and retreat periods, etc.) for religious serving in the diocese (canon 681 §2; see canon 663 §5). Lay persons who perform some ecclesiastical service permanently or temporarily are to receive decent remuneration (*remuneratio*) for their personal and family needs, insurance, social security, and medical benefits (canon 231 §2).

CORRESPONDING CANON OF THE EASTERN CODE: CANON 1030. The Eastern law says that the civil law (*ius civile*, rather than "civil laws," *leges civiles*) on labor and social policy are to be observed *secundum* (after, in the second place to) Church principles. The word used in the Latin code is *iuxta* (next to, along side), indicating that civil laws are to be followed next to Church principles.[168] Also, administrators are to provide a "just remuneration" (*iusta remuneratio*, rather than a "just and decent wage," *iusta et honesta merces*) to employees to provide for themselves and their families.

FINANCIAL REPORTS

> **Can. 1287 – §1. Both clerical and lay administrators of any ecclesiastical goods whatever which have not been legitimately exempted from the power of governance of the diocesan bishop are bound by their office to present an annual report to the local ordinary who is to present it for examination by the finance council; any contrary custom is reprobated.**
>
> **§2. According to norms to be determined by particular law, administrators are to render an account to the faithful concerning the goods offered by the faithful to the Church.**

---

[167] See PCLT, *Nota,* Elementi per configurare l'ambito, p. 26.

[168] ROBERT T. KENNEDY laments that the American translations of both codes translates these two words (*secundum* and *iuxta*) as "according to," thereby presuming to give priority to civil legislation over Church doctrine. In "Temporal Goods," p. 1489, fn. 119.

Canon 1287 explains that two reports are to be made by those who administer any ecclesiastical goods:

1. an annual report to the local ordinary, made by clerical and lay administrators of public juridic persons whose ecclesiastical goods have not been lawfully exempted from the power of governance of the diocesan bishop; the local ordinary is then to present this report to the diocesan finance council (the canon adds that any contrary custom is reprobated by this legislation: see canon 24 §2);

2. an account to the faithful concerning the goods offered by them to the Church; particular law is to determine the specifics of this report.

ANNUAL FINANCIAL REPORTS OF PUBLIC JURIDIC PERSONS. Canon 1284 §2, 8° requires administrators, fulfilling their function with the diligence of a good householder, to prepare a report of administration at the end of each fiscal year. Canon 1287 §1 explains that the recipient of this report is the local ordinary if, and only if,[169] the ecclesiastical goods belong to a public juridic person subject to the power of governance of the diocesan bishop.[170] The local ordinary in turn is to present the report for examination to the diocesan finance

---

[169] There is no requirement in *Book V* that an annual report be presented to the local ordinary by administrators of public juridic persons not subject to the power of governance of the diocesan bishop, or by private juridic persons.

The SACRED CONGREGATION FOR RELIGIOUS AND SECULAR INSTITUTES informed all ordinaries on September 20, 1972 that "religious associations of pontifical right: orders, congregations, institutes, as well as their generalate, procurator, provincial and individual houses... have no obligation to present a balance sheet or render an account of their administration to the local ordinary:" Prot. N.-R.G. 1001/71. In XAVIERUS OCHOA, *Leges Ecclesiae*, vol. 5, n. 4143; *CLD*, vol. 9, p. 911.

[170] CIC/1917, canon 1525 §1 had required only the administrators of churches to surrender annual reports of their administration to the local ordinary. Canon 1287 §1 expands this earlier legislation by requiring that the local ordinary receive such annual reports from administrators of all public juridic persons subject to his power of governance. Among those administrators who must give an annual financial report to the local ordinary by reason of canon 1287 §1 is the pastor of a parish, who administers its goods (see canon 532). In addition, autonomous monasteries must render an annual account of administration to the local ordinary, and the local ordinary has the right to be informed about the financial reports of a religious house of diocesan right (canon 637).

council.[171] Any contrary custom is expressly reprobated, that is, it is unreasonable and does not have the force of law (see canon 24 §2). This is an occasion for the local ordinary to exercise his vigilance role (canon 1276 §1).

Obviously, the diocesan finance council will compare each new financial report to the report from the previous year. It will note observance of civil and canon law on such matters as acts of alienation, acts of extraordinary administration, just wages, insurance coverage, investment of surplus revenue, etc. It may also compare the financial report to the budget proposed for the year being reported, and to the budget proposed for the next fiscal year. It may rely upon the assistance of the diocesan finance officer to provide necessary information together with his or her analysis of the reports. After the diocesan finance council has reviewed the reports, it will offer its comments to the local ordinary (or the diocesan bishop), who may seek clarifications.

In many dioceses, an updated inventory of the goods of the public juridic person is to be submitted with the annual financial report. Particular diocesan law requiring an annual submission of an updated inventory of the goods of a public juridic person together with the annual financial report is a very practical way to assure the regular recording of changes in its stable patrimony and other goods (see 1283, 3°). Nothing prevents this inventory from being reviewed by the diocesan finance council, or at least by the diocesan finance officer.

All juridic persons must have finance councils, or at least two financial counselors (canon 1280). It would be appropriate for the members of these councils (or the consultants) to review the annual reports of administration and, perhaps, even to offer observations on them before they are submitted to the competent authority.

---

[171] An earlier version of the proposed new law had envisioned that the annual report be given by administrators directly to the diocesan finance council who, having examined it, would then present the report to the ordinary: *Communicationes*, 36 (2004), p. 321.

See Thomas J. Paprocki and Richard B. Saudis, "Annual Report to the Diocesan Bishop," in *CFH*, pp. 175-183.

Elsewhere, the code identifies persons other than the local ordinary who are to receive the financial reports to be submitted by administrators. Public associations of the faithful are to make an account of their administration and of expenditures of offerings and alms received to the authority which established them – i.e., the Holy See, the conference of bishops, or the diocesan bishop (canon 319 §2; see canon 312 §1). The diocesan finance officer is to present an annual financial report to the diocesan finance council (canon 494 §4). Finance officers and other administrators of religious institutes, their provinces, and their local communities are to render an account of their administration to the competent authority (canon 636 §2).[172] The parochial administrator, serving a parish retaining its pastor,[173] must render an account to the pastor when he has completed his function (canon 540 §3).[174] Statutes of other public juridic persons would identify the recipients of their annual reports of administration.

Furthermore, the *Directory for the Pastoral Ministry of Bishops* says diocesan bishops should be transparent in revealing the financial status of the diocese, annually and at the conclusion of diocesan projects, when financial reports are to be published:

> It is opportune, moreover, that the diocesan community be kept informed concerning the financial condition of the diocese. Therefore, unless in a special case prudence suggests otherwise, the Bishop will see to the publication of the *financial reports* at the end of every year and at the conclusion of diocesan projects. Likewise, parishes and

---

[172] Canon 741 §1 applies the norm of canon 636 §2 to societies of apostolic life. Canon 718 allows proper law to apply the norm to secular institutes

[173] The diocesan bishop must appoint a parochial administrator when a parish becomes vacant *or* when the pastor, retaining his office, "is prevented from exercising his pastoral function in the parish by reason of captivity, exile or banishment, incapacity or ill health, or some other cause" (canon 539 §1). In addition, the diocesan bishop must appoint a parochial administrator, not a pastor, if a pastor makes recourse against the bishop's decree of his removal (canon 1747 §2).

[174] If the parochial administrator serves a vacant parish, he would render the financial report to the local ordinary, as would a pastor; see canon 540 §1.

other institutions could do the same under the Bishop's oversight.[175]

REPORTS TO DONORS. Canon 1287 §2 requires that administrators render an account to the faithful concerning the goods offered by them to the Church.[176] Particular law[177] is to determine the specifics about this report; presumably, the report would be issued annually. It could be presented to donors at the same time that the administrator gives to the local ordinary the report mentioned in the first paragraph of this canon.

Canon 1287 §2 does not require administrators to give to the faithful a report of *all* income of public juridic persons, but only a report on the goods offered by the faithful.[178] Thus, for example, the report to the faithful is not *required* to identify revenue from grants, the civil government, private agencies, etc. Nonetheless, financial transparency suggests giving the faithful a *complete* report of *all* revenue from *whatever* source.

Inasmuch as the diocesan finance officer routinely administers the goods of the diocese under the authority of the bishop, he or she would render an account to the faithful concerning goods given by them to the diocese.

---

[175] *DPMB*, n. 189 a).

[176] See ROYCE R. THOMAS, "Financial Reports to the Faithful," in *CFH*, pp. 165-174.

[177] This "particular law" can be issued by the conference of bishops (if it chose to do so in accord with canon 455 §1) or by the diocesan bishop. Mandatory expectations can also be found in the statutes of juridic persons.

[178] The *coetus De bonis Ecclesiae temporalibus* rejected the proposal that financial reports give a complete accounting of *all* ecclesiastical goods, not only those which come from the offerings of the faithful. Although the *coetus* admitted that such full disclosure is praiseworthy where it can be done, it concluded that this should not be a requirement of the universal law since in some parts of the world the faithful may not understand the proper purposes for which the Church owns temporal goods. *Communicationes*, 12 (1980), p. 420.

One observes that the norms issued by the USCCB on the implementation of canon 1262 call for disclosure of the monies generated in fund-raising appeals, and the purposes to which those funds are applied. The norms do not, however, require full disclosure of all the assets of the fund-raising group. (The USCCB norms are provided in the commentary on canon 1262.)

CORRESPONDING CANON OF THE EASTERN CODE: CANON 1031.
Eastern canon 1031 §1 simply says that, any contrary custom having
been reprobated, the administrator (not specified as "clerical and lay
administrators") is to render an annual report of administration to
the proper hierarch; the hierarch is not required to present the report
to the eparchial finance council. Eastern canon 1031 §2 requires
administrators, according to particular law, to make an annual report "publicly" (*publice*, not "to the faithful") on goods offered to
the Church (without specifying that these goods are those "offered
by the faithful"). The report on goods offered to the Church is not
mandatory: the local hierarch can establish otherwise "for a grave
reason."

CIVIL LITIGATION

> **Can. 1288 – Administrators are neither to initiate nor
> to contest litigation in a civil forum in the name of a pub-
> lic juridic person unless they have obtained the written
> permission of their own ordinary.**

Every juridic person has a legal representative who represents
the juridic person and acts in its name, both in the civil forum and
the canonical forum. The legal representative of a public juridic person is identified by universal law, particular law, or its own statutes;
the legal representative of a private juridic person is identified in its
statutes only (canon 118).

Canon 1288 forbids administrators of ecclesiastical goods to
initiate or contest civil litigation in the name of the public juridic
person, unless the administrators have the prior written permission
of their own ordinary. An obvious reason for the permission of the
ordinary is the patrimonial risk to which a public juridic person is
subjected by a civil lawsuit, and harm done to the Church by negative
notoriety. If the administrator were to proceed without the ordinary's
written permission, the administrator's action would be illicit (but
not invalid[179]); the administrator, therefore, would be subject to legal

---

[179] VROMANT, p. 192.

action if damage results (see canons 1281 §3; 128).

The ordinary may insist that the administrator refrain from initiating civil litigation. The ordinary cannot insist, of course, that the administrator refrain from civil proceedings if the public juridic person is the defendant, since non-compliance may result in civil ramifications (e.g., contempt of court, fines, etc.). In such a situation, however, the ordinary can prompt the administrator to settle the dispute out of court. This may avoid further negative publicity and, perhaps, result in less harm to the stable patrimony of the public juridic person (see canon 1295).

The canon is operative for public juridic persons[180] involved directly in civil litigation. It does not pertain to actions initiated or contested by an insurance company providing coverage to the public juridic person. Furthermore, "it is generally accepted that actions before 'small claims courts' and various types of similar procedures do not come within this prescription."[181]

This canon requires the ordinary's written permission before the administrator initiates or contests litigation in the *civil* forum. Such permission is not required for the same in the *canonical* forum (see canon 1480).

The "ordinary" mentioned in this canon is either the local ordinary, the major superior of a clerical institute of pontifical right, or the major superior of a clerical society of apostolic life of pontifical right (canon 134 §1). The "ordinary" of other members of religious institutes and societies of apostolic life is the ordinary of their place of domicile or quasi-domicile (canon 103; see canon 107 §1).[182]

---

[180] Inasmuch as one intention of canon 1288 is to avoid negative notoriety for the Church, it may be entirely prudent for administrators of private juridic persons also to be in dialogue with the ordinary before initiating or contesting civil litigation.

[181] MORRISEY, "Temporal Goods," p. 731.

[182] The 1977 *Schema* had also required the permission of one's proper ordinary and of the local ordinary. Some had recommended that permission be required from the ordinary where the litigated object (*res sitae*) is found (rather than from the local ordinary). After considering various possibilities, the *coetus* decided the canon would require only the permission of the proper ordinary. *Communicationes*, 12 (1980), p. 421. CIC/1917, canon 1526, which is the predecessor of canon 1288, had required the permission of the local ordinary or, in an urgent matter, of the vicar forane (who was required to inform the local ordinary immediately of the permission granted).

CORRESPONDING CANON OF THE EASTERN CODE: CANON 1032.
The Eastern discipline does not require the "written" permission of
the hierarch.

ARBITRARY CESSATION OF ADMINISTRATIVE FUNCTION

**Can. 1289 – Even if not bound to administration by the
title of an ecclesiastical office, administrators cannot relinquish their function on their own initiative; if the Church
is harmed from an arbitrary withdrawal, moreover, they
are bound to restitution.**

Canon 1289 is about the function (*munus*) of an administrator,
not only about the office (*officium*). It says that administrators cannot
relinquish their function on their own initiative, even if they do not
perform their task by reason of an ecclesiastical office. Many persons
perform administrative functions, sometimes even on a voluntary
basis, without formal canonical appointment to an ecclesiastical
office. The discipline of this canon includes all these persons. They
must at least inform the competent authority before relinquishing
their administrative function.[183]

If an administrator's arbitrary withdrawal results in harm to
the Church, the administrator must make restitution (see canon
128).[184]

Administrators who perform their function by the title of an
ecclesiastical office cease that function when they lose that office,
which occurs in a number of possible ways: by the passing of a pre-

---

[183] ROBERT T. KENNEDY comments: "The care of real estate, the maintenance of buildings, the keeping of accounts, managing investment portfolios, supervising the work
of employees, and a host of other activities are often performed by such 'unofficial'
administrators who render invaluable service to the Church. Based on long experi-
ence, the Church seeks in canon 1289 to remind all administrators, including unofficial ones, that once they have undertaken to fulfill administrative responsibilities,
they have an obligation not to abandon them suddenly without affording appropriate
authorities ample opportunity to arrange for others to assume the responsibilities."
In "Temporal Goods," p. 1492. See MYERS, "Temporal Goods," p. 878.

[184] The requirement of restitution was added at the recommendation of a consultative
group commenting on the 1977 *Schema. Communicationes*, 12 (1980), p. 422.

determined time, by reaching the legal age limit, by resignation, by transfer, by removal, and by deprivation (canon 184 §1).

Canon 1289 does not forbid those holding the office of administrator from submitting their resignation.

CORRESPONDING CANON OF THE EASTERN CODE: CANON 1033. Eastern canon 1033 forbids an administrator from relinquishing his or her "office or function" (*officium vel munus*) on personal initiative; the legislation therefore omits the clause "even if not bound to administration by the title of an ecclesiastical office" since it would be superfluous.

CHAPTER FIVE

CONTRACTS AND ESPECIALLY ALIENATION
(Title III: Canons 1290-1298)

Title III of *Book V* contains nine canons concerning contracts, particularly those contracts involved in the alienation of ecclesiastical
goods. Canon 1290 "canonizes" civil law in contracts entered into
by ecclesiastical juridic persons, provided the civil law does not
contradict divine law or specific norms of canon law. Canon 1291
requires permission for the valid alienation of ecclesiastical goods
which both constitute the stable patrimony of a public juridic person
and whose value exceeds the sum defined by law. Canon 1292 §§1-
2 identifies the competent authority to define the sum and to give
permission for the alienation, after having collaborated with others.
Canon 1292 §3 requires that prior alienation of parts of a divisible
asset must be reported for the valid alienation of remaining parts.
Canon 1292 §4 mandates full disclosure to those who must give their
counsel or consent before an alienation can be accomplished. Canon
1293 says that, for liceity, alienation of goods exceeding the defined
minimum amount also requires a just cause, a written appraisal by
at least two experts, and observance of other precautions prescribed
by legitimate authority. Canon 1294 explains that, for liceity, an asset
is not ordinarily to be alienated for a price below its appraisal, and
that money resulting from the alienation should either be invested
carefully or expended prudently for the purposes of the alienation.
Canon 1295 applies the norms of canons 1291-1294 to any transaction
which can worsen the patrimonial condition of a juridic person, even
though such a transaction is not an alienation. Canon 1296 identifies
options for the competent authority to pursue when alienations have

occurred which are valid civilly but invalid canonically. Canon 1297 entrusts to the episcopal conference the establishment of norms for leasing ecclesiastical goods. Finally, canon 1298 requires the special written permission of the competent authority for the sale or lease of ecclesiastical goods to the administrators of these goods and their close relatives, unless an asset is worth little.

These canons reflect the discipline of the 1917 *Code of Canon Law* in its canons 1529-1530; 1531 §§1-3; 1532 §4; 1533; 1534 §1; and 1540-1541. Canon 1292 §4 has no predecessor in the first code.

Corresponding canons in the 1990 *Code of Canons of the Eastern Churches* are canons 1034-1035; 1036 §§1, 4; 1038; 1040; and 1042. Latin canons 1294 and 1297 have no corresponding canon in the Eastern code.

CIVIL LAW AND CONTRACTS

Can. 1290 – The general and particular provisions which the civil law in a territory has established for contracts and their disposition are to be observed with the same effects in canon law insofar as the matters are subject to the power of governance of the Church unless the provisions are contrary to divine law or canon law provides otherwise, and without prejudice to the prescript of can. 1547.

Title III is particularly about three specific kinds of contracts:
1. contracts involving alienation of ecclesiastical goods belonging by legitimate designation to the stable patrimony of a public juridic person whose value exceeds the amount established by competent ecclesiastical authority (canons 1291-1294; see canons 1296 and 1298)
2. contracts involving transactions which can worsen the patrimonial condition of a juridic person (canon 1295)
3. contracts involving leases (canon 1297; see canon 1298)[1]

---

[1] "Contract" is also mentioned in canon 1284 §2, 1° regarding insurance policies. Obviously, contracts may be involved in several other issues treated in *Book V*: e.g., employment (canon 1286); pious wills (canons 1299-1301); trusts (canon 1302); foundations (canons 1303-1307), etc.

Canon 1290 requires the Church to observe the provisions of civil law for contracts and their disposition with the same effects in canon law, insofar as the civil law precepts are not contrary to divine law and insofar as the canon law does not provide otherwise. The discipline of canon 1290 is an application to contracts of the more general provision of canon 22:

> **Can. 22 – Civil laws to which the law of the Church yields are to be observed in canon law with the same effects, insofar as they are not contrary to divine law and unless canon law provides otherwise.**[2]

The civil legal prescripts for contracts will vary from jurisdiction to jurisdiction.[3] The contractual capacity of ecclesiastical juridic persons entering contracts is rooted in canon law, not in some provision of the civil law, which the same canon says should generally be observed by these juridic persons.[4]

Canon 1290 mentions canon 1547, by which canon law admits *proofs by witnesses* in an ecclesiastical tribunal in disputed matters concerning contracts, something not necessarily permitted by civil law. Acceptance of proof by witnesses was added after consultation on the 1977 *Schema*, where no reference to such proof had been made. It was believed that this addition would resolve the question in canon law whether or not witnesses can be admitted in the canonical forum if they are excluded in the civil forum in disputes concerning contracts.[5]

Both canon 1290 and canon 22 indicate two exceptions to the absolute "canonization" of civil law: (1) when the civil law is contrary to divine law, and (2) when the canon law provides otherwise

---

[2] There are a number of canons on temporal goods which make reference to careful observance of civil law: canons 1268 (referring to canon 197); 1274 §1; 1284 §2, 2°; 1284 §2, 3°; 1286, 1°; 1299 §2.

[3] See canon 13 §2, 2°.

[4] See MYERS, "Temporal Goods," p. 878. For an extensive treatment of the elements of a contract, see: WILLIAM BASSETT, "A Note on the Law of Contracts and the Canonical Integrity of Public Benefit Religious Organizations," in *CLSA Proceedings*, 59 (1997), pp. 63-67; PÉRISSET, pp. 194-198; SCHOUPPE, pp. 72-88; SIGNIÉ, pp. 148-152.

[5] *Communicationes*, 12 (1980), pp. 427-428.

than civil law. In the matter of temporal goods, there are numerous examples of civil law permitting something contrary to divine law[6] or permitting something for which a different determination is made by canon law, particularly on contracts. Canon law, for example, imposes upon administrators entering contracts the following special requirements:

1. to obtain permission of competent authority for the valid alienation of goods which belong to stable patrimony and whose value exceeds a pre-determined amount (canons 1291, 1292 §§1-3, and 638 §3)

2. to identify a just cause for alienation of goods with a value greater than the defined minimum amount (canon 1293 §1, 1°);

3. to receive written appraisals from experts on goods with a value greater than the defined minimum amount (canon 1293 §1, 2°);

4. to follow precautions prescribed by legitimate authority in alienating goods with a value greater than the defined minimum amount (canon 1293 §2)

5. to refrain normally from alienating ecclesiastical goods at a price under their estimated value (canon 1294 §1)

6. to observe the norms on alienation (canons 1291-1294) in transactions which can worsen the patrimonial condition of a juridic person (canon 1295)

7. to observe particular law established by the conference of bishops in contracts involving leases (canon 1297)

8. to obtain special permission from competent authority before entering into alienation and lease contracts with close relatives (canon 1298)

---

[6] Civil law contradicts divine law, for example, when it mandates providing employment benefits to partners in same-sex unions, abortion, contraception, etc.

In all these contractual concerns, canon law prevails for the Church.[7]

Given the discipline of canon 1290 which generally "canonizes" civil law on contracts, superiors and administrators of public juridic persons must be *most diligent* in understanding the appropriate operative civil laws and in following them when entering into contracts concerning ecclesiastical goods. This is true even if both the contracting parties are public juridic persons.

CONTRACTS ENTERED BY MEMBERS OF INSTITUTES OF CONSECRATED LIFE AND SOCIETIES OF APOSTOLIC LIFE. The code addresses contracts entered into by members of religious institutes in canon 639 §§2-4:

> **Canon 639 – §2. If a member has entered into a contract concerning his or her own goods with permission of the superior, the member must answer for it, but if the business of the institute was conducted by mandate of the superior, the institute must answer.**
>
> **§3. If a religious has entered into a contract without any permission of superiors, he or she must answer, but not the juridic person.**
>
> **§4. It is a fixed rule, however, that an action can always be brought against one who has profited from the contract entered into.**

This is obviously a limitation based in canon law affecting contracts entered into by members of religious institutes. Canon 741 §1 applies the norm of canon 639 §§2-4 to societies of apostolic life. Canon 718 allows proper law to apply the norm to secular institutes.

CORRESPONDING CANON OF THE EASTERN CODE: CANON 1034. Eastern canon 1034 makes no reference to non-observance of civil

---

[7]   Civil law and canon law may also make different determinations in matters of temporal goods not involving contracts: for example, civil law may not require good faith in prescription (see canon 198); civil law may have time periods for prescription which differ from those of canon law (see canon 1270); civil law may not admit proof by witnesses in contract disputes (see canon 1547); etc.

laws which contain provisions contrary to divine law or canon law, or to the admission of proof by witnesses in an ecclesiastical trial involving a contractual dispute.

VALID ALIENATION OF STABLE PATRIMONY

Can. 1291 – The permission of the authority competent according to the norm of law is required for the valid alienation of goods which constitute by legitimate designation the stable patrimony of a public juridic person and whose value exceeds the sum defined by law.[8]

Canon 1254 §1 had already expressed the Church's innate right to alienate its temporal goods independently from civil power in order to pursue the Church's proper purposes.

Canon 1291 says that the competent ecclesiastical authority must give permission for the valid alienation of goods (1) which legitimately constitute the stable patrimony of a public juridic person

---

[8] Canon 1295 requires statutes of juridic persons to conform to the requirements of canon 1291, and adds that canons 1291-1294 must be observed not only for alienation but also for "any transaction [other than alienation] which can worsen the patrimonial condition of a juridic person." This reflects the legislation of canon 1533 of the CIC/1917 which distinguished alienation in a strict sense (*alienatio proprie dicta*) and a broad sense (*quolibet contractus quo conditio Ecclesiae peior fieri possit*). Ambiguity could result.

G. VROMANT comments: "Stricte, pro eo tantum actu per quem dominium directum rei traditae in alterum transfertur.... Lato sensu sumitur alienatio non tantum pro actu quo dominium directum, sed etiam pro omni actu quo ius in re alii conceditur, ita ut dominium directum tantum minuatur.... In hac materia, nomen istud latissime accipitur, uti constat ex can. 1533." In "Book V," pp. 246-247. See also BOUSCAREN-ELLIS-KORTH, p. 835.

Using the distinctions of the 1917 code, one would conclude that canons 1291-1294 of the 1983 code concern alienation in the strict sense (transfer of ownership), but canon 1295 concerns alienation in the broad sense (i.e. acts which do not transfer ownership but which can worsen the patrimonial condition of a juridic person). There remain authors and commentaries who speak of alienation in a strict sense (canons 1291-1294) and in a broad sense (canon 1295). See DE PAOLIS, *De bonis Ecclesiae temporalibus*, pp. 99-100.

The revised code avoids ambiguity. Alienation is treated in canons 1291-1294. Canon 1295 is clearly *not* about alienation. Contemporary canonists should avoid referring to canon 1295 transactions as "acts of alienation in the broad sense"; such transactions are acts of administration in the current law.

and (2) whose value exceeds the sum defined by law (see canon 1292 §1).[9] Stable patrimony refers to those immovable and movable goods which, by legitimate designation of competent authority through an act of extraordinary administration, form the secure basis of a juridic person so that it can perform its works. Stable patrimony is a legally protected good (see the commentary on canon 1285).

Under the 1917 code, alienation was considered as a kind of extraordinary administration.[10] Those drafting the revised legislation made it clear: "*alienatio non est actus extraordinariae administrationis.*"[11] The purpose of administration, even of extraordinary administration, is to preserve the ownership of a temporal good; the purpose of alienation is to pass the ownership of a temporal good to another. The legislation on administration, even of extraordinary administration, is different from that on alienation.

Canon 1291 does *not* say that stable patrimony beyond a certain value *cannot* be alienated; rather, it requires the permission of competent ecclesiastical authority before such alienation can occur *validly*.

Canon 1291 requires consent to alienate goods belonging to the stable patrimony *only* if the value of the goods exceeds the amount defined by the law. Canon 638 §3 explains that the Holy See defines the amount for religious institutes of a region (see canons 718, 741 §1). Canon 1292 §1 says that the conference of bishops is to set minimum and maximum amounts for public juridic persons other than religious institutes in its own territory, and adds:

---

[9] The 1977 *Schema* had required permission for the valid alienation of any stable patrimony. A consultor of the *coetus De bonis Ecclesiae temporalibus* had suggested that permission be required for the valid alienation of stable patrimony whose worth exceeds a certain amount. All the other consultors agreed. *Communicationes,* 12 (1980), pp. 422-423.

[10] CIC/1917, canon 1495 §1 (which is the predecessor of canon 1254 §1 of the current code), identified the right of the Church to *acquire, retain,* and *administer* temporal goods. As a consequence, under the former legislation, alienation was considered an act of extraordinary administration. The 1983 code adds *alienation* to the other three rights of the Church listed in canon 1254 §1.

[11] *Communicationes,* 12 (1980), p. 396. See DE PAOLIS, *De bonis Ecclesiae temporalibus,* p. 98.

- If the value of the stable patrimony is *less than* the minimum amount, permission from a higher competent authority is not required for its alienation. The administrator of the public juridic person may alienate the stable patrimony.

- If the value of stable patrimony is *between* the minimum and maximum amounts, permission from the competent authority (identified in canon 1292 §1) is required for its *valid* alienation.

- If the value of the stable patrimony amount is *greater than* the maximum amount, the *additional* permission of the Holy See is required for its *valid* alienation (canon 1292 §2).[12]

Canon 1291 speaks of "permission" (*licentia*) from competent authority for the *validity* of alienation. Since without this permission the alienation would be invalid canonically, the law really requires the competent authority's *consent*, not merely its permission.[13] If the required consent is not obtained, the act of alienation is invalid (see canons 10; 1292 §2). The person who alienates the ecclesiastical good commits a delict and "is to be punished with a just penalty" (canon 1377).

ACTS OF ALIENATION OF STABLE PATRIMONY.[14] Alienation is a

---

[12] Nonetheless, consent from a competent authority for alienation of stable patrimony valued below the minimum established by the conference of bishops may be mandated by the statutes of the public juridic person (see canon 1291 §2) or by some other particular law.

Likewise, both statutes and particular law may require consent to alienate ecclesiastical goods which do *not* form part of the stable patrimony of a public juridic person. See CONFERENZA EPISCOPALE ITALIANA, "Istruzione in materia amministrativa (2005)," testo approvato dalla 54a Assemblea Generale, Roma (May 30-31, 2005), art. 63.

[13] *Book V* uses the term "permission" (*licentia*) to mean "consent" (*consensus*) in canons 1291, 1292 §2, and 1304 §1. The Eastern code uses the word *consensus* in the corresponding canons (1035 §1, 3°, 1036 §4, and 1048 §2). See also canons 638 §3 and 1190 §2.

[14] The sources for this list, and the following list on acts of administration (which are not to be confused with acts of alienation) are, *passim*: VROMANT, pp. 247-248; BOUSCAREN-ELLIS-KORTH, p. 833; KENNEDY, "Temporal Goods," p. 1494; JORDAN F. HITE, "The Administration of Church Property," in *Readings, Cases, Materials in Canon Law: A Textbook for Ministerial Students*, rev. ed., Jordan Hite and Daniel J. Ward (eds.), Collegeville, The Liturgical Press, 1990, p. 414; DOHENY, *Practical Problems*, pp. 44-50; FRANCIS G. MORRISEY, "The Alienation of Temporal Goods

transfer of ownership by gift, sale, or exchange. If there is no transfer of ownership, there is no alienation.[15] According to various authors, alienation of stable patrimony takes place when one performs the following:

1. To transfer title to the ownership of stable patrimony, including from one public juridic person to another (e.g., from a parish to a diocese, from one religious institute to another, etc.)[16]

---

in Contemporary Practice" in *Studia canonica,* 29 (1995), pp. 295-296, 306-310 (=MORRISEY, "Alienation"); ADRIAN FARRELLY, "Diocesan Finance Council," pp. 161-164; DE PAOLIS, *De bonis Ecclesiae temporalibus,* pp. 105-106; JOHN J. DAN-AGHER, "The New Code and Catholic Health Facilities: Fundamental Obligations of Administrators," in *The Jurist,* 44 (1984), pp. 148-152.

[15] In addition, FRANCIS MORRISEY comments that some canonists consider the establishment of a trust as an act of alienation "since the goods are no longer at the sole disposition of the juridic person. However, personally, it seems that if the trust is carefully established, there would not be an alienation if the funds are being used for their original purpose and are simply being placed in a more secure form of ownership." In "Alienation," p. 296. See MAIDA-CAFARDI, *Church Property,* pp. 234-246.

[16] ROBERT T. KENNEDY says: "A minority view under the 1917 code held that a transfer of property from one province of a religious institute to another province of the same institute should not be considered alienation because members of the same religious family are supposed to help each other and, hence, such a transfer should not be subject to the laws governing restricted alienation. This view was contrary not only to the views of the vast majority of canonists but also to the practice of the Roman Curia. The view still finds occasional expression today, however, and at times is expanded to include transfers from parishes to the diocese, especially in areas where civil-law ownership of church property has been vested in one corporation sole.... Such a view misunderstands the meaning of alienation and the purpose of the Church's laws governing it...." In "Temporal Goods," p. 1495.
Some years ago, a certain confusion was reported involving the sale of stable patrimony by one juridic person (a diocese) to another (a religious institute operating a health system). The diocesan bishop sought permission for the sale from the Congregation for Religious and Secular Institutes, which replied:
"We have received your letter of October 12, 1986, in which you seek permission for the sale of property of the Diocese to the Health System owned and operated by the Sisters of Y. Since the property and the facilities remain in the ownership of a Church entity, there is no need for permission of the Holy See for the transaction." [English original]
This communication caused some to conclude that permission for alienation is not required when the transfer is between public juridic persons in the Church. Nonetheless, the religious institute sought a clarification from the congregation, which replied:
"We are replying to your letter concerning the sale of some diocesan property in the Diocese of X to the Religious Institute of the Sisters of Y. We wish to point out that our letter on the same subject should be understood in light of the following clarification.

2.   To prepare for an act of conveyance of stable patrimony (e.g., to give an option, compromise, security, settlement, etc.)

3.   To use stable patrimony for some purpose other than that for which it was legitimately designated

4.   To transfer to others the "control" of major decision-making in apostolic works owned and operated by a public juridic person (e.g., health care institutions, educational institutions, etc.)[17]

5.   To transfer ownership of real estate which has been legitimately designated as stable capital, even if the proceeds are again legitimately designated as stable patrimony[18]

6.   To burden stable patrimony perpetually or for a long time (e.g., to grant the use or usufruct of property, to grant an easement)

"We intended to convey to the Bishop that he did not require permission from this Congregation for the sale, since the vendor was not a religious institute and therefore this office has no competence in the matter; it is the Congregation for the Clergy which is competent when the property for sale belongs to a diocese and we have forwarded the request of His Excellency to that office. What we meant to say, then, was that this Congregation could not give permission for the sale; not that the permission of the Holy See as such was not required.

"In saying that the ownership remained within Church hands we wished to signify that this would facilitate the granting of the requested permission, but we did not wish to adduce it as a reason for not getting permission or for not needing permission.

"We are grateful that you have brought to our attention the possibility of the letter being misleading. We trust that this matter has now been satisfactorily clarified." [English original]

As a result of this clarification, it is evident that appropriate permission is still needed for alienation of ecclesiastical property by one public juridic person to another. In CLSA, *Roman Replies and Advisory Opinions*, William A. Schumacher and J. James Cuneo (eds.), Washington, CLSA, 1987, pp. 84-86.

[17] As said earlier in this commentary, when an apostolate of a public juridic person is civilly incorporated, alienation does not occur if the public juridic person retains appropriate "reserved powers."

[18] FRANCIS G. MORRISEY reflects that "in the past, the then Congregation for Religious had often held that the sale of real estate which is part of the stable capital of the institute and the application of the proceeds to another capital purpose (such as capital construction or reduction or liquidation of a mortgage on buildings, or to a plant fund) did not constitute a conveyance to which canon 1291 §3 applies, but could be regarded simply as a conversion of capital assets from one form to another. However, examining recent indults, it would appear that this opinion is not followed today by the Congregation for Institutes of Consecrated Life and Societies of Apostolic Life which considers these transactions as alienations." In "Temporal Goods and Their Administration," in *Exegetical Comm*, vol. 2, p. 1685 (=MORRISEY, "Temporal Goods and Their Administration").

ACTS OF ADMINISTRATION (NOT ALIENATION). There is no alienation when there is no transfer of ownership of stable patrimony, or when the goods involved are not part of stable patrimony. Therefore, alienation does *not* take place when one performs the following:

1. To spend money, including invested money,[19] which has not been legitimately designated as stable patrimony (i.e., free capital), whether to pay debts or to make purchases[20]
2. To loan money at a moderate rate of interest, with or without collateral[21]
3. To use goods as collateral for loans[22]
4. To renegotiate or consolidate loans in order to profit the juridic

---

[19] Canon 1284 §2, 6° requires administrators, with the consent of the ordinary, to invest money which is left over after expenses and which can be usefully set aside for the purposes of the public juridic person. Such funds become part of stable patrimony *only* by "legitimate designation" (canon 1291) and not by the mere fact of being invested; therefore, to use funds which have simply been invested but not designated as part of stable patrimony is not an act of alienation. If excess funds have been designated as part of the stable patrimony, however, later use of them would be an act of alienation subject to the norms of the code.

[20] This free capital can even be spent to purchase real estate or to erect edifices, provided that the money involved had not been designated as stable patrimony. See DOHENY, *Practical Problems*, p. 47.

[21] Loans are generally means to earn money. If the one receiving the loan defaults in payment, the loaner would pursue action to recover the ecclesiastical good. Loaning money is an act of administration; depending on the amount, it may be an act of extraordinary administration.

[22] FRANCIS G. MORRISEY comments that "if a juridical person borrows or sells bonds to construct a new edifice, putting up *only* the title of the edifice under construction as collateral, this is not the kind of alienation governed by c. 1291. However, it is generally held that the issuing of bonds constitutes an alienation, at least under the sense of c. 1295. Some reputable canonists also hold that when money is borrowed merely on the general credit of the ecclesiastical corporation, without offering a mortgage or pledge as security, this does not constitute alienation in the sense of c. 1291 because the ownership of ecclesiastical goods is not being transferred to another. Although this opinion is followed in practice in many dioceses and religious institutes, I have serious reservations about it because of the debt incurred. In my opinion, then, the new indebtedness would be subject at least to the norms of c. 1295." In "Alienation," p. 308.

JOHN J. MYERS says: "In a new construction, if the building or buildings to be built are the only security standing behind the bonds or loan, then alienation has not occurred. On the other hand, if other properties might be endangered by the bonds or loan, then alienation is clearly involved and the legal formalities must be observed." In "Temporal Goods," p. 883.

person (e.g., to receive a better rate of interest, to facilitate ease in bookkeeping, etc.)

5. To mortgage property[23]

6. To assume mortgaged property (since the mortgage is not on Church property; rather, the Church acquires partial ownership to property already encumbered by the mortgage, thereby resulting in the Church being in a better position[24])

7. To spend money for the purpose for which it was donated (i.e., to observe the intentions of donors[25])

8. To refuse to accept a gift (since nothing is alienated, but something is merely refused: see canon 1267 §2)

9. To incorporate civilly a part of an ecclesiastical juridic person while retaining ecclesiastical ownership, particularly through articulated reserved powers (such as a religious institute separately civilly incorporating an educational or health care facility, while retaining canonical ownership)

10. To exchange securities for other securities of the same value[26]

---

[23] Regarding mortgaging property, ROBERT T. KENNEDY explains: "A mortgage gives rise to rights in regard to property, and creates the potential of a future loss of ownership in the event of a default in payments on the loan for which the mortgage serves as collateral, but there is no immediate transfer of ownership and, hence, no alienation. The same is true of assuming a mortgage when purchasing property which already has a mortgage on it." In "Temporal Goods," p. 1494.

[24] The ordinary must give permission to accept gifts burdened by a modal obligation or condition (canon 1267 §2; see also canon 1304 §2).

[25] Spending money for its designated purpose is not alienation even if this involves liquidating securities or selling real estate.

[26] FRANCIS G. MORRISEY reflects: "The exchange of securities for securities is generally not governed by the prescriptions on alienation. The norms on administration would apply. If, however, title to real estate is transferred, this is alienation in the strict sense, unless the transfer were for another piece of real estate of the same value (in which case the situation of the ecclesiastical goods is not jeopardized). There are, however, differences of opinion regarding the following case of transfer: some canonists accept that in cases where the sound administration of the goods of the entire juridical person requires that it be unburdened of certain pieces of property, such as land which may no longer be used for Church purposes, vacant land being heavily taxed, land creating ill will toward the Church and its credibility on social concerns, etc., the norms on alienation would not be applicable. Personally, I feel that such situations would give rise to a *legitimate cause* for alienation (see c. 1293), but that the transfer would be subject to the prescriptions governing alienation." In "Alienation," p. 308.

11. To lose temporal goods by prescription (since this is an act of poor administration but not involving a contract: see canons 1268; 1289)

12. To grant an easement to come across or otherwise use one's land in a way that is neither perpetual nor for too long a time[27]

13. To lease one's property (see canon 1297)

14. To surrender ecclesiastical goods to civil governmental authority involuntarily

15. To accept foundations (since there is no transfer of ownership, but the norms of canons 1303-1307 must be observed)

16. To sell old non-precious church furniture (including vestments) and equipment in order to replace it with new furniture and equipment of equal value[28]

These do not involve transfer of ownership of stable patrimony, so they are not acts of alienation. They are acts of administration, and they may be acts of *extraordinary* administration (see canons 638 §1; 1277; 1281) which require special permissions or consents. They may also be transactions which can worsen the patrimonial condition of a public juridic person (canon 1295) which, though not acts of alienation, require observance of the prescriptions of canons 1291-1294.[29]

JOHN J. MYERS says: "If property, including stocks and bonds, is exchanged for property of approximately equal value, no alienation occurs. Transfer of title in exchange for something in a different category, however, is alienation. Some hold that if property were to be sold with the proceeds to be designated as part of the stable patrimony, alienation would not occur. The Code, however, seems to consider any sale of real estate as alienation and subject to the regulations." In "Temporal Goods," p. 883.

[27] If these transactions are perpetual, alienation has occurred. ROBERT T. KENNEDY adds, "If the easement also includes the right to remove minerals, timber, or other natural resources from the land, then, of course, the easement would entail alienation of such resources." In "Temporal Goods," p. 1494, fn. 135.

[28] See the decision of the SACRED CONGREGATION FOR THE COUNCIL (July 12, 1919) in *AAS*, 11 (1919), p. 418.

[29] In commenting on the 1980 *Schema*, Archbishop Joseph Bernardin recommended that the notion of stable patrimony be replaced by a more flexible notion of alienation more appropriate for the contemporary world. The secretariat replied that such a change was unnecessary since canon 1295 applies the norms for alienation to any transaction which can worsen the patrimonial condition of the Church. *Relatio*, p. 288.

Determining what transactions can worsen the patrimonial condition involves an informed and honest analysis of various factors.

Finally, canon 1715 §2 requires that the law on the alienation of ecclesiastical goods is to be observed whenever necessary by those entering agreements or compromises as a method to avoid a trial (see canons 1713-1716). This means that those entering such agreements or compromises must comply with the prescripts of canons 1291-1294. It would be reasonable also that canon 1295 would be observed when these settlements involve transactions whereby the patrimonial condition of a public juridic person may be worsened.

CORRESPONDING CANON OF THE EASTERN CODE: CANON 1035 §1, 3°. The Eastern law requires the written consent of competent authority for the valid alienation of ecclesiastical goods constituting the stable patrimony of a juridic person. No reference is made to the value of these goods exceeding the sum defined by law.

PROCESS FOR VALID ALIENATION OF STABLE PATRIMONY, GOODS GIVEN BY A VOW, AND PRECIOUS GOODS

Can. 1292 – §1. Without prejudice to the prescript of can. 638, §3, when the value of the goods whose alienation is proposed falls within the minimum and maximum amounts to be defined by the conference of bishops for its own region, the competent authority is determined by the statutes of juridic persons if they are not subject to the diocesan bishop; otherwise, the competent authority is the diocesan bishop with the consent of the finance council, the college of consultors, and those concerned. The diocesan bishop himself also needs their consent to alienate the goods of the diocese.

§2. The permission of the Holy See is also required for the valid alienation of goods whose value exceeds the maximum amount, goods given to the Church by vow, or goods precious for artistic or historical reasons.

§3. If the asset to be alienated is divisible, the parts already alienated must be mentioned when seeking per-

mission for the alienation; otherwise the permission is invalid.

§4. Those who by advice or consent must take part in alienating goods are not to offer advice or consent unless they have first been thoroughly informed both of the economic state of the juridic person whose goods are proposed for alienation and of previous alienations.[30]

This canon is not about *spending money which is non-stable patrimony* in order to perform acts of administration. Many dioceses have annual administrative expenditures far in excess of the maximum amount set by the conference of bishops, and no special permission is required in order to operate. Likewise, many religious institutes and societies of apostolic life have expenditures beyond the amount set for the region by the Holy See (see canon 638 §3), and no special permission is required in order to operate. Commonly, money is non-stable patrimony and is spent for routine operations in acts of ordinary administration for which no special permission is required.[31] Rather, this canon is about *alienating stable patrimony* by losing ownership of it. Any money resulting from alienation of stable patrimony must either be invested carefully for the advantage of the Church or expended prudently according to the purposes of the transaction (canon 1294 §2).

Before considering canon 1291, one must recall that canon 638 §3 says that for religious institutes the Holy See defines an amount for the region, and an alienation beyond that amount requires the permission of the Holy See for validity. Canon 741 §1 applies the norm of canon 638 §3 to societies of apostolic life. Canon 718 allows proper law to apply this discipline to secular institutes.

---

[30] Canon 1295 requires statutes of juridic persons to conform to the requirements of this canon, and adds that canon 1292 must be observed not only for alienation but also for "any transaction [other than alienation] which can worsen the patrimonial condition of a juridic person."

[31] The law does require, however, that the diocesan bishop receive the counsel of the diocesan finance council and college of consultors "to place acts of administration which are more important in light of the economic condition of the diocese" as he has designated them (canon 1277). Also, acts of extraordinary administration require involvement of others (see canons 1277, 1281 §1).

Canon 1291 indicates that the value of stable patrimony belonging to public juridic persons other than institutes of consecrated life and societies of apostolic life may fall below the minimum amount, between the minimum and maximum amount, or beyond the maximum amount established by the conference of bishops for its region.[32] If the value is below the minimum amount, no permission is required from competent authority for the valid alienation of stable patrimony.[33]

Those who give their counsel or consent in matters of alienation must first have been thoroughly informed about (1) the economic state of the juridic person to whom the goods belong, and (2) any previous alienations. This information would likely come from the administrator of the public juridic person seeking the permission. The administrator has an obligation to disclose fully the appropriate details so that the counsel or consent is truly informed. At the same time, those giving counsel or consent have the obligation to seek out this information and, once informed, to act responsibly.[34]

If the administrator fails to secure the prescribed permission

---

[32] The 1977 *Schema* had said that one amount would be set by the conference of bishops for its region, and that a special commission of the conference of bishops would be established to confirm any alienation of stable patrimony proposed by a local ordinary beyond the set amount. In light of recommendations on this proposed canon made during the consultation process, the *coetus De bonis Ecclesiae temporalibus* decided that the conference should not limit the legitimate autonomy of each bishop, so the proposed legislation was eliminated. Thereafter, a consultor on the *coetus* proposed that the law require the conference of bishops to establish a "minimum" amount below which no permission for alienation of stable patrimony need be sought, and a "maximum" amount beyond which the Holy See must give permission. This proposal was approved unanimously by the consultors. *Communicationes*, 12 (1980), p. 424.

This canon does not mention that the minimum and maximum amounts must be reviewed by the Apostolic See. Nonetheless, canon 456 requires the review (*recognitio*) of the Holy See before any decree of the conference of bishops obtains binding force. See MYERS, "Temporal Goods," p. 880.

[33] Canon 1298, however, requires special written permission from the competent authority in order to sell or lease ecclesiastical goods to their administrators or to their relatives up to the fourth degree of consanguinity or affinity.

[34] The norm of canon 127 §2 states: "All those whose consent or counsel is required are obliged to offer their opinion sincerely and, if the gravity of the matter requires it, to observe secrecy diligently; moreover, the superior can insist upon this obligation."

before alienating an ecclesiastical good, he or she "is to be punished with a just penalty" (canon 1377).

The value of goods may be determined in a number of ways: (1) the original value; (2) the insured replacement value; (3) the depreciated value; (4) the worth determined for taxation purposes; and (5) the market value.[35] Canon 1293 §1, 2° requires the written appraisal of experts before alienating an asset, and canon 1294 §1 says that ordinarily an asset must not be alienated at a price less than its appraised value.

Canon 1292 §1 makes it clear that the diocesan bishop alone is the agent to alienate diocesan goods; this is beyond the scope of the authority of the diocesan finance officer who only performs "routine" acts of ordinary diocesan administration under the authority of the diocesan bishop (canon 494 §3). Canon 638 §3 likewise makes it clear that the agent to alienate goods of religious institutes is the competent superior with the consent of the council; this is beyond the scope of the authority of the religious finance officer, the superior, or others designated in proper law (canon 636 §1, 638 §2). The diocesan bishop and the competent superior (with the consent of the superior), respectively, are also the agents to enter any transaction which may worsen the patrimonial condition of the public juridic persons they govern (see canon 1295), having observed the discipline of canons 1291-1294.

ALIENATION OF ECCLESIASTICAL GOODS OWNED BY RELIGIOUS INSTITUTES AND SOCIETIES OF APOSTOLIC LIFE. Canon 638 §3 provides legislation concerning the permission required for the alienation of ecclesiastical goods belonging to religious institutes, provinces, and houses (see canon 634 §1) and any other affair which

---

[35] MORRISEY, "Alienation," p. 304. DANIEL J. WARD says that the "valuation of property is the net value, that is, the value after deducting all debts and liabilities on the property." He adds that "[n]ot all canonists accept the interpretation that the evaluation may be based on the net value of the property. It should be noted, however, that there is no authentic interpretation, and, therefore, a person may choose the most favorable interpretation." In "Temporal Goods," p. 204 (see fn. 14).

Moreover, one observes that the particular law of the United States concerning contracts involving leasing, promulgated on June 8, 2007, speaks only of the "market value" of the asset being leased (see the commentary on canon 1297).

can worsen the patrimonial condition of the public juridic person.
The canon states:

> **Canon 638 – §3. For the validity of alienation and of
> any other affair in which the patrimonial condition of a
> juridic person can worsen, the written permission of the
> competent superior with the consent of the council is re-
> quired. Nevertheless, if it concerns an affair which exceeds
> the amount defined by the Holy See for each region, or
> things given to the Church by vow, or things precious for
> artistic or historical reasons, the permission of the Holy
> See itself is also required.**

In these acts of alienation prior written permission is to be granted
by the competent superior with the *consent* of the council. Moreover,
the permission of the Holy See is required also (*insuper* – i.e., in addition to the permission of the competent superior with the council's
consent) if the ecclesiastical good has a value exceeding the amount
defined for the region by the Apostolic See,[36] has been given to the
Church by a vow, or is precious for artistic or historical reasons.

In the United States, the amount for the alienation of ecclesiastical goods of religious institutes is the same as the maximum
amount set for the dioceses of the United States.[37] In Canada,

---

[36] For missionary territories, the competent dicastery of the Apostolic See to define this
amount is the Congregation for the Evangelization of Peoples (*Pastor bonus*, arts.
85-92); for other areas, it is the Congregation for Institutes of Consecrated Life and
Societies of Apostolic Life (*Pastor bonus*, art. 108 §1).

[37] On March 25, 1992, Eduardo Cardinal Martínez Somalo, prefect of the Congregation
for Institutes of Consecrated Life and Societies of Apostolic Life, and Archbishop
Francisco Javier Errázuriz Ossa, secretary, responded to Sister Donna Markhan,
O.P., president of the Leadership Conference of Women Religious, and Brother Paul
Hennessey, C.F.C., president of the Conference of Major Superiors of Men (Prot. N.
SpR275/73). This rescript was an affirmative reply to the request of the two presidents
that the amount be raised from one million to three million dollars. In its reply, the
officials of the congregation requested that the religious institutes continue to exercise
discernment, good management, and prudence. They also asked that the religious
institutes continue to consult the diocesan bishops in these matters. In CLSA, *Roman
Replies and Advisory Opinions*, Kevin W. Vann and Lynn Jarrell (eds.), Washington,
CLSA, 1992, p. 15.
Over a decade later, on December 5, 2003, Archbishop Piergiorgio Silvano Nesti,
C.P., secretary of the Congregation for Institutes of Consecrated Life and Societ-

the same is true.[38]

In addition, if the religious institute is an autonomous monastery (canon 615) or an institute of diocesan right (see canon 589), canon 638 §4 requires that the local ordinary also give his written consent (*consensus in scriptis*).

Canon 741 §1 specifically applies the norms of canon 638 §3 and canon 638 §4 to societies of apostolic life. Canon 718 allows proper law to apply this discipline to secular institutes.

ALIENATION OF ECCLESIASTICAL GOODS OWNED BY OTHER PUBLIC JURIDIC PERSONS.[39] Canon 1292 identifies the "competent authority" who gives permission for the validity of the alienation of stable patrimony owned by others than religious institutes and societies of apostolic life:

- If the value of the stable patrimony is *less than* the minimum amount established by the conference of bishops, permission from a higher competent authority is not required for its alienation. The administrator of the public juridic person may alienate the stable patrimony.

- If the value of the stable patrimony is *between* the minimum and maximum amounts, the permission of competent authority (identified in canon 1292 §1) is required for its *valid* alienation.

  - for juridic persons not subject to the diocesan bishop: the

---

ies of Apostolic Life, responded to Sister Constance Phelps, SCL, president of the Leadership Conference of Women Religious (Prot. N. AG 126-2/03) that the amount was raised to five million dollars. He added, "This includes the annual adjustment linked to the consumer price index, as explained. Since the new limits go into effect for the dioceses in January 1, 2004, it seems appropriate that this authorization also go into effect at the same time." In CLSA, *Roman Replies and Advisory Opinions*, F. Stephen Pedone and James I. Donlon (eds.), Alexandria, CLSA, 2005, p. 14.

[38] This is assured through a telephone call to the secretariat of the CCCB on Friday, August 31, 2007.

[39] POPE PAUL VI gave residential bishops the faculty "[t]o grant permission, for a legitimate reason, to alienate, pledge, mortgage, rent out, or perpetually lease ecclesiastical property and to authorize ecclesiastical moral persons to contract debts to the sum of money determined by the national or regional conference of bishops and approved by the Apostolic See." In apostolic letter *motu proprio Pastorale munus* (November 30, 1963), n. 32: in *AAS*, 56 (1963), p. 10; *CLD*, vol. 6, p. 375.

competent authority is defined in the statutes of these juridic persons
- for juridic persons subject to the diocesan bishop: the competent authority is the diocesan bishop (who must receive the *consent* of the diocesan finance council, the college of consultors, and those concerned)
- for the juridic person of the diocese: the competent authority is the diocesan bishop (who also must receive the *consent* of the diocesan finance council, the college of consultors, and those concerned).[40]

- If the value of the stable patrimony amount is *greater than* the maximum amount, the *additional* (*insuper*)[41] permission of the Holy See is required for its *valid* alienation (canon 1292 §2). The Holy See must also give its permission for the valid alienation of an ecclesiastical good which has been given to the Church by vow, or is precious for artistic or historic reasons.

Canon 1291 speaks of "permission" (*licentia*) from competent authority for the alienation of stable patrimony to be valid. Since without this permission the alienation would be canonically invalid, however, the law really requires the competent authority's *consent*, not merely its permission.[42]

DIVISIBLE GOODS. Canon 1292 §3 requires that if the asset legitimately designated as stable patrimony is divisible, any parts already alienated must be identified. Otherwise, the permission is invalid. Concealing the fact of prior parts having already been

---

[40] In a decision of January 14, 1922 on CIC/1917, canon 1532 §3 (the predecessor of canon 1292 §1 of the revised law), the Sacred Congregation of the Council stated that the ordinary does not have the power to supply the consent of the administrative council (the predecessor of the diocesan finance council) and of the cathedral chapter when these bodies disagree "in the alienation of property and in any other equivalent contract." "*Lauden.* Circa donaria votiva et alienationes," (January 14, 1922), in *AAS*, 14 (1922), pp. 160-161; *CLD*, vol. 1, p. 731.

[41] The permission of the Holy See does not *substitute for* the other permissions. It is required *in addition to* them.

[42] As mentioned previously, *Book V* uses the term "permission" (*licentia*) to mean "consent" (*consensus*) in canons 1291, 1292 §2, and 1304 §1. The Eastern code uses the word *consensus* in the corresponding canons (1035 §1, 3°, 1036 §4, and 1048 §2). See also canons 638 §3 and 1190 §2.

alienated is subreption which, according to canon 63 §1, renders a rescript invalid.

According to a 1922 decision of the Pontifical Council for the Authentic Interpretation of the Canons of the Code, if a public juridic person is simultaneously alienating several separate goods and their total value exceeds the established amount, the permission of the Apostolic See is also required.[43]

ALIENATION OF VOTIVE OFFERINGS. Canon 1292 §2 mentions votive offerings, i.e., goods given to the Church by a vow (*ex voto*). Such votive offerings reflect the piety of the donor[44] and, therefore, regardless of their value, the permission of the Apostolic See is required for their valid alienation.

The Sacred Congregation for the Council issued a decision on January 14, 1922 in which it was determined that even "the mere offering of a gift at the altar or before a sacred image gives rise to a presumption of a vow" unless a contrary intention by the donor can be proven from other sources. Without a contrary indication, therefore, a gift offered at an altar or before a sacred image is considered a votive offering. The Apostolic See must give its permission prior to alienating the good, even if the donor concurs with the alienation.[45]

The Sacred Congregation for the Clergy issued a circular letter on April 11, 1971 on the care of the historico-artistic heritage of the Church. The letter insists that the alienation of precious objects, especially votive offerings, requires the permission of the Apostolic See. Those who fail to receive this permission are subject to ecclesiastical penalties which are not to be remitted unless the damage has first been repaired. The letter directs: "When sending over petitions to obtain the aforesaid permission, the vote of the commission on sacred art as well as that on the sacred liturgy and, if so warranted, that on sacred music and the vote of experts should be clearly indi-

---

[43] PONTIFICAL COMMISSION FOR THE AUTHENTIC INTERPRETATION OF THE CANONS OF THE CODE, *De alienatione bonorum ecclesiasticorum,* (July 20, 1929), in *AAS,* 21 (1929), p. 574. *CLD,* vol. 1, p. 731.

[44] *Communicationes,* 12 (1980), p. 424.

[45] SACRED CONGREGATION OF THE COUNCIL, *"Lauden.* Circa donaria votiva et alienationes,"* (January 14, 1922), in *AAS,* 14 (1922), pp. 160-161; *CLD,* vol. 1, p. 730.

cated. Also, in each case, attention should be given to the current civil law on such matters."

Canon 638 §3 applies the discipline of canon 1292 §2 to votive offerings owned by religious institutes. Canon 741 §1 applies the norm of canon 638 §3 to societies of apostolic life. Canon 718 allows proper law to apply this discipline to secular institutes.

GOODS PRECIOUS FOR ARTISTIC OR HISTORICAL REASONS. Canon 1292 §2 also mentions ecclesiastical goods which are precious for artistic or historical reasons. Obviously, a subjective determination must be made to conclude that an ecclesiastical good has such artistic or historical worth as to make it "precious." The good itself may have minimum monetary value. Nonetheless, if an ecclesiastical good is judged to be precious for artistic or historical reasons, the permission of the Apostolic See is required for its valid alienation.[46]

Canon 638 §3 applies the discipline of canon 1292 §2 to goods precious for artistic or historic reasons owned by religious institutes. Canon 741 §1 applies the norm of canon 638 §3 to societies of apostolic life. Canon 718 allows proper law to apply this discipline to secular institutes.

RELICS AND REVERED IMAGES. Attention must also be given to canon 1190 which absolutely forbids (*nefas est*) the sale of relics. Although the canon does permit that minor relics be given away, the permission of the Apostolic See is required for the valid alienation of (1) relics of great significance; (2) relics honored with great reverence by the people; and (3) images honored in some church with great reverence by the people.[47]

PERMISSION OF THE APOSTOLIC SEE. When the consent of the

---

[46] The SACRED CONGREGATION FOR THE COUNCIL said that the Commission for the Authentic Interpretation of the Canons of the Code must determine whether the ordinary can permit the alienation of a precious object valued under a certain amount. In *Lauden*, p. 160; *CLD*, vol. 1, p. 730.

[47] See APOSTOLIC SACRISTY, "Normae per la concessione delle reliquie del Sanctuario Apostolico," (February 15, 1994), *Notitiae*, 30 (1994), pp. 349-350; English translation in BISHOPS' COMMITTEE ON THE LITURGY, *Newsletter*, 32 (1996), p. 6. The Apostolic Sanctuary issued new norms on relics which permit very small relics to be distributed only for public veneration in a church. It forbids any relic from the Apostolic Sanctuary to be given to individual persons for private veneration.

Apostolic See is required for the valid alienation of certain ecclesiastical goods,[48] the congregations competent to give this permission for public juridic persons of the Latin Church are:

1. Congregation for the Clergy (see *Pastor bonus*, art. 98)
2. Congregation for Institutes of Consecrated Life and Societies of Apostolic Life (in matters affecting institutes of consecrated life and societies of apostolic life: see *Pastor bonus*, art. 108 §1);
3. Congregation for the Evangelization of Peoples (for missionary territories: see *Pastor bonus*, arts. 85-92).

The following information would be transmitted by the competent ecclesiastical authority to the appropriate dicastery of the Apostolic See when petitioning permission for an act of alienation, as appropriate:[49]

1. A brief history of the asset; attached intentions of donors; civil considerations (e.g., as an historic structure); perhaps, a map of the property
2. Explanation of the just cause for the alienation (canon 1293 §1, 1°)
3. Written evaluations by at least two experts (canon 1293 §1, 2°)
4. Notation on observance of any precautions prescribed by legitimate authority (canonical and civil) (canon 1293 §2)
5. Attestation of the consent the appropriate bodies, likely demonstrated through minutes of meetings (canon 1292 §1)

---

[48] In a letter dated January 25, 1988, the apostolic pro-nuncio to the United States communicated the concern of the prefect of the Congregation for the Clergy "that some dioceses in the United States have not been requesting the necessary authorization from the Holy See in order to alienate ecclesiastical goods whose value exceeds the approved maximum amount of one million dollars.... the stipulation of canon 1292 §2 clearly indicates that such permission is required for validity." *CLD* , vol. 12, pp. 750-751.

[49] See MORRISEY, "Alienation," pp. 298-299; MORRISEY, "Temporal Goods and Their Administration," p. 1687; WARD, "Temporal Goods," p. 202.

6. A statement regarding divisible goods, if applicable (canon 1292 §3)

7. The offer to purchase, if available (see canon 1294 §1)

8. An explanation why the asset is being alienated for a price lower than its appraised value, if applicable (canon 1294 §1; see canon 1293 §1, 2°)

9. A statement explaining what will be done with the money to be received (canon 1294 §2)

10. A statement regarding the observance of secular formalities (see canon 1296)

11. In matters concerning religious institutes of pontifical right, a letter from the diocesan bishop stating that he does not object to the transaction (i.e., a *nihil obstat*); for institutes of diocesan right, a letter from the diocesan bishop giving his consent. (The Congregation for Institutes of Consecrated Life and Societies of Apostolic Life has been requiring such a letter.)

Francis G. Morrisey explains that there are three possible procedures used when approaching the Apostolic See for its necessary permission:

> The first is to request permission *in principle* to convey the property; this is usually granted conditionally; then, when a formal offer has been received, it is forwarded (by facsimile, etc.) to the Holy See and a formal approval given; this response is usually given by facsimile or some other appropriate means.
>
> The second approach consists in waiting until a formal offer has been received and then the Holy See is asked to grant the indult. However, this second way of proceeding has the disadvantage that there could be time delays (allowing some forty days for a response) and sometimes this transaction has to be finalized before a reply is received because the offer is valid only for thirty days (or less). In some very urgent cases, permission could prob-

ably be presumed and a message forwarded to the Holy
See advising them of the fact that the transaction has been
finalized, even though the required indult did not arrive
in time.

Thirdly, for some large healthcare systems where
there has been a continued need of indults to finance
construction and renovation projects, a new practice has
been evolving: the Holy See has been granting a blanket
indult allowing the institute to contract accumulated debts
up to a given ceiling, without reference to a particular
transaction.[50]

The Pontifical Council for Legislative Texts has made it clear
that when the Apostolic See gives permission for the alienation of an
ecclesiastical good, it does not assume eventual economic responsibility for the alienation. The Apostolic See, rather, guarantees that
the alienation is in accord with the finality of ecclesiastical property.
The permission to proceed with an act of alienation is an administrative act by the Apostolic See intending to guarantee the good
use of ecclesiastical goods belonging to public juridic persons. The
Roman Pontiff is not bound to respond to the consequences of acts
of economic administration placed by the immediate administrators

---

[50]   MORRISEY, "Alienation," pp. 299-300. Regarding the third approach, Morrisey cites
communications from the Congregation for Institutes of Consecrated Life and Societies of Apostolic Life: August 10, 1991 (Prot. N. 87640/91) and May 14, 1992 (Prot.
N. 82153/89).

DANIEL J. WARD writes: "In the case of alienation, the approval may be sought prior
to or after the agreement to alienate property or fixed capital has been made. In either
case, the agreement should be made subject to the required canonical approvals. If
the approval of the Congregation is sought before the final purchase price has been
agreed upon, all other available information may be sent to the Congregation which
then often gives 'approval in principle.' When the final purchase price has been agreed
upon, it can be faxed to the Congregation for final approval. In such cases, the final
approval is often received within a matter of hours since the Congregation has had
the opportunity to study the matter beforehand.

"In the case of indebtedness, approval may also be sought before final agreement has
been reached. This is particularly important when an institution is seeking financing
through tax-exempt bonds." In "Temporal Goods," pp. 205-206.

of public juridic persons.[51]

PARTICULAR LAW FOR THE UNITED STATES.[52] On March 3, 2006, the USCCB issued a decree promulgating the particular law

---

[51] PCLT, *Nota,* La funzione dell'autorità, p. 32. The *Nota* also observes that the Roman Pontiff is not bound to respond to the consequences of acts of economic administration placed by immediate administrators of ecclesiastical goods because he is not the administrator of this property (as the term "administrator" is used in private law). Rather, he is the supreme administrator of ecclesiastical goods by reason of his primacy of governance and his public position in the Church.

[52] http://www.usccb.org/norms/1292-1.htm (December 1, 2008)

In November, 1985, the NCCB had requested that the maximum amount for alienation be $1,000,000 or a sliding scale based on the $5.00 per capita to a maximum of $5,000,000; the conference had also requested that the apostolic pro-nuncio be empowered to authorize expenses beyond the maximum "when recourse is difficult." The response of the apostolic pro-nuncio (Prot. N. 1782/86/8, April 19, 1986) explained that the Congregation for Bishops, following consultation with the Congregation for the Clergy, set the maximum amount at $1,000,000 (thereby rejecting the proposed sliding scale to a maximum of $5,000,000), and did not empower the apostolic pro-nuncio to authorize expenses beyond that limit when recourse is difficult. The final decree setting the maximum amount at $1,000,000 was promulgated by the NCCB on June 27, 1986.

In November, 1990, the NCCB approved two formulas to determine the maximum amount:

Proposal I – the maximum amount for a given diocese will be calculated according to Catholic population ($5.00 per person) between $1,000,000 and $5,000,000.

Proposal II – the maximum amount assigned to a diocese shall be one of three according to Catholic population:

  1) Dioceses with a Catholic population of over 1,000,000 persons shall have a maximum amount of $5,000,000.

  2) Dioceses with a population between 600,000 and 1,000,000 shall have a maximum of $4,000,000.

  3) Dioceses with fewer than 600,000 persons shall have a maximum of $3,000,000.

These proposals were reviewed by the Congregation for the Clergy which rejected them, and set the maximum for alienation at $3,000,000 to be effective in the interim until a single standard would be set by the NCCB at its November, 1991 meeting (Letter from the Pro-Nuncio, Prot. N. 190357/I, April 16, 1991). In NCCB, *Implementation of the 1983 Code of Canon Law: Complementary Norms*, Washington, NCCB, 1991, pp. 22-24.

In November, 1991, the NCCB set the maximum amount for alienation at $3,000,000. This was reviewed favorably by the Congregation for the Clergy (Letter from the Pro-Nuncio, Prot. N. 1182/I, April 26, 1993). The norm was promulgated by the president of the NCCB on May 21, 1993. See: SHARON EUART (ed.), "Complementary Norms Implementing the 1983 Code of Canon Law by the National Conference of Catholic Bishops," in *The Jurist*, 53 (1993), pp. 411-414. See also CLSA, *Roman Replies and Advisory Opinions*, William A. Schumacher and J. James Cuneo (eds.), Washington, CLSA, 1986, pp. 41-42; *CLD*, vol. 12, p. 750.

for the United States on the minimum and maximum amounts for alienation and any transaction which can worsen the patrimonial condition. The decree follows:

Decree of Promulgation
Canon 1292 §1

On November 13, 2002 the Latin Church members of the United States Conference of Catholic Bishops approved complementary legislation for the implementation of canon 1292 §1 of the Code of Canon Law for the Latin Church dioceses of the United States. The action was granted *recognitio* by the Congregation for Bishops in accord with article 82 of the Apostolic Constitution *Pastor Bonus* and issued by Decree N. 296/84 of the Congregation for Bishops signed by His Eminence Giovanni Battista Cardinal Re, Prefect, and His Excellency Most Reverend Franciscus Monterisi, Secretary, and dated June 3, 2003. On March 31, 2004, a subsequent Decree with the same Protocol Number was issued which granted *recognitio* to the below indicated provisions for a period of two years. By a decree dated January 31, 2006, again with the same aforementioned Protocol Number, the same Congregation decreed the extension of the previous *recognitio* for an additional two year period, a term extended for an additional *biennium* by a decree of March 31, 2008:

Wherefore, and in accord with the prescripts of canon 1292 §1, the United States Conference of Catholic Bishops decrees that:

1. the maximum limit for alienation and any transaction which, according to the norm of law, can worsen the patrimonial condition is $10,000,000 for Dioceses with Catholic populations of half a million persons or more. For other Dioceses the maximum limit is $5,000,000 (cf. can. 1295).

2. the minimum limit for alienation and any transaction which, according to the norm of law, can worsen the patrimonial condition is $1,000,000 for Dioceses with Catholic populations of half a million persons or more. For other Dioceses the minimum limit is $500,000.

3. for the alienation of property of other public juridic persons subject to the Diocesan Bishop, the maximum limit is

$5,000,000 and the minimum limit is $25,000 or 5% of the prior year's ordinary annual income, whichever is higher.

4. both the maximum and minimum amounts within the region are linked to the consumer price index as determined annually by the United States Bureau of Labor Statistics, and reported by the United States Conference of Catholic Bishops to the appropriate offices of the Holy See and to the Conference members.

As President of the United States Conference of Catholic Bishops, I hereby decree that this decree takes effect immediately for all the Latin Church dioceses in the United States.

Given at the offices of the United States Conference of Catholic Bishops in the city of Washington, the District of Columbia, on June 20, 2008.

Francis Cardinal George, O.M.I.
Archbishop of Chicago
President, USCCB
Reverend Monsignor David J. Malloy
General Secretary, USCCB

The application of this decree for calendar year 2009 is identified as follows by the USCCB:[53]

MAY 2009

The USCCB's complementary legislation implementing canon 1292 §1 of the Code of Canon law states that the maximum and minimum sums for alienation of ecclesiastical goods are to be "linked to the consumer price index as determined annually by the United States Bureau of Labor Statistics, and reported by the United States Conference of Catholic Bishops to the appropriate offices of the Holy See and to the Conference members." Accordingly, the adjusted maximum and minimum sums now in effect are as follows:

Maximum: $11,408,000 for populations of 500,000 or more, $5,705,000 for all others (raised from $11,397,000 and $5,699,000 respectively),

---

[53] http://www.usccb.org/norms/1292-1.htm (June 1, 2009)

Minimum: $1,141,000 for populations of 500,000 or more, $575,000 for all others (raised from $1,140,000 and $570,000 respectively),

For other juridic persons subject to the Diocesan Bishop the new maximum sum for alienation is $5,705,000 (raised from $5,699,000) and the minimum is $29,000 (from $28,495) or 5% of prior year's ordinary annual income, whichever is greater.

PARTICULAR LAW FOR CANADA. The CCCB established two particular laws to implement the norm of canon 1292 in Canada. The first decree[54] was approved on October 23, 1984, and reviewed by the Apostolic See on March 8, 1985.[55] It concerns the *minimum* amount for alienation.

Decree No. 10 – In accordance with the prescription of canon 1292, the Canadian Conference of Catholic Bishops hereby decrees that the minimum amount applicable to cases to which this canon applies will be ten per cent (10%) of the maximum amount approved by the Conference.

This decree is effective immediately.

The commentary on this decree explained, among other things, that the maximum amount for alienation since March 26, 1982 had been $1,000,000 CDN.[56] The commentary was later revised by the CCCB Canon Law-Inter-Rite Episcopal Commission on February 18, 1988, and approved by the Permanent Council of the Conference on March 16-17, 1988. The revised commentary[57] explains the decree on canon 1292 at length:

The maximum amount approved for the alienation or conveyance of Church property in Canada is presently fixed at $1,000,000

---

[54] CCCB, *Official Document No. 537* in *Studia canonica*, 19 (1985), pp. 187-191; *CLD*, vol. 11, p. 309. The decree was again issued on March 28, 1988 as *Official Document No. 537-1*, in *Studia canonica*, 22 (1988), pp. 455-457; CCCB, *Complementary Norms to the 1983 Code of Canon Law*, Ottawa, CCCB, 1996, pp. 110-113. In fact, the 1985 and 1988 official documents are identical.

[55] See letter from the Apostolic Nunciature in Canada, Prot. N. 20506 (March 8, 1985), in *Studia canonica*, 19 (1985), p. 189.

[56] *Studia canonica*, 19 (1985), p. 191; *CLD*, vol. 11, p. 310.

[57] *Studia canonica*, 22 (1988), pp. 454-457.

(Sacred Congregation for the Clergy, Prot. No. 167623/III, March 26, 1982).

Acts of alienation of Church property whose value is situated between the minimum and maximum amounts are governed by the prescriptions of canon 1292, §1.

The C.C.C.B. has determined that acts of alienation of Church property whose value is situated between 5% and 10% of the maximum sum approved would be considered to be acts of *major importance* (governed by the prescriptions of canon 1277).

Consequently, in virtue of the present decree, when Church land or buildings are sold, or other transactions entered into which could jeopardize the stable patrimony of a juridical person in the Church, the following norms are to be observed:

- acts under $50,000: the diocesan bishop may carry out these acts on his own;
- acts between $50,000 and $100,000: the diocesan bishop needs to consult the finance council and the college of consultors;
- acts between $100,000 and $1,000,000: the diocesan bishop needs the consent of the finance council, of the college of consultors, and of interested parties;
- acts over $1,000,000: in addition to the consents mentioned immediately above, the consent of the Apostolic See is also required before the transaction can be validly concluded.

Among the acts subject to these requirements, we could mention:

- the sale of Church land and buildings;
- entering into long-term loans or mortgages;
- entering into long-term leases;
- issuing bonds and debentures;
- transfer of corporate ownership to lay boards.

For institutes of consecrated life, the *Code of Canon Law* provides that special sums can be determined for the region. At the present time, the maximum amount for such institutes is $1,000,000.

Canon 638, §3 does not refer to a uniform minimum sum for religious institutes; this is left, then, to proper law.

The second decree[58] was issued on February 10, 1994; its

---

58   CCCB, *Official Document No. 658.* In CANADIAN CANON LAW SOCIETY, *Newsletter,* 20 (June, 1994), p. 29; CCCB, *Complementary Norms to the 1983 Code of Canon Law,* Ottawa, CCCB, 1996, pp. 112-115.

content had been approved by the Canadian Conference of Catholic Bishops on March 20, 1992, and reviewed by the Holy See (see Letter of Apostolic Nunciature, Prot. N. 4211/93, September 8, 1993). It concerns the *maximum* amount for alienation:

> Decree No. 38 – In accordance with the prescriptions of Canon 1292, the Canadian Conference of Catholic Bishops hereby decrees that the maximum amount for the alienation of Church property or for debts which may be contracted without needing recourse to the Holy See be henceforth established at $3,500,000 CDN within all the territory of the Conference. This amount will be annually adjusted according to the cost of living in Canada, taking January 1, 1993, as the point of reference.

The commentary[59] on this decree states:

1. On March 26, 1982, the Congregation for the Clergy had determined that the maximum amount allowed for acts of alienation without the intervention of the Holy See was $1,000,000 CDN. This amount has now been increased to $3,500,000 and applies to acts of alienation, both in the strict sense of sales, conveyances, etc., and in the broad sense of acts which could jeopardize the patrimonial condition of a juridical person.

    In addition, the sum had been indexed, using January 1, 1993, as the benchmark. Thus, each year, revised figures will be determined, depending on the cost of living index.

2. Decree No. 9 of the Conference (*Official Document*, No. 536; see also amended decree, *Official Document*, No. 536-1) provides that non-recurring acts which exceed five per cent (5%) of the maximum amount approved by the Conference are to be considered acts of extraordinary administration.

    Decree No. 10 of the Conference (*Official Document*, No. 537-1) determines that for acts of alienation of property the minimum

---

[59] Ibid., pp. 29-30.

amount applicable in cases to which canons 1292 and 1295 apply is ten per cent (10%) of the maximum amount approved by the Conference.

Therefore, the following amounts would apply:

1) *For acts of extraordinary administration* (goods belonging to the diocese):

Up to $175,000 (5% of the maximum): the diocesan bishop can perform alone acts of extraordinary administration (see revised Decree No. 9)

From $175,000: the diocesan bishop needs the *consent* of the college of consultors and of the diocesan finance committee (Canon 1277).

It should be noted, though, that in virtue of canon 1277, the diocesan bishop is to determine, in view of the financial situation of the diocese, those acts of *major importance* which would require the *advice* of the college of consultors and of the diocesan finance committee.

2) *For acts of alienation:*

Up to $350,000 (10% of the maximum): the diocesan bishop may carry out such acts alone (see Decree No. 10);

From $350,000 to $3,500,000: the diocesan bishop needs the *consent* of the college of consultors, of the diocesan finance committee, and of the interested parties (Canon 1292, §1);

From $3,500,000: in addition to the three consents mentioned immediately above, the consent of the Holy See is also required (Canon 1292, §2).

The application of this decree for calendar year 2009 is identified as follows by the CCCB:[60]

MARCH 2009

...

At its meeting of 17-18 March 2009, after taking into consideration the 2008 national cost-of-living increase of one point two

---

[60] CCCB, Memorandum (February 2008).

percent (1.2%), the Executive Committee determined that the current maximum amount allowed for acts of alienation without the intervention of the Holy See is CAN \$4,736,447 CDN.

…

Therefore, the following amounts would apply:

1) For acts of extraordinary administration (goods belonging to the diocese):
   • Up to \$236,823 CDN (5% of maximum): the diocesan bishop can perform alone acts of extraordinary administration (see revised Decree No. 9);
   • From \$236,823 CDN: the diocesan bishop needs the <u>consent</u> of the college of consultors and the diocesan finance committee (canon 1277)

   It should be noted, though, that in virtue of Canon 1277, the diocesan bishop is to determine, in view of the financial situation of the diocese, those acts of <u>major importance</u> which would require the <u>advice</u> of the college of consultors and the diocesan finance committee.

2) For acts of alienation:
   • Up to \$473,645 CDN (10% of maximum): the diocesan bishop may carry out such acts alone (see Decree No. 10);
   • From \$473,645 CDN to \$4,736,447 CDN: the diocesan bishop needs the <u>consent</u> of the college of consultors, the diocesan finance committee, and the interested parties (canon 1292 §1)
   • Over \$4,736,447 CDN: in addition to the threefold consent mentioned immediately above, the consent of the Holy See is also required (canon 1292 §2).

CORRESPONDING CANONS OF THE EASTERN CODE: CANONS 1036, 1038. Eastern canon 1036 §1 provides that the minimum and maximum amounts are established either by the synod of bishops of a patriarchal Church or by the Apostolic See for Churches *sui iuris*. The alienation of eparchial goods valued between the minimum and maximum amounts needs the consent (*consensus*, not permission for validity) of the eparchial finance council and the college of eparchial consultors. The alienation of goods of a juridic person subject to the eparchial bishop and valued between the minimum and maximum amounts needs the consent of the eparchial bishop, the eparchial finance council, and the college of eparchial consultors. The alienation of goods of a juridic person not subject to the eparchial bishop and valued between the minimum and maximum amounts needs the consent of the authority determined in the typicon or statutes.

Eastern canon 1036 §2 is legislation proper only within the territory of patriarchal Churches.[61] It identifies the various consents required for alienation of goods valued beyond the maximum amount (but not twice that amount) established by the synod of bishops of a patriarchal Church:

- the consent of the patriarch and the permanent synod: if the goods belong to an eparchy, unless the particular law of the same patriarchal Church determines otherwise;
- the consent of the eparchial bishop, the patriarch, and the permanent synod: if the goods belongs to a juridic person subject to an eparchial bishop;
- the consent of the patriarch and the permanent synod: if the goods belong to a juridic person not subject to an eparchial bishop, even of pontifical right.

Eastern canon 1036 §3 also is legislation proper only within the territory of patriarchal Churches. It requires the consent of the patriarch and the synod of bishops of the patriarchal Church (as well as the consents mentioned in canon 1036 §2) for the alienation of (1) goods whose value exceeds twice the maximum amount set by the synod of bishops of the patriarchal Church; (2) precious goods; and (3) goods given to the Church by vow.

Eastern canon 1036 §4 explains that the consent of the Apostolic See is required in other cases if it concerns (1) goods valued

---

[61] CCEO canon 152 says that what is stated in common law (which includes the discipline of *Title XXIII*) concerning patriarchal Churches or patriarchs is to be understand as pertaining also to major archiepiscopal Churches or major archbishops, unless the common law expressly states otherwise or it is evident from the nature of the matter. See JOHN D. FARIS, "The Code of Canons of the Eastern Churches and Temporal Goods," in *CFH*, p. 35.

beyond the amount established or approved by the Apostolic See; (2) precious goods; (3) goods given to the Church by vow.

Eastern canon 1038 §1 corresponds to Latin canon 1292 §4, and mentions those who must give counsel, consent, or "confirmation."[62] Eastern canon 1038 §2 corresponds to Latin canon 1292 §3 but says that "counsel, consent or confirmation are not considered to have been given unless, in seeking them, previous alienations are mentioned." A canon exactly corresponding to Latin canon 1294 §3 is not found in the Eastern law.

ADDITIONAL CANON OF THE EASTERN CODE: CANON 1037. Eastern canon 1037 has no corresponding canon in the Latin legislation. It identifies the counsel or consent needed by the patriarch for the alienation of temporal goods belonging to a patriarchal Church or the patriarch's eparchy. The patriarch needs:

- the counsel of the permanent synod of the patriarchal Church: if the goods belong to the patriarchal Church and are valued between the minimum and maximum amounts established by the synod of bishops;
- the consent of the eparchial finance council and the college of eparchial consultors: if the goods belong to the patriarch's eparchy and are valued between the minimum and maximum amounts established by the synod of bishops (see CCEO, canon 1036 §1, 1°);
- the consent of the permanent synod of the patriarchal Church: if the goods belong to the patriarchal Church or the patriarch's eparchy and are valued beyond the maximum amount established by the synod of bishops (but not twice that amount);
- the consent of the synod of bishops of the patriarchal Church: if the goods belong to the patriarchal Church or the patriarch's

---

[62] JOBE ABBAS comments: "It is unclear why the reference to 'confirmation' remains in CCEO c. 1038. During the iter of CCEO c. 1038, the 'confirmation' was added to the draft of CCEO c. 1038 since the patriarch's confirmation was required in an initial formulation of CCEO c. 1036 §2 [see *Nuntia* 18 (1984) 65 (c. 108 *bis*)]. However, the *Coetus de expensione observationum* totally reformulated the proposed CCEO c. 1036 §2 and changed the patriarch's 'confirmation' into 'consent' [see *Nuntia* 28 (1989) 131 (c. 1051 §2, 2)]." In "Alienating Ecclesiastical Goods in the Eastern Catholic Churches," in *Folia canonica*, 5 (2002), p. 131, fn. 20.

eparchy and are (a) valued beyond twice the maximum amount established by the synod of bishops; (b) precious goods; or (c) goods given to the Church by vow.

ADDITIONAL CANON OF THE EASTERN CODE: CANON 1039. The Eastern code adds canon 1039, which says: "For any alienation, consent is required of those concerned." This same requirement is mentioned in Latin canon 1292 §1.

REQUIREMENTS FOR LICIT ALIENATION OF STABLE PATRIMONY BEYOND THE DEFINED MINIMUM AMOUNT

Can. 1293 – §1. The alienation of goods whose value exceeds the defined minimum amount also requires the following:

1° a just cause, such as urgent necessity, evident advantage, piety, charity, or some other grave pastoral reason;

2° a written appraisal by experts of the asset to be alienated.

§2. Other precautions prescribed by legitimate authority are also to be observed to avoid harm to the Church.[63]

Canon 1293 identifies three requirements for alienating goods belonging to stable patrimony whose value exceeds the defined *minimum* amount:

1. a just cause (e.g., urgent necessity, evident advantage, piety, charity, or some other grave pastoral concern);
2. a written appraisal by experts;
3. precautions to be observed in order to avoid harm to the Church, if these are prescribed by legitimate authority.

The requirements of canon 1294 oblige for the canonical *liceity*, not the *validity*, of the alienation.[64]

---

[63] Canon 1295 requires statutes of juridic persons to conform to the requirements of this canon, and adds that canon 1293 must be observed not only for alienation but also for "any transaction [other than alienation] which can worsen the patrimonial condition of a juridic person."

[64] See BOUSCAREN-ELLIS-KORTH, p. 840.

This canon concerns the alienation of goods belonging to stable patrimony whose value exceeds the defined minimum amount. It does not concern the alienation of goods whose value is below the minimum amount. Indeed, the opinion of experts may be needed to determine the precise value of the ecclesiastical good in order to determine whether it is below or above the defined minimum.

To alienate goods having a value beyond the defined minimum amount requires a just cause. The canon identifies a number of possible just causes: urgent necessity, evident advantage, piety, charity, or some other grave pastoral reason.[65] These just causes, especially the last one, obviously allow broad discretion.[66]

The canon requires the written appraisal of competent experts[67] when the value of a good obviously exceeds the defined minimum amount. The canon speaks of "experts" in the plural (*a peritis*) from which it is understood that the appraisal of at least two experts is required.[68] Obviously, these experts must be persons of honesty and integrity, and competent in the matter about which they are making an appraisal. The appraised value of the good will determine from whom any permission for alienation is required (as defined in canon 1292). Indeed, if the appraised amount is lower than the defined minimum, no permission is required even if it is sold at a

---

[65] CIC/1917, canon 1530 §1, 2°, the predecessor of canon 1293 §1, 1°, had mentioned as examples of a just cause only: "urgent necessity, the evident usefulness of the Church, or piety."

[66] JOHN J. MYERS concludes that the canon identifies "a non-exhaustive list of possible reasons" justifying alienation. He comments specifically about "evident advantage": "Reasons external to the Church may also dictate certain decisions. A situation of economic crisis or collapse in a country or an especially advantageous offer to purchase an asset may indicate a course of action of 'evident usefulness' for the Church." In "Temporal Goods," p. 881.

[67] DANIEL J. WARD observes: "There is no definitive answer as to who may or may not be an expert. Since the opinion of at least two different experts is required, the practical determination of who should be an expert must be considered in light of the cost factor. The Apostolic See has accepted as experts the financial auditors of a juridic person if the auditors have had a long history with the juridic person. The local property tax valuation should be acceptable if this is given at the fair market value or the percentage of the fair market value is stated." In "Temporal Goods," p. 205.

[68] VROMANT, p. 252. This reflects *Regula iuris* 40: "Pluribus locutio duorum numero est contenta."

higher price.[69] The contrary is also true: if the value exceeds the minimum amount, the appropriate permission is required even if, in fact, the good is eventually alienated at an amount lower than its appraised value.

Legitimate authority can also prescribe other "precautions" or guarantees which are to be observed in alienation so that harm does not come to the Church. These precautions "could take the form of public auctions or advertising, requiring certain qualities in the purchaser, a stabilization clause, the posting of a bond when payment is deferred, etc."[70] The "legitimate authority" to define these precautions includes those identified in canon 1292 as competent to grant required permissions.[71] The "legitimate authority" can also be a secular authority.[72]

CORRESPONDING CANON OF THE EASTERN CODE: CANON 1035 §1, 1°-2°, §2. Eastern canon 1035 is about the requisites for alienation of goods "constituting the stable patrimony of a juridic person" (without adding "whose value exceeds the defined minimum amount," as stated in Latin canon 1293 §1). One example of a just cause for such alienation is "a pastoral reason" (instead of "some other grave pastoral reason").

Eastern canon 1035 §1, 3° adds a requirement for alienation of ecclesiastical goods which is not mentioned in the Latin code: "in cases prescribed by law, written consent of the competent authority, without which the alienation is invalid."

---

[69]   See PONTIFICAL COMMISSION FOR THE AUTHENTIC INTERPRETATION OF THE CANONS OF THE CODE, Response (November 24, 1920), in *AAS*, 12 (1920), p. 577; *CLD*, vol. 1, pp. 729-720. See WARD, "Temporal Goods," p. 204.

[70]   LÓPEZ ALARCÓN, "The Temporal Goods," p. 1001.

[71]   JOHN J. MYERS recommends that the episcopal conference "could establish what kinds of transactions, even within the realm of stable capital, are really only ordinary management activities. It could also clarify the limits to borrowing on an extended line-of-credit beyond which higher consultation is needed. The diocesan bishop or other proper superior, then, could apply these even further to a specific situation through particular legislation. Canon 1293, §2 permits the proper authority to set down further requirements for alienation beyond those specified in the Code." In "Temporal Goods," p. 880.

[72]   MORRISEY, "Temporal Goods," pp. 735-736.

ALIENATION BELOW APPRAISED VALUE;
DISPOSITION OF REVENUE RECEIVED

Can. 1294 – §1. An asset ordinarily must not be alienated for a price less than that indicated in the appraisal.

§2. The money received from the alienation is either to be invested carefully for the advantage of the Church or to be expended prudently according to the purposes of the alienation.[73]

Canon 1294 §1 says that ordinarily an asset must not be alienated for a price less than its value indicated in the appraisal by experts, of whom there must be at least two (see canon 1293 §1, 1°). The canon inserts the word "ordinarily" in order to allow the competent authority to exercise discretion; the term had not existed in the 1917 code which had required alienation to the highest bidder, all things considered.[74] For any number of reasons, it can be advisable that an alienation occur at a price lower than the appraisal. The authority competent to allow alienation at this lower amount is the same authority competent to grant permission for the alienation in the first place (see canon 1292).

Canon 1294 §2 directs that money received from an alienation is to be handled in one of two ways. The money is either:

1. to be invested carefully for the advantage of the Church, or

2. to be expended prudently according to the purposes for which the alienation occurred.

---

[73] Canon 1295 requires statutes of juridic persons to conform to the requirements of this canon, and adds that canon 1294 must be observed not only for alienation but also for "any transaction [other than alienation] which can worsen the patrimonial condition of a juridic person."

[74] CIC/1917, canon 1531 §2 had required alienation to be made by public auction or at least enacted following public notice, unless circumstances suggested otherwise, and had expected that the good be sold to the highest bidder, all things considered. The discipline of the 1917 canon is not found in the revised legislation.

WILLIAM J. DOHENY suggested that six points be considered when alienating ecclesiastical goods to the highest bidder: "(1) The good faith and dependability of the prospective purchasers. (2) The financial credit of the prospective purchasers. (3) The method and manner of payment promised. (4) Possibility of litigation and difficulties. (5) Honesty and integrity of prospective purchasers. (6) Use to which the property may or can be adapted by certain purchasers, e.g., theater, dance hall, tavern, race track, etc." In *Practical Problems,* p. 32.

The careful investment of the proceeds from alienation will obviously seek the best return with the lowest risk so that funds and earnings may later be available for proper ecclesiastical purposes. If the proceeds are not invested, they may be prudently spent immediately for the motives prompting the alienation. The law does not specifically require that the proceeds be assigned legitimately by the competent ecclesiastical authority to the stable patrimony of the public juridic person (see canon 1291).[75]

The requirements of canon 1294 oblige for the canonical *liceity*, not the *validity*, of the alienation.[76]

CORRESPONDING CANON OF THE EASTERN CODE: None.

TRANSACTIONS WHICH MAY WORSEN
THE PATRIMONIAL CONDITION

Can. 1295 – The requirements of cann. 1291-1294, to which the statutes of juridic persons must also conform, must be observed not only in alienation but also in any transaction which can worsen the patrimonial condition of a juridic person.

Canon 1295 requires that the legislation of the four preceding canons, 1291-1294, must be reflected in the statutes of juridic persons (although the legislation of these canons is operative even if the legislation is not mentioned in the statutes). It also says that the requirements of these four canons must be observed also in any transaction other than alienation which can worsen the patrimonial condition of a juridic person.

CIC/1917, canon 1533 distinguished alienation "properly so-called" (*proprie dicta*) from contracts by which the condition of

---

[75] CIC/1917, canon 1531 §1 had required the proceeds to be "invested carefully, safely, and usefully in favor of the Church;" no mention was made of expending the proceeds. In a decision on December 17, 1951, the SACRED CONGREGATION OF THE COUNCIL said that the proceeds must be invested in immovable goods: *Cum decreto,* in *AAS,* 44 (1952), p. 44; *CLD,* vol. 3, p. 581. Inasmuch the revised canon now allows expenditure of the proceeds, the restriction of the congregation no longer applies.

[76] BOUSCAREN-ELLIS-KORTH, p. 840.

the Church can worsen (*quo conditio Ecclesiae peior fieri possit*). This distinction led some canonists to consider these "worsening contracts" as acts of alienation "improperly so-called." Put another way, CIC/1917, canon 1533 was said to distinguish alienation "in the strict sense" and alienation "in the wide sense." The revised code avoids ambiguity. Canon 1295 is clearly *not* about alienation. Yet, it requires for certain transactions the same process as acts of alienation.[77]

The statutes, which must conform to canons 1291-1294, are those of public juridic persons, which are governed by the canons of *Book V* (see canon 1257 §2). Including in the statutes the discipline of canons 1291-1294 prevents them from including contrary discipline. This discipline was added to the canon when a consultative organ recommended that the requirements of canons 1291-1294 should be reflected in secular statutes, so that when a transaction is invalid *canonically* it will also be invalid *civilly*.[78] The statutes of private juridic persons are not required to follow the norms of canons 1291-1294, though the statutes may select freely to observe some or all of them.

The requirements of canons 1291-1294 must be observed in any transaction which can worsen the patrimonial condition of a public juridic person. The code considers alienation as a transaction in which ownership is transferred. A transaction which can worsen the patrimonial condition of the public juridic person is *not* alienation;

---

[77] Some authors still consider canon 1295 transactions to be alienation in the broad, not strict, sense. Mariano López Alarcón, for example, says that an act of alienation is to be understood both as one which conveys actual ownership to another and as one which worsens the patrimonial condition of the public juridic person. In light of this, he observes that the code "provides a criterion whereby a potential act of alienation can be identified: the juridical person might be left in a worse patrimonial situation, because of the quality of the goods removed from the patrimony or because of their value in relation to the total value of the patrimony in general. In the same way, it would be necessary to determine whether the goods that replace the ones alienated can be considered to be patrimonial compensation or to have caused a loss, once the purposes of the alienation have been fulfilled." In "Book V," p. 1003.

It must be understood, however, that the 1983 code clearly does *not* consider the transactions in canon 1295 to be acts of alienation. They are not. See the commentary on canon 1291.

[78] See *Communicationes*, 12 (1980), p. 426.

if it were alienation, the code would say so clearly. When an act of alienation occurs, ownership is transferred. When a transaction governed by canon 1295 occurs, ownership is not transferred – but the ownership *is* reasonably judged to be threatened by the transaction. Alienation focuses *ad extra* – on passing an ecclesiastical good to another; a transaction governed by canon 1295 focuses *ad intra* – on protecting ecclesiastical goods which one wishes to retain as stable patrimony.

The threat to the stable patrimony related to canon 1295 must be *reasonable* – i.e., based on prudently evaluated reasons, following appropriate consultation and research. Given diverse circumstances throughout the world, it is impossible to identify actions which may worsen the patrimonial condition of public juridic persons everywhere. What is threatening in one time and place may not be so in another time and place.

Some acts of extraordinary administration (see canons 1277, 1281 §2) may threaten the patrimonial condition of a given public juridic person. All acts of extraordinary administration require the involvement of others. Those acts of extraordinary administration which may threaten stable patrimony, however, also must involve the persons and processes identified in canons 1291-1294.[79] Therefore, some acts of extraordinary administration may require even the permission of the Apostolic See for validity, even though these are not acts of alienation (see canon 1292 §2).

Francis G. Morrisey observes that acts which can worsen the patrimonial condition of a juridic person involve potential loss of ownership, control, or sponsorship. Civil laws must be considered in order to protect these elements. Perhaps "reserved powers" (mentioned earlier in the commentary on canon 1255) protecting the Church's interests would be incorporated into civil legal documents. He adds that canon 1295 "can be of particular relevance when certain joint ventures or collaborative endeavors take place and when the

---

[79] See FEDERICO R. ANZAR GIL, "Actos de administración ordinaria y extraordinaria: normas canónicas," in *Revista española de derecho canónica*, 57 (2000), pp. 66-67.

goods belonging to various juridical persons are commingled, e.g., when two or more parishes jointly operate an educational, charitable or social undertaking, or when two or more religious institutes operate a hospital or other health-care institution."[80]

Reflecting canon 1295, canon 638 §3 says that any transaction by which the patrimonial condition of a religious institute, province, or "canonically erected" house can worsen, requires for validity the written permission of the competent superior and the council. Canon 741 §1 applies the norm of canon 638 §3 to societies of apostolic life. Canon 718 allows proper law to apply the norm to secular institutes.

PERMISSION OF THE APOSTOLIC SEE. When a public juridic person wishes to enter into a transaction which can worsen its patrimonial condition, the competent ecclesiastical superior must contact the appropriate dicastery of the Apostolic See (see the commentary on canon 1292) with the following information, as appropriate:[81]

1. A brief history of the asset; attached intentions of the donors; civil considerations (e.g., as an historic structure); perhaps, a map of the territory

2. Explanation of the just cause for the transaction (canon 1293 §1)

3. The financial condition of the public juridic person

4. The effect of the transaction on the public juridic person

5. Written evaluations of at least two experts, if applicable (canon 1293 §1)

6. Notation on observance of any precautions prescribed by legitimate authority (canonical and civil) (canon 1293 §2)

7. Attestation of the consent of the appropriate bodies, likely demonstrated through minutes of meetings (canon 1292 §1)

8. The proposed means to repay any indebtedness, if applicable

9. A statement regarding the observance of secular formalities (see canon 1296)

---

[80] MORRISEY, "Temporal Goods," p. 736; MORRISEY, "Alienation," pp. 311.

[81] See WARD, "Temporal Goods," p. 203.

10. In matters concerning religious institutes of pontifical right, a letter from the diocesan bishop stating that he does not object to the transaction (i.e., a *nihil obstat*); for institutes of diocesan right, a letter from the diocesan bishop giving his consent. (The Congregation for Institutes of Consecrated Life and Societies of Apostolic Life has been requiring this letter.)

The congregations competent to give permission to enter canon 1295 transactions are the same as those competent to give permission for acts of alienation (see the commentary on canon 1292).

CORRESPONDING CANON OF THE EASTERN CODE: CANON 1042. This canon corresponds almost exactly to Latin canon 1295, but does not require that the statutes of juridic persons must reflect the discipline of the canons on alienation.

ALIENATIONS
VALID CIVILLY, INVALID CANONICALLY

Can. 1296 – Whenever ecclesiastical goods have been alienated without the required canonical formalities but the alienation is valid civilly, it is for the competent authority, after having considered everything thoroughly, to decide whether and what type of action, namely, personal or real, is to be instituted by whom and against whom in order to vindicate the rights of the Church.

Canon 1290 commits the Church to follow the civil law unless its provisions are contrary to divine law or canon law. A reciprocal commitment (i.e., for civil law to follow canon law) is not assured by each secular government. Therefore, it can happen that the civil law recognizes the validity of an act of alienation but canon law does not.

Canon 1296 concerns actions to vindicate the rights of the Church following an act of alienation[82] which is civilly valid but

---

[82] Canon 1296 is about alienation, not about "any transaction which can worsen the patrimonial condition of a juridic person" (canon 1295). Nonetheless, ROBERT T. KENNEDY opines: "The possibility of corrective action of which canon 1296 speaks,

which was done without the required canonical formalities (*solemnitates*) and is therefore canonically invalid. In such a situation, canon law holds that the ecclesiastical goods remain the property of the Church.[83] The competent ecclesiastical authority is to decide on what type of action (personal or real) is to be instituted; who is to initiate that action; and against whom the action will be directed. The action may be *personal* (i.e., directed against a person: here, the administrator who did not observe canon law) or *real* (i.e., directed against a thing [*res*]: here, the ecclesiastical good whose retrieval is sought).[84]

The "competent authority" is the superior of the person responsible for the canonically invalid alienation.[85] This authority

---

however, could by analogy be applied to many canon 1295 transactions as well." In "Temporal Goods," pp. 1505-1506. One will recall that canon 1295 expects the statutes of a public juridic person to conform to the requirements of canons 1291-1294, so that both the canonical and secular fora concur.

One will recall also the discipline of canon 1281 §3 which says that a juridic person has the right to take action or recourse against administrators who have damaged it. See Elizabeth McDonough, "Addressing Irregularities in the Administration of Church Property," in *CFH*, pp. 223-243.

83   This is evident in the communication made on January 28, 1988 by the prefects of the Congregation for Catholic Education and the Congregation for Institutes of Consecrated Life and Societies of Apostolic Life in the matter of establishing a self-perpetuating board of trustees at Saint Louis University Hospital, who wrote: "The authorization of the Holy See is necessary for the sale of Saint Louis University Hospital since the provisions of 1967 of appointing a self-perpetuating board of trustees, a majority of whom were not members of the Missouri Province of the Society of Jesus, did not constitute an alienation of ecclesiastical goods, whose owner, canonically considered, remains the Missouri Province of the Society of Jesus as a public juridic person of the church, and therefore the properties pertaining to Saint Louis University are still to be considered ecclesiastical goods. The action was not a transfer of property, but a change in structure of the governing body of the university." In *Origins*, 27 (1987-1998), p. 631.

To avoid confusion created by this incident, should a public juridic person decide to incorporate civilly one of its apostolates, care must be taken to reserve appropriate powers to the public juridic person. In this way, the control of the ecclesiastical good is not lost and the good is not alienated.

84   This reflects *Regula iuris* 76: "Delictum personae non debet in detrimentum Ecclesiae redundare."

85   This is clearer in Eastern canon 1040 which uses the phrase "the higher authority of the one who carried out the alienation." Clearly, the "competent authority" would not be all those whose permission is required for valid alienation: see Kennedy, "Temporal Goods," p. 1506.

will undoubtedly rely upon the advice of experts before proceeding with any action to vindicate the rights of the Church. These experts may include civil attorneys, the diocesan finance council (whose members are to be "truly expert in financial affairs and civil law" canon 492 §1), the college of consultors, those concerned, etc. Obviously, the competent authority is not the administrator of the public juridic person. Indeed, the administrator would be the person responsible for the invalid alienation; he or she is the person subject to the competent authority. Even if the administrator would seek civil action to rescind an act of alienation, he or she is forbidden "to initiate or contest litigation in a civil forum in the name of a public juridic person" without the prior written permission of his or her own ordinary (canon 1288).

Further, the code requires that an indeterminate penalty be imposed upon an administrator who alienates an ecclesiastical good without the required canonical formalities: "A person who alienates ecclesiastical goods without the prescribed permission is to be punished with a just penalty" (canon 1377). Should a penal trial be initiated against the offender, during the penal trial itself, an injured party is able to bring a contentious action to repair damages incurred personally against one who committed the delict (canon 1729 §1; see also canon 1491).

It can also occur that an act of alienation, recognized as valid by civil law, is held as valid *but illicit* in canon law (see canons 1293-1294). In such a case, the one harmed has the right to bring canonical action (see canon 1400 §2) against the administrator who illicitly but validly alienated the temporal good (but not against the recipient of the good who has received it validly). The administrator illegitimately inflicted damage on another by his or her juridic act, whether out of malice or negligence, and is obliged to repair damages (see canon 128).

This canon not only underscores the importance of carefully following canonical norms in acts of alienation, but also the importance of inserting appropriate aspects of the discipline of the code into civil legal documents which would secure the interests of the Church before the secular society (e.g, the articles of incorporation and bylaws of corporations). The civil documents may say, for example, that an alienation which is invalid canonically is also invalid civilly.

CORRESPONDING CANON OF THE EASTERN CODE: CANON 1040. The Eastern code changes the term "competent authority" in the Latin code to the phrase "the higher authority of the one who carried out the alienation." Eastern canon 1040 makes no mention of "real or personal" action. It also says that invalid alienation is enacted "against the prescripts of canon law" (rather than "without the required canonical formalities").

LEASING ECCLESIASTICAL GOODS

> **Can. 1297 – Attentive to local circumstances, it is for the conference of bishops to establish norms for the leasing of Church goods, especially regarding the permission to be obtained from competent ecclesiastical authority.**

Canon 1297 requires the conference of bishops to establish norms for the leasing of Church goods. "A lease is a contract by which property, whether movable or immovable, is let to another for his [or her] use for a determined time at a specified price or rent."[86] A contract involving leasing is *not* a contract involving alienation (see canons 1291-1294). Nor is every contract involving leasing to be treated as a contract involving a transaction which can worsen the patrimonial condition of the lessor (see canon 1295); were the contrary true, there would be no need for separate legislation on leasing.

Canon 1297 is another example of an occasion requiring the action of the conference of bishops concerning temporal goods. The conference is expected to establish norms governing the entire matter of leasing of ecclesiastical goods. The norms are particularly to include reference to the permission to be obtained from competent

---

[86] BOUSCAREN-ELLIS-KORTH, p. 844.

ecclesiastical authority when entering a lease agreement.[87]

A lease contract involving a public juridic person must also conform to the appropriate norms of civil law (see canon 1290).[88] Indeed, during the process of drafting the proposed revised code, consideration was given to require the Church simply to observe civil laws when leasing goods.[89] In the end, however, the promulgated law requires not only observance of civil law but also observance of the particular ecclesiastical law on leasing promulgated by the conference of bishops.

The 1917 code had contained elaborate legislation on leasing temporal goods (CIC/1917, canons 1541-1543). The 1983 code greatly simplifies the earlier norms, and assigns to the conference of bishops the task of establishing particular law on leases.

PARTICULAR LAW FOR THE UNITED STATES.[90] On June 8, 2007, the USCCB issued a decree promulgating the particular law for the United States on the leasing of Church goods. The decree follows:

---

[87] In 1990 an institute of women religious sought permission from the Congregation for Religious Institutes and Societies of Apostolic Life to enter into an eight and a half year lease with a Catholic university. The university intended to spend significant sums on the property. The religious institute also requested permission to alienate the property to the university upon the expiration of the lease, should both parties agree. Since it would be impossible in 1990 to determine the fair market value of the property in 1998, a formula was mutually agreed upon by the parties: each party would select an appraiser who would determine the fair market value which would be the average of the two appraisals if the lower of the two appraisal was 90% or more of the higher; if the lower was less than 90% of the higher appraisal, a third appraiser, mutually acceptable, would make the final determination. The petition carried the favorable *votum* of the diocesan bishop. The rescript from the Apostolic See granted the requested permissions, said that canons 1292-1294 were to be observed, but did not require the diocesan bishop to serve as executor. In CLSA, *Roman Replies and Advisory Opinions*, Kevin W. Vann and Lynn Jarrell (eds.), Washington, CLSA, 1992, pp. 15-16.

[88] See NICHOLAS P. CAFARDI, "Leasing Ecclesiastical Goods," in *CFH*, pp. 207-214, esp. pp. 210-212.

[89] See *Communicationes*, 12 (1980), p. 427.

[90] http://www.usccb.org/norms/1297.htm (December 1, 2008) See PAPROCKI, "Recent Developments," pp. 275-278; LEGAL RESOURCE CENTER FOR RELIGIOUS, "Commentary on USCCB Complementary Norms Implementing Canon 1297 on Leasing Ecclesiastical Goods," (April 14, 2008), manuscript, 7 pp.

In November, 1985, the NCCB had included two norms for leasing of ecclesiastical goods in the complementary norm on acts of extraordinary administration (canon 1277); these were: (5) To lease church property when the annual lease income ex-

Decree of Promulgation
Canon 1297

On November 13, 2002, the members of the United States Conference of Catholic Bishops legitimately approved complementary legislation for the implementation of canon 1297 of the Code of Canon Law for the dioceses of the United States. The action was granted *recognitio* by the Congregation for Bishops in accord with article 82 of the Apostolic Constitution *Pastor Bonus* and issued by Decree N. 778/2005 of the Congregation for Bishops signed by His Eminence Giovanni Battista Cardinal Re, Prefect, and His Excellency Most Reverend Francesco Monterisi, Secretary, and dated May 2, 2007.

Wherefore, and in accord with the prescripts of canon 1297, the United States Conference of Catholic Bishops decrees that the following norms shall govern the leasing of Church property:

1. Prior to leasing of ecclesiastical goods owned by a diocese, the diocesan bishop must hear the finance council and the college of consultors, when the market value of the goods to be leased exceeds $400,000.

2. Prior to leasing of ecclesiastical goods owned by a diocese, the diocesan bishop must obtain the consent of the finance council and the college of consultors when the market value of the property to be leased exceeds $1,000,000 or the lease is to be for 3 years or longer.

3. The valid leasing of ecclesiastical goods owned by a parish or other public juridic person subject to the governance of the diocesan bishop requires consent of the diocesan bishop when the market value of the goods to be leased exceeds $100,000 or the lease is to be for 1 year or longer.

4. The valid leasing of ecclesiastical goods owned by a pontifical institute of consecrated life or society of apostolic life requires, in addition to the consent of the competent major superior and council, the *nihil obstat* of the diocesan bishop when the market

---

ceeds the minimum limit. (6) To lease church property when the value of the leased property exceeds the minimum and the lease is for more than nine (9) years. The complementary legislation on acts of extraordinary administration never received the *recognitio* of the Apostolic See. NCCB, *Implementation of the 1983 Code of Canon Law: Complementary Norms*, Washington, NCCB, 1991, p. 21.

value of the property to be leased exceeds $1,000,000 or the lease is to be for 3 years or longer.

5. The valid leasing of ecclesiastical goods by any public juridic person requires the consent of the Holy See when the market value of the goods exceeds $5,000,000.

As President of the United States Conference of Catholic Bishops, I hereby decree that the effective date of this decree for all the dioceses of the United States Conference of Catholic Bishops will be August 15, 2007.

Given at the offices of the United States Conference of Catholic Bishops in the city of Washington, the District of Columbia, on the 8th day of June, in the year of our Lord 2007.

Most Reverend William S. Skylstad, Bishop of Spokane
President, USCCB
Reverend Monsignor David J. Malloy,
General Secretary, USCCB

The particular law for the United States can be summarized as follows:

Owner of the Ecclesiastical Good	Market Value (and Length of Lease)	Counsel, Consent, *Nihil Obstat*
Diocese	$400,000+	diocesan bishop must receive counsel of diocesan finance council and college of consultors
Diocese	$1,000,000+ or lease for 3+ years	diocesan bishop must receive consent of diocesan finance council and college of consultors
Parish or other public juridic person subject to the diocesan bishop	$100,000+ or lease for 1+ year(s)	diocesan bishop must give consent
Pontifical Institute of Consecrated Life or Society of Apostolic Life	$1,000,000+ or lease for 3+ years	competent major superior and council must give consent; diocesan bishop must give *nihil obstat*
Any public juridic person	$5,000,000+	Holy See must give consent

Particular Law for Canada.[91] On December 1, 1987 the CCCB promulgated the following as particular law enacting canon 1297 in Canada. This legislation had been approved by the CCCB on October 24, 1985 and reviewed by the Congregation for Bishops on January 10, 1987 (Prot. N. 6/84).

Decree No. 16 – In accordance with the prescriptions of c. 1297, the Canadian Conference of Catholic Bishops hereby decrees that the following norms shall be observed when it is a question of leasing or renting ecclesiastical goods:

1. Lands and buildings for which no immediate or long-term use for Church purposes is foreseen should not be retained indefinitely;

2. The leasing of ecclesiastical property, when the lease extends over a period of two years, constitutes an act of extraordinary administration, and is subject to the prescriptions of c. 1277, or, in the case of institutes of consecrated life, of c. 638 §1;

3. Any leasing or renting of ecclesiastical property for a period extending beyond thirty continuous days shall be done in writing, observing all applicable civil and particular laws;

4. Normally, the Church property shall not be leased for less than the current comparable rates. If, however, in particular circumstances, the property is to be leased for less than these rates, the written permission of the Ordinary is to be obtained beforehand, except in the case of institutes of consecrated life of pontifical right where the permission of the major superior shall be obtained.

5. Any leasing of ecclesiastical property without change to charitable or other organizations, if the duration of the lease extends beyond three months, requires the written consent of the Ordinary, or, in the case of institutes of consecrated life of pontifical right, of the major superior;

6. If the total amount of rent to be paid exceeds the maximum

---

[91] CCCB, *Official Document No. 575* in *Studia canonica* 22 (1988), pp. 200-203; CCCB, *Complementary Norms to the 1983 Code of Canon Law*, Ottawa, CCCB, 1996, pp. 116-119.

amount determined for acts of alienation of ecclesiastical goods, and if the lease has a duration of more than nine years, the permission of the Holy See is also to be obtained beforehand.

This decree is effective one month after the date of promulgation.

The commentary[92] on this decree states:

This decree applies both to property owned by dioceses and to that owned either by institutes of consecrated life (cf. canons 635, §1; 718) or by societies of apostolic life (cf. canon 741). It applies to the *leasing* of buildings or of space within them, even for charitable purposes. However, it does not apply directly to the *renting* of non ecclesiastical property from others for Church purposes.

"Property" in this decree refers not only to lands and buildings, but also to air space or underground areas, as in the case of easements or similar servitudes.

Written permission is now required in many instances before Church property may be legitimately leased to others.

According to canon 1277 (see also Decree No. 9, C.C.C.B. *Official Document*, no. 536), when the property belongs to a diocese, the *consent* of the finance council and of the college of consultors is required before acts of extraordinary administration may be carried out. Thus, if the lease were to be for a period of more than two years, such consent would be required beforehand.

The permission of the Apostolic See is required if two conditions co-exist simultaneously:

– the lease is for *more* than nine years duration;
– *and* the total rent or compensation to be received exceeds $1,000,000 (according to Decree no. 10, C.C.C.B. *Official Document*, no. 537).

---

[92] *Studia canonica*, 22 (1988), pp. 202-205.

In other cases, permission may be granted by the Ordinary or, if such is within his or her competence according to the institute's legislation, by the appropriate major superior.

Any applicable prescriptions of civil legislation (for instance as found in articles of incorporation, etc.) would also have to be observed.

CORRESPONDING CANON OF THE EASTERN CODE: None.

ALIENATIONS AND LEASES TO CLOSE RELATIVES

Can. 1298 – Unless an asset is of little value, ecclesiastical goods are not to be sold or leased to the administrators of these goods or to their relatives up to the fourth degree of consanguinity or affinity without the special written permission of competent authority.

Canon 1298 requires the special written permission of competent authority (*specialis competentis auctoritatis licentia scripto data*) for the sale or lease of ecclesiastical goods (unless they have little value) to the administrators of these goods or to their relatives up to the fourth degree of consanguinity or affinity. The obvious purpose for this canon is to avoid abuses and even the appearance of impropriety.[93]

The competent authority will obviously need to determine the value of the ecclesiastical good involved in the alienation or lease. He may rely upon the inventory mentioned in canon 1283, 2° when making this determination. The inventory is to indicate the goods of the public juridic person and the value of each; it would also indicate what ecclesiastical goods constitute stable patrimony. The competent

---

[93] Other canons also intend to avoid abuse and the appearance of impropriety in the matter of ecclesiastical goods: e.g., canon 492 §3 excludes close relatives of the diocesan bishop from being members of the diocesan finance council; canon 1448 forbids tribunal officials from serving in trials involving close relatives; and canon 1456 forbids tribunal officials from accepting any gift on the occasion of a trial. See also canon 478 §2 which forbids the diocesan bishop from appointing as vicars general or episcopal vicars his relatives by consanguinity up to the fourth degree.

authority may also rely upon the appraisal of experts to determine the value of an asset (see canon 1293 §1, 2°).

The permission of the competent ecclesiastical authority is to be written and "special." The emphasis on "special" written permission indicates that the permission is to be for a determined sale or lease. A general permission is not permitted.

Canon 1298 mentions persons related to the administrator of ecclesiastical goods up to the fourth degree of consanguinity or affinity. Consanguinity is a relationship based on common blood, regardless of the marital status of any ancestors. Affinity is a relationship based on a valid marriage, even if not consummated, and existing between a person and the blood relatives of that person's spouse. Relationships are computed through lines (direct or collateral) and degrees (successive generations). The laws about consanguinity and affinity are found in canons 108-109. The prohibition of canon 1298 encompasses those related to the administrator by blood (consanguinity) or marriage (affinity) up to the fourth degree.[94]

If the administrator violates this canon and the alienation is valid in civil law, he or she is subject to the discipline of canon 1296, above.

CORRESPONDING CANON OF THE EASTERN CODE: CANON 1041. This canon requires the "special permission" (but not the "special *written* permission") of the competent authorities mentioned in Eastern canons 1036-1037 to sell or lease ecclesiastical goods to persons related to administrators by consanguinity or affinity up to the fourth degree.

---

[94] Canon 1298 excludes relatives "up to" the fourth degree, not "up to, and including" the fourth degree.

CHAPTER SIX

PIOUS WILLS IN GENERAL AND PIOUS FOUNDATIONS
(Title IV: Canons 1299-1310)

Title IV of *Book V* contains twelve canons concerning pious wills in general and pious foundations. Canon 1299 §1 asserts the rights of persons to give their goods for pious causes through an act *inter vivos* or through an act *mortis causae*. Canon 1299 §2 mandates the observance of civil laws, if possible, for dispositions *mortis causae* and admonishes heirs to fulfill the intention of the testator when civil laws are not observed. Canon 1300 requires the diligent observance of the wills of the faithful who give their resources for pious causes. Canon 1301 asserts the right of the ordinary to be the executor of all pious wills; other executors must render an account to him. Canon 1302 is legislation on pious trusts. Canons 1303-1307 are general legislation on pious foundations. Canon 1308 concerns the reduction of Mass obligations. Canon 1309 concerns the transfer of the Mass obligations of pious foundations. Finally, canon 1310 concerns the reduction, moderation, and commutation of pious wills.

These canons reflect the discipline of the 1917 *Code of Canon Law* in its canons 1489 §1; 1513-1517; 1544 §1; 1545-1549; and 1551 §1. Several canons have no predecessor in the first code: canons 1303 §2; 1308 §§2-5; 1309 and 1310 §3.

All the canons of Title IV have corresponding canons in the 1991 *Code of Canons of the Eastern Churches*: canons 1043-1054.

DISPOSITIONS FOR PIOUS CAUSES
INTER VIVOS AND MORTIS CAUSAE; OBLIGATIONS OF HEIRS

> **Can. 1299 – §1. A person who by natural law and canon law is able freely to dispose of his or her goods can bestow goods for pious causes either through an act *inter vivos* or through an act *mortis causa*.**
>
> **§2. In dispositions *mortis causa* for the good of the Church, the formalities of civil law are to be observed if possible; if they have been omitted, the heirs must be admonished regarding the obligation, to which they are bound, of fulfilling the intention of the testator.**

Title I of *Book V* had identified a number of ways whereby the Church is able to acquire temporal goods, including by free-will gifts from the faithful. Title II had provided norms for the administration of ecclesiastical goods; specifically, it had expressed the freedom and obligation of the Christian faithful to support the Church (canon 1261).[1] Title IV of *Book V* provides legislation on particular ways in which the Church may acquire goods from the faithful (i.e., pious wills, pious trusts, and pious foundations), and how those goods are to be administered.[2]

It is important to understand carefully certain technical terms found in, or related to, the content of Title IV:

- *pious cause*[3] (canon 1299) – an undertaking for a spiritual or supernatural motive, to merit grace or to glorify God, or in satisfaction for one's sins or those of others[4] (see canons 114 §2; 1254 §2); a pious cause may be one of two kinds:

---

[1] Title IV contains one norm on alienation of ecclesiastical goods, a topic addressed in Title III: canon 1303 §2 addresses the disposition of goods belonging to a non-autonomous pious foundation when the time has passed for it to be held by a public juridic person.

[2] See VROMANT, p. 143.

[3] *Pious cause* is mentioned several times in the code: canons 325 §2; 956; 1299 §1; 1300; 1302 §1; 1301 §3; 1310 §1. A similar term, *pious works*, is found in canon 1245.

[4] Giving a temporal good simply to fulfill some merely humanitarian or philanthropic cause, no matter how generous or noble the gift may be, is not considered a "pious cause." A pious cause must have a spiritual or supernatural motive. See VROMANT, p. 137; BOUSCAREN-ELLIS-KORTH, p. 821.

ecclesiastical – a pious cause whose goods are "ecclesiastical goods," i.e., those which are established as a public juridic person (an autonomous foundation) or which are given to another public juridic person (a non-autonomous foundation); these goods are governed by the norms of *Book V*

lay – a pious cause whose goods are not "ecclesiastical goods," i.e., those which are established as a private juridic person (e.g., an autonomous foundation),[5] or which are given to a private juridic person or to a physical person (e.g., some pious trusts)

- *pious will* (canons 1300-1301) – a temporal good given for one or more pious causes; pious wills are made in one of two ways:

inter vivos – by transfer of ownership while the donor remains alive; it is contractual (see canon 1290) and therefore must be accepted by the recipient; once accepted, it is irrevocable

mortis causa – by transfer of ownership upon the death of the donor; this may be done by two distinct instruments:

last will and testament[6] – the final declaration for the disposition of one's temporal goods upon one's death; it is not contractual and, therefore, it need not be accepted before the donor's death by the beneficiary; it can be revoked as long as the testator lives[7]

---

[5] Canon 1303 §1, 2° explains that a *non-autonomous* foundation cannot be entrusted to a *private* juridic person.

[6] Several terms apply to the receipt of the temporal goods *mortis causa:*

An *heir (heres)* is a person, physical or juridic, who is legally entitled to the estate (i.e., to all property and incumbrances upon it) of the deceased.

An *inheritance (hereditas)* is the property of the deceased accepted by the heir.

A *legacy (legatum)* is a specific gift made by a last will and testament from a person's estate; it is to be delivered to the *legatee (legatarius)* by the heir or by the executor or administrator of the estate. Canonists have disputed whether the legatee has the *ius in re* (i.e., the actual ownership of the gift still in the possession of the heir) or merely the *ius ad rem* (i.e., the right to demand the gift from the heir). See BOUSCAREN-ELLIS-KORTH, pp. 795-796; VROMANT, pp. 139-140.

[7] VROMANT, pp. 139-140.

gift in contemplation of death (donatio mortis causa) – an instrument whereby a temporal good is given to another in anticipation of death with the understanding that the donor can revoke it before death; the ownership of the temporal good is transferred at death; it is contractual (see canon 1290) and, therefore, it must be accepted by the recipient before the donor's death[8]

- *pious trust*[9] (canon 1302) – a pious will given by a donor (called a *trustor*) which demands continued administration by a third party (called a *trustee*) who "owns" and administers it in order that its income and/or principle benefit a pious cause
- *pious foundation* (canons 1303-1310) – temporal goods (an *endowment*) given perpetually or at least for a long period of time with the obligation to perform one or more pious causes in return for the revenue; the code identifies two kinds of foundations:

    autonomous foundations – a juridic person, public or private,[10] comprised of temporal goods destined for one or more pious causes; since they are juridic persons, autonomous foundations are perpetual (see canon 120 §1)

---

[8] VROMANT, pp. 138-139.

[9] Several terms apply to the receipt of the temporal goods by a trust, which is the transfer of ownership to one person for the benefit of another. A trust can be established either by an act *inter vivos* or an act *mortis causa*. To establish a trust, four elements must converge:

(1) Property (*fideicommisum*): a temporal good transferred to one person for the benefit of another.

(2) A trustee (*fiduciarius*): a physical or juridic person distinct from the beneficiary to whom ownership of the good is transferred with the obligation to administer it for the beneficiary.

(3) A beneficiary (*fideicommisssarius*): a physical or juridic person, or a pious cause, for whose benefit the temporal good is to be administered by the trustee according to the will of the donor.

(4) Actual transfer of the property (*fiducia*): the transfer of the temporal good to the trustee so he or she can administer it for the benefit of the beneficiary. See BOUSCAREN-ELLIS-KORTH, p. 796; VROMANT, pp. 140-141.

[10] If the autonomous foundation is *public*, its goods are ecclesiastical goods (see canon 1257 §1). If the autonomous foundation is *private*, its goods are not ecclesiastical goods (see canon 1257 §2).

> *non-autonomous foundations* – temporal goods given to
> an already existing *public* (not private) juridic person, with
> the obligation to perform one or more pious causes from
> the earnings (but not from the principle); this is a kind of
> pious trust, and the juridic person is the "trustee" of the
> temporal good

Title IV is placed at the end of *Book V*, as if forming an appendix,[11] since some of its legislation does not concern "ecclesiastical goods" (as that term is defined in canon 1257 §1). "Ecclesiastical goods" belong to public juridic persons. Sometimes pious wills are entrusted to physical persons (as can be the case with a pious trust, canon 1302) or established as private juridic persons (as can be the case with an autonomous foundation: see canon 1303 §1, 1°). In these cases, the goods are not "ecclesiastical goods."

Canon 1299 mentions three laws to which consideration must be given with pious causes: natural law, canon law, and civil law. It is important that those giving temporal goods for pious causes, and those receiving them, be aware of the norms in all three categories. *Natural law* gives the right to dispose of their temporal goods to all persons who have the use of reason (see canons 97 §2; 99) and are able to act freely.[12] *Civil law* may place certain restrictions on, or require certain formalities in, the disposition of temporal goods; these are accepted by the Church if they do not contradict natural law or canon law. *Canon law* requires that a person not place a juridic act out of force, grave fear, malice, ignorance or substantial error; if these factors are present, the act may be invalid or subject to recissory action (see canons 125-126). Canon law may place certain restrictions

---

[11] On April 21, 1970, the *coetus De iure patrimoniali Ecclesiae* observed that the goods entrusted by a pious will to a physical person or to an institute which lacks juridic personality are unable to be considered "ecclesiastical goods." Therefore, the *coetus* agreed to place the canons on pious wills in general with those of pious foundations instead of with the canons on acquiring goods (where they had been in the CIC/1917, canons 1513-1516). The norms on pious wills and pious foundations would properly follow the canons dealing with temporal goods in general. *Communicationes*, 37 (2005), pp. 263-264. All these canons on pious wills and pious foundations are considered "as if an appendix" to the preceding canons. *Communicationes*, 5 (1973), p. 101. See also *Communicationes*, 37 (2005), pp. 267-268.

[12] See DE PAOLIS, *De bonis Ecclesiae temporalibus*, p. 111.

on physical persons in the exercise of their right to bestow temporal goods (see canon 668 concerning restrictions placed on religious). Canon law may also place certain restrictions on juridic persons in doing the same (see canon 1285 concerning donations made by administrators of public juridic persons).

Canon 1299 §1 says that persons who by natural law and canon law can freely dispose of their goods may do so in one of two ways: (1) through an act *inter vivos*, or (2) through an act *mortis causa*.[13] The remaining canons in Title IV explain that these donations can be in the form of pious wills, pious trusts, and pious foundations.

Canon 1299 §1 does not defer to civil law (as the code does in the matter of contracts: canon 1290; see canon 22). Rather, this canon focuses on the rights of persons in natural and canon law to dispose their temporal goods for pious causes, even should the civil law say the contrary. The canon does not suggest, however, that legitimate civil legal formalities should be disregarded irresponsibly. Civil law may place certain restrictions on the disposition of goods, or may require certain formalities to dispose of them. If the civil law eliminates one's natural and canonical right to dispose of goods, however, the civil legislation does not prevail in the law of the Church.[14] If it simply establishes formalities within which one may exercise the natural and canonical right, the civil legislation should be observed.

Canon 1299 §2 explains that, if possible, the formalities of civil law are to be observed in the disposition of goods given for the good of the Church[15] *mortis causa* (i.e., both by last will and testa-

---

[13] Canon 1299 is virtually identical to CIC/1917, canon 1513. The first code, however, used *mortis causa* in canon 1513 §1 and *ultimis voluntatibus* in canon 1513 §2. The revised law uses *mortis causa* in both paragraphs.

[14] For example, the civil law may not recognize the validity of a will made by a minor without parental approval, but canon law would recognize it if the minor had adequate reason and freedom. In such a situation, the canon law would prevail for purposes of the Church, even though the civil law may not recognize the validity of the minor's act.

[15] The term *Church* here does not have the restricted meaning assigned by canon 1258; instead, it also refers to private juridic persons. CIC/1917, canon 1513 §3 had referred to last wills given "for the good of the Church." The 1977 *Schema* had spoken of dispositions given "for pious causes" but the 1980 *Schema* returns to the language of

ment[16] and *donatio mortis causa*). The purpose of observing civil legal formalities is to avoid conflict and confusion after the donor has died. The code recognizes that, in some instances, compliance with the formalities of civil laws may have been ignored or may be impossible to observe. Even in such cases, the Church nonetheless accepts the intention of the donor as binding. If the deceased has failed to observe the civil legal formalities, the heirs should be informed of the deceased's intention (if they do not know about it) and must be admonished (*moneri debent*)[17] concerning their obligation to fulfill that intention. This admonition serves to remind the heirs that their obligation does not cease simply because the will of the deceased may not be recognized by civil authorities. The admonition is to be made by the ordinary, who is the "executor of all pious wills" (canon 1301 §1).

The norm of canon 1299 §2 concerns only goods given to the Church *mortis causa*, not to those given *inter vivos*. If the formalities of civil law are not observed in dispositions *inter vivos*, the contract is not considered valid (see canon 1290).[18]

For the Latin Church, the Congregation for the Clergy is the competent dicastery of the Apostolic See dealing with Mass obligations, pious wills in general, and pious foundations (*Pastor bonus*, 97, 2°).

CORRESPONDING CANON OF THE EASTERN CODE: CANON 1043. This canon corresponds almost exactly to Latin canon 1299, but East-

---

the CIC/1917 and speaks of dispositions given "for the good of the Church," which without change became promulgated law.

[16] Canon 668 §1 specifically requires that, at least before perpetual profession, members of religious institutes "make a will which is to be valid also in civil law."

[17] Canon 1299 §2 parallels CIC/1917, canon 1513 §2. On February 17, 1930, the PONTIFICAL COMMISSION FOR THE AUTHENTIC INTERPRETATION OF THE CANONS OF THE CODE explained that the word *moneantur* is a precept and not a mere exhortation. In *AAS,* 22 (1930), p. 196; *CLD,* vol. 1, p. 725. Recalling this, on June 8, 1967 the *coetus De bonis Ecclesiae temporalibus* agreed that the stronger phrase, *moneri debent*, should replace *moneantur. Communicationes,* 36 (2004), pp. 266-267.
Later, the *coetus* decided to omit the phrase "*ex iustitia*" which had appeared in the 1977 *Schema* since its inclusion may appear "too rigid." *Communicationes,* 12 (1980), p. 429.

[18] DE PAOLIS, *I beni temporali*, p. 229; DE PAOLIS, *De bonis Ecclesiae temporalibus*, pp. 112-113.

ern canon 1043 §2 mentions only "last wills" (*ultimae voluntates*), not all "dispositions *mortis causae*."[19]

PIOUS WILLS

> **Can. 1300 – The legitimately accepted wills of the faithful who give or leave their resources for pious causes, whether through an act *inter vivos* or through an act *mortis causa*, are to be fulfilled most diligently even regarding the manner of administration and distribution of goods, without prejudice to the prescript of can. 1301, §3.**

Canon 1300 concerns *pious wills*, that is, dispositions of temporal goods by the faithful[20] for pious causes. It obliges the competent persons to fulfill diligently the legitimately accepted wills of the faithful who give their resources for pious causes (whether *inter vivos* or *mortis causa*). There is no obligation to preserve the principal except in the case of *pious foundations*.

The canon governs pious wills which have been "legitimately accepted."[21] The current code requires a "just cause" to refuse a donation (canon 1267 §2). It requires permission from the ordinary for public juridic persons to refuse gifts "in matters of greater importance" and "to accept offerings burdened by a modal obligation or condition" (canon 1267 §2). It also requires the written permission of the ordinary for the valid acceptance of a non-autonomous pious foundation by a public juridic person (canon 1304 §1). Such provisions protect the Church from donations which may impose an

---

[19] Robert Kennedy observes that the Eastern code uses the same phrase (*"ultimae voluntates"*) as had CIC/1917, canon 1513 §2. He comments: "This should not be understood, however, as a narrowing of the scope of this canon to last wills and testaments, since in canonical tradition the expression 'last wills' includes all acts by which one disposes of all or part of one's goods as of one's death, including a gift in contemplation of death (*donatio mortis causa*)." "Temporal Goods," pp. 1511-1512.

[20] Perhaps the term "faithful" (*fidelis*) could instead have been "person" (*persona*) to reflect that even those who are not members of the Christian faithful can establish pious wills for pious causes. See De Paolis, *De bonis Ecclesiae temporalibus*, p. 111.

[21] CIC/1917, canon 1514, the predecessor of this canon, did not contain this phrase.

obligation not in keeping with the proper purposes of the Church (see canon 1254 §2), or which may excessively burden the Church.

The intention of the donor governs pious causes, and it is to be observed most diligently both in the administration of goods (see canon 1284 §2, 3°) and the distribution of goods. The donor may make certain specifications about the administration of the goods, such as requiring that money be placed in specific investments. The donor may also make certain specifications about the distribution of goods – e.g., regarding their quality (e.g., the particular piece of property), the place (the locale for the distribution of goods), or the time (the days when certain obligations are to be fulfilled).[22] No such stipulations regarding administration or distribution, however, can contradict the right of the ordinary to be executor of all pious causes (canon 1301 §1); should such a stipulation be attached to last wills and testaments, it is to be considered non-existent (*non appositae*) (canon 1301 §3).

The application of this canon is not restricted to gifts given only to public juridic persons. It concerns any goods given for a pious cause also to private juridic persons.

CORRESPONDING CANON OF THE EASTERN CODE: CANON 1044. This canon corresponds almost exactly to Latin canon 1300, which speaks of the "Christian faithful" instead of the "faithful," and of "their goods" (*bona sua*) rather than "their resources" (*facultates suae*).

ORDINARY AS EXECUTOR OF ALL PIOUS WILLS

Can. 1301 – §1. The ordinary is the executor of all pious wills whether *mortis causa* or *inter vivos*.

§2. By this right, the ordinary can and must exercise vigilance, even through visitation, so that pious wills are fulfilled, and other executors are bound to render him an account after they have performed their function.

§3. Stipulations contrary to this right of an ordinary

---

[22] See BOUSCAREN-ELLIS-KORTH, p. 820.

attached to last wills and testaments are to be considered non-existent.

Canon 1301 says that the ordinary has the right and obligation to exercise vigilance so that the intentions expressed in pious wills (whether *inter vivos* or *mortis causa*) are fulfilled. In this sense, he is said to be the executor of all pious wills. Stipulations in last wills and testaments contrary to this right are to be considered non-existent (*non appositae*). If other executors are involved (as will normally be the situation), after they have performed their role, they must render an account to the ordinary who exercises his role of vigilance over the administration of the ecclesiastical goods of public juridic persons subject to him (see canon 1276 §1).

The ordinary (see canon 134 §1) is the one with jurisdiction over the entity to receive favor from the disposition, regardless of the residence of the donor or the place of the donor's death.[23] The power of the ordinary is ordinary executive power (see canon 135 §§1, 4) and, as such, can be delegated (see canon 137).

If the ordinary who has the right and obligation to exercise vigilance is the diocesan bishop, he may entrust this function to the diocesan finance officer (canon 1278). The ordinary may exercise his right through visitation. If the ordinary is the diocesan bishop, he may make the visitation mentioned in canon 1301 §2 on the occasion of the visitation mentioned in canon 396.

The canon envisions the possibility of "other executors" in addition to the ordinary.[24] Among the potentially several executors, the ordinary has a prominence based on his exercise of vigilance and evidenced in his receiving an account from the other executors when they have completed their function. The ordinary's function as executor is founded in the universal law of the Church, not in a grant by the donor or testator. The term *executor* is used here "not in the civil law sense but in the canonical sense of having the

---

[23] For religious who do not have a religious ordinary, the ordinary is the local ordinary (see canon 103). See DE PAOLIS, *I beni temporali*, p. 230.

[24] CIC/1917, canon 1515 §2 had said these other executors were "delegated." This is omitted in the revised law.

responsibilities of an administrator of property."[25] The ordinary is exercising his executive authority (canon 135) and his vigilance (see also canons 325 §1; 392 §2; 1276; 1302 §2).[26] He serves as the executor *ex officio*.[27]

In the early days of drafting the proposed legislation, one consultor suggested that the text make no mention of the ordinary as the executor of pious wills, but simply explain that he has the right and duty to exercise vigilance over the actual executors of these wills. The relator of the *coetus*, however, said that the law must identify the ordinary as executor, since in some parts of the world others do not perform the function of executor and the ordinary must do it.[28]

During the consultation on the 1977 *Schema*, some had observed that making the ordinary to be the executor of all pious wills was too burdensome. The *coetus De bonis Ecclesiae temporalibus* responded that having the ordinary as the executor of all pious wills affirms his power of vigilance to see that pious wills are fulfilled, and his obligation to serve as executor personally when there is no other executor. Generally, the ordinary will simply perform the vigilance function, something which is not overly burdensome.[29]

Stipulations in last wills and testaments contrary to this right and duty of the ordinary as executioner are to be considered nonexistent (*non appositae*). This is an obvious exception to the repeated insistence that the intentions of donors be respected. Donors are

---

[25] JORDAN F. HITE, "The Administration of Church Property," in *Readings, Cases, Materials in Canon Law: A Textbook for Ministry Students*, rev. ed., Jordan Hite and Daniel J. Ward (eds.), Collegeville, The Liturgical Press, 1990, p. 417. See also KENNEDY, "Temporal Goods" p. 1513.

[26] DANIEL J. WARD explains the ordinary's role as executor in this way: "'Executor' in the code is not the same as executor in the civil law. This is obvious from the canon, which recognizes other executors. Rather, executor is used to describe the ordinary's general duty: to ensure that the disposition is fulfilled. This is the general duty of the ordinary, whether the disposition is a bequest or a gift. The ordinary, therefore, has supervisory powers, such as seeking enforcement of the disposition in the civil courts since the ordinary is the principal representative of the recipient of the bequest or gift." In "Bequests and Gifts to the Church under the Code of Canon Law," in *The Catholic Lawyer*, 30 (1986), p. 278 (=WARD, "Bequests and Gifts").

[27] VROMANT, p. 148.

[28] *Communicationes*, 36 (2004), p. 268.

[29] *Communicationes*, 12 (1980), p. 429.

not able to express intentions which are beyond the scope of their power (here, beyond their power is the right of the Church to expect that ordinaries will exercise vigilance over the fulfillment of pious wills). Since ordinaries exercise their vigilance for the very purpose of fulfilling pious wills, any requirement that the ordinary not do so could frustrate the very intention of the donor.

Canon 325 §2 specifically states that a private association of the faithful is "subject to the authority of the local ordinary according to the norm of can. 1301 in what pertains to the administration and distribution of goods which have been donated or left to it for pious causes." Private associations of the Christian faithful may, or may not, be juridic persons (see canon 322 §1). If they are juridic persons, they must be *private* ones.[30]

CORRESPONDING CANON OF THE EASTERN CODE: CANON 1045. This canon corresponds almost exactly to Latin canon 1301.

PIOUS TRUSTS

Can. 1302 – §1. A person who has accepted goods in trust for pious causes either through an act *inter vivos* or by a last will and testament must inform the ordinary of the trust and indicate to him all its movable and immovable goods with the obligations attached to them. If the donor has expressly and entirely prohibited this, however, the person is not to accept the trust.

§2. The ordinary must demand that goods held in trust are safeguarded and also exercise vigilance for the execution of the pious will according to the norm of can. 1301.

§3. When goods held in trust have been entrusted to a member of a religious institute or society of apostolic life and if the goods have also been designated for some place or diocese or for the assistance of their inhabitants or [their][31] pious causes, the ordinary mentioned in §§1 and

---

[30] See PAGÉ, p. 416.
[31] The word "their," inserted by this author to the CLSA translation, may help avoid ambiguity.

**2 is the local ordinary; otherwise, it is the major superior
in a clerical institute of pontifical right and in clerical
societies of apostolic life of pontifical right or the proper
ordinary of the member in other religious institutes.**

Canon 1302 concerns a pious trust, that is, a pious will in
which goods are accepted from a donor (called the *trustor*) by a
third party (called the *trustee*)[32] who owns[33] them and administers
them for pious causes according to the will of the donor. A pious
trust is established either *inter vivos* or by a last will and testament.
The trustee, who may be a physical or juridic person, administers
the temporal goods over a period of time. The earnings and/or the
goods themselves are used to benefit the pious cause.

Trustees are not to be confused with executors of pious wills
(canon 1301). Executors of a pious will perform their role once and
have no ownership of the temporal good (i.e., they have no *ius in re*);
when the pious will has been fulfilled, the executors' role ceases.
Those to whom a pious trust has been given, however, have ownership
of the temporal good (i.e., they have a *ius in re*) which they administer
over a period of time according to the will of the trustor. [34]

Nor is a pious trust to be confused with a non-autonomous
pious foundation (canon 1303), although both involve pious causes.
A pious trust is received by a physical or juridic person, but a non-
autonomous pious foundation can be entrusted only to a public juridic
person. A pious trust may be fulfilled in a rather brief time, but a
non-autonomous pious foundation lasts for a long period of time
(as determined by particular law). A pious trust does not require
maintaining an endowment, but a non-autonomous pious founda-

---

[32] CIC/1917, canon 1516 §1, the predecessor of canon 1302, had allowed only clerics
or religious to be trustees. The revised code allows for anyone to be a trustee.

[33] The ownership enjoyed by a trustee is not absolute *dominium*, as understood in
classical Roman law. The temporal good must be used for the purposes identified by
the donor. The trustee cannot freely dispose of it as he or she may wish. Hence, the
trustee enjoys a "qualified" ownership of the temporal good.

[34] VROMANT, p. 142; KENNEDY, "Temporal Goods," p. 1514.

tion involves an endowment whose earnings are used to pursue a pious cause.[35]

Nonetheless, every non-autonomous pious foundation is a pious trust inasmuch as the ownership of temporal goods is given to a public juridic person who, for a long period of time, uses the revenue of the endowment to perform a pious cause. Put another way, every non-autonomous pious foundation is a trust, but not every trust is a non-autonomous pious foundation.

A trustor may designate gifts either *inter vivos* or by a last will and testament *only*. The former is contractual, and latter is not. The code does not allow a trust to be established as a *donatio mortis causa*, in contemplation of death, which is also contractual, because in such a case the donor retains until the moment of death the right to revoke ownership which had been passed to another. In a trust, ownership is transferred to the trustee either during the donor's lifetime or upon the donor's death and is irrevocable.

The trustee who accepts these goods must inform the ordinary of the immovable and movable goods of the trust and of the terms for distributions. The ordinary, according to canon 1301, is the executor of all pious wills, exercising vigilance to assure that they are properly fulfilled. If the donor forbids the trustee to inform the ordinary of the trust, such that the ordinary cannot exercise his canonical responsibilities as executor, the trustee must not accept the gift. If the trust is offered *inter vivos*, the donor may select to revoke the prohibition and permit the ordinary to be informed. If the trust is offered by a last will and testament, the refusal would frustrate the intention of the deceased donor; in this situation, it may be more appropriate to invoke the norm of canon 1301 §3 (that stipulations contrary to the

---

[35] VROMANT, p. 302; BOUSCAREN-ELLIS-KORTH, pp. 847-848.

DANIEL J. WARD says that a non-autonomous pious foundation "would be a long-term trust fund, in the canonical sense, managed by an ecclesiastical institution such as a diocese, a monastery, or an institution of higher learning." In "Bequests and Gifts," p. 279. See also KENNEDY, "Temporal Goods," p. 1516.

An autonomous foundation is *not* a pious trust since the goods themselves are established as a juridic person, rather than "*entrusted*" to an already existing one (as is the case with a non-autonomous pious foundation).

right of the ordinary in last wills and testaments are to be considered non-existent) and simply ignore the prohibition.[36]

The ordinary, for his part, must demand that the goods are safeguarded and expended according to the purposes of the trust. He must exercise vigilance over the execution of the pious will, even through visitation (canon 1301). If the ordinary is the diocesan bishop, he may entrust this vigilance to the diocesan finance officer (canon 1278).

If the goods have been entrusted to a member of a religious institute (canon 607 §2) or a society of apostolic life (canon 731 §1), the "ordinary" is the person with jurisdiction over the pious cause which benefits from the trust. He is either:

1. the local ordinary, if the goods have been designated for some place or diocese, or for the assistance of their inhabitants or for their pious causes; or

2. the major superior (in a clerical religious institute of pontifical right and in clerical societies of pontifical right) or the proper ordinary (in other religious institutes), if the goods have been designated for some other purpose. The "proper ordinary" for members of these "other religious institutes" is the "local ordinary" (see canons 103; 107 §1).[37]

The trustee is bound to observe the prescripts imposed by a donor (see canons 1284 §2, 3°, 1299 §2). The trustee cannot change the trustor's intention in establishing the trust, nor can the ordinary (see canon 1267 §1).

CORRESPONDING CANON OF THE EASTERN CODE: CANON 1046. Eastern canon 1046 §1 mentions trusts established through an act *inter vivos* or an act *mortis causae* (reference is not made only to a

---

[36] ROBERT T. KENNEDY suggests that the last clause of canon 1302 §1, since it speaks of the donor (*donator*), applies *only* to trusts established *inter vivos*. Compare canon 1299 §2 which concerns dispositions given *mortis causa* and speaks of a *testator* rather than a *donator*. Pious causes given *inter vivos* are contractual, so they require acceptance. Pious causes given by last wills and testaments are not contractual. "Temporal Goods," p. 1515.

[37] The proper law of a secular institute would need to address goods are given in trust to one of its members (see canon 718).

310 CHURCH PROPERTY

"last will and testament," *ex testamento*).[38] It requires a list of all goods (not qualified as "movable and immovable") with obligations attached (*omnia talia bona cum onoribus adiunctis*). The proposed trustee must inform his or her own hierarch (*hierarcha proprius*) of the trust. Eastern canon 1046 §2 refers only to the hierarch's vigilance mentioned in Eastern canon 1045 §2 (which corresponds to Latin canon 1301, the whole of which is referred to in Latin canon 1302 §2). Eastern canon 1046 §3 mentions that the "local hierarch" (without reference to other hierarchs) must be informed of goods held in trust and designated "for churches of a place or of some eparchy, for the Christian faithful who have a domicile there, or for the assistance of [their] pious causes."

PIOUS FOUNDATIONS:
AUTONOMOUS AND NON-AUTONOMOUS

Can. 1303 – §1. In law, the term pious foundations includes:

1° *autonomous pious foundations*, that is, aggregates of things (*universitates rerum*) destined for the purposes mentioned in can. 114, §2 and erected as a juridic person by competent ecclesiastical authority;

2° *non-autonomous pious foundations*, that is, temporal goods given in some way to a public juridic person with the obligation for a long time, to be determined by particular law, of celebrating Masses and performing other specified ecclesiastical functions or of otherwise pursuing the purposes mentioned in can. 114, §2, from the annual revenues.

§2. If the goods of a non-autonomous pious foundation have been entrusted to a juridic person subject to a diocesan bishop, they must be remanded to the institute mentioned in can. 1274, §1 when the time is completed unless some other intention of the founder had been expressly manifested; otherwise, they accrue to the juridic person itself.

---

[38] Thereby, the Eastern code permits the establishment of a pious trust through a *donatio mortis causae* and a last will and testament.

One may make a gift to the Church by means of a pious foundation, that is, by donating goods with the obligation, perpetual or lasting for a long time, to perform one or more pious causes.[39] The principal (called the *endowment*) is preserved but the income is spent for the pious cause. Canon 1303 §1 defines the two kinds of pious foundations:[40]

1. *autonomous pious foundations*,[41] i.e., aggregates of things (*universitas rerum*) erected as a (public or private) juridic person (which is perpetual: canon 120 §1) by competent ecclesiastical authority and destined for the works of piety, works of the apostolate, or works of spiritual or temporal charity (see canon 114 §2)

2. *non-autonomous pious foundations*, i.e., temporal goods given in some way (i.e., *inter vivos* or *mortis causa*) to a *public* juridic person[42] with the long-term obligation (to be determined by particular law) to use annual revenues:
   a. to celebrate Masses;[43]

---

[39] Pious foundations involve goods given with a long-term obligation. Goods given to the Church with the understanding that they will be used rather soon are not pious foundations. CIC/1917, canon 1544 §2 had addressed the contractual nature of foundations: "A foundation, legitimately accepted, by its nature parallels the contract formula, *do ut facias* [= I give that you do]." Although this norm is not found in the 1983 code, its doctrine still applies. Any pious foundation, autonomous or non-autonomous, involves a donation which, once accepted, imposes a contractual obligation.

[40] CIC/1917, canon 1544 §1 called "foundations" those which the revised code calls "non-autonomous foundations." The canonical equivalent of the "autonomous foundations" of the revised code were simply known as "non-collegiate ecclesiastical institutes" in CIC/1917, canons 1489-1494.

[41] See canon 115 §2 which describes an *autonomous foundation:* "An aggregate of things (*universitas rerum*), or [*seu*] an autonomous foundation, consists of goods or things, whether spiritual or material, and either one or more physical persons or a college directs it according to the norm of law and the statutes." Canon 1303, §1, 1° refers to an autonomous *pious* foundation.

[42] On December 17, 1969, the *coetus De iure patrimoniali Ecclesiae* agreed that only *public* juridic persons could receive (what became known as) non-autonomous pious foundations by a vote of 5 to 3 (with one abstention). *Communicationes,* 37 (2005), p. 237.

[43] Masses obliged to be offered through a foundation are commonly called *foundation Masses* (or *founded Masses*). Other Masses are commonly called *manual Masses* (from the Latin, *manus*, hand: offerings for these Masses are "handed" over to the priest). This terminology, *manual Masses* and *foundation Masses*, was used in CIC/1917, canon 826.

    b. to perform other specified ecclesiastical functions; or

    c. to pursue in some other way works of piety, works of the apostolate, or works of spiritual or temporal charity (see canon 114 §2).

KINDS OF PIOUS FOUNDATIONS: AUTONOMOUS AND NON-AU-TONOMOUS. An *autonomous foundation* is a foundation erected as a *private* or *public* juridic person by competent ecclesiastical authority. It is governed by its statutes and the universal law on juridic persons. The *non-autonomous pious foundation* is a foundation entrusted to an already existing *public* juridic person; competent authority must give permission for the juridic person to accept the temporal good.

An autonomous foundation is itself a juridic person established by competent ecclesiastical authority. It holds its endowment for itself, not for a third party (so it is not a trustee). Before establishing it as a juridic person, the competent ecclesiastical authority is bound to make sure the juridic person will possess the means which are foreseen to be sufficient to achieve its designated purpose, as is the case before erecting any juridic person (see canon 114 §3). Put another way, at the time of its foundation, every juridic person must have at least the *capacity* for stable patrimony. As a juridic person, an autonomous pious foundation is perpetual (see canon 120 §1).

A non-autonomous pious foundation is not a juridic person. It is a kind of pious trust (see canon 1302) entrusted to a public juridic person (but not to a private juridic person).[44] The public juridic person is the trustee. Annual revenues are to be distributed for a pious cause, but the endowment itself is not to be distributed. The ordinary must give his permission in writing for the valid acceptance of such a foundation, and is to do so only if he has legitimately determined

---

[44] DANIEL J. WARD comments: "The non-autonomous pious foundation which is a trust or fund established for a long period of time and administered by an ecclesiastical institution, is not a separate juridic person. Therefore its management is dual, that is, governed by the terms of the trust or fund and by the law governing the ecclesiastical institution, which may be either collegial or non-collegial.... The dual nature of the governance would be similar to a trust established at a financial institution since a financial institution not only must comply with the terms of the trust, but also with its own procedures of administration and accountability." In "Trust Management Under the New Code of Canon Law," in *The Jurist,* 44 (1984), p. 139 (=WARD, "Trust Management").

that the public juridic person receiving the foundation can satisfy the new obligation (see canon 1304). Particular law is to determine the duration of the non-autonomous foundation; it is not necessarily perpetual, though of course it may be.

DURATION OF PIOUS FOUNDATIONS. An autonomous foundation, since it is a juridic person, is perpetual (canon 120 §1). The temporal goods given to a non-autonomous foundation are to be entrusted "for a long period of time" (*in diuturnum tempus*). The 1917 code had said that the goods could be entrusted to a foundation perpetually (*in perpetuum*) or for a long period (CIC/1917, canon 1544 §1). Those preparing the 1977 *Schema* did not forbid perpetual endowments but left the determination to particular law.[45] The group was undoubtedly aware that economic fluctuations may make it imprudent to accept perpetual obligations.[46] Early in the process of drafting the proposed new law, one consultor of the *coetus De bonis Ecclesiae temporalibus* mentioned that the phrase "for a long time" would mean a period of 40 to 50 years.[47] During consultation on the 1977 *Schema*, many suggested that non-autonomous pious foundations should not be established perpetually; modern economic conditions are such that it would be difficult to have stable income to fulfill obligations *in perpetuum*. The consultors agreed, and the 1980 *Schema* simply said that non-autonomous pious foundations are to be established "for a long period of time" as determined by particular law.[48]

---

[45] One consultor of the *coetus De bonis Ecclesiae temporalibus* observed that the ordinary, who is to exercise vigilance over the fulfillment of the conditions, would promulgate particular law with attention given to local circumstances. After significant discussion, the *coetus* determined that the duration of a foundation should not be established by the conference of bishops, but instead by the ordinary. *Communicationes*, 36 (2004), p. 280.

[46] The preface of the 1977 *Schema* mentions that the *coetus* permitted the establishment of a perpetual non-autonomous pious foundation for the sake of those who wished to establish one. The *coetus* added that particular law can impose suitable conditions to prevent problems which may arise from perpetual foundations: in 1977 *Schema*, Preface, pp. 6-7. See also *Communicationes*, 5 (1973), p. 102; 12 (1980), p. 431; 36 (2004), pp. 278-279.

[47] *Communicationes*, 36 (2004), p. 278.

[48] *Communicationes*, 12 (1980), p. 431.
ROBERT T. KENNEDY observes: "It was apparently not the intention of the revisers

Given the significant and rapid changes in contemporary
society, there may be great prudence in not having perpetual foundations. If perpetual foundations are established (as autonomous
pious foundations) or accepted (as non-autonomous pious foundations owned by public juridic persons), however, some provision
for possible modifications should be made with an indication of
the authority competent to make the changes (see canons 1308 §2,
1309, and 1310 §1).

Obviously, civil legislation must also be observed carefully
in the matter of ecclesiastical foundations, autonomous and non-
autonomous (see canon 1290). Civil lawyers in particular will provide helpful guidance in this.

If persons wish to make a donation that does not last "perpetually" or "for a long time" (e.g., for forty years, as many commentators
on the 1917 code applied the phase),[49] they would establish a "pious
trust" (canon 1302) rather than a pious foundation. Donors must be
informed of this option.

EXTINCTION/COMPLETION OF PIOUS FOUNDATIONS. The goods
of an autonomous foundation are handled according to the norm
of canon 123 should it become extinct. These goods would be al-
located according to the foundation's statutes. If the statutes give no
indication, the goods go to "the juridic person immediately superior,
always without prejudice to the intention of the founders and donors
and acquired rights."

---

of the code, however, to prohibit perpetual obligations, but simply to acknowledge
modern economic reality by not supposing such obligations to be undertaken frequently enough to warrant mention in universal law, and by leaving to particular
law the enactment of whatever relevant regulations may be thought advisable." In
"Temporal Goods," p. 1516, fn. 222.

DANIEL J. WARD explains about the duration of a non-autonomous pious foundation:
"Under traditional canonical jurisprudence, 'long-term' would be forty years. Under
the new code, particular law must define 'long-term,' but if particular law would not
so define, then it would seem that forty years would be the presumptive time period.
The time period does not mean that the pious foundation actually would last the
requisite time period, but that it be at least capable of lasting that period, which would
be true if the [non-autonomous] pious foundation were established for an indefinite
period." In "Bequests and Gifts," p. 279.

[49] See BOUSCAREN-ELLIS-KORTH, p. 848.

The goods of a non-autonomous foundation are handled according to the norm of canon 1303 §2 when its time is completed. The canon says that if the goods of a non-autonomous pious foundation have been entrusted to a public juridic person subject to the diocesan bishop, the goods must be remanded to the diocesan "institute for clergy support" (canon 1274 §1) when the time is completed, unless the founder has expressly manifested otherwise. Emphasis is clearly placed on the donor's intention.[50] Therefore, special assistance should be given to founders so they will determine, as the law allows, where the goods will accrue when the non-autonomous foundation ceases. Absent such a determination and in places where the "institute for clergy support" has not been established, it would be consistent with the law for the goods of the completed non-autonomous foundation to be used for the purposes for which the institute of canon 1274 §1 is envisioned. Obviously, even in dioceses where the "institute for clergy support" exists, founders may wish their funds to accrue eventually to some other pious cause.

If the goods of a non-autonomous pious foundation had been entrusted to a public juridic person *not* subject to the diocesan bishop (e.g., a religious institute), they eventually accrue to that public juridic person itself.

COMPETENT AUTHORITY TO ERECT/ACCEPT PIOUS FOUNDATIONS. Canon 1303 §1, 1° speaks of the action of the "competent authority" to erect an autonomous pious foundation, but does not define precisely who that authority is. Canon 1304 §1 speaks of the written permission of the "ordinary" for a public juridic person to accept validly a non-autonomous pious foundation, which indicates that any ordinary (that is, a local ordinary [i.e., diocesan bishop, vicar general, or episcopal vicar], and a major superior of a clerical religious institute of pontifical right and of clerical society of apostolic life, c. 134 §1) is a "competent authority" to give this written permission. Some canonists indicate that there is an argument to

---

[50] The intention of the donor is highlighted in a number of canons: 121; 122; 123; 326 §2; 531; 616 §1; 706, 3°; 954; 1267 §3; 1284 §2, 3°; 1300; 1302 §1; 1303 §2; 1304 §1; 1307 §1; and 1310 §2.

allow only the "local ordinary" to be the competent authority both to erect autonomous pious foundations and to accept a non-autonomous pious foundation.[51]

CORRESPONDING CANON OF THE EASTERN CODE: CANON 1047. This canon corresponds almost exactly to Latin canon 1303. The purposes for establishing both autonomous and non-autonomous foundations are identified as "works of piety, the apostolate, or charity, whether spiritual or temporal." Although mention is not made specifically of the celebration of the Eucharist (as the Latin code does concerning non-autonomous foundations), certainly included among the "works of piety" could be the celebration of the Divine Liturgy. Also, inasmuch as the Eastern code does not distinguish private and public juridic persons, non-autonomous foundations are said to be entrusted simply to "a juridic person."

PIOUS FOUNDATIONS:
REQUIREMENTS FOR ESTABLISHMENT AND ACCEPTANCE

Can. 1304 – §1. For a juridic person to be able to accept a foundation validly, the written permission of the ordinary is required. He is not to grant this permission before he has legitimately determined that the juridic person can satisfy both the new obligation to be undertaken and those already undertaken; most especially he is to be on guard so that the revenues completely respond to the attached obligations, according to the practice of each place or region.

§2. Particular law is to define additional conditions for the establishment and acceptance of foundations.

---

[51] See ROBERT GEISINGER, pp. 228-231. He argues that CIC/1917, canons 1489-1494 required "non-collegial ecclesiastical institutions" (e.g., hospitals, orphanages, and other similar institutions), which were considered "foundations," to depend on the local ordinary for approval and vigilance. He comments that "there has been a recent argument advanced encouraging a return to dependence on the local ordinary. An effect, indeed the prompting motive of this, would appear to be not to accept religious major superiors of clerical institutes of pontifical right and of clerical societies of apostolic life of pontifical right (ordinaries) as ecclesiastical authorities competent to erect juridic persons in the form of pious autonomous foundations. This is an unresolved question, both academically and practically." (pp. 230-231)

Canon 1304 §1 concerns only *non-autonomous* foundations, i.e., foundations accepted by a *public* juridic person (see canon 1303 §1, 2°). *Autonomous* foundations are not accepted by a juridic person, but are (public or private) juridic persons themselves which are erected by a written decree. The cautions (i.e., the ability to fulfill the obligation and sufficient revenues that correspond to those obligations) in canon 1304 §1 would obviously be observed by the authority competent to erect the autonomous pious foundation. Canon 114 §3 permits the competent ecclesiastical authority to confer juridic personality only on aggregates which "pursue a truly useful purpose" and "possess the means which are foreseen to be sufficient to achieve their designated purpose" i.e., the means at least to achieve stable patrimony.[52]

Canon 1304 §1 legislates that the ordinary must give his written permission for the *valid* acceptance of a non-autonomous foundation. It adds that the ordinary is to grant his written permission only after he has legitimately determined that the public juridic person can satisfy the new obligation to be undertaken in addition to other obligations already had. He is especially to make sure that the revenues completely respond to the new obligations to be accepted, according to local practices. Since only *public* juridic persons can accept a non-autonomous foundation, it follows that the goods of the foundation are "ecclesiastical goods" (see canon 1257 §2), over the administration of which the ordinary exercises careful vigilance (see canon 1276 §1).

A public juridic person has absolutely no obligation to accept a foundation (see canon 1267 §2). If it chooses to accept a foundation, then it must receive the written permission of the ordinary *for validity*.[53] It will be helpful if the public juridic person also makes its request in written form and provides thorough details to allow the ordinary to give his permission in an informed manner. It may hap-

---

[52] See WARD, "Trust Management," p. 138.

[53] CIC/1917, canon 1546 §1 did not say the written permission of the ordinary was required for *validity*. The great majority of the members of the *coetus De bonis Ecclesiae temporalibus* favored that the consent of the ordinary be for validity. *Communicationes*, 36 (2004), p. 281.

pen that the ordinary, in his role as executor of all pious wills (canon 1301 §1), may need to investigate some details (e.g., the amount of Mass offerings) before permitting the public juridic person to accept the foundation. Requiring the ordinary's permission reflects the norm of canon 1267 §2 which requires his permission whenever accepting a gift burdened by a modal obligation or condition.[54]

If the public juridic person chooses not to accept the foundation, for whatever reason, if the gift is given *inter vivos*, the donor can select another public juridic person to accept it. If the gift is *mortis causa*, recourse may be made to canon 1309 in the matter of transferring Mass obligations.

Canon 1304 §1 speaks of "permission" (*licentia*) from the ordinary for the valid acceptance of a foundation.[55] Therefore, the law really requires the "consent" of the competent authority, not merely its permission. If the "permission" is not given, the acceptance is invalid. Since the establishment of a non-autonomous pious foundation is the establishment of a kind of pious trust, the competent authority giving permission to accept it is the ordinary identified in canon 1302 §3.

Canon 1304 §2 says particular law is to define additional conditions for the *establishment* of an autonomous foundation and *acceptance* of temporal goods by a non-autonomous foundation. Unlike canon 1304 §1 which concerns only non-autonomous foundations, canon 1304 §2 concerns both kinds of foundations: autonomous and non-autonomous.[56] The particular law may establish requirements not only for the *liceity* but also for the *validity*

---

54 ROBERT T. KENNEDY observes: "Requiring a public juridic person to obtain authorization from the ordinary to accept a non-autonomous foundation echoes the general norm requiring public juridic persons to obtain permission when accepting any gift to which is attached a condition or modal obligation (canon 1267 §2) and, since the authorization required by canon 1302 is for validity, in effect makes the acceptance of a non-autonomous foundation an act of extraordinary administration." In "Temporal Goods," p. 1518.

55 *Book V* uses the term "permission" (*licentia*) to mean "consent" (*consensus*) in canons 1291, 1292 §2, and 1304 §1. The Eastern code uses the word *consensus* in the corresponding canons (1035 §1, 3°, 1036 §4, and 1048 §2). See also canons 638 §3 and 1190 §2.

56 See JOBE ABBAS, "Establishment of Autonomous and Non-Autonomous Pious Founda-

of the establishment or acceptance.[57]

CORRESPONDING CANON OF THE EASTERN CODE: CANON 1048. Eastern canon 1048 §1 does not have a corresponding canon in the Latin law: "Autonomous pious foundations can be erected only by an eparchial bishop or another higher authority." Eastern canon 1048 §2 concerns only the acceptance of "non-autonomous" foundations for which the written "consent" (not the written "permission") of one's own hierarch is required. The hierarch is to be on guard that the revenues completely respond to attached obligations "according to the practices of his own Church *sui iuris*" (not "according to the practice of each place or region"). Eastern canon 1048 §3 speaks of particular law determining other conditions "without which pious foundations cannot be erected or accepted."

PIOUS FOUNDATIONS: INVESTMENT OF THE ENDOWMENT

Can. 1305 – Money and movable goods, assigned to an endowment, are to be deposited immediately in a safe place approved by the ordinary so that the money or value of the movable goods is protected; as soon as possible, these are to be invested cautiously and usefully for the benefit of the foundation, with express and specific mention made of the obligation; this investment is to be made according to the prudent judgment of the ordinary, after he has heard those concerned and his own finance council.

---

tions" in *CLSA AO3*, p. 343 (=Abbas, "Establishment"); LUIGI CHIAPPETTA, *Il Codice di Diritto Canonico: Commento Giuridico-Pastorale*, 2nd ed., Rome, Dehoniane, 1996, vol. 2, p. 574.

ROBERT J. KENNEDY, however, concludes that canon 1304 §2 (taken in conjunction with canon 1304 §1) concerns only non-autonomous pious foundations and focuses on "the wisdom of accepting and the manner of establishing" them. In "Temporal Goods," p. 1518, esp. fn. 226.

[57] Examples of issues which may be addressed by particular law are: the length of the duration of the non-autonomous pious foundation, the disposition of the endowment of an autonomous foundation should it become extinct (see canon 123) or of a non-autonomous pious foundation when its time is completed (see canon 1303 §2), the frequency of actuarial studies to monitor the growth of the endowed funds, etc.

Canon 1305 concerns the prudent handling of money and movable goods assigned to the endowment of a pious foundation. The canon seemingly concerns both autonomous pious foundations which are established as *public* juridic persons, and non-autonomous pious foundations which by law are accepted only by a *public* juridic person. The canon does not provide mandatory legislation for autonomous pious foundations established as *private* juridic persons over which the ordinary would have less immediate supervision.[58]

The money and movable goods are to be deposited immediately (*statim*) in a safe place approved by the ordinary.[59] As soon as possible thereafter, they are to be invested cautiously and usefully for the benefit of the foundation, with express mention of this obligation. This investment is to be made according to the prudent judgment of the ordinary, formulated after he has received the counsel (but not necessarily the consent) of those concerned and of his own finance council. He could also direct any subsequent changes in the manner of investing, after he has again received the counsel of those concerned and his finance council.

The consultation of the ordinary with those concerned and his own finance council (see canons 1304; 1302 §2; 1284 §2, 6°) is required for the validity of the ordinary's action (see canon 127 §2, 2°). If the ordinary is the local ordinary, the finance council is the diocesan finance council. If he is the ordinary of a religious institute

---

[58] ROBERT T. KENNEDY argues that canon 1305 concerns only non-autonomous pious foundations. Autonomous pious foundations are themselves juridic persons and, as such, are governed by their own statutes. Since many autonomous pious foundations are often *private* juridic persons, it would not be appropriate for the ordinary to closely supervise them, as canon 1305 requires. In "Temporal Goods," pp. 1518-1519.
At the same time, however, some autonomous pious foundations are *public* juridic persons which are subject to the power of governance of the ordinary (see canons 1276 §1; 1279; 1281 §1; etc.) Specifically, canon 1284 §2, 6° requires that an administrator receive consent of the ordinary to invest surplus funds for the juridic person. Therefore, there is reason to conclude that canon 1305 would also apply to autonomous pious foundations which are *public* juridic persons subject to the ordinary.

[59] CIC/1917, canon 1547 had required the ordinary to *select* the safe place for immediate deposit. The revised law simply requires that he *approve* the safe place, giving the responsible person the authority to select it for the ordinary's approval. The *coetus De bonis Ecclesiae temporalibus* overwhelmingly agreed that the ordinary must approve the safe place. *Communicationes*, 36 (2004), p. 283.

or a society of apostolic life, the function of the finance council may be fulfilled by two financial advisors if the institute or society does not have its own finance council (canon 1280; see canons 635 §1 and 741 §1).

In making the investment, the ordinary must keep in mind the intentions of the donor who may stipulate the manner of administering pious wills (see canon 1300) – in this instance, the manner of investing.

CORRESPONDING CANON OF THE EASTERN CODE: CANON 1049. This Eastern canon legislates for both autonomous and non-autonomous pious foundations (since the Eastern code does not have *private* juridic persons.) It requires the hierarch to "designate" (not merely "approve") a safe place for immediate deposit of the money and movable goods. He is to give his prudent judgment on their more permanent investment after consulting those concerned and "the competent council" (rather than "his own finance council").

PIOUS FOUNDATIONS: DOCUMENTATION

Can. 1306 – §1. Foundations, even if made orally, are to be put in writing.

§2. One copy of the charter is to be preserved safely in the archive of the curia and another copy in the archive of the juridic person to which the foundation belongs.

Canon 1306 §1 says that foundations, although they can be made orally, are to be recorded in writing. This refers only to *non-autonomous* pious foundations. Autonomous pious foundations, since they are juridic persons (canon 1301 §1, 1°), are established by a decree of the competent authority (canon 114 §1) which, like all decrees, must be in writing (canon 51; see canon 37). It is not possible to establish an autonomous pious foundation orally. Therefore, one properly concludes that canon 1306 §1 concerns only non-autonomous foundations.

The written document will clearly define the goods and purposes of the foundation. This will provide proof of the establishment, operation, duration, and pious causes of the foundation, in accord with the wishes of the donors. These issues would be addressed in the statutes of the autonomous pious foundation, as is the case with all juridic persons (see canon 117). The written document guides the service of successive administrators.

Canon 1306 §2 requires that one copy of the charter (*tabularum exemplar*) of the foundation is to be preserved securely in the archive of the curia (i.e., the curia of the diocesan bishop or the curia of the major superior). A second copy is to be preserved in the archive of the public juridic person to which the non-autonomous foundation belongs. Indicating that the pious foundation belongs to a juridic person reveals that canon 1306 §2 pertains only to non-autonomous pious foundations, since an autonomous pious foundation is itself a juridic person which does not belong to another. In the case of autonomous pious foundations, the governing statutes would be preserved by the juridic person itself.

CORRESPONDING CANON OF THE EASTERN CODE: CANON 1050. The Eastern law has no norm corresponding to Latin canon 1306 §1; it makes no provision for the oral establishment of foundations. The Eastern canon requires that a copy of the "document of the foundation" (*documentum fundationis*), rather than a "copy of the charter" (*tabularum exemplar*), is to be placed in the archive of the "juridic person," rather than the archive of the "juridic person to whom the foundation belongs."

PIOUS FOUNDATIONS: RECORDS OF OBLIGATIONS ACCEPTED AND FULFILLED

Can. 1307 – §1. A list of the obligations incumbent upon pious foundations is to be composed and displayed in an accessible place so that the obligations to be fulfilled are not forgotten; the prescripts of cann. 1300-1302 and 1287 are to be observed.

§2. In addition to the book mentioned in can. 958, §1, another book is to be maintained and kept by the pastor or rector in which the individual obligations, their fulfillment, and the offerings are noted.

Canon 1307 concerns recording the obligations incumbent upon pious foundations.[60] Canon 1307 §1 requires the composition of a list of these obligations. The list is to be displayed in such a place that the obligations will not be forgotten or disregarded. The placement of the displayed document is left to the discretion of the competent authority. A list identifying liturgical obligations may logically be displayed in the sacristy where it would serve as a ready reminder to those fulfilling the duties. The canon also requires the observance of the prescripts of canons 1300-1301 (on pious wills), canon 1302 (on pious trusts),[61] and 1287 (on financial reports to the local ordinary and the faithful).

Canon 1307 §2 requires that the pastor or rector[62] keep a special book listing *all* the obligations (including Mass obligations), their fulfillment, and the offerings. If the obligations include the celebrations of Masses, this book is to exist *in addition to* the book in which the pastor or rector regularly records Mass offerings (see canon 958 §1).

If the autonomous foundation is a juridic person subject to the diocesan bishop, or if the non-autonomous foundation has been entrusted to a juridic person subject to the diocesan bishop, their administrators are required to make an annual report to the local

---

[60]   ROBERT T. KENNEDY concludes that this canon refers to non-autonomous pious foundations. The obligations of autonomous pious foundations (which are juridic persons) are indicated in their statutes. In "Temporal Goods," p. 1520. It may be argued, however, that the discipline of canon 1307 applies also to autonomous pious foundations, inasmuch as the purpose of canon 1307 is to prevent those responsible from forgetting the obligations which are to be fulfilled. In the case of autonomous foundations, those responsible to fulfill obligations may not have routine access to its statutes, but should have routine access to the list of obligations presented in the document required by canon 1307. The recollection of obligations is important both for autonomous and non-autonomous pious foundations.

[61]   A non-autonomous pious foundation is a pious trust (entrusted to a public juridic person as trustee) established by a pious will for a pious cause, so the discipline of canon 1302 applies. An autonomous pious foundation is *not* a pious trust, but is itself a juridic person.

[62]   The pastor (*parochus*) is the proper pastor (*pastor*) of a parish (canons 519, 515 §1); a parish can exist without a church. The rector is a priest to whom is entrusted the care of some church which is neither parochial, capitular, nor connected to a house of a religious community or a society of apostolic life which celebrates in it (canon 556).

ordinary, who in turn is to submit it for examination to the diocesan
finance council (canon 1287 §1). In addition, all administrators of a
juridic person are to give an accounting to the faithful concerning
goods offered to it, according to the norms of particular law (canon
1287 §2). These reports, to the local ordinary and to the faithful,
would indicate the fulfillment of the obligations of a pious foundation.

CORRESPONDING CANON OF THE EASTERN CODE: CANON
1051. Like the Latin code, the Eastern law specifies that canons
1044-1046 (which correspond to Latin canons 1300-1302) are to be
observed, but adds the additional requirement of observing Eastern
canon 1031 concerning an annual report to the proper hierarch and a
public account of goods given to the Church. Also, the Eastern code
makes no reference to the additional book recording offerings for the
Divine Liturgy; it simply directs that a book recording individual
obligations, their fulfillment, and the offering is to be held and kept
by the pastor or rector of a church.

MASS OBLIGATIONS: REDUCTIONS

**Can. 1308 – §1. A reduction of the obligations of
Masses, to be made only for a just and necessary cause,
is reserved to the Apostolic See, without prejudice to the
following prescripts.**

**§2. If it is expressly provided for in the charters of
the foundations, the ordinary is able to reduce the Mass
obligations because of diminished revenues.**

**§3. With regard to Masses independently founded
in legacies or in any other way, the diocesan bishop has
the power, because of diminished revenues and for as long
as the cause exists, to reduce the obligations to the level of
offering legitimately established in the diocese, provided
that there is no one obliged to increase the offering who
can effectively be made to do so.**

**§4. The diocesan bishop also has the power to
reduce the obligations or legacies of Masses binding an
ecclesiastical institute if the revenue has become insuf-**

ficient to pursue appropriately the proper purpose of the institute.

§5. The supreme moderator of a clerical religious institute of pontifical right possesses the same powers mentioned in §§3 and 4.

Canons 1308-1310 concern modifications of obligations coming from pious wills. Canon 1308 regulates the reduction of Mass obligations.[63] Canon 1309 addresses the transfer of Mass obligations (to days, churches, or altars different from those determined in the foundation), without reducing them. Canon 1310 concerns modifications in obligations attached to a foundation.

Canon 1308 addresses the reduction of Mass obligations, not their elimination. Such a reduction is to be made only for a "just and necessary cause."[64] A "necessary" cause implies that, were the reduction not made, the intention of the donor would be frustrated because the intended obligation would not be fulfilled. Several norms apply in diverse circumstances:

1. The reduction is reserved to the Apostolic See, except as provided below (canon 1308 §1).[65]
2. The reduction can be made by the ordinary:
   a. if the charter of the foundation expressly gives him this power, and
   b. if the revenues are diminished (canon 1308 §2).
3. If the Masses are independently founded in legacies or in any other way and the revenues are diminished, the reduction can be made by the diocesan bishop (or, by the supreme moderator of a clerical religious institute of pontifical right); however,

---

[63] Mass obligations are not subject to prescription (canon 199, 5°). They are governed by canons 945-958. Canon 1308 concerns the reduction of Mass obligations *attached to a foundation* (i.e., a *foundation Mass*), not manual Mass obligations. See DAVID R. PERKIN, "Canonical Rights to Reduce and to Transfer Mass Obligations," in *CLSA AOI*, pp. 421-423; PAUL ZIELKINSKI, "Pious Wills and Mass Stipends in Relation to Canons 1299-1310," in *Studia canonica*, 19 (1985), pp. 115-154.

[64] The phrase "just and necessary" appears only twice in the code: canon 1308 §1 and canon 1310 §1.

[65] This general norm certainly pertains to *manual* Masses.

a. he can make the reduction only for so long as the cause exists,[66]

b. he must make the reduction to the level legitimately established in the diocese, and

c. he must see that there is no one who is obliged to increase the offering who can effectively be made to do so (canon 1308 §3).

4. If the obligations or legacies of Masses bind an ecclesiastical institute and the revenue has become insufficient to pursue appropriately the proper purpose of the institute, the reduction can be made by the diocesan bishop (or, by the supreme moderator of a clerical religious institute of pontifical right) (canon 1308 §4).

A reduction in Mass obligations is a decrease in their number, not in the nature of the obligation itself. Normally, a reduction in Mass obligations is reserved to the Apostolic See (i.e., to the Congregation for the Clergy – see *Pastor Bonus*, 97, 2°). The last four paragraphs of canon 1308 provide *three exceptions* to this general rule.

The first exception (canon 1308 §2) allows the ordinary to reduce Mass obligations attached to foundations (autonomous and non-autonomous).[67] He can make this reduction *only* if the charter

---

[66] Canon 1308 is about the *reduction* (not the *elimination*) of Mass obligations attached to a foundation. The PONTIFICAL COMMISSION FOR THE AUTHENTIC INTERPRETATION OF THE CANONS OF THE CODE ruled on July 14, 1922 that the ordinary can reduce the obligations of Masses, owing to diminished revenue, if such power is expressly given in the articles of foundation. *AAS*, 14 (1922), p. 529; *CLD*, vol. 1, p. 726. Some commentators (e.g., Vermeersch-Creusen and Cocchi) in the past held that, if the revenue is eliminated through no fault of it holders, the Mass obligations cease. See WOYWOOD, vol. 2, p. 221. Attention should be given to canon 949 of the 1983 code: "A person obliged to celebrate and apply Mass for the intention of those who gave an offering is bound by the obligation even if the offerings received have been lost through no fault of his own." (This same discipline is found in CIC/1917, canon 829.) It appears, therefore, that Mass obligations attached to a foundation can never be eliminated, except by the Apostolic See (see canon 1310 §3).

[67] Canon 1308 §1 reflects in part the legislation of PAUL VI, apostolic letter *motu proprio Firma in traditione* (June 13, 1974), in *AAS*, 66 (1974), p. 311; *CLD*, vol. 8, p. 533. See also the "Facultates circa missarum stipendia a Summo Pontifice sacris romanae curiae congregationis concessae et normae de earum usu," in *Commentarium pro religiosis et missionariis*, 56 (1975), pp. 90-91.

of the foundation expressly permits this *and* the revenues are diminished. When advising persons who wish to make pious wills for the celebration of Masses, it may be prudent to recommend that the donors see to it that the foundation document gives the ordinary the power to reduce Mass obligations should the revenues diminish. The donor may also be encouraged to give the ordinary in the same foundation document the permissions to transfer Mass obligations to different days, churches, or altars (see canon 1309).

The second exception (canon 1308 §3)[68] allows the diocesan bishop (and the supreme moderator of clerical religious institutes of pontifical right: see canon 1308 §5) to reduce Mass obligations attached to foundations (autonomous and non-autonomous) which are "founded independently" (*quae sint per se stantia* – i.e., founded *only* for the celebration of Masses and not for any other pious causes).[69] He can make this reduction if the revenues are diminished and provided that (*dummodo*)[70] there is no one obliged to increase the offerings who can be effectively made to do so. The reduction, however, is to be only to the amount of Mass offerings established by canon 952 and can continue only for as long as the reduction of revenues exists. If the income again becomes sufficient to fulfill the Mass obligations, they must be fulfilled. The discipline of canon 1308 §3 applies when the local ordinary had not been given the power to reduce Mass obligations by the foundation document (see canon 1308 §2).

The third exception (canon 1308 §4)[71] allows the diocesan bishop (and the supreme moderator of clerical religious institutes of pontifical right: see canon 1308 §5) to reduce Mass obligations binding an ecclesiastical institute (e.g., a Catholic school, health care facility, etc.). Canon 1308 §4 does not concern "foundation Masses." The Mass obligations here have not been entrusted to a foundation

---

[68] This canon reflects the discipline of POPE PAUL VI, apostolic letter *motu proprio Pastorale munus* (November 30, 1963), n. 11, in *AAS*, 56 (1963), p. 12; *CLD*, vol. 6, p. 372.

[69] See KENNEDY, "Temporal Goods," p. 1522, fn. 234.

[70] See canon 39.

[71] This canon reflects the discipline of POPE PAUL VI, apostolic letter *motu proprio Pastorale munus* (November 30, 1963), n. 12, in *AAS*, 56 (1963), p. 12; *CLD*, vol. 6, pp. 372-373.

(autonomous or non-autonomous), but rather to an ecclesiastical institute, with the accompanying modal obligation (see canon 1267 §2) to offer Masses.[72] The law permits the above-mentioned authorities to reduce these obligations if the revenue has become insufficient for the institute to pursue appropriately its proper purpose.

The power of the ordinary (canon 1308 §2), the diocesan bishop (canon 1308 §§3-4), and the supreme moderator of a clerical religious institute of pontifical right (canon 1308 §5) is "ordinary power of governance" (canon 131 §1) and, as such, can be delegated (canon 137 §1) since canon 1308 does not forbid delegation.

CORRESPONDING CANON OF THE EASTERN CODE: CANON 1052. Eastern canon 1052 §1 makes no reference to the "just and necessary cause" for the reduction of Mass obligations and omits the phrase "without prejudice to the following prescripts." Eastern canon 1052 §2 refers to the "document of the foundation" (*documentum foundationis*) rather than the "charter of the foundations" (*tabula foundationum*). Eastern canon 1052 §3 omits the phrase "independently founded in legacies or in any other way." Eastern canon 1052 §4 omits reference to "legacies" and clarifies more precisely that the revenues have become insufficient to pursue "those purposes which, at the time of the acceptance of the obligations, could have been obtained." Eastern canon 1052 §5 extends the power mentioned in canon 1052 §§3-4 to "superiors general of clerical religious institutes or societies of common life in the manner of religious of pontifical or patriarchal right." Significantly, Eastern canon 1052 §6 is absent in the Latin law: "An eparchial bishop can delegate the powers mentioned in §§3 and 4 only to a coadjutor bishop, auxiliary bishop, protosyncellus or syncellus, excluding any subdelegation."

FOUNDATION MASS OBLIGATIONS: TRANSFERS

Can. 1309 – The authorities mentioned in can. 1308 also have the power to transfer, for an appropriate cause, the

---

[72] See KENNEDY, "Temporal Goods," p. 1522.

obligations of Masses to days, churches, or altars different from those determined in the foundations.

Canon 1309 addresses the transfer of Mass obligations to days, churches, or altars different than those determined in the foundations.[73] It does not concern the reduction of Mass obligations (legislation about which is in canon 1308). The transfer can be done for an appropriate cause (*congrua causa*). The competent authorities are those listed in the preceding canon.

This canon only concerns the transfer of Mass obligations attached to foundations. Mass obligations binding another ecclesiastical institute (but not attached to a foundation: see canon 1308 §4) cannot, therefore, be transferred by virtue of canon 1309.

Canon 1309 says that the power to transfer foundation Mass obligations rests with the authorities mentioned in canon 1308 – i.e., the Apostolic See and all ordinaries.[74] This ordinary power of governance (canon 131 §1) can be delegated (canon 137 §1), since canon 1309 does not forbid delegation.

As is the case with canon 1308, when advising persons who wish to make pious wills for the celebration of Masses, it may be prudent to recommend that the donors see to it that the ordinary be given in the foundation document the power to transfer Mass obligations to different days, churches, or altars.

CORRESPONDING CANON OF THE EASTERN CODE: CANON 1053. The canon requires a "just cause" (rather than an "appropriate cause") to transfer the obligations of celebrating the "Divine Liturgy" to different "days or institutes" (rather than to different "days, churches, or altars").

---

[73] This reflects the legislation found in POPE PAUL VI, apostolic letter *motu proprio Firma in traditione* (June 23, 1974), in *AAS*, 66 (1974), p. 311; *CLD*, vol. 8, p. 533.

[74] Since canon 1308 §2 speaks of "the ordinary," it is reasonable to conclude that canon 1309 gives all ordinaries the power to transfer Mass obligations. See DE PAOLIS, *I beni temporali*, p. 237; KENNEDY, "Temporal Goods," p. 1532.

FOUNDATIONS: REDUCTIONS, MODERATIONS, COMMUTATIONS (NOT INVOLVING MASSES)

> **Can. 1310 – §1. The ordinary, only for a just and neces-sary cause, can reduce, moderate, or commute the wills of the faithful for pious causes if the founder has expressly entrusted this power to him.**
>
> **§2. If through no fault of the administrators the fulfillment of the imposed obligations has become impos-sible because of diminished revenues or some other cause, the ordinary can equitably lessen these obligations, after having heard those concerned and his own finance council and with the intention of the founder preserved as much as possible; this does not hold for the reduction of Masses, which is governed by the prescripts of can. 1308.**
>
> **§3. In other cases, recourse is to be made to the Apostolic See.**

Canon 1310 concerns the reduction, moderation, and commu-tation of the pious wills of the faithful in matters other than Mass obligations (which are governed by canon 1308). Canon 1310 §1 says that such actions can be performed by the ordinary:

1. for a just and necessary cause; and
2. only if the founder of the pious will has expressly entrusted this power to him.

When advising persons who wish to make pious wills for purposes other than the celebration of Masses, it may be prudent to recommend that the donors see to it that the foundation document give the ordinary the express power to reduce, moderate, or commute pious wills for a "just and necessary cause."[75] To make the reduction, moderation, or commutation due to mere convenience does not suf-fice. A "necessary" cause implies that, were the reduction not made, the intention of the donor would be frustrated because the imposed obligation would not be fulfilled.

---

[75] The phrase "just and necessary" appears only twice in the code: canon 1308 §1 and canon 1310 §1.

Canon 1310 §2 adds that, even if the founder has not authorized the ordinary to reduce, moderate, or commute the obligations imposed by the pious wills of the faithful, the ordinary may nonetheless equitably lessen them:

1. if through no fault of the administrators the fulfilment of the obligations has become impossible because of reduced revenues or some other cause,

2. if he has first consulted those concerned and his own finance council,

3. if the intention of the founder is preserved as much as possible, and

4. if the reduction does not concern Mass offerings (the reduction of Mass obligations is governed by canon 1308).

Otherwise, recourse is to be made to the Apostolic See (canon 1310 §3).

The canon speaks of "reduction, moderation, and commutation" of pious wills. A reduction (*reductio*) is a decrease in the number of acts of an obligation without changing the nature of the obligation itself (e.g., to issue three scholarships rather than four). A modification (*moderatio*) is a specific determination adjusting conditions secondary or accessory to the fulfillment of the obligation (e.g., to determine that scholarships will be directed only to persons of a determined category). A commutation (*commutatio*) concerns the substitution of one pious cause for another (e.g., providing food for the poor instead of educating catechists in the missions).[76]

Canon 1310 §2 says, in order to equitably lessen the obligations, the ordinary must first receive the counsel (but not necessarily the consent) of his own finance council and of those concerned. Failure

---

[76] See BOUSCAREN-ELLIS-KORTH, p. 821. These commentators add: "*Interpretation* of a pious last will is not the same as commutation. Since the Ordinary is the executor of all pious wills, he has the right to interpret them if necessary. This should be done by determining the exact wishes of the donor as expressed in the document establishing a foundation, or as expressed in his last will and testament even though it be invalid at civil law, or as determined from the testimony of reliable witnesses, and so on." (p. 822) See also VROMANT, p. 155.

to make these mandated consultations results in an invalid alteration of the pious will by the ordinary (see canon 127).

In circumstances other than those identified above in this canon, the Apostolic See must make the reduction, moderation, or commutation of the pious wills.

Finally, it is obvious that the legislation in canon 1310 is strictly canonical. The operative civil law requirements must also be taken into consideration.

CORRESPONDING CANON OF THE EASTERN CODE: CANON 1054. Eastern canon 1054 §2 requires the hierarch to consult "the competent council" (rather than "his own finance council"). Eastern canon 1054 §3 says that in other cases the Apostolic See or "the patriarch" (who "is to act with the consent of the permanent synod") is to be approached.

CONCLUSION

The Church has its origin in God; it is not a human creation. It has an "innate right" from God to temporal goods in order to achieve its principal purposes, which are primarily: "to order divine worship, to care for the decent support of ministers, and to exercise works of the sacred apostolate and of charity, especially toward the needy" (canon 1254 §2). At the same time, the Church has an "innate right" to require from the Christian faithful "those things which are necessary for the purposes proper to it" (canon 1260). The Church exercises this innate right "independently from civil power" (canon 1254 §1), and claims the right "to acquire temporal goods by every just means of natural or positive law permitted to others" (canon 1259).

This commentary, while focusing on the several canons dealing with ecclesiastical property in *Book V* and elsewhere, makes it obvious that ecclesiastical goods are owned within the *communio* of the Church.[1] When he promulgated the 1983 *Code of Canon Law*, Pope John Paul II said that canon law should show the Church "as a *communio*" so as to reveal the relations which exist between the particular churches and the universal Church, and between collegiality and primacy.[2] Two years later, the participants of the 1985 extraordinary Synod of Bishops said that "[t]he ecclesiology of *communio* is the central and fundamental idea of the [Second Vatican Council's]

---

[1]   For reflections on the fundamental principles governing the Church's care of ecclesiastical goods, see JOHN A. RENKEN, "The Principles Governing the Care of Church Property," in *The Jurist*, 68 (2008), pp. 136-177; D'SOUZA, pp. 467-498.

[2]   JOHN PAUL II, apostolic constitution *Sacrae disciplinae leges*, in *AAS*, 75:2 (1983), p. xxii; English translation, *Code of Canon Law: Latin-English Edition*, prepared under the auspices of the CLSA, Washington, CLSA, 1999, pp. xxx.

documents."[3] The conciliar documents, which reflect *"communio ecclesiology,"* are the basis for the canons of the code.[4]

By reason of baptism, all the Christian faithful are in the full *communio* of the Church when they "are joined with Christ in its visible structure by the bonds of the profession of faith, the sacraments, and ecclesiastical governance" (canon 205). This Church is "constituted and organized in this world as a society" and "subsists in the Catholic Church governed by the successor of Peter and the bishops in *communio* with him" (canon 204 §2). The Roman Pontiff, who is the successor of Peter, and the bishops, who are the successors of the Apostles, constitute one college (canon 330) whose head is the Roman Pontiff (canon 336). In fulfilling his role, "the Roman Pontiff is always in *communio* with the other bishops and with the universal Church" (canon 333 §2). The conciliar Dogmatic Constitution on the Church, *Lumen gentium*, speaks of the *communio* of the Churches which is based in the unity of the college of bishops with the Roman Pontiff:

---

[3]   SYNOD OF BISHOPS, Final Report *Ecclesia sub verbo Dei mysteria Christi celebrans pro salute mundi*, (December 7, 1985), Vatican City State, Libreria editrice Vaticana, 1985; English translation in *Origins*, 15 (1985-1986), p. 448. See JOHN A. RENKEN, "'*Duc in altum!*' *Communio:* Source and Summit of Church Law," in *The Jurist*, 63 (2003), pp. 22-69.

[4]   When promulgating the 1983 code, POPE JOHN PAUL II had reflected about the conciliar influence on the revised code: "[T]he reform of the [1917] Code of Canon Law appeared to be definitely desired and requested by the [Second Vatican] Council which devoted such great attention to the Church.

"As is obvious, when the revision of the Code was first announced [in 1959] the council was an event of the future. Moreover, the acts of the magisterium and especially its doctrine on the Church would be decided in the years 1962-1965; however, it is clear to everyone that John XXIII's intuition was very true, and with good reason it must be said that his decision was for the long-term good of the Church.

"Therefore, the new Code which is promulgated today necessarily required the previous work of the council. Although it was announced together with the ecumenical council, nevertheless it follows it chronologically because the work undertaken in its preparation, which had to be based upon the council, could not begin until after the latter's completion....

"[The revised Code] corresponds perfectly with the teaching and the character of the Second Vatican Council. Therefore not only because of its content but also because of its very origin, the Code manifests the spirit of this council in whose documents the Church, the universal 'sacrament of salvation,' (dogmatic constitution on the Church, *Lumen gentium*, nn. 1, 9, 48), is presented as the people of God and its hierarchical constitution appears based on the college of bishops united with its head." In *Sacrae disciplinae leges*, pp. xxvii-xxviii.

The Roman Pontiff, as the successor of Peter, is the perpetual and visible source and foundation of the unity both of the bishops and of the whole company of the faithful. The individual bishops are the visible source and foundation of unity in their particular churches, which are constituted after the model of the universal Church; it is in these and formed out of them that the one and unique Catholic Church exists. (n. 23)[5]

The Church is essentially a *communio* of baptized believers united in faith and sacramental celebrations in union with the Roman Pontiff and the college of bishops in *communio* with him. Within the Church, juridic persons own temporal goods under the supreme authority, administration and stewardship of the Roman Pontiff so that the Church can achieve its proper purposes. All the Christian faithful have the freedom and duty to assist in the work of the Church by uniting and sharing their resources. This reveals that *communio* is the fundamental principle guiding the code's legislation on temporal goods.

The Church is a *communio*, which is experienced in multiple manifestations throughout the world. On May 28, 1992, the Congregation for the Doctrine of the Faith issued *Communionis notio*, the Letter on Certain Aspects of the Church as a Communion.[6] This letter explains that the universal Church has given rise to different local churches:

Indeed, according to the fathers [see: Clement of Rome, Shepherd of Hermas], ontologically the Church-mystery, the Church that is one and unique, precedes creation and gives birth to the particular churches as her daughters. She expresses herself in them; she is the mother and not the offspring of the particular churches. Furthermore, the

---

5   FLANNERY 1, p. 376.
6   CONGREGATION FOR THE DOCTRINE OF THE FAITH, Letter on Certain Aspects of the Church as a Communion *Communionis notio* (May 28, 1992), in *AAS*, 85 (1993), pp. 838-850; English translation in *Origins*, 22 (1992-1993), pp. 108-112.

Church is manifested temporally on the day of Pentecost in the community of the 120 gathered around Mary and the twelve Apostles, the representatives of the one unique Catholic Church and the founders-to-be of the local churches, who have a mission directed to the world. From the first the Church speaks all languages.

From the Church, which in its origins and first manifestation is universal, have arisen the different local churches as particular expressions of the one unique Church of Jesus Christ. Arising within and out of the universal Church, they have their ecclesiality in her and from her. Hence the formula of the Second Vatican Council: *The Church in and formed out of the churches (Ecclesia in et ex ecclesiis)* is inseparable from this other formula, *the churches in and formed out of the Church (ecclesiae in et ex Ecclesia)*. Clearly the relationship between the universal Church and the particular churches is a mystery and cannot be compared to that which exists between the whole and the parts in a purely human group or society. (n. 9)

Within this ecclesial *communio*, the Church cares for its property. To do so effectively, several norms on ecclesiastical goods apply the principle of subsidiarity whereby effective determinations are prudently made at the most appropriate local level. The Church owns temporal goods to achieve its proper purposes. Administrators of ecclesiastical goods exercise vigilance over the property which has been entrusted to their oversight, and collaborate with others to do the same. They assure the decent support of those who serve the Church. They are very careful to respect and implement the intentions of donors. They observe and apply, as appropriate, the principles of civil law to assure that Church property is protected in the secular forum for the proper purposes of the Church, now and in future generations. They are transparent in their stewardship and render accounts of their service.

All the norms of the code concerning the Church's care for its property will necessarily be reflected both in particular legislation and in the daily activities of those who are stewards of the Church's material blessings. The code's norms will remain nothing more than words, however, unless and until their spirit and discipline are woven into the ordinary fabric of the life of all the Christian faithful. To weave this fabric appropriately is precisely the challenge presented to the People of God, and is the reason for which the legislation on ecclesiastical goods continues to call all to a grateful stewardship for God's gifts which is both responsible and effective within the *communio* of the Church. Temporal goods are entrusted to the Church for the well-being of all the faithful, especially for the salvation of our souls, which forever remains the "supreme law of the Church" (canon 1752).

TEMPORAL GOODS IN INSTITUTES OF CONSECRATED LIFE AND SOCIETIES OF APOSTOLIC LIFE
(Canons 634-640, 718, 741)

The treatment of the Latin Church's legislation[1] on temporal goods would be incomplete without some consideration given to the few specific norms in the 1983 code governing temporal goods in institutes of consecrated life (i.e., religious institutes and secular institutes) and societies of apostolic life. These norms have been discussed in appropriate places in the preceding text of this commentary. Nonetheless, the norms are gathered in this appendix where a brief commentary will be given to each canon. They are found in *Book II* of the code, which is entitled *The People of God*.[2] Only nine canons provide specific legislation on temporal goods: seven for religious institutes, one for secular institutes, and one for societies of apostolic life. Except for these norms and any proper law approved for these groups, the institutes and societies are governed by the norms of *Book V* in matters of ecclesiastical goods.[3]

---

[1] For an extensive comparison of the Latin and Eastern legislation on the temporal goods and the consecrated life, see JOBE ABBAS, *The Consecrated Life: A Comparative Commentary on the Eastern and Latin Codes*, Ottawa, Saint Paul University, 2008.

[2] All the canons are in *Part III: Institutes of Consecrated Life and Societies of Apostolic Life*. Canons 634-640 on the temporal goods of religious institutes are in *Section I: Institutes of Consecrated Life, Title II: Religious Institutes, Chapter II: The Governance of Institutes, Article 3: Temporal Goods and Their Administration*. Canon 718 on the temporal goods of secular institutes is found in *Section I: Institutes of Consecrated Life, Title III: Secular Institutes*. Canon 741 on the temporal goods of societies of apostolic life is found in *Section II: Societies of Apostolic Life*.

[3] See SCHOUPPE, pp. 219-239.

OWNERSHIP OF TEMPORAL GOODS BY RELIGIOUS INSTITUTES

Can. 634 – §1. As juridic persons by the law itself, institutes, provinces, and houses are capable of acquiring, possessing, administering, and alienating temporal goods unless this capacity is excluded or restricted in the constitutions.

§2. Nevertheless, they are to avoid any appearance of excess, immoderate wealth, and accumulation of goods.

Canon 634 explains that religious institutes[4] (their provinces[5] and their houses[6]) are juridic persons *ipso iure* (see canon 114 §1);

---

[4] Canon 607 §2 defines a *religious institute*: "A religious institute is a society in which members, according to proper law, pronounce public vows, either perpetual or temporary which are to be renewed, however, when the period of time has elapsed, and lead a life of brothers or sisters in common." The religious institute is governed by a *supreme moderator*, defined in canon 622: "The supreme moderator holds power over all the provinces, houses, and members of an institute; this power is to be exercised according to proper law. Other superiors possess power within the limits of their function." The supreme moderator is also considered to be a *major superior* (see canon 620, in the following footnote).

[5] Canon 621 defines a *religious province*: "A grouping of several houses which constitutes an immediate part of the same institute under the same superior and has been canonically erected by legitimate authority is called a province." The provincial superior is considered in law to be a *major superior*, defined in canon 620: "Those who govern an entire institute, a province of an institute or a part equivalent to an institute, or an autonomous house, as well as their vicars, are major superiors. Comparable to these are an abbot primate and a superior of a monastic congregation, who nonetheless do not have all the power which universal law grants to major superiors."

[6] Canon 608 describes a *"constituted" religious house*: "A religious community must live in a legitimately established house under the authority of a superior designated according to the norm of law. Each house must have at least an oratory in which the Eucharist is to be celebrated and reserved so that it is truly the center of the community."

In addition to "constituted" religious houses, the code identifies *"canonically erected" religious houses*, which are defined in canon 609 §1: "Houses of a religious institute are erected by the authority competent according to the constitutions, with the previous written consent of the diocesan bishop." Canon 609 §2 adds that the additional permission of the Apostolic See is required to erect a monastery of nuns.

Only a "canonically erected" religious house has juridic personality (canon 634 §1). Also, a "canonically erected" house is not always identified with a building where religious live (individual religious may, in fact, live alone or in a very small group, but belong to a "canonically erected" house).

therefore, they can acquire, possess,[7] administer, and alienate temporal goods. It also acknowledges that their constitutions (proper law) can exclude or restrict this capacity. Nonetheless, all religious institutes are to avoid any appearance of excess, immoderate wealth, and accumulation of goods.

Canon 634 §1 is a specific application of the discipline of preliminary canons in *Book V.* Since religious institutes, provinces, and houses are public juridic persons *ipso iure*, they are able to acquire, retain/possess, administer, and alienate temporal goods (which, since they belong to public juridic persons, are called "ecclesiastical goods:" see canons 1257 §1, 635 §1).

While the common law on religious institutes permits the ownership of temporal goods, canon 634 §1 adds that the fundamental proper law of a religious institute (i.e., its constitution) can exclude or restrict this right to own temporal goods.[8]

Canon 634 §2 says that, even if a religious institute can own temporal goods without any restrictions, it is to avoid all appearance of excess, immoderate wealth, and accumulation of goods. This is in keeping with the evangelical counsel of poverty which is described in canon 600:

> **Can. 600 – The evangelical counsel of poverty in imitation of Christ who, although he was rich, was made poor for us, entails, besides a life which is poor in fact and in spirit and is to be led productively in moderation and foreign to earthly riches, a dependence and limitation in the use and disposition of goods according to the proper law of each institute.**

---

[7] "To possess" (*possidere*) temporal goods (canon 634 §1) is the same as "to retain" (*retinere*) them (canon 1254 §1).

[8] FRANCIS G. MORRISEY comments: "The constitutions of some institutes limit the right of possession of provinces, and especially of houses, by determining that all surplus funds are to be given on a regular basis to the next higher unit for the good of the institute. In some communities, even the right of possession does not exist. The goods belong either to the Holy See, or to syndics who hold them in trust." In "Temporal Goods and Their Administration," p. 1674. See also SUGAWARA, "Le norme sui beni temporali," pp. 419-420.

Avoiding "any appearance of excess, immoderate wealth and accumulation of goods" will involve an analysis of local circumstances, sincerity, transparency, and faith.

The *acquisition* of the goods of these religious institutes, provinces, and houses is governed by canons 1259-1272. The *administration* of their goods is governed by canons 638 §§1-2 and canons 1273-1289. The *alienation* of their goods is governed by canons 638 §§3-4 and canons 1290-1298. Pious wills, trusts, and non-autonomous foundations related to religious institutes are governed by canons 1299-1310.

It must be understood that canons 634-640 apply to all goods owned by a religious institute, even if these goods have been separately incorporated in civil law. Such goods continue to be "ecclesiastical goods" (see canon 1257 §1). If a religious institute staffs an apostolate not belonging to the institute, however, the religious institute obviously does not own the goods of that apostolate. Such goods are "ecclesiastical goods" only if the apostolate owning them is a public juridic person.[9]

GOODS OWNED BY RELIGIOUS INSTITUTES: COMMON AND PROPER LAWS

> **Can. 635 – §1. Since the temporal goods of religious institutes are ecclesiastical, they are governed by the prescripts of Book V, *The Temporal Goods of the Church*, unless other provision is expressly made.**
>
> **§2. Nevertheless, each institute is to establish suitable norms concerning the use and administration of goods, by which the poverty proper to it is to be fostered, protected, and expressed.**

Canon 635 §1 says that the temporal goods of religious institutes (which are considered "ecclesiastical goods" since religious

---

9   See JORDAN F. HITE, "Religious Institutes (Canons 607-709)" in *The Code of Canon Law: Text and Commentary*, commissioned by the CLSA, James A. Coriden, Thomas J. Green, and Donald E. Heintschel (eds.), New York, Paulist, 1985, p. 485 (=HITE, "Religious Institutes").

institutes, provinces, and houses are public juridic persons *a iure*: canon 634 §1, and all temporal goods owned by public juridic persons are called "ecclesiastical goods": canon 1257 §2) are governed by the prescripts of *Book V, The Temporal Goods of the Church*, unless other provision is expressly made in canons 634-640. Further, the proper law of each religious institute takes precedence over the common law found in these canons.

From this, it follows that all the temporal goods belonging to these religious institutes, provinces, and houses are considered ecclesiastical goods even if they have been separated civilly. This means, for example, that if a religious institute owns and operates a health care or educational institution, the goods of these apostolic works are "ecclesiastical goods" of the religious institute, even if the works are separately civilly incorporated. Likewise, if these apostolates have been established as public juridic persons separated from the institute, the goods are also "ecclesiastical goods" since they belong to the Church (see canon 1258), whether or not the apostolates are also separately civilly incorporated. If, however, a religious institute or another public juridic person does not own the apostolic endeavors, the norms of *Book V* do not apply and the temporal goods are not "ecclesiastical goods."

Obviously, any temporal goods owned personally by a member of a religious institute are not considered "ecclesiastical goods" (see canon 1257).

Canon 635 §2 calls for the proper law[10] to establish suitable

---

[10]   The proper law of a religious institute includes the fundamental code (or constitutions) and supplementary statutes. In common parlance in religious institutes, *Book I* refers to the *constitutions* or *fundamental code* which contains "fundamental norms regarding governance of the institute, the discipline of members, incorporation and formation of members, and the proper object of the sacred bonds," and which can be changed only with the consent of the competent ecclesiastical authority – e.g., by the Apostolic See for institutes of pontifical right (see canon 587 §§1-3). *Book II* refers to the *statutes* or *rules*, whose preparation and revision generally belong to the general chapter (see canon 587 §4). *Book III* refers to various handbooks or directories which are required by the code: for temporal goods (canon 635 §2), for formation of members (canon 659 §3), for procedures for chapters and elections (canon 632), and for general governance (canons 617, 627). See MICHAEL A. O'REILLY, "The Proper Law of Institutes of Consecrated Life and of Societies of Apostolic Life"

norms concerning the use and administration of the ecclesiastical
goods of an institute. The fundamental code (constitutions) "should
include the key elements for ordinary and extraordinary administration, as well as for acts of alienation of the temporal goods of the
institute."[11] Any less fundamental norms are typically found in a
financial directory or handbook specifically established to govern
the ecclesiastical goods of religious institutes.

This finance directory may be developed with the collaboration
of persons truly expert in financial and legal matters, and approved by
the competent ecclesiastical authority of the religious institute (e.g.,
by the general chapter, or by the major superior with the consent of
the council). Francis G. Morrisey comments about the contents of
the finance directory:

> The finance directory can spell out the capacity of each
> level of government to acquire, possess, administer and
> alienate its own goods. It can establish norms for ac-
> counting procedures and specify the way in which annual
> reports and financial statements are to be presented. We
> can also expect to find in the directory norms relating to
> the inventory of goods, their classification as immovable,
> precious (historical, cultural), or as free capital. Likewise,
> policies relating to gifts (canon 640) and hiring practices
> for employees could be spelled out.[12]

Elsewhere, Morrisey provides more details regarding issues
which may wisely be addressed in the financial directory.[13]

---

in *Canonical Studies Presented to Germain Lesage, O.M.I.*, Michel Thériault and
Jean Thorn (eds.), Ottawa, Saint Paul University, 1991, pp. 302-303; SUGAWARA,
"Amministrazione e alienazione dei beni temporali," p. 255.

[11] ROSE M. MCDERMOTT, "Institutes of Consecrated Life and Societies of Apostolic
Life," in *New Commentary on the Code of Canon Law*, commissioned by the CLSA,
John P. Beal, James A. Coriden, and Thomas J. Green (eds.), New York, Paulist,
2000, p. 754.

[12] MORRISEY, "Temporal Goods and Their Administration," p. 1676.

[13] FRANCIS G. MORRISEY, "The Directory for the Administration of Temporal Goods
in Religious Institutes," in *Unico Ecclesiae servitio: Canonical Studies Presented
to Germain Lesage, O.M.I.*, Michel Thériault and Jean Thorn (eds.), Ottawa, Saint
Paul University, 1991, pp. 267-285.

1. Financial reports: canon 636 §2 requires that financial officers and other administrators periodically render an account to the competent authority (a financial report is made periodically to the Apostolic See)[14]

2. Preparation of budgets: canon 1284 §3 invites, but does not mandate, preparation of budgets of projected income and expenditures[15]

3. Acts of ordinary and extraordinary administration: canon 638 §1 requires proper law to determine the limits of ordinary administration and to define what is necessary for a valid act of extraordinary administration; the detailed procedure for these acts should be identified in the directory

4. Acts of alienation, and acts which can worsen the patrimonial condition of the institute: canon 638 §3 requires permission of the Apostolic See for these acts if the amounts exceed the maximum amount established by the Apostolic See for each region (see canons 1291-1295); the detailed procedure for these acts should be identified in the directory

5. Relationship of the treasurer to the institute, and the specific duties and qualifications of the treasurer: canon 636 says the treasurer (who administers the goods of the institute under the direction of the superior) is to be distinct from the superior, but does not specify that the treasurer must be a member of the institute

6. Definition of stable patrimony: stable patrimony (see canons 1285, 1291) should be carefully identified in an inventory, which is regularly updated (see canon 1283, 2°-3°)

7. Investment policies (long-term and short-term)

---

[14] The periodic reports to the Apostolic See are to present, among many other things, the economic condition of the institute or society, with a general notation on any economic difficulties. See CONGREGATION FOR RELIGIOUS AND SECULAR INSTITUTES, circular letter, *Criteria de notitiis ad statum et vitam religiosorum et societatum vitae apostolicae spectantibus, quae cum Sede Apostolica, quibus temporis intervalis, communicanda sunt* (January 2, 1988), in *AAS*, 80 (1988), p. 105.

[15] Annual budgets, however, are *required* for dioceses; they are prepared by the diocesan finance council (canon 493) and guide the work of the diocesan finance officer (canon 494 §3).

8. Norms for wills and legacies left to the institute
9. Insurance programs
10. Policies for borrowing and lending money
11. Norms for contributions of local communities to provinces, and of provinces to the general administration of the institute
12. Depending on the size of the institute, other issues such as: a) administration of property not owned by the institute; b) the common use of community equipment; c) purchasing of major equipment; d) accounting procedures; e) entering into contracts with dioceses; f) hiring of employees; g) custody of archival material; h) concern for close relatives of community members in cases of illness, old age, etc.; i) funeral and burial policies; j) hospitality; k) vacations, home leave for missionaries, returning missionaries; l) durable power of attorney for health care; m) sabbatical; n), extended therapy, etc.

FINANCE OFFICERS IN RELIGIOUS INSTITUTES

Can. 636 – §1. In each institute and likewise in each province which is governed by a major superior, there is to be a finance officer, distinct from the major superior and constituted according to the norm of proper law, who is to manage the administration of goods under the direction of the respective superior. Insofar as possible, a finance officer distinct from the local superior is to be designated even in local communities.

§2. At the time and in the manner established by proper law, finance officers and other administrators are to render an account of their administration to the competent authority.

Canon 636 §1 requires a finance officer (commonly called a "treasurer" or a "bursar") in each religious institute and in each province which is governed by a major superior. The finance officer is to be distinct from the major superior: their offices are incompatible (see canon 152). The finance officer is to be constituted according to the norm of proper law (not necessarily the constitutions), which may indicate how the finance officer is designated, etc.[16]

The duty of the finance officer is to administer the goods of the institute or province under the direction of the respective superior[17] in accord with the norms of *Book V* (see canons 1273-1289), the common law for religious institutes (canon 638 §§1-2), and the proper law of the individual religious institute. The law adds that even *local* communities are to have a finance officer who, insofar as possible, is to be distinct from the local superior.[18]

Canon 636 §2 requires the proper law of the religious institute to establish the frequency and manner of accounts of administra-

---

[16] Interestingly, the code does not specify that the finance officers must be members of the religious institute, though such would seem preferable. The appointment of a finance officer to administer the ecclesiastical goods obviously does not preclude the service of others well qualified in finances, civil law, and canon law. See ROSEMARY SMITH, "The Governance of Institutes," in *New Commentary on the Code of Canon Law*, commissioned by the CLSA, John P. Beal, James A. Coriden, and Thomas J. Green (eds.), New York, Paulist, 2000, p. 800; MORRISEY, "Temporal Goods and Their Administration," p. 1678.

[17] VELASIO DE PAOLIS observes that "canon 636, which refers to administration of the temporal goods of religious, deserves special attention. After stating that the general or provincial econome must be different from the major superior, the code says that he or she is to administer the goods under the direction of the respective superior. In this case the superior has not only supervision but the direction itself, which evidently is something more, since direction also implies a real right to dispose of the goods themselves. As a matter of fact, canon 638, §2 states that 'besides the superiors, even the other officials appointed for that purpose in their proper law can, within the purview of their office, validly make expenditures and perform juridical acts of ordinary administration.' The religious superiors, therefore, have not only supervision but can also perform administrative acts that are proper to economes. In their own purview, religious superiors have more power than local ordinaries in their diocesan purview. The reason is very simple if we understand the typical setup of religious institutes and the religious vows. The diocesan ordinary, even with regard to *diocesan* church goods, cannot dispose of them." In "Temporal Goods... Consecrated Life," pp. 352-353.
ADAM MAIDA and NICHOLAS CAFARDI reflect: "This treasurer is the person who actually carries on the administration of the public juridic person's property, manages its investments, handles its property, pays its bills, and collects its income under the direction of the competent superior." In *Church Property*, p. 47.

[18] The last sentence in canon 636 §1 may seem ambiguous and interpreted to mean either that a local treasurer is to be designated insofar as possible, or that the local treasurer is to be distinct from the local superior insofar as possible. The terminology was much clearer in CIC/1917, canon 516 §3 which legislated that the local superior can be the local finance officer if necessary, though it is preferable that these roles be distinguished.

tion to be given by the finance officers and other administrators to the competent authority. Universal law requires that accounts of administration must be drawn up at the end of each fiscal year (canon 1284 §2, 8°), but proper law may require more frequent financial reports. Attention must also be given to canon 1287 §2 which requires administrators of all public juridic persons to render a financial account to the faithful concerning the goods which the faithful have offered to it.

Universal law also requires that every juridic person have a finance council or at least two councilors who assist the administrator (canon 1280). Since they are public juridic persons *a iure* (canon 634 §1), the norm of canon 1280 applies to religious institutes, provinces, and canonically erected houses. Proper law will determine whether the various levels of governance will have a finance council or simply financial counselors.

RELIGIOUS INSTITUTES AND THE LOCAL ORDINARY

> **Can. 637 – The autonomous monasteries mentioned in can. 615 must render an account of their administration to the local ordinary once a year. Moreover, the local ordinary has the right to be informed about the financial reports of a religious house of diocesan right.**

This canon applies specifically the more general discipline of canon 636 §2. It identifies two religious communities which must report their financial administration to the local ordinary:

(1) the autonomous monasteries mentioned in canon 615[19] must render him an annual account of their administration;

Yuji Sugawara comments that the phrase "insofar as possible" allows consideration to be given to the size and nature of the community. He adds that, in case of necessity, it is possible to designate one finance officer for distinct groups or local communities. In "Amministrazione e alienazione dei beni temporali," pp. 260-261, fn. 12.

[19] Canon 615 defines an "autonomous monastery" and entrusts it to the special vigilance of the diocesan bishop: "An autonomous monastery which does not have another major superior besides its own moderator and is not associated to another institute of religious in such a way that the superior of the latter possesses true power over such

(2) religious houses of diocesan right must inform him about their finances.[20]

Although the canon speaks only of reports from religious *houses* of diocesan right, nothing prevents the local ordinary from requesting and receiving a comprehensive report concerning the administration of the entire religious institute of diocesan right.

The local ordinary has a close relation with these two kinds of institutes, evidenced also in the requirement that he must give written consent (*consensus in scriptis*) in certain cases of alienation (see canon 638 §4), notwithstanding the norm of canon 586 which establishes the just autonomy of life, especially of governance, in all religious institutes:

> **Can. 586 – §1. A just autonomy of life, especially of governance, is acknowledged for individual institutes, by which they possess their own discipline in the Church and are able to preserve their own patrimony intact, as mentioned in can. 578.**
>
> **§2. It is for local ordinaries to preserve and safeguard this autonomy.**

The law does not require religious institutes of pontifical right to give annual financial reports to the local ordinary.[21]

ACTS OF ORDINARY AND EXTRAORDINARY ADMINISTRATION; ALIENATION; TRANSACTIONS WORSENING PATRIMONIAL CONDITION

> **Can. 638 – §1. Within the scope of universal law, it belongs to proper law to determine acts which exceed the limit and manner of ordinary administration and to es-**

---

a monastery as determined by the constitutions is entrusted to the special vigilance of the diocesan bishop according to the norm of law."

[20] Canon 594 explains that, without prejudice to the norm of canon 586, "an institute of diocesan right remains under the special care of the diocesan bishop."

[21] See SACRED CONGREGATION FOR RELIGIOUS AND SECULAR INSTITUTES, Private Letter (September 30, 1972) in XAVERIUS OCHOA, *Leges ecclesiae*, vol. 5, n. 4143; *CLD*, vol. 9, p. 991.

tablish what is necessary to place an act of extraordinary administration validly.

§2. In addition to superiors, the officials who are designated for this in proper law also validly incur expenses and perform juridic acts of ordinary administration within the limits of their function.

§3. For the validity of alienation and of any other affair in which the patrimonial condition of a juridic person can worsen, the written permission of the competent superior with the consent of the council is required. Nevertheless, if it concerns an affair which exceeds the amount defined by the Holy See for each region, or things given to the Church by vow, or things precious for artistic or historical reasons, the permission of the Holy See itself is also required.

§4. For the autonomous monasteries mentioned in can. 615 and for institutes of diocesan right, it is also necessary to have the written consent of the local ordinary.

This canon is an adaptation and application of canons 1281 and 1291-1295 to religious institutes, provinces, and canonically erected houses. It addresses acts of ordinary administration (canon 638 §2), acts of extraordinary administration (canon 638 §1), transactions which can worsen the patrimonial condition of a juridic person (canon 638 §§3-4), and acts of alienation (canon 638 §§3-4).[22] The common law for religious institutes does not make reference to acts of ordinary administration more important in light of economic conditions, as the universal law does for dioceses (canon 1277).

ACTS OF EXTRAORDINARY ADMINISTRATION. Canon 638 §1 concerns extraordinary administration. It requires the proper law of a religious institute (1) to determine acts which exceed the limit[23] and

---

[22] See XAVERIUS OCHOA, "Acquisitio, distributio ac destinatio bonorum temporalium Ecclesiae institutorumque perfectionis ad mentem Concilii Vaticani II," in *Commentarium pro religiosis et missionariis*, 51 (1970), pp. 22-33.

[23] YUJI SUGAWARA comments that the limit (*finis*) of extraordinary administration must also take into account the spirit and proper purposes of religious institutes approved in the Church which reflect the proper ends for which they, as public juridic persons, possess and administer ecclesiastical goods (see canon 1254 §1). In "Amministrazione e alienazione dei beni temporali," pp. 257-258.

manner of ordinary administration, and (2) to establish the necessary formalities to place a valid act of extraordinary administration.[24] These two distinct determinations are for the religious institute, its provinces, and its canonically erected houses. The proper law defining these acts and formalities must be within the scope of the universal law. Velasio De Paolis comments about canon 638 §1:

> These norms of common law must be spelled out in the proper law of religious, specifying which are acts of ordinary administration and which are acts of extraordinary administration, when just the advice or when the consent of certain people or certain bodies is required, which is the authority competent to grant authorizations and how such authorizations are to be granted on various levels.[25]

Book V states that acts of extraordinary administration for dioceses are to be determined by the conference of bishops (canon 1277). Such acts for juridic persons subject to him are to be determined by the diocesan bishop after he receives the counsel of the finance council (canon 1281 §1). Such acts for other juridic persons are determined in their statutes (canon 1281 §1).

ACTS OF ORDINARY ADMINISTRATION. Canon 638 §2 concerns ordinary administration. It explains that incurring expenses and performing juridic acts of ordinary administration (within the limits of their function) can be performed validly by superiors and by other officials designated for such activity by proper law.[26] The finance officer may be a person so designated; others would likely

---

[24] See SUGAWARA, "Amministrazione e alienazione dei beni temporali," p. 259.

[25] DE PAOLIS, "Temporal Goods... Consecrated Life," p. 355.

[26] JORDAN F. HITE proposes who may be designated to perform acts of ordinary administration: "Those others than superiors who may perform acts of ordinary administration would be treasurers; investment officers or committees; fund-raisers; a president, chief executive officer, or director of a school, hospital, or retreat center. The officers should be named and the acts they can perform should be defined in the appropriate proper law or civil documents if applicable." In "Religious Institutes," p. 487.

be designated as well. The persons competent to perform acts of *extraordinary* administration must be defined clearly in proper law, as stated in canon 638 §1.

Canon 638 §2 gives superiors the right to perform acts of ordinary administration. While such acts of superiors are valid and licit, attention must be given to canon 636 §1 which requires the designation of a finance officer for each institute, province, and, insofar as possible, in local communities. Some would argue that the law does not envision that the superiors routinely perform acts of ordinary administration, though such acts would be both valid and licit; such routine acts would more appropriately be performed by finance officers.[27]

ACTS OF ALIENATION AND ACTS WHICH CAN WORSEN THE PATRIMONIAL CONDITION OF THE RELIGIOUS INSTITUTE. Canon 638 §3 concerns alienation and any transaction other than alienation which can worsen the patrimonial condition of a juridic person. It reflects the discipline of canons 1291-1295. It requires the written permission[28] of the competent superior (as determined by proper law) with the *consent* of the council[29] for the *validity* of alienation and of any other transaction in which the patrimonial condition of a juridic person can worsen.[30] Moreover, the canon requires the permission of

---

[27] See SUGAWARA, "Amministrazione e alienazione dei beni temporali," pp. 262-263.

[28] In some circumstances, depending on the amount and the level of governance involved, an act of alienation may require the written permission of more than one superior and consent of more than one council.

[29] The faculties of the competent superior, with the consent of the council and for a just cause, to alienate ecclesiastical goods of a religious institute were granted by the SECRETARIAT OF STATE, rescript *Cum admotae* (November 30, 1964), n. 9, in *AAS*, 56 (1964), pp. 374-378; *CLD*, vol. 6, pp. 147-152 (for cleric religious institutes of pontifical right); and the SACRED CONGREGATION FOR RELIGIOUS, decree *Religionum laicalium* (May 31,1966), in *AAS*, 59 (1967), pp. 362-364; *CLD*, vol. 6, pp. 153-156 (for male and female lay religious institutes of pontifical right). For related faculties granted to diocesan bishops, see POPE PAUL VI, apostolic letter *motu proprio Pastorale munus* (November 30, 1963), in *AAS*, 56 (1964), pp. 5-12; *CLD*, vol. 6, pp. 370-378.

[30] DANIEL J. WARD suggests that "[a]s a general rule, however, all indebtedness would be considered to have an adverse effect." Therefore, whenever a religious institute incurs significant indebtedness, its patrimonial condition can be worsened; the written permission of the competent superior with the consent of the council is required. In "Temporal Goods," p. 199.

the Holy See is also (*insuper*) needed *for validity* if it concerns:

1. a transaction that exceeds the amount defined by the Holy See;[31] or

2. goods given to the Church by a vow; or

3. goods precious for artistic or historical reasons.

For the information to be communicated to the Apostolic See when seeking the required permission to alienate goods of the religious institute, see the commentary on canon 1292.[32]

In addition, canon 638 §4 requires the written consent of the local ordinary if the religious institute is:

1. the autonomous monastery mentioned in canon 615; or

2. an institute of diocesan right.

In the case of the alienation of ecclesiastical goods of religious institutes of pontifical right, it has been the practice of the Congregation for Institutes of Consecrated Life and Societies of Apostolic Life to request a letter from the local diocesan bishop stating that he has no objection to the proposed transaction which would take place in his diocese (i.e., a *nihil obstat*).[33] If a religious institute of diocesan

---

[31] FRANCIS G. MORRISEY observes that if the Holy See has not determined the amount for a given region, the amount applied would properly be that established by the conference of bishops. He adds: "However, it often happens that a province is situated in one territory and the generalate in another, and that different maximum amounts have been authorized for each. Sometimes it is said that the generalate can authorize only the amount determined for the region where it is situated, even if at the provincial or local levels, a higher amount is in effect. However, in practice, it seems that the higher sum can be used, either that which is in effect in the territory where the alienation will take place, or that which applies in the territory of the generalate." In "Temporal Goods and Their Administration," p. 1683.

[32] See also JOAN DE LOURDES LEONARD, "Temporal Goods: Canons 634-640," in *A Handbook on Canons 537-746*, Jordan Hite, Sharon Holland, and Daniel Ward (eds.), Collegeville, The Liturgical Press, 1985, pp.108-111.

[33] CONGREGATION FOR INSTITUTES OF CONSECRATED LIFE AND SOCIETIES OF APOSTOLIC LIFE, Circular Letter (21 December 2004), Prot. N. 971/2004. ROBERT GEISINGER comments about this communication: "...always respecting the full autonomy of institute governance (which the *ordinarius loci* must honor) as regards the disposition of its own goods, the Congregation has established the practice of requesting the local ordinary's opinion of the proposed sale, even though this is not required by canon law (cann. 586-593; 634-638). Therefore, in the spirit of can. 1293 §2, the dicastery asks that the institute inform the local ordinary of the place of alienation so as to hear from him should he have any opinion, especially if he himself were to

right seeks to alienate its ecclesiastical goods situated in another diocese, it must present to the Apostolic See a letter of *consent* from the local ordinary of the general house, and a letter expressing the *nihil obstat* of the local ordinary where the asset to be alienated is located. Whether he is writing a letter of consent or a letter expressing his *nihil obstat*, the diocesan bishop should state clearly that he will assume no financial responsibility for the endeavor.[34]

APPLICATION OF CANON 638 §3 IN THE UNITED STATES AND CANADA. In the United States, the maximum amount for the alienation of ecclesiastical goods of religious institutes is the same as that for the dioceses of the United States.[35] In Canada, the same is true.[36]

---

have interest in acquiring the property for pastoral needs in his own diocese. This ideally serves not only the mutual relations between the institute and bishops, but also may lessen the risk of impoverishing the relative ecclesiastical patrimony." He adds that this circular letter "formalizes, explains, and publicizes a developing expectation which is now clearly a *praxis curiae* requirement." (p. 244, fn. 12)

[34] MORRISEY, "Temporal Goods and Their Administration," p. 1688.

[35] On March 25, 1992, Eduardo Cardinal Martínez Somalo, prefect of the Congregation for Institutes of Consecrated Life and Societies of Apostolic Life, and Archbishop Francisco Javier Errázuriz Ossa, secretary, responded to Sister Donna Markhan, O.P., president of the Leadership Conference of Women Religious, and Brother Paul Hennessey, C.F.C., president of the Conference of Major Superiors of Men (Prot. N. SpR275/73). This rescript was an affirmative reply to the request of the two presidents that the amount be raised from one million to three million dollars. In its reply, the officials of the congregation requested that the religious institutes continue to exercise discernment, good management, and prudence. They also asked that the religious institutes continue to consult the diocesan bishops in these matters. In CLSA, *Roman Replies and Advisory Opinions*, Kevin W. Vann and Lynn Jarrell (eds.), Washington, CLSA, 1992, p. 15.

Later, on December 5, 2003, Piergiorgio Silvano Nesti, C.P., secretary of the Congregation for Institutes of Consecrated Life and Societies of Apostolic Life, responded to Sister Constance Phelps, SUL, president of the Leadership Conference of Women Religious (Prot. N. AG 126-2/03) that the amount was raised to five million dollars. He added, "This includes the annual adjustment linked to the consumer price index, as explained. Since the new limits go into effect for the dioceses in January 1, 2004, it seems appropriate that this authorization also go into effect at the same time." In CLSA, *Roman Replies and Advisory Opinions*, F. Stephen Pedone and James I. Donlon (eds.), Alexandria, CLSA, 2005, p. 14.

[36] This is assured through a telephone call to the secretariat of the CCCB on Friday, August 31, 2007.

DEBTS OF RELIGIOUS INSTITUTES AND THEIR MEMBERS

Can. 639 – §1. If a juridic person has contracted debts and obligations even with the permission of the superiors, it is bound to answer for them.

§2. If a member has entered into a contract concerning his or her own goods with the permission of the superior, the member must answer for it, but if the business of the institute was conducted by mandate of the superior, the institute must answer.

§3. If a religious has entered into a contract without any permission of superiors, he or she must answer, but not the juridic person.

§4. It is a fixed rule, however, that an action can always be brought against one who has profited from the contract entered into.

§5. Religious superiors are to take care that they do not permit debts to be contracted unless it is certain that the interest on the debt can be paid off from ordinary income and that the capital sum can be paid off through legitimate amortization within a period that is not too long.

Canon 639 §§1-3 concerns accountability for debts and obligations:

1. If a juridic person has contracted debts and obligations, even with the permission of the superiors: the juridic person is accountable.

    This would apply if a religious province has incurred debts and obligations with the permission of the provincial superior. The province, not the entire institute, is responsible.

2. If a member has entered into a contract concerning his or her personal goods with the permission of the superior: the member is accountable.[37]

---

[37] GEISINGER, pp. 246-258, discusses a variety of personnel issues regarding individual religious: debts of candidates and persons in formation, personal wealth of religious and those in formation, goods acquired in religious life, wills and testaments, administration of temporal goods of externs, accountability in particular circumstances, finances of members absent with or without permission, poverty violations as cause for dismissal from the institute, infirmity and possible dismissal, etc.

3. If a member has conducted business of the institute by mandate
    of the superior: the institute is accountable.

    This is an application of canons 1281 §3 (see also canons
    1289 and 1296). Rosemary Smith comments on the complexi-
    ties which may be involved in this situation: "The canonical
    principal is deceptively simple as stated but may have serious
    ramifications. For instance, if a member of the institute is as-
    signed or missioned to a particular apostolate by the superior,
    it is sometimes difficult to distinguish between actions and li-
    ability for which the institute is responsible and those for which
    the individual member is responsible. Civil actions seeking res-
    titution and/or damages have varied considerably in assigning
    responsibility. The proper law of the institute should distinguish
    clearly between personal and institutional responsibility."[38]

4. If a member has entered a contract without any permission of
    superiors: the member is accountable.

    Canon 639 §4 mentions the fixed rule that an action can always
    be brought against one who has profited from a contract which was
    entered into. This is an application of canons 1281 §3 and 1296.

    Canon 639 §5 admonishes religious superiors not to allow debts
    to be contracted unless it is certain that:

1. the interest on the debt can be paid off from ordinary income;
    and

2. the capital debt can be paid off through legitimate amortization
    within a period that is not too long.

    This is an application of canon 1284 §2, 5° and an effort to
    avoid a transaction which can worsen the patrimonial condition of a
    religious institute (see canon 1295). The canon leaves it to the prudent
    judgment of the superior to determine the length of a given loan. The
    superior, of course, will take into consideration the importance of
    the temporal good for whose purchase the loan is proposed.

---

[38] SMITH, p. 805. Attention should be given to assure proper liability insurance coverage.

COLLECTIVE WITNESS TO CHARITY AND POVERTY

Can. 640 – Taking into account local conditions, institutes are to strive to give, as it were, a collective witness of charity and poverty and are to contribute according to their ability something from their own goods to provide for the needs of the Church and the support of the poor.

Canon 640 says that, aware of local conditions, religious institutes should strive to give collective witness of charity and poverty. In addition, they are to contribute as they can to provide for the needs of the Church and the support of the poor. This canon must be understood in light of canon 1285, which permits administrators, within the limits of ordinary administration, to make donations for the sake of piety and Christian charity only from movable goods not belonging to stable patrimony.

SUPPRESSION OF INSTITUTES OF CONSECRATED LIFE AND ALLOCATION OF THEIR TEMPORAL GOODS

Can. 584 – The suppression of an institute pertains only to the Apostolic See; a decision regarding the temporal goods of an institute is also reserved to the Apostolic See.

Canon 584 concerns the suppression of any institute of consecrated life (i.e., both religious institutes and secular institutes). The suppression pertains exclusively to the Apostolic See, whether the institute is of pontifical or diocesan right. Likewise, the allocation of the ecclesiastical goods of a suppressed institute of consecrated life also pertains to the Apostolic See.

This canon relates to canon 123 which says that upon the extinction of a public juridic person (e.g., an institute of consecrated life), the allocation of its goods, patrimonial rights, and obligations is governed by universal law (i.e., canon 584) and its statutes. Obviously, the Apostolic See will take into account the intention of donors and acquired rights, also in accord with canon 123.

SUPPRESSION OF RELIGIOUS HOUSES AND ALLOCATION OF
THEIR TEMPORAL GOODS

**Can. 616 – §1. The supreme moderator can suppress
a legitimately erected religious house according to the
norm of the constitutions, after the diocesan bishop has
been consulted. The proper law of the institute is to make
provision for the goods of the suppressed house, without
prejudice to the intentions of the founders or donors or
to legitimately acquired rights.**

**§2. The suppression of the only house of an institute
belongs to the Holy See, to which the decision regarding
the goods in that case is also reserved.**

**§3. To suppress the autonomous house mentioned in
can. 613 belongs to the general chapter, unless the constitutions state otherwise.**

**§4. To suppress an autonomous monastery of nuns
belongs to the Apostolic See, with due regard to the prescripts of the constitutions concerning its goods.**

Canon 616 provides legislation on the suppression of religious
houses and monasteries and the allocation of their goods upon suppression. Four distinct scenarios are addressed:

1. When the only religious house of a religious institute is to be
    suppressed, the suppression must be done by the Holy See which
    also decides on the allocation of its ecclesiastical goods (canon
    616 §2).

2. When a religious house of canons regular or of monks under
    the governance and care of its own moderator (i.e., the autono-
    mous house mentioned in canon 613) is to be suppressed, the
    suppression is done by general chapter, unless the constitutions
    state otherwise (canon 616 §3).

3. When an autonomous monastery of nuns is to be suppressed, the
    suppression must be done by the Holy See, and the constitution
    of the monastery governs the allocation of its goods (canon 616
    §4).

4. When any other religious house is to be suppressed, the sup-

pression is done by the supreme moderator (in accord with the constitution of the religious institute and after the diocesan bishop has been consulted), and the proper law of the institute is to be observed in the allocation of its ecclesiastical goods (canon 616 §1).

Canon 616 §1 specifically states that, in the suppression of a religious house other than the only one of the institute, to be observed are the intentions of the founders or donors and any legitimately acquired rights. These intentions and rights must also be observed in the other scenarios addressed in canon 616 §§2-4, in conformity with the legislation on the extinction of any juridic person provided in canon 123.

TEMPORAL GOODS AND SECULAR INSTITUTES

Can. 718 – The administration of the goods of an institute, which must express and foster evangelical poverty, is governed by the norms of Book V, *The Temporal Goods of the Church*, and by the proper law of the institute. Likewise, proper law is to define the obligations of the institute, especially financial ones, towards members who carry on work for it.

Canon 718 is the only canon which concerns the temporal goods of secular institutes.[39] It says simply that the administration of the goods of a secular institute must express and foster evangelical poverty, and this administration is governed by the norms of *Book V, The Temporal Goods of the Church*.[40] Sharon Holland observes that while this canon makes reference to evangelical poverty, such poverty "is not to be equated with the collective witness expected of

---

[39] Canon 710 defines a *secular institute*: "A secular institute is an institute of consecrated life in which the Christian faithful, living in the world, strive for the perfection of charity and seek to contribute to the sanctification of the world, especially from within."

[40] See FABIO MARINI, "Gli istituti secolari: amministrazione dei beni temporali e personalità giuridica (can. 718)," in *Quaderni di diritto ecclesiale*, 20 (2007), pp. 402-414.

religious institutes [canon 640]. Because of the whole manner of life and ministry of secular institutes, they are less likely to own many houses, institutions, or designated funds than religious institutes which require these to support their members."[41]

The canon adds that the proper law of each secular institute is to define the financial (and other) obligations of the secular institute toward members who work for it. Such proper law would especially address the sustenance of members "engaged full-time in internal services or works of the institute."[42]

TEMPORAL GOODS AND SOCIETIES OF APOSTOLIC LIFE

> **Can. 741 – §1. Societies and, unless the constitutions determine otherwise, their parts and houses are juridic persons and, as such, capable of acquiring, possessing, administering, and alienating temporal goods according to the norms of the prescripts of Book V, *The Temporal Goods of the Church*, of cann. 636, 638, and 639, and of proper law.**
>
> **§2. According to the norm of proper law, members are also capable of acquiring, possessing, administering, and disposing of temporal goods, but whatever comes to them on behalf of the society is acquired by the society.**

This is the only canon which concerns the temporal goods of societies of apostolic life[43] and their members.

Canon 741 §1 explains that societies of apostolic life and, unless the constitutions say otherwise, their parts and houses are juridic persons *ipso iure* (see canon 114 §1). Since this is so, they are able

---

[41] SHARON HOLLAND, "Secular Institutes," in *New Commentary on the Code of Canon Law*, commissioned by the CLSA, John P. Beal, James A. Coriden, and Thomas J. Green (eds.), New York, Paulist, 2000, p. 879.

[42] Ibid.

[43] Canon 731 §1 defines *societies of apostolic life*: "Societies of apostolic life resemble institutes of consecrated life; their members, without religious vows, pursue the apostolic purpose proper to the society and, leading a life in common as brothers or sisters according to their proper manner of life, strive for the perfection of charity through the observance of the constitutions."

to acquire, possess, administer, and alienate temporal goods. These actions are to be done according to:

1.   the norms of *Book V, The Temporal Goods of the Church,*
2.   the norms of canons 636, 638, and 639, and
3.   the proper law of the society itself.

Canon 741 §2 says that, according to the proper law of the society, its members also are able to acquire, possess, administer, and alienate their personal temporal goods. Anything coming to members on behalf of the society, however, is acquired by the society.

REFERENCES TO TEMPORAL GOODS OUTSIDE BOOK V

The following table lists those canons related to temporal goods which are located outside of *Book V* of the *Code of Canon Law.*

Canon	Description
121	allocation of goods when juridic persons are merged
122	allocation of goods when a juridic person is divided
123	allocation of goods when a juridic person becomes extinct
191 §1	an office holder being transferred receives remuneration from the current office until taking possession of the new office
222	obligation of all the faithful to assist the needs of the Church
231 §2	remuneration (*remuneratio*) of lay persons who serve the Church
263	provision is to be made to maintain the seminary, support the students, pay the teachers, and meet other seminary needs
264	special collection for the seminary; diocesan tax for the seminary
281	clergy remuneration and benefits
282 §2	clerics are to use their excess goods for the good of the Church and works of charity
285 §4	restrictions on clergy involvement with secular goods (management, providing surety, signing promissory notes)
286	restrictions on clergy involvement in business or trade
319	administration of temporal goods of public associations of the Christian faithful

325	administration of temporal goods of private associations of the Christian faithful
326 §2	allocation of temporal goods of an extinct private association of the Christian faithful
392 §2	duty of the diocesan bishop to exercise vigilance over the administration of goods
418 §2, 2°	a bishop being transferred receives his entire remuneration from his current diocese until he takes canonical possession of the new diocese
492	composition of the diocesan finance council
493	functions of the diocesan finance council
494	appointment and functions of the diocesan finance officer
510 §4	presumption that alms given to a church which is both parochial and capitular are given to the parish
531	presumption that offerings given when a certain function is performed belong to the parish; the diocesan bishop is competent to establish prescripts for the allocation of these offerings and the remuneration of clergy fulfilling the same function
532	pastor as legal representative of the parish, and his responsibility to take care that parochial ecclesiastical goods are administered according to canons 1281-1288
537	parish finance council
551	application of canon 531 to parochial vicars
584	the Apostolic See decides on the destination of the ecclesiastical goods of a suppressed institute of consecrated life
616	allocation of the goods of suppressed religious houses and monasteries
634-640	temporal goods of religious institutes
668	personal goods of individual religious
670	obligation of a religious institute to provide for the needs of its members
672	application of canons 285-286 to members of religious institutes
681 §4	the contract between the diocesan bishop and competent religious superior is to address economic matters
702	obligation of a religious institute to departing members

718	temporal goods of secular institutes
741	temporal goods of societies of apostolic life and their members
791, 4°	annual offering for the missions
848	limits on offerings for administration of the sacraments
945-958	Mass offerings
1181	funeral offerings
1333 §4	restitution of revenue and benefits received illegitimately by a suspended cleric
1350 §1	provision of decent support for a penalized cleric who is not dismissed from the clerical state
1350 §2	provision for a person dismissed from the clerical state who is truly in need because of the penalty
1375	facultative penalty for those who impede the legitimate use of sacred goods
1377	preceptive penalty for alienation of ecclesiastical goods without permission
1380	preceptive penalty for celebrating or receiving a sacrament through simony
1385	preceptive penalty for illegitimate profit-making from Mass offerings
1386	preceptive penalty for bribery
1419 §2	competent tribunal for cases involving temporal goods represented by the bishop
1489	fines for advocates and procurators accepting financial (and other) favors
1649	judicial expenses and gratuitous legal assistance
1715 §2	norms on alienation of ecclesiastical goods are to be observed in agreements and compromises (i.e., in actions entered to avoid trials)
1741, 5°	poor administration of temporal affairs with grave damage to the Church as a reason for legitimate removal of a pastor

THE ACTION OF COMPETENT AUTHORITIES INVOLVING ECCLESIASTICAL GOODS IN BOOK V

The following tables list those canons on temporal goods which identify a number of instances when the competent authority can or must take some action.[1]

CONFERENCE OF BISHOPS[2]

CANON	ACTION
1262	to establish norms governing appeals
1265 §2	to establish norms for begging for alms to be observed by all, including mendicants
1272	to direct the governance of benefices, where they exist, through norms agreed to and approved by the Apostolic See, so that gradually the income and, insofar as possible, the endowment are gradually transferred to the "institute for clergy support" (canon 1274 §1)
1274 §2	to take care that there is an institute to provide for the social security of clerics where social provision for them does not yet exist
1274 §4	to establish an appropriate association for various dioceses or its whole territory to fulfill the diocesan obligations mentioned in canon 1274 §§ 2-3

---

[1] See SCHOUPPE, pp. 176-179, 183-187.

[2] On November 8, 1983, before the revised Code became operative, Agostino Cardinal Casaroli, Secretary of State, communicated with the presidents of the world's conferences of bishops reminding them of the need to develop particular legislation as required by the 1983 Code. He made specific reference to several canons in *Book V* for which particular legislation *must* be made: canons 1262, 1272, 1277, 1292 §1, 1297. In *Communicationes*, 15 (1983), pp. 135-139; *CLD*, vol. 11, pp. 5-8.

1277	to define acts of extraordinary diocesan administration
1292 §1	to define the minimum and maximum amounts for alienation
1297	to establish norms for leasing Church goods

DIOCESAN BISHOP

CANON	ACTION
1261 §1	to admonish the faithful of their obligation to assist the needs of the Church, and to urge them to fulfill it (see canon 222 §1)
1263	to hear the diocesan finance council and the presbyteral council before imposing a moderate tax, proportionate to their income, for diocesan needs upon public juridic persons subject to him
1263	to hear the diocesan finance council and the presbyteral council before imposing an extraordinary and moderate exaction, in case of grave necessity, upon other physical and juridic persons
1271	to assist in procuring those means which the Apostolic See needs in order to offer service properly to the universal Church
1274 §1	to establish a special institute to collect goods or offerings to support the clerics who serve the diocese, unless this is provided in some other way
1274 §3	to establish a common fund to satisfy obligations for persons (other than clerics) who serve the Church, to meet various diocesan needs, and to assist poorer dioceses
1277	to obtain the counsel of the diocesan finance council and the college of consultors to place acts of administration which are more important in light of the economic condition of the diocese
1277	to obtain the consent of the diocesan finance council and the college of consultors to place acts of extraordinary diocesan administration (as such acts are defined by the conference of bishops)
1278	to entrust to the diocesan finance officer, if he so chooses, (1) the vigilance over administration over all goods belonging to public juridic persons subject to him (canon 1276 §1), and (2) the power to appoint suitable physical persons to

	administer the goods of public juridic persons subject to him if no other administrator is identified by law, the charter of the foundation, or the statutes (canon 1279 §2)
1281 §1	to define acts that exceed the limit and manner of ordinary administration for juridic persons subject to him, after he has heard the finance council, if their statutes are silent
1292 §1	to receive the consent of the diocesan finance council, the college of consultors, and those concerned, when the value of the stable patrimony to be alienated is between the minimum and maximum amounts set by the conference of bishops and when the object belongs to the diocese, or to a juridic person subject to the diocesan bishop (see canon 1295)
1308 §3	to reduce Masses independently founded in legacies or in any other way to the level of offering legitimately established in the diocese, as long as diminished revenues exist, provided there is no one obliged to increase the offering who can effectively be made to do so
1308 §4	to reduce the obligations or legacies of Masses binding an ecclesiastical institute if the revenue has become insufficient to pursue appropriately the proper purpose of the institute

PROVINCIAL BISHOPS

CANON	ACTION
1264, 1°	to fix the fees for acts of executive power granting a favor or for the execution of rescripts of the Apostolic See (these fees are to be approved by the Apostolic See)
1264, 2°	to set a limit on the offerings on the occasion of the administration of sacraments and sacramentals

LOCAL ORDINARY

CANON	ACTION
1265	to give written permission for any private person (physical or juridic), without prejudice to the right of religious mendicants, to beg for alms for any pious or ecclesiastical institute or purpose, according to norms established by the conference of bishops
1266	to order a special collection for specific parochial, diocesan, national, or universal purposes to be gathered in all churches and oratories which are, in fact, habitually open to the faithful, including those of religious institutes

| 1287 §1 | to receive an annual report from clerical and lay administrators of any ecclesiastical goods not exempt from the power of governance of the diocesan bishop; the local ordinary is to present it for examination to the diocesan finance council |

ONE'S OWN ORDINARY

CANON	ACTION
1265 §1	to give written permission for any private person (physical or juridic), without prejudice to the right of religious mendicants, to beg for alms for any pious or ecclesiastical institute or purpose, and according to norms established by the conference of bishops
1288	to give written permission for administrators to initiate or contest civil litigation in the name of a public juridic person

ORDINARY

CANON	ACTION
1267 §2	to give permission, in matters of greater importance, to refuse offerings which are given to a public juridic person
1267 §2	to give permission for a public juridic person to accept offerings burdened by a modal obligation
1276 §1	to exercise careful vigilance over the administration of all goods belonging to public juridic persons subject to him
1276 §2	to issue special instructions, within the limits of universal and particular law, for the entire matter of the administration of ecclesiastical goods
1279 §1	to intervene in the case of negligence by an administrator
1279 §2	to appoint suitable physical persons to administer the goods of public juridic persons subject to him if no other administrator is identified by law, the charter of the foundation, or the statutes
1281 §1	to give the written faculty for administrators validly to place acts exceeding ordinary administration
1283, 3°	to receive the oath of office before the administrator begins to function that he or she will administer well and faithfully
1284 §2, 6°	to give consent for an administrator to invest money which remains after expenses and which can be set aside usefully for the purposes of the juridic person

1301 §1	to be the executor of all pious wills, whether *mortis causa* or *inter vivos*
1301 §2	to exercise vigilance that pious wills are fulfilled, and to receive an account from other executors when they have completed this function
1302 §1	to be informed when one has accepted goods in trust for pious causes, with an indication of its movable and immovable goods and the obligations attached
1302 §2	to demand that goods held in trust are safeguarded
1302 §2	to exercise vigilance for the execution of pious wills (see canon 1301)
1304 §1	to give written permission for a juridic person to accept a non-autonomous foundation validly
1305 §1	to render prudent judgment, after hearing those concerned and his own finance council, on the investment of money and movable goods assigned to the endowment of a pious foundation
1308 §2	to reduce Mass obligations because of diminished revenues if this power is expressly given in the charters of the foundations
1309	to transfer, for an appropriate cause, the obligations of Masses to days, churches, or altars different from those determinated in foundations
1310 §1	to reduce, moderate, or commute the wills of the faithful for pious causes, for a just and necessary cause, if the founder has expressly entrusted this power to him
1310 §2	to lessen obligations (other than Mass obligations) imposed by founders when their fulfillment, through no fault of the administrators, has become impossible because of diminished revenue; the ordinary must first hear those concerned and his own finance council, and must intend to preserve the intention of the founder as much as possible

TABLE OF CORRESPONDING CANONS[1]

1983 CIC	1990 CCEO	1917 CIC
1254 §1	1007	1495 §1
1254 §2	1007	1496
1255	1009 §1	1495 §2
1256	1008 §2	1499 §2
1257 §1	1009 §2	1497 §1
1257 §2	x	x
1258	x	1498
1259	1010	1499 §1
1260	1011	1496
1261 §1	x	1513
1261 §2	x	x
1262	x	x
1263	1012	1504, 1506
1264	1013 §1	1507 §1
1265 §1	1015	1503

---

[1]   The identification of corresponding canons of the 1917 code and the 1983 code are taken, for the most part, from *Codex iuris canonici, auctoritate Ioannis Pauli II promulgatus, fontium annotatione et indice analytico-alphabetico auctus*, Libreria editrice Vaticana, 1989, pp. 341-356; English translation *Code of Canon Law: Latin-English Edition*, prepared under the auspices of the CLSA, Washington, CLSA, 1999, p. 645.

1983 CIC	1990 CCEO	1917 CIC
1265 §2	x	1624
1266	1014	1505
1267 §1	1016 §2	1536 §1
1267 §2	1016 §3	1536 §2
1267 §3	1016 §1	x
1268	1017	1508, 1509
1269	1018	1510
1270	1019	1511
1271	x	x
1272	x	x
1273	1008 §1	1518
1274 §1	1021 §1	x
1274 §2	1021 §2	x
1274 §3	1021 §3	x
1274 §4	x	x
1274 §5	x	x
1275	x	x
1276	1022	1519
1277	263 §4	1520 §3
1278	x	x
1279 §1	1023	1182 §2
1279 §2	x	1521 §1
1280	x	x
1281 §1	1024 §1	1527 §1
1281 §2	1024 §2	x
1281 §3	1024 §3	1527 §2
1282	x	1521 §2
1283	1025-1026	1522
1284 §1	1028 §1	1523
1284 §2, 1°	1028 §2, 1°	1523, 1°

1983 CIC	1990 CCEO	1917 CIC
1284 §2, 2°	1020 §1	x
1284 §2, 3°	1028 §2, 2°	1523, 2°
1284 §2, 4°	1028 §2, 3°	1523, 3°
1284 §2, 5°	1028 §2, 4°	x
1284 §2, 6°	1028 §2, 5°	1523, 4°
1284 §2, 7°	1028 §2, 6°	1523, 5°
1284 §2, 8°	1028 §2, 7°	x
1284 §2, 9°	1028 §2, 8°	1523, 6°
1284 §3	1028 §3	x
1285	1029	1535
1286	1030	1524
1287	1031	1525
1288	1032	1526
1289	1033	1528
1290	1034	1529
1291	1035 §1, 3°	1530 §1, 3°
1292 §1	1036 §1	1532 §3
1292 §2	1036 §4	1532 §1
1292 §3	1038 §2	1532 §4
1292 §4	1038 §1	x
1293	1035 §1, 1°-2°, §2	1530, §1, 1°-2°, §3
1294 §1	x	1531 §1
1294 §2	x	1531 §3
1295	1042	1533
1296	1040	1534 §1
1297	-x	1541
1298	1041	1540
1299	1043	1513
1300	1044	1514
1301	1045	1515

1983 CIC	1990 CCEO	1917 CIC
1302	1046	1516
1303 §1, 1°	1047 §1, 1°	1489 §1
1303 §1, 2°	1047 §1, 2°	1544 §1
1303 §2	1047 §2	x
1304 §1	1048 §2	1546
1304 §2	1048 §3	1545
1305	1049	1547
1306	1050 §2	1548
1307	1051	1549
1308 §1	1052 §1	1551 §1
1308 §2	1052 §2	x
1308 §3	1052 §3	x
1308 §4	1052 §4	x
1308 §5	1052 §5	x
1309	1053	x
1310 §1	1054 §1	1517 §1
1310 §2	1054 §2	1517 §2
1310 §3	1054 §3	x

BIBLIOGRAPHY

Primary Sources

Acta Apostolicae Sedis, Rome, 1909-present.

CANADIAN CONFERENCE OF CATHOLIC BISHOPS, *Complementary Norms to the 1983 Code of Canon Law*, Ottawa: CCCB, 1996.

Codex canonum Ecclesiarum orientalium, auctoritate Ioannis Pauli PP. II promulgatus, fontium annotatione auctus, Libreria editrice Vaticana, 1995; English translation *Code of Canons of the Eastern Churches: Latin-English Edition, New English Translation*, prepared under the auspices of the CLSA, Washington: CLSA, 2001.

Codex iuris canonici, auctoritate Ioannis Pauli II promulgatus, fontium annotatione et indice analytico-alphabetico auctus, Libreria editrice Vaticana, 1989; English translation *Code of Canon Law: Latin-English Edition*, prepared under the auspices of the CLSA, Washington: CLSA, 1999.

Codex iuris canonici Pii X Pontificis Maximi iussu digestus Benedicti Papae XV auctoritate promulgatus, Typis polyglottis Vaticanis, 1917; English translation EDWARD N. PETERS (ed.), *The 1917 Pio-Benedictine Code of Canon Law*, San Francisco:Ignatius Press, 2001.

CONGREGATION FOR BISHOPS, *Directory for the Pastoral Ministry of Bishops,* Vatican City State: Libreria editrice Vaticana, 2004.

CONGREGATION FOR THE CLERGY, Decree *Mos igitur*, Regulations on the Stipends Accepted by a Priest for the Celebration of Masses (February 22, 1991), in *AAS*, 83 (1991), pp. 443-446; English translation in *Origins,* 20 (1990-1991), pp. 705-706.

CONGREGATION FOR RELIGIOUS AND SECULAR INSTITUTES, letter, *Criteria de notitiis ad statum et vitam religiosorum et societatum vitae apostolicae spectantibus, quae cum Sede Apostolica, quibus temporis intervalis, communicanda sunt* (January 2, 1988), in *AAS*, 80 (1988), pp. 104-105.

ITALIAN EPISCOPAL CONFERENCE, "Istruzione in materia amministrativa (2005)," testo approvato dalla 54a Assemblea Generale, Roma (May 30-31, 2005).

JOHN PAUL II, apostolic constitution *Sacrae disciplinae leges*, in *AAS*, 75:2 (1983), pp. vi-xiv; English translation, *Code of Canon Law: Latin-English Edition*, prepared under the auspices of the CLSA, Washington: CLSA, 1999, pp. xxvii-xxxii.

JOHN PAUL II, apostolic constitution on the Roman Curia *Pastor bonus*, (June 28, 1988), in *AAS*, 80 (1088), pp. 841-930; English translation in *Code of Canon Law: Latin-English Edition*, prepared under the auspices of the CLSA, Washington: CLSA, 1999, pp. 679-751.

NATIONAL CONFERENCE OF CATHOLIC BISHOPS, *Implementation of the 1983 Code of Canon Law: Complementary Norms*, Washington: NCCB, 1991.

PAUL VI, *motu proprio Ecclesiae sanctae, Normae ad quaedam exequenda SS. Concilii Vaticani II Decreta statuuntur* (August 6, 1966), in *AAS*, 58 (1966), pp. 757-787; English translation in *CLD*, vol. 6, pp. 264-298.

PAUL VI, apostolic letter *motu proprio Firma in traditione* (June 13, 1974), *AAS*, 66 (1974), pp. 308-311; English translation in *CLD*, vol. 8, pp. 531-533.

PAUL VI, apostolic letter *motu proprio Pastorale munus* (November 30, 1963), in *AAS*, 56 (1964) pp. 5-12; English translation in *CLD*, vol. 6, pp. 370-378.

PONTIFICAL COMMISSION FOR THE REVISION OF THE CODE OF CANON LAW, *Codex Iuris Canonici, Schema Novissimum post consultationem S.R.E. Cardinalium, episcoporum conferentiarum, dicasteriorum curiae romanae, universitatum facultatumque ecclesiarum necnon superiorum institutorum vitae consecratae recognitum, iuxta placita Patrum Commissionis deinde emendatum atque Summo pontifici praesentatum*, Vatican City, 1982.

_____ *Relatio: complectens synthesim animadversionem ab Emm.mis atque Exc.mis patribus commissionis ad novissimum schema Codicis Iuris Canonici exhibitarum, cum responsibus a secre-*

taria et consultoribus datis, Vatican City State: Typis polyglottis Vaticanis, 1981.

_____ *Schema Codicis Iuris Canonici, iuxta animadversiones S.R.E. Cardinalium, episcoporum conferentiarum, dicasteriorum curiae romanae, universitatem facultatumque ecclesiarum necnon superiorum institutorum vitae consecratae recognitum,* Vatican City State: Typis polyglottis Vaticanis, 1980.

_____ *Schema canonum libri V: De iure patrimoniali Ecclesiae,* Vatican City State: Typis polyglottis Vaticanis, 1977.

_____ (1971-1983), PONTIFICAL COMMISSION FOR THE AUTHENTIC INTERPRETATION THE CODE OF CANON LAW(1984-1989), PONTIFICAL COUNCIL FOR THE INTERPRETATION OF LEGISLATIVE TEXTS (1989-1999), PONTIFICAL COUNCIL FOR LEGISLATIVE TEXTS (1999-present), "Coetus studiorum 'De bonis Ecclesiae temporalibus,'" in *Communicationes,* 5 (1973), pp. 94-13; 9 (1977) pp. 273; 12 (1980), pp. 388-435; 16 (1984), pp. 27-37; 36 (2004), pp. 236-333; 37 (2005), pp. 116-138, 186-303.

PONTIFICAL COUNCIL FOR THE INTERPRETATION OF LEGISLATIVE TEXTS. *Congregatio Plenaria diebus 20-29 octobris 1981 habita,* Vatican City State: Typis polyglottis Vaticanis, 1991.

PONTIFICAL COUNCIL FOR LEGISLATIVE TEXTS. *Decretum* De recursu super congrugentia inter legem particularem et normam codicalem [Recourse against a general decree which establishes a diocesan *tributum*] (February 8, 2000), in *Communicationes,* 32 (2000), pp. 15-23. Commentary by Jesús Miñambres, in *Ius Ecclesiae,* 13 (2001), pp. 271-276.

_____ *Decretum* De recursu super congrugentia inter legem particularem et normam codicalem [Recourse against diocesan norms on the clergy remuneration fund] (April 29, 2000), in *Communicationes,* 32 (2000), pp. 162-167.

_____ Instruction *Dignitas connubii,* Vatican City: Libreria editrice Vaticano, 2005.

_____ *Nota* La funzione dell'autorità ecclesiastica sui beni ecclesiastici (February 12, 2004), in *Communicationes,* 36 (2004), pp. 24-32.

_____ *Nota* Elementi per configurare l'ambito di responsabilità canonica del Vescovo diocesano nei riguardi dei presbyteri incardinati nella propria diocesi e che esercitano nella medesima il loro ministero (February 12, 2004), in *Communicationes*, 36 (2004), pp. 33-38; unofficial English translation in *Studies in Church Law*, 3 (2007), pp. 29-39.

_____ *Nota* La 'recognitio' nei documenti della Sancta Sede (April 28, 2006), in *Communicationes*, 38 (2006), pp. 10-17.

SACRED CONGREGATION FOR RELIGIOUS, decree *Religionum laicalium* (May 31,1966), in *AAS*, 59 (1967), pp. 362-364; English translation in *CLD*, vol. 6, pp. 153-156.

SECOND VATICAN COUNCIL, Declaration on Religious Liberty *Dignitatis humanae* (December 7, 1965), in *AAS*, 58 (1966), pp. 929-941; English translation in FLANNERY 1, pp. 799-812.

_____ Decree on the Ministry and Life of Priests *Presbyterorum ordinis* (December 7, 1965), in *AAS*, 58 (1966), pp. 991-1024; English translation in FLANNERY 1, pp. 863-902.

SECRETARIAT OF STATE, rescript *Cum admotae* (November 30, 1964), in *AAS*, 56 (1964), pp. 374-378; English translation in *CLD*, vol. 6, pp. 147-152.

SYNOD OF BISHOPS, document *Convenientes ex universo,* Justice in the World (November 30, 1971) in *AAS,* 63 (1971), pp. 923-942; English translation in *Origins,* 1 (1971-1972), p. 383, 385-386, 393-398, FLANNERY 2, pp. 695-710.

_____ document *Ultimis temporibus*, Ministerial Priesthood (November 30, 1967), in *AAS*, 63 (1971), pp. 898-922; English translation in FLANNERY 2, pp. 672-694.

_____ "Final Report," (1985) in *Origins*, 15 (1985-1986), pp. 444-450.

Books/Commentaries

ABBAS, JOBE. *The Consecrated Life: A Comparative Commentary on the Eastern and Latin Codes*, Ottawa: Saint Paul University, 2008.

ABBO, JOHN A. and JEROME D. HANNAN. *The Sacred Canons: A Concise Presentation of the Current Disicplinary Norms of the Church*, 2 vols., Saint Louis: B. Herder Book Co., 1952.

ANZAR GIL, FEDERICO R. *La Administración de los Bienes Temporales de la Iglesia*, 2nd rev. ed., Salamanca: Universidad de Salamanca, 1993.

ARRIETA, JUAN I. (ed.). *Enti ecclesiastici e controllo dello stato: Studi sull'Istruzione CEI in materia amministrativa*, Istituto di Diritto Canonico San Pio X, Study N. 5, Venice: Marcianum Press, 2007.

BEAL, JOHN P., JAMES A. CORIDEN, and THOMAS J. GREEN (eds.). *New Commentary on the Code of Canon Law*, commissioned by The CLSA, New York: Paulist Press, 2000.

BEGUS, CRISTIAN. *Diritto patrioniale canonico*, Vatican City: Lateran University Press, 2007.

BOUSCAREN, T. LINCOLN, ADAM ELLIS, and FRANCIS N. KORTH. *Canon Law: A Text and Commentary*, 4th rev. ed., Milwaukee: Bruce Publishing Co., 1963.

CATHOLIC HEALTH ASSOCIATION. *The Search for Identity: Canonical Sponsorship of Catholic Healthcare*, Saint Louis: CHA, 1993.

COGAN, PATRICK (ed.). *CLSA Advisory Opinions, 1984-1993*, Washington: CLSA, 1995.

CONN, JAMES and LUIGI SABBARESE (eds.). *Iustitia in caritate: Miscellanea di studi in onore di Velasio de Paolis*, Rome: Urbaniana University Press, 2005.

CONSORTI, PARLOG. *La remunerazione del clero. Dal sistema beneficiale agli Istituti per sostentamento del clero*, Torino: Ed. Giapphichelli, 2000.

CORIDEN, JAMES A., THOMAS J. GREEN and DONALD HEINTSCHEL (eds.). *The Code of Canon Law: A Text and Commentary*, commissioned by the CLSA, New York: Paulist Press, 1985.

DE PAOLIS, VELASIO. *De bonis Ecclesiae temporalibus: Adnotationes in Codicem, Liber V*, Rome: Gregorian University, 1986.

_____ *I beni temporali della Chiesa*, Bologna: Dehoniane, 1995.

DINGAN, PATRICIA J. *A History of the Legal Incorporation of Catholic Church Property in the United States, 1784-1932*, Washington: The Catholic University of America, 1933.

DOHENY, WILLIAM J. *Practical Problems in Church Finances: A Study of the Alienation of Church Resources and the Canonical Restrictions on Church Debt*, Milwaukee: Bruce Publishing Co., 1941.

ESPELAGE, ARTHUR (ed.). *CLSA Advisory Opinions, 1994-2000*, Washington: CLSA, 2002.

_____ (ed.). *CLSA Advisory Opinions, 2001-2005*, Alexandria: CLSA, 2006.

FLANNERY, AUSTIN (ed.). *Vatican Council II: The Conciliar and Post-Conciliar Documents*, vol. 1, new rev. ed., Northport, New York: Costello Publishing Co., 1996.

_____ (ed.). *Vatican Council II: More Post-Conciliar Documents*, vol. 2, new rev. ed., Northport, New York: Costello Publishing Co., 1998.

FOX, JOSEPH (ed.). *Render Unto Caesar: Church Property in Roman Catholic and Anglican Church Law,* Rome: Pontifical University of Saint Thomas Aquinas *in Urbe*, 2000.

HITE, JORDAN. *A Primer on Public and Private Juridic Persons: Applications to the Healthcare Ministry,* Saint Louis: The Catholic Health Association, 2000.

HUELS, JOHN M. *Empowerment for Ministry,* New York: Paulist Press, 2003.

_____ *The Pastoral Companion: A Canon Law Handbook for Catholic Ministry*, 3rd rev. ed., Quincy: Franciscan Herald Press, 1995.

KORTH, FRANCIS N. *Canon Law for Hospitals: Administration of Temporal Goods*, Saint Louis: Catholic Health Association for the United States and Canada, 1963.

MAIDA, ADAM J. *Ownership, Control, and Sponsorship of Catholic Institutions,* Harrisburg: Pennsylvania Catholic Conference, 1975.

_____ *Issues in the Labor-Management Dialogue: Church Perspectives*, Saint Louis: The Catholic Health Association of the United States, 1982.

_____ and NICHOLAS P. CAFARDI. *Church Property, Church Finances, and Church-Related Corporations,* Saint Louis: The Catholic Health Association of the United States, 1984.

MARZOA, ÁNGEL, JORGE MIRAS and RAFAEL RODRÍGUES-OCAÑA (eds.). *Exegetical Commentary on the Code of Canon Law*, ERNEST CAPARROS (Eng. ed.), 9 vols., Chicago: Midwest Theological Forum, 2004.

McDERMOTT, ROSE. *The Consecrated Life: Cases, Commentaries, Documents, Readings*, Alexandria: CLSA, 2006.

McGOWAN, M.D. *The Canonical Status of Catholic Health Care Facilities in the Province of New Brunswick in Light of Recent Provincial Government Legislation,* Lewiston: Mellen Press, 2000.

McGRATH, JOHN J. *Catholic Institutions in the United States: Canonical and Civil Law Status,* Washington: The Catholic University of America, 1968.

McKenna, Kevin E., Lawrence A. DiNardo, and Joseph W. Pokusa (eds.), *Church Finance Handbook,* Washington: CLSA, 1999.

Ngundu, M. *Comment gérer les bens de l'Église?* Kinshasa: Baobab, 1998.

Périsset, Jean-Claude. *Les biens temporals de l'Église,* Paris: Éditions Tardy, 1996.

Perlasca, Alberto. *Il concetto di bene ecclesiastico,* Tesi Gregoriana, 24, Roma: Pontificia Università Gregoriana, 1997.

Schouppe, Jean-Pierre. *Droit canonique des biens,* Montréal: Wilson and Lafleur, 2008.

Shannon, P. and D.M. Wilson. *Disposition of Real Estate by Religious Institutes,* Washington: NATRI, 1987.

Signié, Jean Marie. *Paroisses et administration des biens: Un chemin vers l'autosuffisiance des Églises d'Afrique,* Paris: L'Harmattan, 2007.

Smith, Rosemary, Warren Brown and Nancy Reynolds (eds.). *Sponsorship in the United States Context: Theory and Practice,* Washington: CLSA, 2006.

Vromant, G. *De bonis Ecclesiae temporalibus,* 3rd rev. ed., Brussels: Éditions De Schuet, 1953.

Woywood, Stanislaus and Callistus Smith. *A Practical Commentary on the Code of Canon Law,* rev. ed., 2 vols., New York: Joseph F. Wagner, Inc., 1948.

Wrenn, Lawrence G. *Authentic Interpretations on the 1983 Code,* Washington: CLSA, 1993.

Dissertations/Theses

Antoine, Rajeh. *I beni temporali nella Chiesa Maronita in Libano,* Rome: Pontificia Università Lateranense, 1999.

Asdorian, Kathleen. *Piercing the Corporate Veil in a Religious Institution: A Search for Assets,* Washington: The Catholic University of America, 2006.

Balvo, Charles. *The Administration of Temporal Goods and Diocesan Finance Councils,* Rome: Pontifical Gregorian University, 1984.

Barrett, John D. *A Comparative Study of the Councils of Baltimore and the Code of Canon Law,* Washington: The Catholic University of America, 1932.

BIFFI, GISUEPPE. *Le pie voluntà e le pie fondazioni nel Codice di Diritto Canonico e nella legislazione civile,* Rome: Pontificia Università Lateranense, 1996.

BUCCI, ALESSANDRO. *Proprietà e gestione con atti di prassi amministrativa dei beni temporali della Chiesa,* Rome: Pontificia Università Lateranense, 2002.

CHAMBLEE, ANNA MARIA. *Public Juridic Persons and Statutes: The Application of Canon 117 to Parishes,* Washington: The Catholic University of America, 2006.

CISTERNINO, MARCO. *L'uso dei beni temporali da parte dei chierici dal Concilio Vaticano II al CJC 1983,* Rome: Pontificia Università Lateranense, Pontificii Instituti Utriusque Juris, 1999.

CLEARY, JOHN FRANCIS. *Canonical Limitations on the Alienation of Church Property,* Washington: The Catholic University of America, 1936.

CONLON, DANIEL C. *Canonical and Civil Legal Issues Surrounding the Alienation of Catholic Health Care Facilities in the United States,* Rome: Pontifical University of Saint Thomas Aquinas in Urbe, 2000.

DEMERS, FRANÇOIS. *The Temporal Administration of the Religious House of a Non-Exempt Clerical Pontifical Institute,* Washington: The Catholic University of America, 1961.

DIGNAN, PATRICK J. *A History of the Legal Incorporation of Catholic Church Property in the United States (1784-1932),* New York: P.J. Kennedy, 1935.

DOYLE, JERALD A. *Civil Incorporation of Ecclesiastical Institutions: A Canonical Perspective,* Ottawa: Saint Paul University, 1989.

EGBUNA, MIRIAM P. *The Right to Acquire, Possess, Administer and Alienate Ecclesiastical Goods in Religious Institutes,* Rome: Pontifical Gregorian University, 1993.

EMEH, MARTINS. *Canon 1277: Acts of Extraordinary Administration by the Diocesan Bishop,* Washington: CUA, 2007.

EZENWA, ANNE MARIE. *Ecclesial and Nigerian Legal Perspectives on Employment of Workers: Application of Canon 1286, 1°,* Ottawa: Saint Paul University, 1999.

FARRELLY, ADRIAN G. *The Diocesan Finance Council: A Historical and Canonical Study,* Ottawa: Saint Paul University, 1987.

FRUGÉ, DONALD J. *The Taxation Practices of the United States Bishops in Relation to the Authority of Bishops to Tax According to the*

Code of Canon Law and Proposed Revisions, Washington: The Catholic University of America, 1982.

GIRASOLI, N. *Significato ecclesiale dei beni temporali della Chiesa*, Rome: Pontifical Gregorian University, 1990.

GOODWINE, JOHN A. *The Right of the Church to Acquire Temporal Goods*, Washington: The Catholic University of America, 1941.

GRAZIAN, FRANCESCO. *La nozione di amministrazione e di alienazione nel Codice di Diritto Canonico*, Tesi Gregoriana, 55, Rome: Pontificia Università Gregoriana, 2002.

HESTON, EDWARD L. *The Alienation of Church Property in the United States: An Historical Synopsis and Commentary*, Washington: The Catholic University of America, 1941.

KEALY, ROBERT T. *Diocesan Financial Support: Its History and Canonical Status,* Rome: Pontifical Gregorian University, 1986.

KOHLS, EUGENE C. *An Interpretation of Canon 1500: The Division of Property and Debts in the Division of a Territorial Moral Person,* Rome: Pontifical Lateran University, 1966.

KUNG MIN, NAM. *L'Istituto diocesano per il sostentamento del clero a norma del canone 1274 §1 con riferimento all'attuazione del sostentamento del clero nella Chiesa coreana,* Rome:Pontificia Università Urbaniana, 1995.

LAHEY, JOHN A. *Faithful Fulfillment of the Pious Will: A Fundamental Principle of Church Law as Found in the 1983 Code of Canon Law,* Washington: The Catholic University of America, 1987.

MALÉ, P. *The Role of Temporal Goods in the Life and Mission of the Church: Towards an Understanding and Application of Church Property Law in Mission Territories According to Canon 254 of the 1983 Code of Canon Law,* Rome: Pontifical Lateran University, 2003.

MCKEVITT, AMADEUS. *The Canons on Alienation of Book V of the 1983 Code of Canon Law,* Washington: The Catholic University of America, 1984.

ROCHE, GARRETT T. *The Poor in the Code of Canon Law and the "Option for the Poor" in the Teaching of Pope John Paul II*, Rome: Pontifical Gregorian University, 1993.

SANTI, MARY. *Canonical Standards for Lay Employees in the Church*, Washington: The Catholic University of America, 2006.

TAYLOR, CHRISTINE. *Canon 1284, §2, 2° and the Corporation Sole*, Washington: The Catholic University of America, 2006.

WISDO, NANCY. *Canons 231 and 1286: The Responsibility in Canon Law for Church Administrators to Provide Health Insurance for Lay Employees*, Washington: The Catholic University of America, 2006.

VOWELL, T. *The Acts of Financial Administration by Diocesan Bishops According to the Norm of Canon 1277*, Ottawa: Saint Paul University, 1991.

Articles/Chapters in Books

ABBAS, JOBE. "Establishment of Autonomous and Non-Autonomous Pious Foundations," in *CLSA Advisory Opinions, 2001-2005*, Arthur J. Espelage (ed.), Alexandria: CLSA, 2006, pp. 343-344.

_____ "The Temporal Goods of the Church," in *The Two Codes in Comparison*, Kanonkia, vol. 7, Rome: Pontificio Istituto Orientale, 1977, pp. 177-205.

AMOS, JOHN R. "Hiring and Salary for Parochial School Teachers," in *CLSA Advisory Opinions, 1994-2000*, Arthur J. Espelage (ed.), Washington: CLSA, 2002, pp. 411-412.

ARMSTRONG, CHRISTOPHER. "Alienation of Church Property and Consultation," in *CLSA Advisory Opinions, 1994-2000*, Arthur J. Espelage (ed.), Washington: CLSA, 2002, pp. 421-422.

BEAL, JOHN P. "From the Heart of the Church to the Heart of the World: Ownership, Control, and Catholic Identity of Institutional Apostolates in the United States," in *Sponsorship in the United States Context: Theory and Praxis*, Rosemary Smith, Warren Brown, and Nancy Reynolds (eds.), Alexandria: CLSA, 2006, pp. 31-48.

BINZER, JOSEPH R. and WILLIAM J. KING. "Alienation and Acts of Extraordinary Administration," in *CLSA Advisory Opinions, 2001-2005*, Arthur J. Espelage (ed.), Alexandria: CLSA, 2006, pp. 337-339.

CAFARDI, NICHOLAS P. "Alienation of Church Property," in *Church Finance Handbook*, Kevin E. McKenna, Lawrence A. DiNardo, and Joseph W. Pokusa (eds.), Washington: CLSA, 1999, pp. 247-266.

_____ "L'autorità di imporre le tasse da parte del vescovo diocesano secondo quanto previsto dal canone 1263," in *Attuali problemi di interpretazione del Codice di diritto canonico*, Bruno Esposito (ed.), Rome: Millennium, 1977, pp. 127-138.

_____ "Assessment of Parish Income for Diocesan Needs," in *CLSA Advisory Opinions, 1994-2000*, Arthur J. Espelage (ed.), Washington: CLSA, 2002, pp. 399-402.

_____ [and] DONALD J. FRUGÉ, "Alienation of Objects Precious by Reason of Artistic or Historical Significance," in *CLSA Advisory Opinions, 1994-2000*, Arthur J. Espelage (ed.), Washington: CLSA, 2002, pp. 417-421.

_____ "The Bishop's Power to Tax All Parish Funds," in *CLSA Advisory Opinions, 1984-1993*, Patrick J. Cogan (ed.), Washington: CLSA, 1995, pp. 410-416.

_____ and JORDAN T. HITE. "Civil and Canonical Requirements for a Clergy Retirement Fund," in *CLSA Advisory Opinions, 1984-1993*, Patrick J. Cogan (ed.), Washington: CLSA, 1995, pp. 416-419.

_____ "Leasing Ecclesiastical Goods," in *Church Finance Handbook*, Kevin E. McKenna, Lawrence A. DiNardo, and Joseph W. Pokusa (eds.), Washington: CLSA, 1999, pp. 207-215.

CARRAGHER, MICHAEL. "Pious Cause and Public Benefit," in *Miscellanea in onore del Prof. José Castaño*, Angelo Urru (ed.), Rome: Millennium, 1997, pp. 119-171

CHALMERS, MARGARET POLL. "Right of Ownership and Administration of Catholic Cemetery," in CLSA, *Roman Replies and Advisory Opinions*, Joseph J. Koury and Shiobhan M. Verbeek (eds.), Washington: CLSA, 2007, pp. 92-93.

CHOPKO, MARK. "Control of and Administration for Separately-Incorporated Works of the Diocesan Church: A Constitutional, Statutory, and Judicial Evaluation of the Experiences of U.S. Dioceses," in *Public Ecclesiastical Juridic Persons and their Civilly Incorporated Apostolates (e.g., Universities, Healthcare Institutions, Social Service Agencies) in the Catholic Church in the U.S.A.: Canonical-Civil Aspects: Acts of the Colloquium*, Rome: Pontifical University of Saint Thomas Aquinas *in Urbe*, 1998, pp. 65-95.

COCCOPALERMO, FRANCESCO. "Diritto patrimoniale della Chiesa," in *Il diritto nel mistero della Chiesa*, Tarcisio Bertone, et al. (eds.), Rome: Libreria editrice della Pontificia Università Lateranense, 1980, vol. 4, pp. 1-70.

CORIDEN, JAMES and FREDERICK MCMANUS. "The Present State of Roman Catholic Law Regarding Colleges and Sponsoring Religious

Bodies," in *Church and State*, P.R. Moots and E.M. Gaffney (eds.), Notre Dame: University of Notre Dame Press, 1979, pp. 141-153.

COUNCE, PAUL D. "Transfer of Diocesan Money to Private Foundation," in *CLSA Advisory Opinions, 1994-2000*, Arthur J. Espelage (ed.), Washington: CLSA, 2002, pp. 397-399.

CUSACK, BARBARA. "Forgiveness of Parish Debt by Diocese," in *CLSA Advisory Opinions, 2001-2005*, Arthur J. Espelage (ed.), Alexandria: CLSA, 2006, pp. 339-340.

_____ "Pious Foundations and Mass Intentions," in *CLSA Advisory Opinions, 1994-2000*, Arthur J. Espelage (ed.), Washington: CLSA, 2002, pp. 426-428.

DALY, WILLIAM P. "Remuneration for Church Employees," in *Church Finance Handbook*, Kevin E. McKenna, Lawrence A. DiNardo, and Joseph W. Pokusa (eds.), Washington: CLSA, 1999, pp. 53-59.

DE PAOLIS, VELASIO. "L'amministrazione dei beni: soggetti cui è demandata in via immediata e loro funzioni (cc. 1279-1289)," in *I Beni temporali della Chiesa*, Studi Giuridici, 50, Vatican City: Libreria editrice Vaticana, 1999, pp. 59-82.

DINARDO, LAWRENCE A. "The Inventory of Property," in *Church Finance Handbook*, Kevin E. McKenna, Lawrence A. DiNardo, and Joseph W. Pokusa (eds.), Washington: CLSA, 1999, pp. 151-163.

DIPIETRO, MELANIE. "Incorporated Apostolates," in *Church Finance Handbook*, Kevin E. McKenna, Lawrence A. DiNardo, and Joseph W. Pokusa (eds.), Washington: CLSA, 1999, pp. 279-303.

_____ "The Interfacing of Canonical principles and American Law in the Negotiation of Joint Ventures Between Church-Related and Non-Church-Related Corporations," in *Public Ecclesiastical Juridic Persons and their Civilly Incorporated Apostolates (e.g., Universities, Healthcare Institutions, Social Service Agencies) in the Catholic Church in the U.S.A.: Canonical-Civil Aspects: Acts of the Colloquium*, Rome: Pontifical University of Saint Thomas Aquinas *in Urbe*, 1998, pp. 181-229.

_____ "A Juridic Meaning of Sponsorship in the Formal Relationship Between a Public Juridic Person and a Healthcare Corporation in the United States," in *Sponsorship in the United States Context: Theory and Praxis*, Rosemary Smith, Warren Brown, and Nancy Reynolds (eds.), Alexandria: CLSA, 2006, pp. 101-122.

DONLAN, JAMES I. "Priests' Remuneration and Mass Stipends," in *CLSA Advisory Opinions, 2001-2005*, Arthur J. Espelage (ed.), Alexandria: CLSA, 2006, pp. 254-256.

D'SOUZA, VICTOR G. "General Principles Governing the Administration of Temporal Goods of the Church," in *In the Service of Truth and Justice: Festschrift in Honour of Prof. Augustine Mendonça, Professor Emeritus*, Victor G. D'Souza (ed.), Bangalore: Saint Peter's Pontifical Institute, 2008, pp. 467-498.

DUNN, BEVERLY K. [and] LYNDA ROBITAILLE. "Canon Law and the Observance of Labor Law," in *CLSA Advisory Opinions, 1994-2000*, Arthur J. Espelage (ed.), Washington: CLSA, 2002, pp. 412-416.

EASTON, FREDERICK E. "The Diocesan Finance Officer," in *Church Finance Handbook*, Kevin E. McKenna, Lawrence A. DiNardo, and Joseph W. Pokusa (eds.), Washington: CLSA, 1999, pp. 125-134.

ERDÖ, PÉTER. "Chiesa e beni temporali: principi fondamentali del magistero del Concilio Vatican II (cann. 1254-1256)," in *I Beni temporali della Chiesa*, Studi Giuridici, 50, Vatican City: Libreria editrice Vaticana, 1999, pp. 21-35.

FALCHI, FRANCESCO. "Le pie volontà (cann. 1299-1302 et 1310)," in *I Beni temporali della Chiesa*, Studi Giuridici, 50, Vatican City, Libreria editrice Vaticana, 1999, pp. 163-223.

FALTIN, DANIEL. "Diritto di proprietà ed uso dei beni temporali da parte della Chiesa," in *Problemi e prospettive di diritto canonico*, Ernesto Cappellini (ed.), Brescia: Editrice Queriniana, 1977, pp. 227-240.

FAVERGIOTTI, ANNA. "Il Fondamento dell'Obligazione Tributaria nello Stato Moderno e nel Diritto Canonico Latino e Orientale," in *Incontro fra Canoni d'Oriente e d'Occidente*, Raffaele Coppola (ed.), Bari: Cacucci Editore, 1994, pp. 571-582.

FARIS, JOHN D. "The Code of Canons of the Eastern Churches and Temporal Goods," in *Church Finance Handbook*, Kevin E. McKenna, Lawrence A. DiNardo, and Joseph W. Pokusa (eds.), Washington: CLSA, 1999, pp. 29-43.

FAVERGIOTTI, ANNA. "Il fondamento dell'obbligazione tributaria nello stato moderno e nel diritto canonico ed orientale: Note comparative," in *Atti del Congresso Internazionale: Incontro fra canoni d'oriente e d'occidente*, Raffaele Coppola (ed.), 3 vols., Bari: Cacucci editore, 1994, vol. 2, pp. 571-582.

FELICIANI, GIORGIO. "La nozione di bene culturale nell'ordinamento canonico," in *Iustitia in caritate: Miscellanea di studi in onore di Velasio de Paolis*, James J. Conn and Luigi Sabbarese (eds.), Rome: Urbaniana University Press, 2005, pp. 445-455.

FITZSIMMONS, EUGENE J. "Mass Offerings and Stole Fees," in *Church Finance Handbook*, Kevin E. McKenna, Lawrence A. DiNardo, and Joseph W. Pokusa (eds.), Washington: CLSA, 1999, pp. 97-109.

FLOWERS CONTI, JOY. "Liability Issues for Related Church Entities," in *Public Ecclesiastical Juridic Persons and their Civilly Incorporated Apostolates (e.g., Universities, Healthcare Institutions, Social Service Agencies) in the Catholic Church in the U.S.A.: Canonical-Civil Aspects: Acts of the Colloquium*, Rome: Pontifical University of Saint Thomas Aquinas *in Urbe*, 1998, pp. 97-179.

FOX, JOSEPH. "Introductory Thoughts about Public Juridic Persons and Their Civilly Incorporated Apostolates," in *Public Ecclesiastical Juridic Persons and their Civilly Incorporated Apostolates (e.g., Universities, Healthcare Institutions, Social Service Agencies) in the Catholic Church in the U.S.A.: Canonical-Civil Aspects: Acts of the Colloquium*, Rome: Pontifical University of Saint Thomas Aquinas *in Urbe*, 1998, pp. 231-258.

FRANK, JOSEPH A. "Insurance and Ecclesiastical Goods," in *Church Finance Handbook*, Kevin E. McKenna, Lawrence A. DiNardo, and Joseph W. Pokusa (eds.), Washington: CLSA, 1999, pp. 215-222.

FRUGÉ, DONALD J. "Diocesan Finance Council and a Capital Campaign," in *CLSA Advisory Opinions, 1994-2000*, Arthur J. Espelage (ed.), Washington: CLSA, 2002, pp. 406-409.

GOLDEN, PAUL L. "Leasing Church Property Owned by a Religious Institute," in *CLSA Advisory Opinions, 2001-2005*, Arthur J. Espelage (ed.), Alexandria: CLSA, 2006, pp. 340-343.

_____ "Mass Offerings Held in an interest Bearing Account," in CLSA, *Roman Replies and Advisory Opinions*, Joseph J. Koury and Shiobhan M. Verbeek (eds.), Washington: CLSA, 2007, pp. 77-78.

GRAZIAN, FRANCESCO. "Amministrazione e gestione dei beni nell'ordiamento canonico," in *Enti ecclesiastici e controllo dello stato: Studi sull'Istruzione CEI in materia amministrativa*, JUAN I. ARRIETA (ed.), Istituto di Diritto Canonico San Pio X, Study N. 5, Venice: Marcianum Press, 2007, pp. 61-70.

HITE, JORDAN. "Religious Institutes (canons 607-709)," in *The Code of Canon Law: Text and Commentary*, commissioned by the CLSA, James A. Coriden, Thomas J. Green, and Donald E. Heintschel (eds.), New York: Paulist, 1985, pp. 470-524.

————— "The Temporal Goods of Religious Institutes," in *Church Finance Handbook*, Kevin E. McKenna, Lawrence A. DiNardo, and Joseph W. Pokusa (eds.), Washington: CLSA, 1999, pp. 45-52.

HOLLAND, SHARON. "Canonical Reflections on Civilly Incorporated Apostolates," in *Public Ecclesiastical Juridic Persons and their Civilly Incorporated Apostolates (e.g., Universities, Healthcare Institutions, Social Service Agencies) in the Catholic Church in the U.S.A.: Canonical-Civil Aspects: Acts of the Colloquium*, Rome: Pontifical University of Saint Thomas Aquinas *in Urbe*, 1998, pp. 325-341.

————— "Secular Institutes," in *New Commentary on the Code of Canon Law*, commissioned by the CLSA, John P. Beal, James A. Coriden, and Thomas J. Green (eds.), New York: Paulist, 2000, p. 879.

HUBER, MATTHEW P. "Ecclesiastical Financial Administrators," in *Church Finance Handbook*, Kevin E. McKenna, Lawrence A. DiNardo, and Joseph W. Pokusa (eds.), Washington: CLSA, 1999, pp. 113-124.

HUELS, JOHN. "Indeterminate Mass Obligations," in CLSA, *Roman Replies and Advisory Opinions*, Joseph J. Koury and Shiobhan Verbeek (eds.), Washington, CLSA, 2007, pp. 79-80.

KASLYN, ROBERT. "The Christian Faithful," in *New Commentary on the Code of Canon Law*, commissioned by the CLSA, John P. Beal, James A. Coriden, and Thomas J. Green (eds.), New York: Paulist, 2000, pp. 241-290.

KEALY, ROBERT L. "Taxation, Assessments and Extraordinary Collections," in *Church Finance Handbook*, Kevin E. McKenna, Lawrence A. DiNardo, and Joseph W. Pokusa (eds.), Washington: CLSA, 1999, pp. 77-90.

KENNEDY, ROBERT J. "The Temporal Goods of the Church," in *New
    Commentary on the Code of Canon Law*, commissioned by the
    CLSA, John P. Beal, James A. Coriden, and Thomas J. Green
    (eds.), New York: Paulist, 2000, pp. 1449-1525.
KING, WILLIAM J. "Mandated Diocesan Centralized Financial Service," in
    CLSA Advisory Opinions, 2001-2005, Arthur J. Espelage (ed.),
    Alexandria: CLSA, 2006, pp. 331-336.
_____ "Sponsorship by Juridic Persons," in *Sponsorship in the United
    States Context: Theory and Praxis*, Rosemary Smith, Warren
    Brown, and Nancy Reynolds (eds.), Alexandria: CLSA, 2006,
    pp. 49-72.
LEONARD, JOAN DE LOURDES. "Temporal Goods: Canons 634-640," in
    A Handbook on Canons 537-746, Jordan Hite, Sharon Holland,
    and Daniel Ward (eds.), Collegeville: The Liturgical Press,
    1985, pp. 99-114.
LONGHITANO, ADOLFO. "L'amministrazione dei beni: la funzione di
    vigilanza del vecsoco diocesano (cann. 1276-1277)," in *I Beni
    temporali della Chiesa*, Studi Giuridici, 50, Vatican City: Libre-
    ria editrice Vaticana, 1999, pp. 83-102.
LÓPEZ ALARCÓN, MARIANO "Book V: The Temporal Goods of the
    Church," in *Code of Canon Law Annotated*, 2nd rev. ed., Ernest
    Caparros and Hélène Aubé (eds.), Montréal: Wilson and Lafleur,
    2004, pp. 963-1016.
_____ "Book V: The Temporal Goods of the Church, Introduction (cc.
    1254-1258)," in *Exegetical Comm*, vol. 4, pp. 1-40.
MAIDA, ADAM. "The *Code of Canon Law* of 1983 and the Property of
    the Local Church," in *The New Code of Canon Law: Proceed-
    ings of the Fifth International Congress of Canon Law*, Michel
    Thériault and Jean Thorn (eds.), Ottawa: Saint Paul University,
    1986, pp. 743-753.
MARCUZZI, PIERO GIORGIO. "Le fondazioni pie (cann. 1303-1310)," in *I
    Beni temporali della Chiesa*, Studi Giuridici, 50, Vatican City:
    Libreria editrice Vaticana, 1999, pp. 225-264.
McDONOUGH, ELIZABETH. "Addressing Irregularities in the Administra-
    tion of Church Property," in *Church Finance Handbook*, Kevin
    E. McKenna, Lawrence A. DiNardo, and Joseph W. Pokusa
    (eds.), Washington: CLSA, 1999, pp. 223-243.
McDONOUGH, KEVIN M. "The Diocesan and Parish Finance Council,"

in *Church Finance Handbook*, Kevin E. McKenna, Lawrence A. DiNardo, and Joseph W. Pokusa (eds.), Washington: CLSA, 1999, pp. 135-149.

METZ, RENÉ. "Temporal Goods in the Church (cc. 1007-1054)," in *A Guide to the Eastern Code*, George Nedungatt (ed.), Kanonika, 10, Rome: Pontificio Istitutio Orientale, 2002, pp. 689-712.

MIÑAMBRES, JESÚS. "Beni ecclesiastici: nozione, regime giuridico e potere episcopale (cann. 1257-1258)," in *I Beni temporali della Chiesa*, Studi Giuridici, 50, Vatican City: Libreria editrice Vaticana, 1999, pp. 7-20.

_____ "La responsabilità nella gestione dei beni ecclesiastici dell'ente diocesi," in *Enti ecclesiastici e controllo dello stato: Studi sull'Istruzione CEI in materia amministrativa*, JUAN I. ARRIETA (ed.), Istituto di Diritto Canonico San Pio X, Study N. 5, Venice: Marcianum Press, 2007, pp. 71-86.

_____ "Il Romano Pontifice garante ultimo della destinazione dei beni ecclesiastici," in *Iustitia in caritate: Miscellanea di studi in onore di Velasio de Paolis*, James J. Conn and Luigi Sabbarese, Rome: Urbaniana University Press, 2005, pp. 431-443.

MISTÒ, LUIGI. "La gestione amministrativa della parrocchia e la questione della perequazione tra gli enti ecclesiastici," in *Enti ecclesiastici e controllo dello stato: Studi sull'Istruzione CEI in materia amministrativa*, JUAN I. ARRIETA (ed.), Istituto di Diritto Canonico San Pio X, Study N. 5, Venice: Marcianum Press, 2007, pp. 87-96.

MORRISEY, FRANCIS G. "Basic Concepts and Principles," in *Church Finance Handbook*, Kevin E. McKenna, Lawrence A. DiNardo, and Joseph W. Pokusa (eds.), Washington: CLSA, 1999, pp. 3-15.

_____ "Canonical Issues to Anticipate and Resolve in Mergers and Joint Ventures Involving Catholic Health-Care Institutions," in *Magister Canonistarum*, Federico R. Anzar Gil (ed.), Bibliotheca Salmanticensis, Estudia 163, Salamanca: Universidad de Salamanca, 1994, pp. 215-236.

_____ "The Directory for the Administration of Temporal Goods in Religious Institutes," in *Unico Ecclesiae Servitio: Canonical Studies Presented to Germain Lesage, O.M.I.*, Ottawa: Saint Paul University, 1991, pp. 267-285.

_____ "Establishment of a Lay Board and Alienation of Property," in *CLSA Advisory Opinions, 1994-2000*, Arthur J. Espelage (ed.), Washington: CLSA, 2002, pp. 422-424.

_____ "The Expression of Church Law in Canonical and Civil Documents," in Catholic Health Association, *The Search for Identity: Canonical Sponsorship of Catholic Healthcare*, Saint Louis: Catholic Health Association, 1993, pp. 49-58.

_____ "Leasing of Goods," in *CLSA Advisory Opinions, 1984-1993*, Patrick J. Cogan (ed.), Washington: CLSA, 1995, pp. 419-421.

_____ "New Canon Law on Temporal Goods Reflects Vatican II's Influence," In *The New Canon Law: Perspectives on the Law, Religious Life, and the Laity*, Saint Louis: Catholic Health Association, 1983, pp. 38-44.

_____ "Religious Institute's Finance Council," in *CLSA Advisory Opinions, 1994-2000*, Arthur J. Espelage (ed.), Washington: CLSA, 2002, pp. 409-410.

_____ "Responsibility for Liabilities of Priests When a Diocese is Divided," in *CLSA Advisory Opinions, 1994-2000*, Arthur J. Espelage (ed.), Washington: CLSA, 2002, pp. 16-17.

_____ "The Temporal Goods of the Church," in *The Canon Law: Letter and Spirit: A Practical Guide to the Code of Canon Law*, Gerard Sheehy, et al. (eds.), prepared by the CLSA OF GREAT BRITAIN AND IRELAND in association with the CANADIAN CANON LAW SOCIETY, Collegeville: The Liturgical Press, 1995, pp. 707-747.

_____ "Temporal Goods and Their Administration," in Ángel Marzoa, Jorge Miras and Rafael Rodrígues-Ocaña (eds.), *Exegetical Commentary on the Code of Canon Law*, Ernest Caparros (Eng. ed.), 9 vols, Chicago: Midwest Theological Forum, 2004, vol. 2, pp. 1672-1692.

_____ [and] MADELEINE WELCH. "Establishment of a Lay Board and Alienation of Property," in *CLSA Advisory Opinions, 1994-2000*, Arthur J. Espelage (ed.), Washington: CLSA, 2002, pp. 422-424.

MOSCA, VINCENZO. "Il ruolo della gerarchia nell'amministrazione comunale dei beni della Chiesa," In *Iustitia in caritate: Miscellanea di studi in onore di Velasio de Paolis*, James J. Conn and Luigi Sabbarese (eds.), Rome: Urbaniana University Press, 2005, pp. 387-409.

MYERS, JOHN J. "The Temporal Goods of the Church," in *The Code of Canon Law: Text and Commentary*, commissioned by the CLSA, James A. Coriden, Thomas J. Green, and Donald E. Heintschel (eds.), New York: Paulist, 1985, pp. 857-890.

NAVARRO, LUIS. "L'acquisto dei beni temporali: Il finanziamento della Chiesa (cann. 1259-1272)," in *I Beni temporali della Chiesa*, Studi Giuridici, 50, Vatican City: Libreria editrice Vaticana, 1999, pp. 37-58.

OKULIK, LUIS. "Gestione economica e distribuzione delle responsabilità negli istituti di vita consacrata," in *Enti ecclesiastici e controllo dello stato: Studi sull'Istruzione CEI in materia amministrativa*, JUAN I. ARRIETA (ed.), Istituto di Diritto Canonico San Pio X, Study N. 5, Venice: Marcianum Press, 2007, pp. 97-115.

ONCLIN, WILLIE. "De personalitate morali vel canonica," in *Acta conventus canonistarum, Romae diebus 20-25 mai 1968 celebrati*, Rome: Typis polyglottis Vaticanis, 1968, pp. 121-157.

O'REILLY, MICHAEL A. "The Proper Law of Institutes of Consecrated Life and of Societies of Apostolic Life," in *Unico Ecclesiae Servitio: Canonical Studies Presented to Germain Lesage, O.M.I.*, Ottawa: Saint Paul University, 1991, pp. 287-303.

PAGÉ, ROCH. "Associations of the Christian Faithful," in *New Commentary on the Code of Canon Law*, commissioned by the CLSA, John P. Beal, James A. Coriden, and Thomas J. Green (eds.), New York: Paulist, 2000, pp. 398-422.

PALESTRO, VITTORIO. "La disciplina canonica in materia di alienzatione e di locazione (cann. 1291-1298)," in *I Beni temporali della Chiesa*, Studi Giuridici, 50, Vatican City: Libreria editrice Vaticana, 1999, pp. 141-162.

PAPROCKI, THOMAS J. and RICHARD B. SAUDIS. "Annual Report to the Diocesan Bishop,"in *Church Finance Handbook*, Kevin E. McKenna, Lawrence A. DiNardo, and Joseph W. Pokusa (eds.), Washington: CLSA, 1999, pp. 175-183.

PERKIN, DAVID R. "Canonical Rights to Reduce and to Transfer Mass Obligations," *CLSA Advisory Opinions, 1984-1993*, Patrick J. Cogan (ed.), Washington: CLSA, 1995, pp. 421-423.

PERRY JOSEPH N. "Support for the Church," in *Church Finance Handbook*, Kevin E. McKenna, Lawrence A. DiNardo, and Joseph W. Pokusa (eds.), Washington: CLSA, 1999, pp. 63-76.

POKUSA, JOSEPH. "Introduction to a Church Finance Handbook: Background for the Law on Temporal Goods," in *Church Finance Handbook*, Kevin E. McKenna, Lawrence A. DiNardo, and Joseph W. Pokusa (eds.), Washington: CLSA, 1999, pp. vii-xvii.

PRESAS BARROSA, CONCEPCIÓN. "La conservación del patrimonio historico eclesiastico en el Codigo de la Iglesia oriental," in *Incontro fra canoni d'orientale e d'occidente*, Raffaele Coppola (ed.), Bari, Cacucci Editore, 1994, pp. 607-610.

———— "El patrimonio artístico de la Iglesia en el 'Codex iuris canonici' y en el 'Codex canonum Ecclesiarum orientalium:'" Aproximaciones al respecto," in *Ius in vita et in missione Ecclesiae*, Vatican City: Libreria editrice Vaticana, 1994, pp. 791-801.

PROVOST, JAMES. "Responsibility for Liabilities of Priests When a Diocese is Divided," in *CLSA Advisory Opinions, 1994-2000*, Arthur J. Espelage (ed.), Washington: CLSA, 2002, pp. 17-18.

———— "Right of the Diocesan Bishop to Levy a Tax on a Juridic Person Subject to Him," in *CLSA Advisory Opinions, 1984-1993*, Patrick J. Cogan (ed.), Washington: CLSA, 1995, pp. 408-410.

———— "Use of Parish Funds for Gifts," in *CLSA Advisory Opinions, 1994-2000*, Arthur J. Espelage (ed.), Washington: CLSA, 2002, pp. 410-411.

RENKEN, JOHN A. "Canon 1263: Parish Financial Goals," in CLSA, *Roman Replies and Advisory Opinions*, Joseph J. Koury and Shiobhan M. Verbeek (eds.), Washington, CLSA, 2008, pp. 122-124.

———— "Parishes, Pastors, and Parochial Vicars," in *New Commentary on the Code of Canon Law*, commissioned by the CLSA, John P. Beal, James A. Coriden, and Thomas J. Green (eds.), New York: Paulist, 2000, pp. 673-724.

ROVERA, VIRGINIO. "I beni temporali della Chiesa," in *La normativa del nuovo codice*, Ernesto Cappellini (ed.), Brescia, Queriniana, 1983, pp. 273-294.

———— "Il libro V: I beni temporali della Chiesa," in *Il nuovo codice di diritto canonico*, Luigi Mistò (ed.), Turin: Editrice di Ci, 1987, pp. 223-241.

SALERNO, FRANCESCO. "L'amministrazione dei beni: la funzione primaziale del Romano Pontifice," in *I Beni temporali della Chiesa*, Studi Giuridici, 50, Vatican City: Libreria editrice Vaticana, 1999, pp. 103-104.

SUGAWARA, YUJI. "Le norme sui beni temporali negli istituti religiosi (can. 635)," in *Iustitia in caritate: Miscellanea di studi in onore di Velasio de Paolis*, James J. Conn and Luigi Sabbarese, Rome: Urbaniana University Press, 2005, pp. 411-429.

THOMAS, ROYCE R. "Financial Reports to the Faithful," in *Church Finance Handbook*, Kevin E. McKenna, Lawrence A. DiNardo, and Joseph W. Pokusa (eds.), Washington: CLSA, 1999, pp. 165-174.

URRU, ANEGLO. "Incidenza della simonia nel Codice attuale," in *Miscellanea in onore del Prof. José Castaño*, Angelo Urru (ed.), Rome. Millenium, 1997, pp. 103-117.

VARVARO, WILLIAM A. "The Bishop's Right to Tax Parish Income," In *CLSA Advisory Opinions, 1994-2000*, Arthur J. Espelage (ed.), Washington: CLSA, 2002, pp. 402-403.

WALKOWIAK, DAVID J. "Ordinary and Extraordinary Administration," in *Church Finance Handbook*, Kevin E. McKenna, Lawrence A. DiNardo, and Joseph W. Pokusa (eds.), Washington: CLSA, 1999, pp. 185-206.

WARD, DANIEL. "Religious Institute Raising Funds in Diocese," in *CLSA Advisory Opinions, 1994-2000*, Arthur J. Espelage (ed.), Washington, CLSA, 2002, pp. 403-405.

_____ "Temporal Goods," in CLSA, *Procedural Handbook for Institutes of Consecrated Life and Societies of Apostolic Life*, Washington: CLSA, 2001, pp. 195-208.

WATERS, IAN B. "Bishop's Responsibility in Parish Financial Matters," in *CLSA Advisory Opinions, 1994-2000*, Arthur J. Espelage (ed.), Washington: CLSA, 2002, pp. 405-406.

_____ "Transfer of Property from Religious Congregation to Diocese," in *CLSA Advisory Opinions, 1994-2000*, Arthur J. Espelage (ed.), Washington: CLSA, 2002, pp. 416-417.

WELCH, MADELINE. "Establishment of a Lay Board and Alienation of Property," in *CLSA Advisory Opinions, 1994-2000*, Arthur J. Espelage (ed.), Washington: CLSA, 2002, pp. 425-426.

ZALBIDEA, DIEGO. "La legislazione particolare di alcune conferenze episcopali sull'alienazione dei beni appartenenti a patrimonio stabile," in *Enti ecclesiastici e controllo dello stato: Studi sull'Istruzione CEI in materia amministrativa*, JUAN I. ARRIETA (ed.), Istituto di Diritto Canonico San Pio X, Study N. 5, Venice: Marcianum Press, 2007, pp. 87-96.

Articles

ABBAS, JOBE. "Alienating Ecclesiastical Goods in the Eastern Catholic Churches," in *Folia canonica*, 5 (2002), pp. 125-147.

_____ "The Temporal Goods of the Church: A Comparison of the Eastern and Latin Codes of Canon Law," in *Periodica*, 83 (1994), pp. 669-714.

ADAMI, FRANCO E. "I controlli canonici e civili sull'amministrazione dei beni temporali ecclesiastici," in *Monitor ecclesiasticus*, 111 (1986), pp. 69-85.

ANZAR GIL, FEDERICO. "Acts de administración ordinaria y extraordinaria: normas canónicas," in *Revista española de derecho canónica*, 57 (2000), pp. 41-70.

_____ "El fondo diocesano para la sustentación del clero (c. 1274 §1)," in *Revista española de derecho canónico*, 48 (1991), pp. 619-647.

AUSTIN, RODGER J. "The Search for Identity: Canonical Perspectives on Diocesan Development Funds," in *CLSANZ Newsletter*, 1 (1997), pp. 12-25.

_____ "Temporal Goods Within the Church. Some Canonical Reflections," in *CLSANZ Newsletter*, 2 (1992), pp. 8-20.

BAINBRIDGE, STEPHEN M. and AARON H. COLE. "The Bishop's Alter Ego: Enterprise Liability and the Catholic Priest Sex Abuse Scandal," *Journal of Catholic Legal Studies,* 46 (2007), pp. 65-106.

BALBONI, DANTE. "La conservazione e la tutela dei monumenti e dei beni artistici," in *Monitor ecclesiasticus*, 111 (1986), pp. 109-121.

BARRETT, MATTHEW J. "The Theological Case for Progressive Taxation as Applied to Diocesan Taxes or Assessments under Canon Law in the United States," in *The Jurist,* 63 (2003), pp. 312-365.

BASSETT, WILLIAM W. "The American Civil Corporation, the 'Incorporation Movement,' and the Canon Law of the Catholic Church," in *The Journal of College and University Law*, 25 (Spring, 1999).

_____ "A Note on the Law of Contracts and the Canonical Integrity of Public Benefit Religious Organizations," in *CLSA Proceedings*, 59 (1997), pp. 61-86.

_____ "Relating Canon and Civil Law," in *The Jurist*, 44 (1984), pp. 3-18.

_____ "Religious Organizations: Their Identity in a Secular World," in *CLSANZ Proceedings*, (1995), pp. 17-50.

BELLINI, PIERO. "Potestas Ecclesiae circa temporalia: concezione tradizionale e nuove prospettive," in *Ephemerides iuris canonici*, 24 (1968), pp. 68-154.

BENNETT, AUSTIN P. "The Practical Effects on the Fiscal Administration of Church Finances of Book Five: The Law Regarding Church Possessions," in *CLSA Proceedings*, 42 (1980), pp. 171-178.

BECKER, ROBERT C. and JAMES A. SERRITELLA. "Problems of Ecclesiastical and Religious Organizations," in *The Jurist*, 44 (1984), pp. 48-66.

BERTOLINO, RINALDO. "La nuova legislazione canonica e beni culturali ecclesiali," in *Diritto ecclesiastico*, 93 (1982), pp. 250-308.

BUCCI, ALESSANDRO. "Le radice storiche della formazione giuridica del concetto di bene ecclesiastico," in *Apollinaris*, 77 (2004), pp. 357-414.

BUDNEY, LINDA A. "The Parish as Employee," in *CLSA Proceedings*, 64 (2002), pp. 59-72.

BUNGE, A.W. "Los consejos de asuntos económicos," in *Anuario Argentino de Derecho Canónico*, 5 (1998), pp. 45-70.

_____ "Órganos y oficios de ayuda al obispo diocesano en la administración de los bienes temporales," in *Anuario Argentino de Derecho Canónico*, 7 (2000), pp. 29-46.

BUSSO, A.D. "El obispo, administrador de los bienes eclesiásticos," in *Anuario Argentino de Derecho Canónico*, 7 (2000), pp. 13-28.

CAFARDI, NICHOLAS P. "Bequests for Masses: Doctrine, History, and Legal Status," in *Duquesne Law Review*, 20 (1982), pp. 403-427.

_____ "Closing Churches, Merging Institutes, Dividing Dioceses and Other Developments in Church Property," in *CLSA Proceedings*, 52 (1990), pp. 222-234.

CAMPBELL, PETER E. "The New Code and Religious: Some Civil Law Considerations," in *The Jurist*, 44 (1984), pp. 81-109.

CHOPKO, MARK E. "An Overview of the Parish and the Civil Law," in *The Jurist*, 67 (2007), pp. 194-226.

COCCOPALERMO, FRANCESCO. "Considerazioni sui beni della Chiesa," in *La scuola cattolica*, 107 (1979), pp. 299-317.

_____ "La consultività del consiglio pastorale parrocchiale e del consiglio per gli affari economici della parrocchia (cc. 536-537)," in *Quaderni di diritto ecclesiale*, 1 (1988), pp. 60-65.

_____ "Quaestiones de parochia in novo codice," in *Periodica*, 73 (1984), pp. 403-404.

COLOMBO, MARINO. "L'istituto per il sostentamento del clero e problemi connessi," in *Monitor ecclesiasticus*, 111 (1986), pp. 87-108.

CONLON, DANIEL C. "The McGrath Thesis and Its Impact on a Canonical Understanding of the Ownership of Ecclesiastical Goods," in *CLSA Proceedings*, 64 (2002), pp. 73-96.

CORBELLINI, GIORGIO. "Note sulla formazione del can. 1274 (e dei cann. 1275 e 1272) nel 'Codex iuris canonici'," in *Ius ecclesiae*, 8 (1996), pp. 465-507.

CORRECCO, EUGENIO. "Dimettersi dalla Chiesa per ragioni fiscali," in *Apollinaris*, 55 (1982), pp. 461-502.

COSTA, MAURIZIO. "Paupertas presbyteralis," in *Periodica*, 88 (1999), pp. 231-257, 437-466.

DALLA TORRE, GIUSEPPE. "Annotazione sui beni ecclesiastici nel nuovo Codice di diritto canonico," in *L'Amico del Clero*, 65 (1983), pp. 275-280, 310-317, 360-366, 463-469; 66 (1984), pp. 31-39, 70-78.

DALY, BRENDAN. "Use of Clergy Trust Fund to Pay Lay Pastoral Workers," in CLSA, *Roman Replies and Advisory Opinions*, Joseph J. Koury and Shiobhan M. Verbeek (eds.), Washington: CLSA, 2007, pp. 94-97.

DANAGHER, JOHN J. "The New Code and Catholic Health Facilities: Fundamental Obligations of Administrators," in *The Jurist*, 44 (1984), pp. 143-152.

DANEELS, FRANS. "De dioecesanis corresponsabilitatis organis," in *Periodica*, 74 (1985), pp. 301-324.

DE ANGELIS, AGOSTINO. "I consigli per gli affari economici: statuti e indicazzioni applicative," in *Montor ecclesiasticus*, 111 (1986), pp. 57-68.

_____ "Note per l'amministrazione dei beni parrocchiali," in *Orientamenti pastorali*, 32 (1984), pp. 4-5, 113-126.

DE PAOLIS, VELASIO, "Adnotatione ad responsum authenticum circa canonem 1263," in *Periodica*, 80 (1991), pp. 108-127.

_____ "Alcune osservazioni sulla nozione di amministrazione dei beni temporali della Chiesa," in *Periodica*, 88 (1999), pp. 91-140.

_____ "I beni temporali nel Codice di diritto canonico," in *Monitor ecclesiasticus*, 111 (1986), pp. 9-30.

_____ "Les biens temporals au regard du Code de Droit canonique," in *L'année canonique*, 47 (2005), pp. 7-36.

_____ "De bonis Ecclesiae temporalibus in novo Codice Iuris Canonici," in *Periodica*, 73 (1984), pp. 113-151.

_____ "De paroeciis institutis religiosis commissis vel committendis," in *Periodica*, 74 (1985), pp. 389-417.

_____ "Dimenzione ecclesiale dei beni temporali destinati a fini ecclesiali," in *Periodica*, 84 (1995), pp. 77-103.

_____ "Negozio Giuridico, 'quo condicio patrimonialis personae iuridicae peior fieri possit' (cf. c. 1295)," in *Periodica*, 83 (1994), pp. 493-528.

_____ "Nota sul significato di 'bene ecclesiale'," in *Periodica*, 84 (1995), pp. 155-160.

_____ "Questiones miscellaneae," in *Periodica*, 73 (1984), pp. 451-486.

_____ "Schema canonum Libri V: De iure patrimoniali Ecclesiae," in *Periodica*, 68 (1979), pp. 677-713.

_____ "Il sostentamento del clero dal concilio al Codice di diritto canonico," in *Quaderni di diritto ecclesiale*, 2 (1989), pp. 35-46.

_____ "Temporal Goods of the Church in the New Code with Particular Reference to Institutes of Consecrated Life," in *The Jurist*, 43 (1983), pp. 343-360.

DURAND, JEAN-PAUL. "Biens ecclésiastiques, droit canonique et droit français: Propos conclusifs," in *L'année canonique*, 47 (2005), pp. 75-86.

ÉCHAPPÉ, OLIVIER. "Les 'biens' des associations d'église," in *L'année canonique*, 47 (2005), pp. 51-62.

FALTIN, DANIEL, "De recto usu bonorum ecclesiasticorum ad mentem Concilii Vaticani II," in *Apollinaris*, 40 (1967), pp. 409-441.

_____ "De retributione et praevidentia sociali presbyterorum iuxta doctrinam concilii Vaticani II," in *Apollinaris*, 46 (1973), pp. 366-393.

FARRELLY, ADRIAN. "Acts of Extraordinary Administration and Acts of Alienation," in *CLSANZ Newsletter*, 1 (2004), pp. 49-40.

_____ "The Diocesan Finance Council: Functions and Duties according to the *Code of Canon Law*," in *Studia canonica*, 23 (1989), pp. 149-166.

FELICIANI, GIORGIO. "La notion de bien culturel en droit canonique," in *L'année canonique* 47 (2005), pp. 63-74.

FITZGERALD, MICHAEL. "The Canon Law Implications of the Physician/ Hospital Organization in the United States of America," in *Studia canonica*, 22 (1988), pp. 27-65.

FOLMER, JOHN J. "The Canonization of Civil Law: The Law of Personal Injury," in *CLSA Proceedings*, 46 (1984), pp. 46-65.

FÓRNÉS, J. "Régimen juridico-patrimonial y financiación de la Iglesia desde la perspective de la liberdad religiosa," in *Ius canonicum*, 36 (1996), pp. 13-61.

FOSTER, JOHN. "To Protect by Civilly Valid Means: Reorganization and the Canonical-Civil Restructuring of Dioceses and Parishes," in *CLSA Proceedings*, 70 (2008), pp. 102-127.

FRUGÉ, DONALD J. "Diocesan Taxation of Parishes in the United States, Sign of *Communio* or Source of Tension?" in *CLSA Proceedings*, 60 (1998), pp. 68-81.

_____ "Taxes in the Proposed Law," in *CLSA Proceedings*, 44 (1982), pp. 274-288.

GALDI, F. "L'economo nel nuovo codice di diritto canonico," in *Amico del clero*, 68 (1986), pp. 120-129.

GAUTHIER, ALBERT. "Juridical Persons in the *Code of Canon Law*," in *Studia canonica*, 25 (1991), pp. 77-92.

GEISINGER, ROBERT. "Some Ongoing Considerations in Canon Law for Treasurers General of Religious Institutes," in *Periodica*, 96 (2006), pp. 227-259.

GEMMA, A. "La povertà religiosa tra codice di diritto canonico e vangelo," in *Apollinaris*, (1996), pp. 263-275.

GIACON, B.A. "L'amministrazione dei beni ecclesiastici nel nuovo Codice di diritto canonico," in *Palestra del clero*, 62 (1983), pp. 915-927.

GILLET, F. "Gli istituti diocesani per il sostentamento del clero," in *Amico del clero*, 67 (1985), pp. 175-181.

GONZÁLEZ, J. "Alienation of Church Goods: Why and How?" in *Boletin eclesiastico de Filipinas*, 81 (2005), pp. 426-435.

GONZÁLES GREÑÓN, J. "El párroco y la administración de los bienes eclesiásticos," in *Anuario Argentino de Derecho Canónico*, 11 (2004), pp. 397-430.

GRAMLICH, MIRIAM L. "New Directions: Towards Congregational Divestiture of Property," in *Review for Religious*, 39 (1980), pp. 434-440.

GRANT, TERENCE T. "Social Justice in the 1983 Code of Canon Law: An

Examination of Selected Canons," in *The Jurist*, 49 (1989), pp. 112-145.

GRAUDER, PETER. "Der Kirchenaustritt und seine Folgen," in *Theologische-praktische Quartalschrift*, 132 (1984), pp. 64-75.

GRAZIAN, FRANCESCO. "Patrimonio stabile: istituto dimenticato?" in *Quaderni di diritto ecclesiale*, 16 (2003), pp. 282-296.

GREEN, THOMAS. "Shepherding the Patrimony of the Poor: Diocesan and Parish Structures of Financial Administration," in *The Jurist*, 56 (1996), pp. 706-734.

GREINER, PHILIPPE. "Les biens de paroisses dans le contexte des diocèses français," in *L'année canonique*, 47 (2005), pp. 37-50.

HALL, K.A. "Facing the Risk – Liability Insurance Checklist," in *CCCC Bulletin*, 4 (1998), p. 5.

HEINTSCHEL, DONALD. "Canon Law and Civil Law: The Convergence of Two Systems," in *CLSA Proceedings*, 44 (1982), pp. 375-380.

HEREDIA, C.I. "El obispo y la vigilancia de los bienes eclesiásticos de la Iglesia," in *Anuario Argentino de Derecho Canónico*, 7 (2000), pp. 47-64.

HERMANN, DONALD H.J. "The Code of Canon Law Provisions on Labor Relations," in *The Jurist* 44 (1984), pp. 153-193.

HITE, JORDAN. "Church Law on Property and Contracts," in *The Jurist*, 44 (1984), pp. 117-133.

_____ "Property Issues for Religious," in *CLSA Proceedings*, 48 (1986), pp. 163-177.

HOLLENBACH, DAVID. "Corporate Investments, Ethics, and Evangelical Poverty: A Challenge to American Religious Orders," in *Theological Studies*, 34 (1973), pp. 265-274.

HOWARTH, JOSEPH. "Juridic Person or Private Association: Choosing a Canonical Structure," in *Health Progress*, (September, 1986), p. 51.

HUELS, JOHN. "Stipends in the Code of Canon Law," in *Worship*, 57 (1983), pp. 215-224.

JACQUES, ROLAND. "Posséder en pauverté: Le droit de proprieté d'une congrégation," in *Praxis juridique et religion*, 3 (1986), pp. 205-216.

KASLYN, ROBERT J. "Accountability of Diocesan Bishops: A Significant Aspect of Ecclesial Communion," in *The Jurist,* 67 (2007), pp. 109-152.

KEALY, ROBERT L. "Methods of Diocesan Incorporation," in *CLSA Proceedings*, 48 (1986), pp. 163-177.

KENNEDY, ROBERT T. "McGrath, Maida, Michiels: Introduction to a Study of the Canonical and Civil Law Status of Church-Related Institutions in the United States," in *The Jurist*, 50 (1990), pp. 351-401.

――― "The Declaration on Religious Liberty Thirty Years Later: Challenges to the Church-State Relationship in the United States," in *The Jurist*, 55 (1995), pp. 479-503.

KING, WILLIAM J. "The Corporation Sole and Subsidiarity," in *CLSA Proceedings*, 63 (2003), pp. 107-134.

LE TOURNEAU, DOMINIQUE. "Les conseils pour les affaire economique: origine, nature," in *Il diritto ecclesiastico*, 99 (1988), pp. 609-627.

LOBO, P.I. "Régimen jurídico de los tributos en el Código de 1983," in *Anuario Argentino de Derecho Canónico*, 10 (2003), pp. 181-244.

LÓPEZ ALARCÓN, MARIANO. "La administración de los bienes eclesiasticos," in *Ius canonicum*, 24 (1984), pp. 87-121.

LUCAS, BRIAN. "Diocesan Assets and Risk Management," in *CLSANZ Newsletter*, 1 (2008), pp. 57-65.

MAIDA, ADAM J. "Canon Law Implications of Real Estate Transactions – Impact of the New Canon Law," in *The Catholic Lawyer*, 27 (1982), pp. 218-225.

――― "Canonical and Legal Fallacies of the 'McGrath Thesis on Reorganization of Church Entities'," in *The Catholic Lawyer*, 19 (1973), pp. 275-286, 288-289.

――― and NICHOLAS P. CAFARDI. "Charitable Trust Helps Ensure Catholic Hospitals' Identity," in *Hospital Progress*, 63 (1982), pp. 32-36, 62.

MALLETT, JAMES K. "Temporalities Under the Revised Code," in *The Catholic Lawyer*, 29 (1984), pp. 187-194.

MANZANARES, JULIO. "De stipendio pro missis ad intentionem 'collectivam' celebratis iuxta decretum 'Mos igitur'," in *Periodica*, 80 (1991), pp. 579-608.

MARCHESE, M. "Il laico e l'amministrazione dei beni della Chiesa," in *Quaderni di diritto ecclesiale*, 3 (1989), pp. 329-340.

MARCHI, TINO. "Enti ecclesiastici e loro atti di straordinario amministrazione secondo le nuove norme canoniche e civili," in *Amico del clero*, 68 (1986), pp. 339-369.

_____ "La remunerazione dei chierici nel nuovo codice," in *Monitor ecclesiasticus*, 109 (1984), pp. 187-195.

MARINI, FABIO. "Gli istituti secolari: amministrazione dei beni temporali e personalità giuridica (can. 718)," in *Quaderni di diritto ecclesiale*, 20 (2007), pp. 402-414.

MARTÍN DE AGAR, JOSÉ, "Note sul diritto particolare delle conferenze episcopali," in *Ius ecclesiae*, 2 (1990), pp. 593-623.

MATTHEWS, KEVIN. "Calculating Matters of Extraordinary Administration and Alienation within Australia," in *CLSANZ Newsletter*, 1 (1999), pp. 35-37.

MAURO, TOMMASO. "La disciplina delle persone giuridiche, le norme sui beni ecclesiastici e sul loro regimine con riferimento all'ordinamento statale," in *Monitor ecclesiasticus*, 109 (1984), pp. 379-396.

MBALA-KYÉ, A. "Les fondations paroissiales comme élément de l'auto-financement des Églises en Afrique. La prévision par la conversion," in *Praxis juridique et religion*, 15 (1988), pp. 3-38.

MCDONOUGH, ELIZABETH. "Bona ecclesiastica," in *Review for Religious*, 66 (2007), pp. 95-100.

MESTER, STEFANO. "I beni temporali della Chiesa (le novità apportate dal nuovo codice)," in *Apollinaris*, 57 (1984), pp. 49-59.

METZ, RENÉ. "Les responsables des biens des églises dans la pespective de Vatican II comparée à celle du Code de 1917," in *Prawo Kanoniszne*, 20 (1977), pp. 53-65.

MIÑAMBRES, JESÚS. "Evoluzione nella prassi amministrativa della Chiesa in Italia: dalla 'Istruzione in materia amministrativa' del 1992 a quella del 2005," in *Ius Ecclesiae*, 18 (2006), pp. 199-216.

_____ "Il tributo diocesano ordinario come strumento di governo," in *Ius ecclesiae*, 16 (2004), pp. 619-637.

MIRAGOLI, E. "L'obolo di San Pietro, tra le esigenze della carità e dell'amministrazone (c. 1271)," in *Quaderni di diritto ecclesiale*, 5 (1992), pp. 67-77.

MISTÒ, LUIGI. "I beni temporali della Chiesa, commento al Libro V del Codice di Diritto Canonico," in *La scuola cattolica*, 119 (1991), pp. 45-59, 301-343.

MODDE, MARGARET MARY. "Private Association: Opportunity for Laity," in *Health Progress* (September, 1986), pp. 46-50.

MOLLOY, THOMAS E. "The Canonization of Civil Law: The Law on Labor Relations," in *CLSA Proceedings*, 46 (1984), pp. 43-45.

MONCION, JEAN. "L'Église peut-elle agir comme toute autre puissance financière?" in *Studia canonica*, 14 (1980), pp. 423-430.

_____ "L'Institut religieux et les biens temporels," in *Studia canonica*, 20 (1986), pp. 355-365.

_____ "Should a Religious Congregation provide a Reserve Fund or Pension Plan for Its Members?" in *Studia canonica*, 8 (1974), pp. 183-190.

MONTAN, AGOSTINO. "I religiosi e il sostentmento del clero: applicazione del nuovo sistema nelle parrocchie affidate agli istituti religiosi," in *Quaderni di diritto ecclesiale*, 3 (1989), pp. 71-81.

MORENO ANTON, MARIA G. "Algunas consideraciones en torno al concepto de bienes eclesiasticos en el CIC de 1983," in *Revista española de derecho canónico*, 44 (1987), pp. 71-92.

MORIN, ANDRÉ A. "Des origines de le fiducie, un exemple concret des racines institutionnelles des droits occidentaux dans le droit canonique," in *Ius ecclesiae*, 7 (1995), pp. 481-493.

MORRISEY, FRANCIS G. "Acquiring Temporal Goods for the Church's Mission," in *The Jurist*, 56 (1996), pp. 594-596.

_____ "The Alienation of Temporal Goods in Contemporary Practice," in *Studia canonica*, 29 (1995), pp. 293-316.

_____ "Challenges for the Proper Administration of Temporal Goods in the Light of Changing Circumstances," Unpublished paper presented at the Eastern Regional Conference of Canonists, Charleston, South Carolina (May 5-7, 2008).

_____ "Juridic Status: Canonical Provisions, Possible Applications," in *Health Progress*, (September, 1986), pp. 41-45.

_____ "Ordinary and Extraordinary Administration: Canon 1277," in *The Jurist*, 48 (1988), pp. 709-726.

_____ "The Temporal Goods of the Diocesan Church," in *CLSANZ Newsletter*, 2 (2002), pp. 24-36.

MOSCA, VINCENZO. "Povertà e amministrazione dei beni negli istituti religiosi," in *Quaderni di diritto ecclesiale*, 4 (1990), pp. 234-263.

MOSTAZA RODRIGUEZ, ANTONIO. "El nuevo derecho patrimonial de la Iglesia," in *Estudios eclesiásticos*, 58 (1983), pp. 183-216.

MYERS, JOHN J. "Church Approval Necessary for Activity to be Truly Catholic," in *Health Progress*, 68 (1987), pp. 70, 74.

_____ "The Diocesan Fiscal Officer and the Diocesan Finance Council," in *CLSA Proceedings*, 44 (1982), pp. 181-188.

NEDUNGATT, GEORGE. "Temporal Goods in the Church," in *Vidyajyoti*, 64 (2000), pp. 205-214, 283-291, 367-377.

―――― "Who Is the Administrator of Church Property? The Answer of the Ecumenical Councils," in *Folia canonica* 4 (2001), pp. 117-133.

NICORA, ATTILIO. "Tratti caratteristici e motivi ispiratori del nuovo sistema di sostentamento del clero," in *Amico del clero*, 71 (1989), pp. 340-354.

O'BRIEN, MARY JUDITH. "Instructions for Parochial Temporal Administrators," in *Catholic Lawyer*, 41 (2001), pp. 113-143.

ODCHIMAR, NEREO P. "Decent Support and Social Security for the Clergy Under the 1983 Code of Canon Law," in *Philippiniana sacra*, 18 (1983), pp. 511-538.

OCHOA, XAVERIUS. "Acquisitio, distributio ac destinatio bonorum temporalium Ecclesiae institutorumque perfectionis ad mentem Concilii Vaticani II," in *Commentarium pro religiosis et missionariis*, 51 (1970), pp. 22-33.

―――― "Ratio bonorum temporalium in Ecclesia et institutis perfectionis post Concilium Vaticanum II," in *Commentrium pro religiosis et missionariis*, 48 (1969), pp. 339-348.

OKULIK, L. "La potestad tributaria del obispo diocesano y la interpretación del canon 1263 del CIC," in *Anuario Argentino de Derecho Canónico*, 11 (2004), pp. 431-449.

ORSI, JOÃO CARLOS. "O princípio de subsidiaridade e a sua aplicabilidade no Livro V do Código de Direiro Canônico," in *Apollinaris*, 78 (2005), pp. 399-412.

PAPROCKI, THOMAS J. "Recent Developments Concerning Temporal Goods, Including Complementary USCCB Norms," *CLSA Proceedings*, 70 (2008), pp. 257-284.

PASSICOS, JEAN. "Rapports droit général et particulier: Une contribution diocésaine imposée aux processes confiées à des religieux," in *L'année canonique*, 47 (2005), pp. 114-117.

PERLASCA, ALBERTO. "I beni delle persone giuridiche private," in *Quaderni di diritto ecclesiale*, 12 (1999), pp. 380-393.

―――― "Commento al canone 1284," in *Quaderni di diritto ecclesiale*, 11 (1998), pp. 382-394.

PIÑERO CARRION, M.J. "L'aspetto patrimoniale ed economico della trasformazione del beneficio nell'ufficio," in *Monitor ecclesiasticus*, 96 (1971), pp. 432-463.

PROVOST, JAMES and RICHARD A. HILL. "Stole Fees," in *The Jurist*, 45 (1985), pp. 321-324.

REDAELLI, CARLO. "Le persone giuridiche come strumenti per organizzare le attività diocesane e parrocchiale," in *Quaderni di diritto ecclesiale*, 17 (2004), pp. 25-40.

_____ "Patrimonio degli enti che fanno parte della diocesi e loro attività," in *Amico del clero*, 75 (1993), pp. 113-127.

RENKEN, JOHN A. "The Collaboration of Civil Law and Canon Law in Church Property Issues," in *Studies in Church Law*, 4 (2008), pp. 43-80.

_____ "'Duc in altum!' Communio: Source and Summit of Church Law," in *The Jurist*, 63 (2003), pp. 22-69.

_____ "Pastoral Councils: Pastoral Planning and Dialogue Among the People of God," in *The Jurist*, 53 (1993), pp. 132-154.

_____ "Particular Law on Temporal Goods," in *Studies in Church Law*, 4 (2008), pp. 447-454.

_____ "Penal Law and Financial Malfeasance," in *Studia canonica*, 41 (2008), pp. 5-57.

_____ "Pious Wills and Pious Foundations," in *Philippine Canonical Forum*, 10 (2008), pp. 69-110.

_____ "The Principles Guiding the Care of Church Property," in *The Jurist*, 68 (2008), pp. 136-177.

_____ "Temporal Goods in the Latin and Eastern Codes: A Comparative Study," in *Studies in Church Law*, 5 (2009).

RINCON-PEREZ, TOMAS. "El decreto de la Congregation para el Clero sobre accumulation de estependios (22-II-91)," in *Ius canonicum*, 31 (1991), pp. 627-656.

_____ "La responsibilità del vescovo diocesano nei confronti dei beni ecclesiastici," in *Quaderni di diritto ecclesiale*, 4 (1991), pp. 317-335.

RIVELLA, MAURO. "Beni temporali e associazioni di consacrati," in *Quaderni di diritto ecclesiale*, 12 (1999), pp. 363-370.

_____ "L'Istruzione in materia amministrativa 2005 della Conferenza Episcopale Italiana," in *Ius ecclesiae*, 18 (2006), pp. 187-197.

_____ "La remunerazione del lavoro eccclesiale," in *Quaderni di Diritto Ecclesiale*, 19 (2006), pp. 175-184.

ROCHE, GARRETT J. "The Poor and the *Code of Canon Law*: Some

Relevant Issues in Book II," in *Studia canonica*, 30 (1996), pp. 177-219.

_____ "The Poor and Temporal Goods in Book V of the Code," in *The Jurist*, 55 (1995), pp. 299-348.

ROEBER, CAROLYN A. "Sponsorship of Ministries of Individual Religious," in *CLSA Proceedings*, 56 (1994), pp. 171-196.

ROVERA, VIRGINIO. "De structuris oeconomicis in Ecclesia renovandis," in *Periodica*, 65 (1971), pp. 197-250.

_____ "Il libro V: I beni temporali della Chiesa," in *La scuola cattolica*, 112 (1984), pp. 337-355.

RUOTOLO, RICCARDO. "I ricorsi per diritti del sostentamento del clero," in *Monitor ecclesiasticus*, 113 (1988), pp. 62-71.

SACKETT, FRED and PETER E. CAMPBELL. "Religious Treasurers in the Revised Code: Six Practical Cases," in *CLSA Proceedings*, 46 (1984), pp. 71-97.

SCHLICK, JEAN. "Vers une autonomie financière des Églises catholiques d'Afrique subsaharienne? Réalisations pastorales et institution-nelles après *Ecclesia in Africa*," in *Praxis juridique et religion*, 12-13 (1995-1996), pp. 5-58.

SCHMITZ, HERIBERT. "Die Bestimmungen des c. 1271 CIC zum Benefi-zialrecht," in *Arkiv für Katholisches Kirchenrecht*, 155 (1986), pp. 443-460.

SHEA, PATRICK J. "Parish Finance Councils," in *CLSA Proceedings*, 68 (2006), pp. 169-188.

SOLS LUCÍA, A. "La fundación pía no autónoma en el actual CIC," in *Revista española de derecho canónico*, 50 (1993), pp. 519-552.

SUGAWARA, YUJI. "Amministrazione e alienazione dei beni temporali degli istituti religiosi nel Codice (Can. 638)," in *Periodica*, 97 (2007), pp. 251-282.

TESTERA, FLORENCIO. "Cases and Inquiries: Lay Persons in the Admin-istration of Ecclesiastical Property," in *Boletin eclesiastico de filipinas*, 62 (1986), pp. 639-650.

_____ "Ecclesiastical Financial Management," in *Philippiniana sacra*, 18 (1983), pp. 495-510.

_____ "The Temporal Patrimony of the Parish and its Administration," in *Boletin eclesiastico de filipinas*, 62 (1986), pp. 43-60.

TING PONG LEE, IGNATIUS. "De bonorum in missionibus adscriptione," in *Commentarium pro religiosis et missionariis*, 57 (1976), pp. 222-237.

_____ "Quaedam de bonorum assignatione in missionibus criteria crisi subiiciuntur," in *Commentarium pro religiosis et missionariis*, 57 (1976), pp. 335-348.

URSO, P. "Le strutture amministrative della diocesi," in *Quaderni di diritto ecclesiale*, 4 (1991), pp. 336-347.

VALLINI, AGOSTINO. "I criteri ispiratori del nuovo diritto sui beni della Chiesa. Dal Concilio Vaticano II al nuovo Codice di diritto canonico," in *Aspernas*, 33 (1986), pp. 65-77.

VIZZARI, ANGELO. "Il consiglio diocesano per gli affari economici," in *Monitor ecclesiasticus*, 119 (1994), pp. 269-290.

VON USTINOV, HUGO A. "El régimen canónico de los bienes de propiedad de las personas juridicas privadas," in *Anuario Argentino de Derecho Canónico*, 13 (2006), pp. 187-213.

WARD, DANIEL. "Bequests and Gifts to the Church Under the Code of Canon Law," in *The Catholic Lawyer*, 30 (1986), pp. 276-285.

_____ "Trust Management Under the New Code of Canon Law," in *The Jurist*, 44 (1984), pp. 134-142.

WATERS, IAN B. "A Tribunal Case Concerning Clergy Remuneration," in *CLSANZ Proceedings*, (2000), pp. 55-60.

WIEDENHOFER, SIEGFRIED. "Kircke, Geld und Glaube," in *Theologische-praktische quartalschrift*, 142 (1994), pp. 169-185.

ZALBIDEA GONZÁLEZ, DIEGO. "Antecedentes del patrimonio estable (c. 1291 del CIC de 1983)," in *Ius canonicum*, 47 (2007), pp. 141-175.

_____ "El patrimonio estable en el CIC de 1983," in *Ius canonicum*, 47 (2008), pp. 553-589.

ZANNONI, G. "I beni temporali della Chiesa nel nuovo Codice di diritto canonico," in *Amico del clero*, 69 (1987), pp. 154-161.

ZIELINSKI, PAUL J. "Pious Wills and Mass Stipends in Relation to Canons 1299-1310," in *Studia canonica*, 19 (1985), pp. 115-154.

INDEX

ST PAULS

This book was produced by ST PAULS/Alba House, the Society of St. Paul, an international religious congregation of priests and brothers dedicated to serving the Church through the communications media.

For information regarding this and associated ministries of the Pauline Family of Congregations, write to the Vocation Director, Society of St. Paul, 2187 Victory Blvd., Staten Island, New York 10314-6603. Phone (718) 982-5709; or E-mail: vocation@stpauls.us or check our internet site, www.vocationoffice.org